Gr… & Water Lilies

The life and work of Paul Bennett

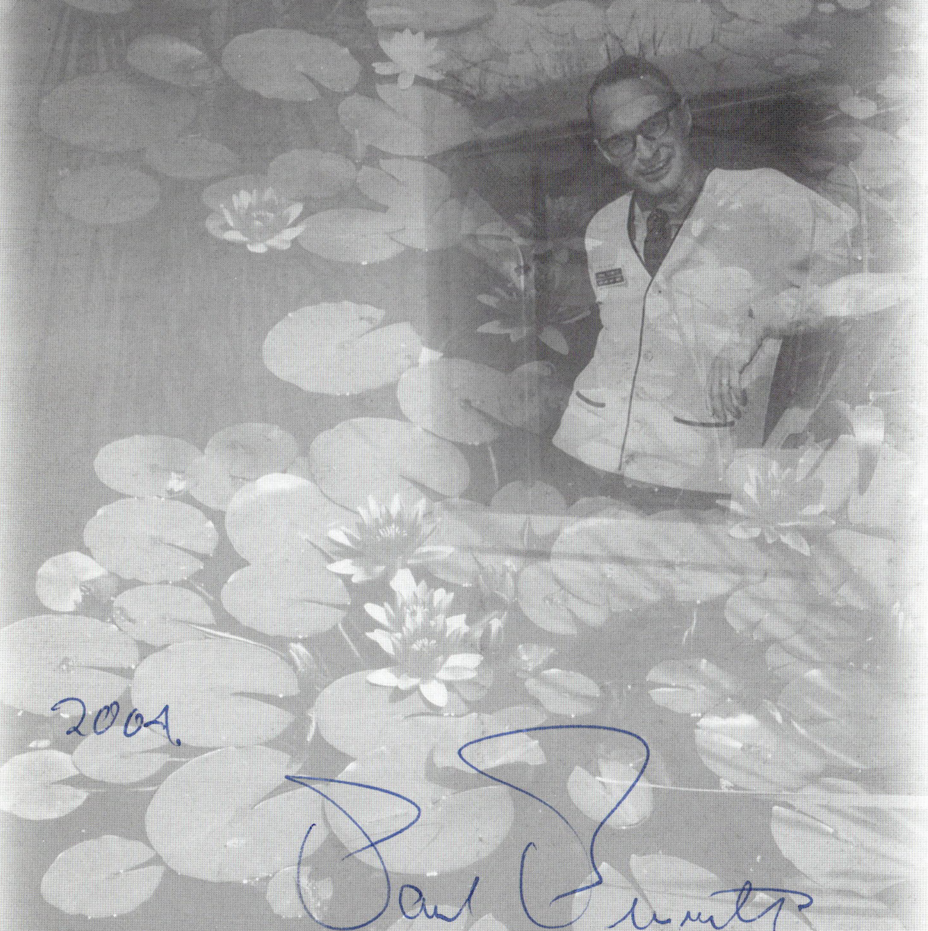

2004.

Paul Bennett

by Paul Bennett

Grass roots and water lilies: the life and work of Paul Bennett

Published by Paul Bennett
43 Dorset Street West
Port Hope, Ontario Canada L1A 1E9

Printed by Haynes Printing, Cobourg, Ontario
Cover and text design by Marc Mireault
Manuscript entry by Andrew Chatwood

National Library of Canada Cataloguing in Publication

Bennett, Paul, 1928-
Grass roots and water lilies: the life and work of Paul Bennett by Paul Bennett.

Includes index.
ISBN 0-9733570-0-2

1. Bennett, Paul, 1928- 2. Art museum directors—Ontario, Southern. 3. Art critics—Ontario, Southern—Biography. I. Title.

N89.2.B45A3 2003 709'.2 C2003-903773-8

Contents

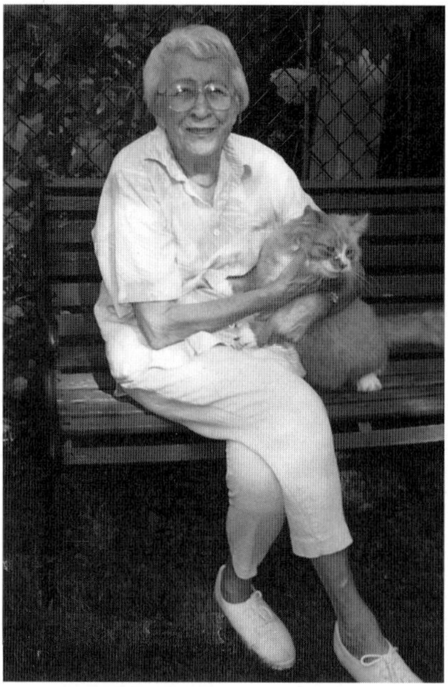

Dedicated to my sister Joan

Introduction

Although this is an autobiography, I have not referred to all aspects of my life; in fact, I have deliberately left out mention of a number of minor positions that I held. I decided that I would concentrate on my own personal development and also the development of the visual arts, especially in the areas away from Toronto, where I may have had a small hand in moving them forward.

The book is a curious merging of two approaches to recording history. First, concerning myself, I write in a somewhat facetious style relating personal anecdotes; second, I write in a factual style relating the history of the Visual Arts in Ontario. I, like most other people, do have more than one side to my nature. I do hope that this merging is a successful one.

In all of my professional positions over the years, I kept a separate personal record of all my monthly reports to my Boards: budgets, a complete set of newspaper clippings, monthly bulletins, and so on. In 1991 I donated these sets to the archives of the Art Gallery of Ontario (into which the Art Institute of Ontario had merged), the Robert McLaughlin Gallery of Oshawa, the Ontario Crafts Council and the Gallery Stratford. As far as I could at the time, I made duplicate copies of all of the important papers and it is these that I have used as a resource for this book.

Finally, why the name, Grass Roots and Water Lilies? The first part is easy: "grass roots" always refers to the beginning of something that is sturdy, continuing, and growing upward. I would like to think that my work helped to create such an atmosphere for the growth of the Visual Arts in this province. The second part refers to me and for me is equally important. Gay people in the past have been referred to as "lilies" — take, for example, the early gay club in Toronto that was called the "Maison du Lys" — the House of Lilies, I would like to think that I did mature and flower and become someone worthwhile.

The water lily is a beautiful flower. It may be an obtuse reference but I bear it proudly.

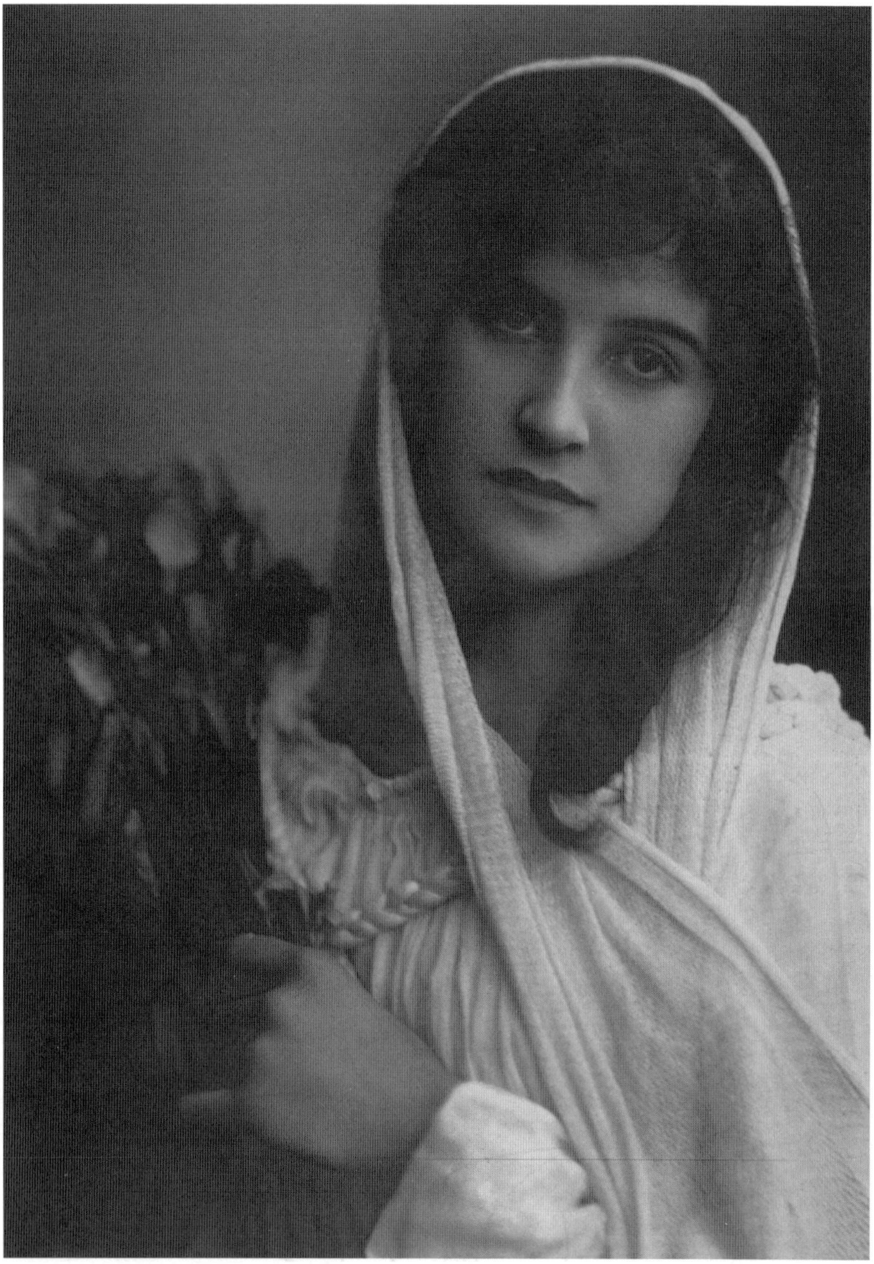

My mother — Grace Winnifred Maidens, 1893-1963

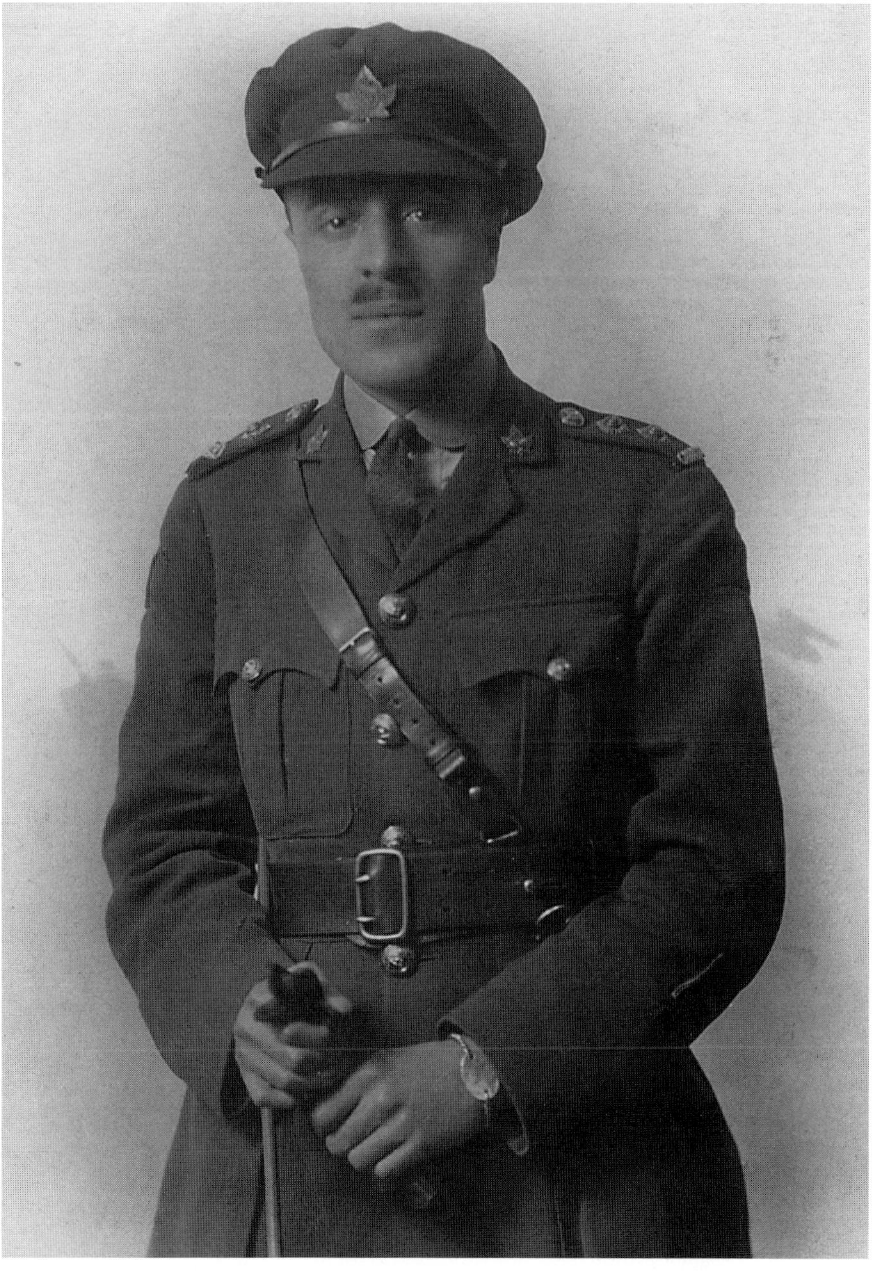

My father — Lieutenant David Leonard Bennett, 1894-1965

Chapter One

Ghosts and Things Nocturnal

I wake in the night with an idea. Uncle Grant's Revenge, my grandfather's clock, has just chimed four-thirty. Uncle Grant and I used to fight just about half the time; in fact, he disinherited me. After his death, my two sisters who had inherited his estate gave me his prize possession, his clock. Now the clock chimes every fifteen minutes and I am forced to think of him although he has not been around for ten years.

My idea is the fact that I must have a chapter in my book about ghosts. I live in an old house that began life as a tavern back in 1860. I hear the sound of a body coming through the cat door from my sister's apartment. I look over the edge of the big Victorian bed that is my home at night and I see a ghostly figure quietly glide across the floor toward the door of my study. Marmie, short for Marmalade (I call him Pumpkin), our almost twenty-pound, maybe Maine Coon, once a stray, cat moves across the pine floor and goes into my study to take a drink out of the bowl that accommodates Andy, my Dalmatian-mix dog. Then he takes up his position as guard on one side of the hall above the crook in the wall where he can look through the balustrade and see the dancing figures of the past on the stairway.

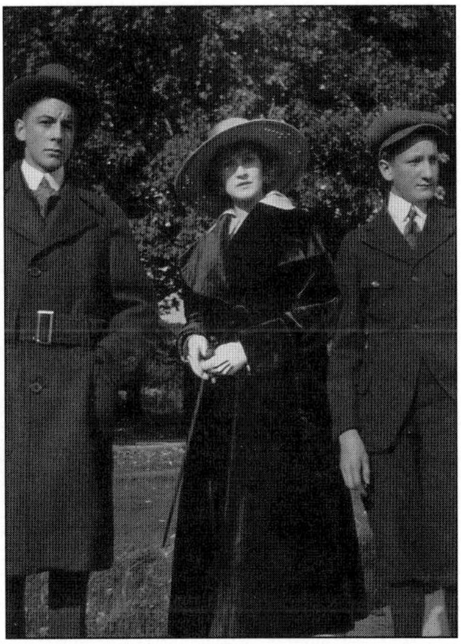

Andy stays asleep under the clavichord and so I turn over, knowing all is well and go back to sleep.

I have seen these shadows from time to time; they are an unruly bunch, bobbing up and down with excitement. Marmie especially likes to watch them at the bottom of the stairs when we are playing bridge. I look out the door of the card room and see him, eyes intent on a small space in the middle of the floor; then he pounces but never seems to catch the object of his interest, maybe a phantom mouse? He is watching and there may come a day...

My ideas come when I wake at night. I am getting old and beginning to lose words in my train of thought. I had better start to write...

Back in 1917 in Belleville, Ontario, one night in January my mother was playing the piano in the darkened room. The moon was streaming in the French windows, one of my uncles was resting in the old Morris chair, and my grandmother was upstairs asleep. Suddenly my mother looked up over the music rack and saw my father coming up out of the trenches leading his platoon. He waved them on with his right arm as he was carrying his revolver in his left hand. Suddenly shells were bursting around the group and machine gun bullets were piercing the dawn, Dad waved his men on, ran forward, grabbed his right arm up near the shoulder, spun around and fell. The sergeant moved up and took his place and the wave of men moved across no man's land at Vimy Ridge. Mother screamed and everybody came running. The old house on Victoria Avenue came to life as whiskey, kept only for medicinal purposes, was poured down Mother's throat.

Dad, the dashing young Englishman, had come to Belleville in 1912 from St. Albans in England to be near his brother who had arrived before him and his cousin who had been born here. He worked in the telephone service. He had married my mother just before he disappeared overseas with the waves of Canadian men called to defend King and country. When I was young I found love letters to my mother that revealed how young and lonely my father had felt in the trenches.

My mother was put to bed. The next day she wrote a letter to my father describing exactly what had happened. My father received the letter but did not answer at the time. At Easter came the famous assault at Vimy Ridge led by Canadians when, as historians state, Canada came of age as a nation. It was the first time in the First Great War that all the Canadian troops had come together and acted as one unit. My father was badly wounded in the upper right arm, he walked five miles to a dressing station and eventually returned to London where he was admitted to hospital; (The humerus of his right arm had been fractured by machine gun fire, but a skilled doctor saved the nerve so that he had the use of his right arm for the rest of his life, although his right arm was some inches shorter than his left one, he hid it well.) Mother had written in her letter that she could not understand why, in the vision, she had seen my father carrying his revolver in his left hand when he was right-handed. Dad wrote her back from hospital and explained that when he had gone over the top blood poisoning had disabled his right hand and consequently he had transferred his revolver to the left.

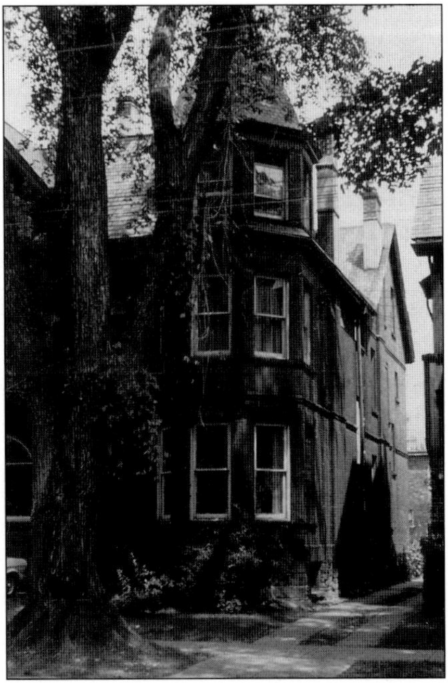

In the mid-sixties I rented a house on Bedford Road in Toronto. My bedroom was the biggest room in the house, at the front of the building on the second floor. The bedroom was equal in size to the living room and front hall directly below it. There was a tower in my room in the corner surrounded by four windows.

I was playing the piano late one evening when suddenly I sensed that I was not alone in the room. There was the faint outline of a woman over in the opposite corner but she was very indistinct. I was not frightened; my German Shepherd dog, Jannes, was asleep under the piano and did not appear disturbed by this apparition. The woman faded away and disappeared. My guest seemed to approve of me and began to appear about once a month on a regular basis. Occasionally I would suddenly awake in the middle of the night and I would sit up and find her watching me. Gradually I sensed or somehow knew more and more about her.

She was dressed in the fashion of the First World War and was waiting for her fiancé to return from the war. But he had been killed; still she waited as if she would not accept that verdict.

If ever I spoke about her to somebody she would disappear for a period as if only I, alone, was to know of her vigil. This was especially true if I, somehow, seemed to joke about her. For example, the best way to draw attention to yourself at a cocktail party is to mention a true ghost story. As you talk the room will grow quiet in chilly anticipation and everybody listens. But my ghost would disappear for a long period of time, her disapproval very strong.

Once when visiting my sister who owned an antique store I found that she had a World War One wedding dress complete with attendant bridesmaid's dresses in her store. The outfits had never been finished as if the wedding had never taken place. There was a bill with the dress from the T. Eaton Co., thus authenticating the date. I asked my sister if I could take the complete set of outfits to that company. I knew that they had a museum of their old stock and might be interested in buying the dresses. I brought the outfits to Bedford Road and all hell broke loose. My ghost was very upset, stairs creaked, doors opened by themselves, a T.V. left by itself suddenly increased in volume. I used to collect old melodeons or pump organs; three of these were sitting in the dining room where notes would sound in the night. I took the dresses to Eaton's but the store was not interested in them. I returned them as quickly as I could to my sister and the house quieted down.

My apparition was at peace again, content to stand always in the same place and listen to my music.

I received a Canada Council grant in 1967-1968 and I went off to Europe for almost a year. I left the house and my furniture in the care of John Lee, an old friend of mine, who had sublet the third floor from me. John had a new roommate. The first night after he moved in he woke up in the small hours of the night and cried out — the figure of a young girl in a long flowing dress was hovering over his bed! He had never been told about my resident ghost who normally lived on the floor below. I had never known her to move outside my bedroom but perhaps she was looking for me.

I returned to Toronto and decided for a variety of reasons to give up the house. I moved to an apartment on Hillsboro Avenue. In those days when anybody moved one borrowed or rented a small truck and friends helped you to make the move. A friend was helping me carry one of my melodeons, a small keyboard reed organ made in the nineteenth century, from the truck to the front door. As we approached the door, it swung open by itself. We went into the lobby and up to the elevator and my floor light came on by itself and the elevator door opened. I cried out, "She is coming with me!" — but maybe she did not like the heights or the spareness of modern architecture because that was her goodbye and I never saw or heard from her again.

Chapter Two

Genes

Jabez Thomas Bennett, 1858-1926

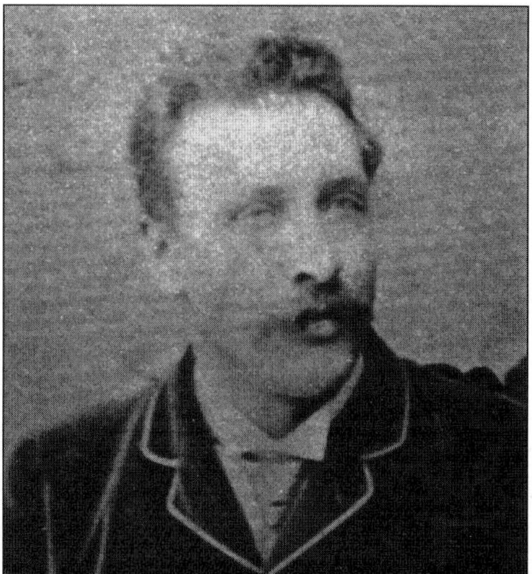

Both of my grandfathers' families originally came from Cornwall, England. On my father's side, many years ago my Uncle Ern, my father's oldest brother, sent me a set of four photographs of ancestors, all from Cornwall. The earliest of these was born in the eighteenth century.

First in line was John Bennett, 1765-1825, who came from a community named Linkinhorne. Then there was another John Bennett, 1800-1877, also from Linkinhorne. Next in line was Thomas Smith Bennett, 1832-1912, from the community of Egloskerry. Then came my grandfather, Jabez Thomas Bennett, 1858-1926, whose home was in St. Albans. I was able to add my father's picture to the group, David Leonard Bennett, 1894-1965, also of St. Albans, and myself, Paul David Bennett, 1928-20?? originally from Toronto.

I have this set of six pictures all combined in sequence, in one frame, hanging on the wall of my bedroom. All the portraits look like photographs, even the first one (which seems impossible because it seemingly was taken a few years before photography was invented?) I must add that Grandfather Bennett appears to have lived in London for a while before he moved to St. Albans. Both Uncle Ern and Auntie Eve, the two oldest of my father's siblings, were born in London while all the others were born at Priory Park in St. Albans.

My father never talked very much about his early life in England. He arrived in Canada in 1912, at the age of eighteen, and went to the city of Belleville to join his brother, my Uncle Jake, and a cousin, Hector Bennett-Post. He had been engaged in the telephone service in St. Albans, his hometown just north of London, England. In Canada, to quote a newspaper article in St. Albans, he was "rising rapidly in the telephone service" in Belleville when he joined the army at the outbreak of World War One. He married my mother just prior to going overseas.

Dad arrived in Canada in the summer months. He was wearing a huge Russian bearskin coat that practically reached to the ground and had a very large collar. I have a picture of him in this coat and standing on the steps of the YMCA where he was living in Belleville. As a child I remember seeing that picture and wondering about the grandfather who would give such a coat to a son going away to an unknown country. Dad sold the coat shortly after he arrived.

My grandfather was the stereotypical Englishman of the late nineteenth-early twentieth century. He had eight children, actually ten but two died in infancy — the perfect-sized family. Queen Victoria had eight children. He was middle class, upwardly mobile, and ready to try anything new, ready to gamble on a business venture and eccentric in his own interests. He was concerned with the plight of the underprivileged and thought about the betterment of the average man. He was a manufacturer of bicycles, a stamp dealer, an importer of silk and violins, a musician of note and a teacher of many instruments. He was an inventor; an innovator and a businessman who made money easily and just as easily lost it.

My grandmother's maiden name was Mary Everest. She was nicknamed "Ninny". A forebear had been Sir George Everest who spent twenty years, 1820 to 1840, in India doing a trigonometrical survey of that country. While he was map-making he suffered recurring bouts of malaria and often instructed his staff from his bed. When he went back to England he became the President of the Royal Society, and Mount Everest was named in his honour in the 1860s.

I learned a great deal about my grandfather when I finally visited St. Albans in 1956. I took pictures of the large house, Priory Park. Uncle Lionel told me it had boasted two drawing rooms and many bed-

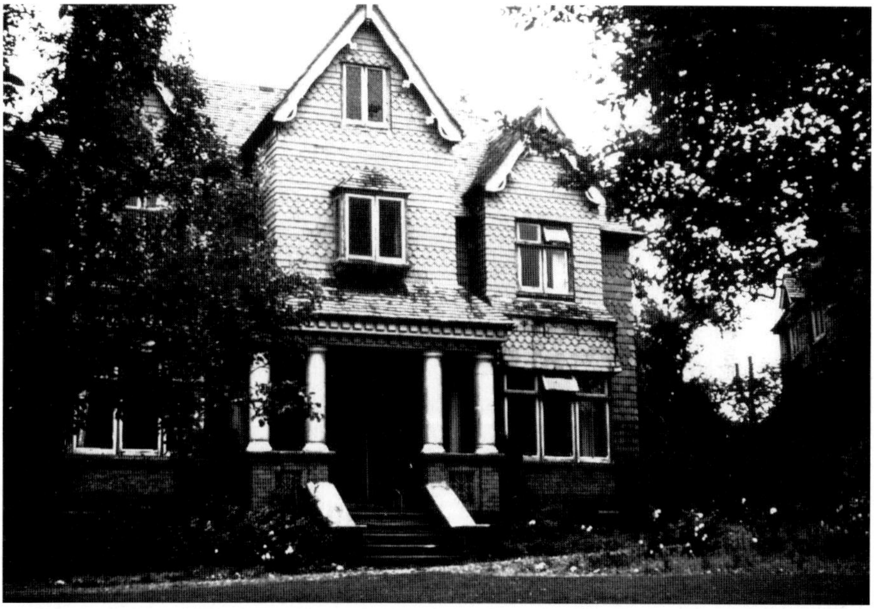

rooms. Its gardens backed onto the garden of Uncle Will, Grandfather's brother. As there was a pedestrian right-of-way dividing the two gardens, the two brothers wanted to have easy access between the two houses: one wanted a bridge over the lane and the other wanted to dig a tunnel. They could not agree on which to do and so they did both. First a small bridge was built. Two of Dad's brothers used to watch a lady teacher pass along the road each day and they were certain that she wore a wig; they took a line and a fish hook and — sure enough it was a wig!! Next Grandfather started a tunnel under the road. The tunnel was partially completed when they discovered another tunnel that evidently had run to a monastery in the Middle Ages, or might even be older as they found some Roman coins in it. The children were forbidden to go near the mouth of this tunnel, as it was feared that it ran under the river.

Grandfather and his brother, Uncle Will, owned a bicycle factory; it was one of the biggest bicycle factories in the country at the time and was capable of turning out one hundred bicycles a week!! The first bicycles were made under the brand name "The Bennett Scorcher Cycle Company". There was a showroom and sales office on the Strand in London, and the Scorcher was the first cheap bicycle in England.

The three girls in the family were jealous that the five boys could have bicycles and they could not as it was impossible to ride with long skirts. Grandfather with his inventive bent cut out the cross bar and lowered it and thus invented the girl's bicycle. But he was a careless businessman: he never bothered to take out a patent and so he lost his monopoly. He was careless in other ways. Each week Auntie Eve used to go to the factory office and go through the wastebaskets in her father's office to rescue the cheques that he had thrown out along with the envelopes after he had received letters. He often used to leave the window wide open by his desk as he opened his mail. Often cheques would blow out the windows and somebody would have to go out and search the garden for them.

Grandfather Bennett heard about wonderful prospects for making money in South Africa. He launched a very expensive advertising campaign to sell his bicycles there but it was a failure and he lost a fortune. Grandfather attempted to reorganize and he bought out his brother's half share of the company. Indeed Auntie Marge told me that her father made the money and Uncle Will lost it. The company gradually sank into oblivion. Finally when I visited Uncle Ern in 1956 he had only recently closed the last remnant of the company. He had made bicycles all his life, finally under the name "Grandex". At the end he had one helper and they were making three-wheeled bicycles for delivery boys.

Grandfather Bennett wanted to have the first of everything that came along. He had the first wireless in St. Albans. He was mad over wireless telegraphy. He had one machine that did not work well and so he bought a big one from the Daily Mail in London that took up the whole of one side of the dining room. He would invite as many as twenty friends and neighbours in for an evening but not be able to make the wireless work. Then he would stay up half the night listening to it after the company had departed.

The family had the first car in St. Albans. One Sunday Grandfather Bennett decided to take his youngest son, Lionel, his daughter, Marge, and a cousin for a ride. There were too many passengers to fit in the car, and so Granddad drove, accompanied by a female relative, and the children were put in a wicker trailer. They went merrily out onto the London Road. The trailer happily parted company with the car and went into a ditch. Marge and the cousin got out, left young Lionel in the cart, and pulled the whole contraption home. Completely oblivious, Granddad and his companion went on in noise and exhaust fumes and did not return for an hour.

Grandfather Bennett was a wonderful musician, as I have been told by a number of English relatives. He could play many instruments and taught lessons on a number of them giving all of his students their own instruments. His own favourites were the violin and cello. It is interesting how talent descends in a family: my Uncle Jake, who originally came to Canada before Dad, played the cello all his life. It was his great love. My father had an excellent voice, my sister Jane developed a glorious soprano voice and my sister Joan has composed music all her life including a musical called *Loyalties*. As for me, I am a baritone and have sung in church choirs for over fifty years.

Grandfather, at one point, went into the business of importing violins from France. He would take out the original labels and substitute "Stradivarius" labels, and then sell the instruments in North America!! I have often seen such instruments at country auctions, poor in quality and rich in label, and wondered if Grandfather Bennett's deeds have come back to haunt me.

More of my opportunistic grandfather's imports: this man of business realized that Queen Victoria was very old and would die within a reasonable time. He expected that every person in Britain would need a black armband and women of fashion, in particular, would need black dresses. He went to France to the great silk-making centre of Lyon, and buying a vast quantity of black silk and velvet imported it into England. Grandfather again was a little ahead of his time for Queen Victoria lived longer than he expected so that it took a long time to recapture his original investment. Eventually the materials were needed and then that venture was allowed to fade into oblivion.

Grandfather Bennett was interested in the Salvation Army; in fact for a period of time each week on a regular basis he would buy new drums for the Salvation Army bands because on the weekends when the bands were on parade in London people would throw stones through them. General William Booth became a friend of my grandfather's and visited St. Albans a number of times. When he stayed at Priory Park lavish preparations were made for the great man. The guests were given the best guest rooms. General Booth would sit in the drawing room and the children were brought in and introduced to him. My Auntie Marge, in her seventies, still remembered the tone of Booth's voice, when he put his hand on her head and said, "God bless you, Marjorie Catherine". My father remembered being pushed forward and his father said, "And this is little David". Later, on one occasion a tea wagon was rolled in laden, with dainties and the afternoon tea paraphernalia. General Booth looked at it and said, "I do not drink tea; I am a Christian", much to my Grandmother's chagrin. At a later visit he had changed his ideas somewhat: he would deign to drink tea but it had to be made in his own silver teapot. In the long run, my grandfather gave a great deal of money to the Salvation Army.

Grandfather was always inventing or enquiring. He invented a ship that would not sink. He was interested in movie cameras and actually made some movies on the lawn at Priory Park. Long before people knew much about genes, he became very interested in eugenics — the adverse effects of people not marrying suitable partners, the effects of mentally defective people producing defective offspring, and so on. He carefully guarded his family to make sure that each one married the right "strain". I wonder how he managed to allow my father to come to Canada and marry my mother without his permission!

Again he was ahead of his time in being something of a "health nut". My Aunt told me that the big house somewhat resembled a hospital: everybody had an iron bed with a hard mattress. Exercise was tremendously important. Tennis was played by the whole family on the three tennis courts at the bottom of the garden. Weather permitting, tennis was almost constantly played by a group of about thirty people including cousins, aunts, uncles and a few friends. Uncle Lionel, the youngest of the boys, told me about this obsession with tennis. He said that he started playing tennis at six years of age and swore that he would play for fifty years. (He stopped when he was fifty-six!). Variations in age and ability must have produced some interesting games. Lionel told me that when he was three, his oldest brother

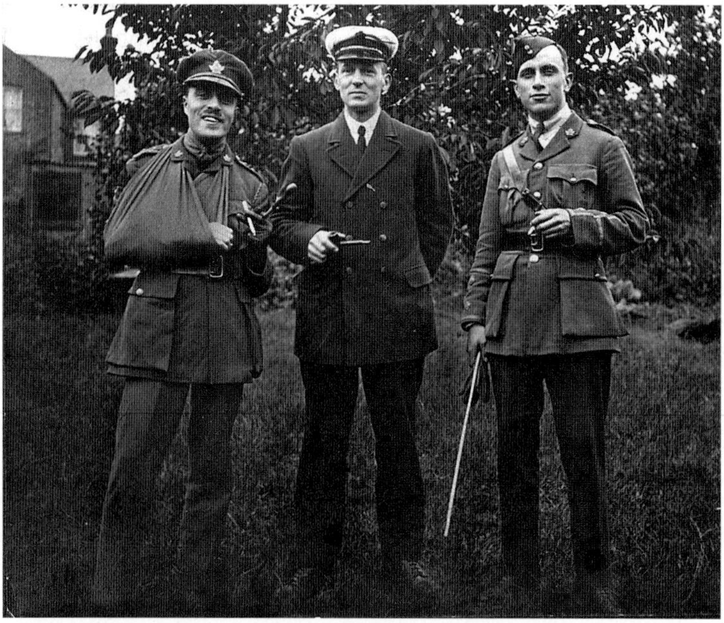

Lieutenant David L. Bennett with brothers Don Bennett, gunner with artillery in Egypt, and Lieutenant Jake Bennett of the British Flying Corp.

Ern was twenty-three and married. In fact Lionel was closer in age to Uncle Ern's oldest son.

After my father was wounded at Vimy Ridge he spent a great deal of time in hospital in London. When he was able he journeyed down to St. Albans with his wounded arm in a sling. He often brought friends with him from the hospital who would join in the family activities.

Lionel told me about a letter he had received from my father just before Vimy Ridge. It had been written just prior to the great attack. Dad was sure, in the letter, that he would be killed. He stated that if he was wounded he prayed it would be anywhere but in his right arm, as he wanted to be able to draw the rest of his life. Ironically, he was wounded in that very arm. But twelve successive operations saved the nerve and the arm. He did not draw or paint for a while but eventually he was able to do so.

Grandfather Bennett's interest in health took some funny turns. When all of the family went to the seaside he would walk along the edge of the shore, dodging the incoming waves and reaching out with his cane to loop it around the neck of some very young unsuspecting swimmer and pull him to shore, telling him of the danger of being in the water.

My Auntie Marge told me wistfully that Christmas was always wonderful. The first inkling of it would come early in the season when her mother would take out a huge vat and put all the ingredients in it to make fifty-three Christmas puddings. The puddings were stored in the attic. There was one for each Sunday dinner all through the year and the biggest for Christmas dinner itself. On Christmas morning there would not be a rush to open presents as there is today. Uncle Lionel swore to me that he could remember the Christmas when he was two years old. He desperately wanted a wheelbarrow and had been promised one. Early Christmas morning he remembered looking down the long curving staircase that led to the ground floor; and thinking that he would never be able to get down that vast long stair. He kept wondering where the wheelbarrow had been hidden. Finally he managed the journey and he found it.

Later in the day would come the time when the drawing room doors would be opened with great fanfare and there would be a beautiful tree decorated and lit with live candles. The thought of the fire hazard posed by those candles causes shivers to run up and down my spine.

I never did get an explanation as to why the family fortunes declined. It is obvious that in spite of his talents in so many directions, my Grandfather was basically a bad businessman. The end of the nineteenth century was a time of tremendous expansion in Britain and elsewhere. That business climate plus imaginative enterprise created a situation where my Grandfather could try to spread himself to South Africa, North America and France. He was a true entrepreneur in a climate where social values were changing, where the common man was beginning to believe that he had a place in the world. Grandfather sold inexpensive bicycles for that reason; he attempted to build a garden city for people of small income. Once again he and Uncle Will were partners. The idea was that each family could have a self-contained home complete with its own garden plot, an idea from the future for that period of time. I am sure that he might be interested in knowing that Priory Park was eventually demolished and a modern subdivision — complete with individual gardens – was built in the St. Albans area.

While researching this chapter I have come to gradually realize that perhaps I did inherit something from my Grandfather Bennett. He was interested in making life better for the average man; I have spent a good part of my life in developing an interest in the visual arts at a grass roots level. Perhaps we were both working on the same wavelength.

Sister Marjorie Bennett, M.B.E.

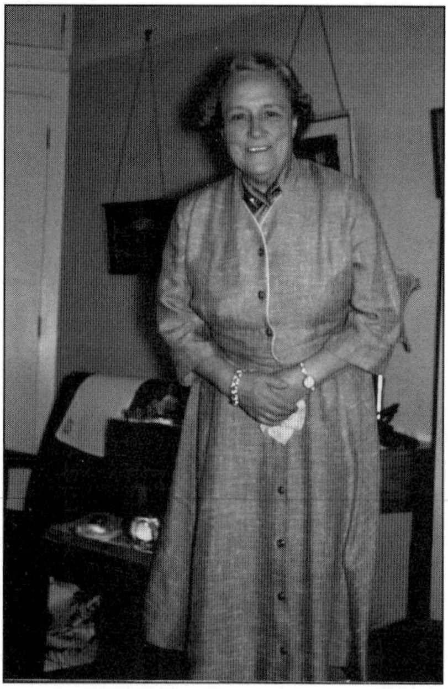

My father told me that his sister, my Auntie Marge, wanted very much to be a nurse during the First World War. Her father objected as she was very young, but he allowed her to go to London as a Nurse's Aid thinking that the drudgery of the job would put her off a nursing career. But he was wrong, and eventually Auntie Marge became one of the most notable nurses in England.

There were eight children in the family, five boys and three girls. Four of the boys were in the forces in World War One. I have a copy of the *Herts Advertiser* and the *St. Albans Times*, dated April 21st 1917. There is an article on a page devoted mostly to casualty lists of local boys. The article's heading is, "A

Quartette of Brave Brothers" and in it describes my father and his three brothers. It states, "Another of the many patriot families of St. Albans is that of Mr. and Mrs. Thomas Bennett, of Priory Park, four of whose son's photos are here produced. They are (1) Lieutenant David Bennett (22) of the Canadian Contingent, who, we regret to say, has been severely wounded, the humerus of the right arm having been fractured by machine gun fire; (2) Lieutenant Jake Bennett (24) who was also with the Canadians but has recently transferred to the British Flying Corps, (3) Gunner Don Bennett (19) who is with the artillery in Egypt: and (4) the youngest son Mr. Lionel Bennett, (18 in July), who at present is in the City of Midland Bank, St. Albans but who is joining up in a short time (when he would come of age). The article goes on to say that Dad "had gone to Canada three years earlier, was married a few days before leaving for England, and was wounded at the storming of Vimy Ridge."

With such a family, naturally, my Auntie Marge wanted to join in the war effort too. She went to London to St. Mary's Hospital, Paddington, where as a V.A.D. she scrubbed floors and emptied bedpans, not returning to St. Albans until the war ended. She stayed at home for a while; her father died in 1926 and she stayed on until her mother died. Back in London she trained at St. Mary's, worked for a while at Guy's Hospital, London and then returned to St. Mary's in 1939 where she remained for the rest of her career.

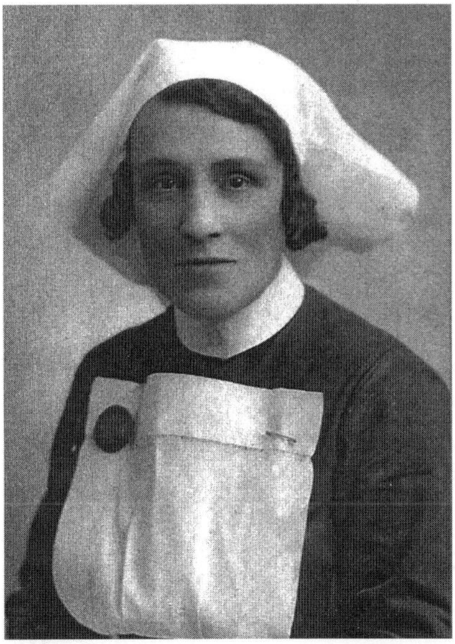

I met Auntie Marge on two visits that I made to England. First, in the summer of 1956 when I travelled around Europe with three friends, we stayed in London for some days and I arranged to see Auntie Marge. I made an appointment by phone and went to meet her. I went into a ward where I saw someone who bore a startling resemblance to my father, but of course it was my aunt who was in a somewhat quaint nurse's uniform; a full starched dress covered by a white pinafore, and a small white ruffled cap standing on the top of her head with a large bow under her chin. We had a wonderful visit and she showed me around the wards. I arranged to go back for an evening. This time I was directed to her room and found Marge in a very smart tailored grey suit. Her room was large with two windows and a cupboard at each end, a comfortable continental bed, two armchairs, and a few antiques from her family home. There was a watercolour painting by my father on the wall. We had a lovely supper and spent a wonderful evening going over family news and the recent war.

My next visit to Auntie Marge was on December 1st in 1968. She was then living at Ewelme in Oxfordshire, retired; she had been awarded a grace and favour position in charge of the Cloisters Alms House. This sinecure was the gift of a grateful nation for her work during the war. Again we talked all evening. This time I had a tape recorder with me and the following information mostly comes from that tape.

Auntie Marge had never wanted to be a Matron, she was proud of the fact that she was a ward sister. When she retired she was in charge of four large wards. She was an examiner for the General Nursing Council of England and she lectured first year medical students. One of her wards was the staff ward for doctors and medical students.

There was a best seller in 1957, written by a New Zealander, June Opie. It was called *Over My Dead Body* and related the true experiences of a young girl who came to England from New Zealand by way of the Suez Canal. In Egypt she contracted polio and became terribly sick when she got to London. She was taken to St. Mary's Hospital and was a patient in one of Auntie Marge's wards. She was there for three years. Marge described June Opie as a very beautiful girl, almost six feet tall, deeply tanned when she first arrived and with long blond hair falling to her waist. She went into an iron lung; at one point she could only lift one finger. Then gradually the cure took hold, she became the darling of the ward and should have been moved to another ward but Auntie Marge prevailed and kept her there. There were many concerts put on for the patients by famous musicians. June Opie was wheeled out and attended many of them and became well known to such luminaries as Yehudi Menuhin. Eventually the day came when June Opie left St. Mary's in a wheelchair by ambulance and was taken to a liner that took her back home. She claimed that Auntie Marge's care, humour, understanding, skill and love were the guiding factors in her cure. She dedicated her book to her Mother and to Marjorie Bennett, S.R.N.

I asked Auntie Marge about World War Two and the air raids. How did they affect the hospital? She said that there were seventy patients in the ward instead of the regular forty. In the wards on the ground floor were patients with the usual sicknesses, and the regular routines were kept going. There was an air raid shelter for the hospital but only the maids used it; nobody else went down to it. Auntie Marge slept in her own room and would draw the curtains to cut out the war, the destruction, the fires and the chaos. She usually was so tired that she fell asleep immediately. A couple of times fires were started on the roof and the top of the hospital; nobody panicked and the student nurses and doctors were well trained to put them out.

Marge said that the young nurses were wonderful. She could be handing a teen-age nurse-in-training a bowl of soup; when a crash would come, and later she would find out that a wall nearby in the neighbourhood had taken a hit and collapsed. But the nurse's hand would not even shake as it took the bowl from Marge, I am sure that it was the confidence inspired by Auntie Marge that created that steadiness.

I asked her about her role in the development of penicillin. She began by explaining that St. Mary's was a research hospital, and she talked with great admiration about Alexander Fleming and his laboratories. She wondered if, had the laboratories suffered a direct hit by bombs, penicillin would have ever been discovered? In fact she always maintained that St. Mary's Hospital was under special divine protection because of the special penicillin research there. It was the only London hospital not seriously damaged during the blitzkrieg.

Here is her part in this miracle; she was asked to prepare two wards of patients, (carefully selected for being in advanced stages of disease). But just before these scheduled tests with the drug an emergency arose. A three-week-old baby, the daughter of a St. Thomas Hospital doctor, was admitted to St. Mary's. The child would have been dead by morning of septicemia. The decision was made to administer a small dose of penicillin and the child incredibly was improved dramatically by the morning! When Marge told me this I will never forget the wonder in her voice and the look in her eyes as she said it. The experimental wards ran for nine months; the drug was being made right at the hospital. As it was in very short supply, very small doses were administered. Auntie Marge said that every case was a miracle: the patients got better and it happened every time. When the experimental period was over the wards were returned to their regular use. All penicillin produced then went to the armed forces. If it were not for this drug then patients all over England, almost dead, would never have survived.

In 1959 Auntie Marge retired. A marvellous dinner was held in her honour. Every doctor and nurse that she had trained or who had worked in the wards with her was contacted. One hundred of them accepted the invitation.

When I visited her at Ewelme she had been there for nine years, in charge of the Cloisters Alms House. She had her own cottage with a garden. There was an ancient church of flint with a crenellated tower, below which was a courtyard surrounded by the cottages built of brick in a herringbone pattern; they were covered in moss and conveyed a feeling of great age. The Duke and Duchess of Norfolk had founded the Alms Houses in 1443; and they were maintained financially on the interest accruing from the rental of rich farm lands left for that purpose. Each day the inmates, including my Auntie Marge, when attending church, would say a prayer for the souls of the two founders.

Marge was involved in a programme to rebuild the interiors of the houses. The exteriors, because of their antiquity, could not be touched. Each rebuilt dwelling was to have a living room, a bedroom, a small kitchen and a bathroom. Auntie Marge confided in me that she felt the present interiors were old, damp, badly planned and just plain awful.

That was the last time I saw my Auntie Marge. I heard that she had been given the M.B.E. (Order of a Member of the British Empire) especially for her work in penicillin. In 1969 she went to Buckingham Palace where she met the Queen. Her younger brother, Don, and two of my cousins, Tony and Pam, accompanied her. She died at Ewelme in 1973, a wonderful, cheerful, talented, compassionate, dedicated woman.

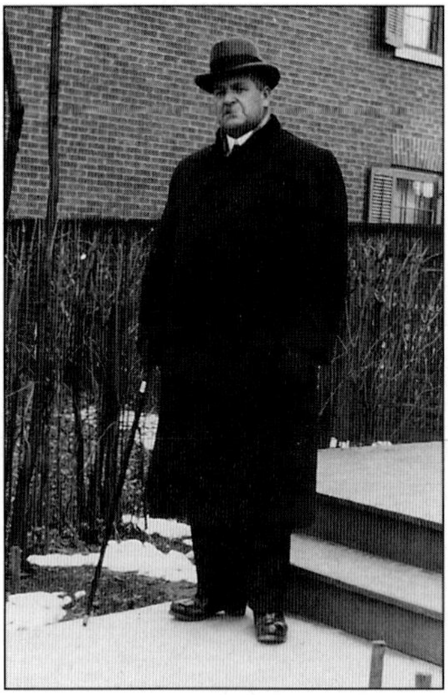

John Maidens 1863-1934

Both my father's and my mother's families originally came from Cornwall. My mother's maiden name was Maidens. Grandfather Maiden's great-great grandfather was the only survivor of four brothers who fought in the Napoleonic Wars. He fought in the Peninsular War and later at Waterloo. In later life he recalled a time when he and his fellow soldiers were being pursued while crossing the Pyrenees. The British were carrying a huge load of plunder which, unfortunately, they had to dump down a crevasse in order to lighten their loads so that they could travel more quickly and eventually elude their pursuers.

Our ancestor later recalled how the Duke of Wellington visited his troops in the terrible rain while they were waiting for the coming battle of Waterloo. The next day great-great grandfather fought until he was wounded and he remembered that as he was lying in the field, seemingly dead, he must have moved and caught the attention of a French officer who, seeing him, came over and slashed him with his sword from the chin to the navel!! Incredibly his victim survived, reared up on one elbow and shot the galloping officer dead. He not only lived to tell the tale but also to come to Canada where he settled near Hastings, Upper Canada, on a farm. When he died and was "laid out" as the custom was then, his clothes were open in the casket to display the long scar. One of our greatest family treasures is the iron tinderbox, complete with original flint and striking iron, which was carried at Waterloo.

Our maternal grandfather, John Maidens, was born in Percy Township near Hastings, where he grew up on the family farm, He decided, with the rapid increase in the economy in the late nineteenth century, that he would go into the retail business. His first job was selling shoes in a Norwood store. One fall he went to the Norwood Fair and met a young woman, Jenny Fanning; they were attracted to each other. The lady turned up at the shoe store (by accident?) and bought a pair of shoes. Grandfather waited on her and, as it was considered ladylike to have small feet in those days, she bought shoes that were a size too small for her. Shortly the couple was married. They lived in Norwood until, at the age of twenty-three, Grandfather decided to move to Havelock and open a general store. Havelock at that time was a thriving community because there the Canadian Pacific Railway had a roundhouse and other facilities for servicing the locomotives. Havelock not only supplied the local people but also the trappers and lumberjacks from the area north of the town.

After a few years all was not well. Grandfather had a large thriving store complete with a bakery — but there was a very big problem in collecting what was owing to him. In those days it was customary to run accounts until the harvest was in or until the lumberjack received his seasonal wages or a trapper had sold his pelts. Also there was further reason for dissatisfaction; Havelock was becoming a very rowdy town and taverns were always overflowing on Saturday nights with rough, drunken men.

My mother remembers her mother telling a lurid story. One Saturday night an Indian rushed into the store, seeking safety from a very drunk white man who was wielding a long knife. The two men circled the pot-bellied stove in the middle of the store until my grandfather, who was a very tall, powerfully built man, grabbed the Indian shoved him behind the counter, and then chased the attacker from his store. He gave the man shelter for the night and protected him until he saw him on his way the next morning. The Indian was very grateful and promised to come back in the spring and tell Grandfather the whereabouts of a secret silver mine. Unfortunately he was drowned running logs during that winter. As for the mine — other accounts of a mine known only to the Indians have surfaced from time to time.

There was a catastrophic fire in Grandfather's store that almost wiped him out. He decided to move to the other, quieter end of town and open his business there, but trade did not follow him and the store did not prosper. Finally, Grandfather decided to become a commercial traveller. The family was growing and my grandparents decided to move to Belleville where they hoped to find better social and educational opportunities for their children.

Grandfather was a commercial traveller for the next thirty-five years. He was the representative of George Phillips and Company of Montreal and he handled cut glass. This was the great Brilliant Period in the history of cut glass manufacture, never really equalled since. Grandfather loved and cherished the products that he sold. The ambitious farm lad had entered a new century of opportunity for himself and his family. Grandfather travelled right across Canada and would be away a month at a time. My mother used to say proudly that her father knew exactly how to pack his trunks with his samples and had never broken a piece of glass in all his years of travel.

The family were staunch members of the Methodist Church and later of the United Church of Canada. They belonged to the Tabernacle Church in Belleville. Old timers in Belleville have told me that in the early days people would wait outside to watch the Maidens family go into church. My mother and her two older sisters, Della and Leah, were all extremely beautiful and the five boys were handsome. Grandfather was a member of the Board of the church from the time he moved to Belleville. Also he was a class leader in the church for thirty years.

Grandfather was a local preacher for many years and engaged in work of an evangelistic nature. In this regard he was well known throughout southeastern Ontario. He loved preaching; in fact the story is told that as a young boy he would stand on a large stone out in the fields of his father's farm and preach to the four winds. A cousin of mine, quite by chance, came upon the scripts of some of Grandfather's sermons. He said that you would not believe today what he preached

— a mixture of hell fire and brimstone mixed with a message urging the protection of Protestant women and children from the invasion over the borders by other religions! Incredible how really decent people, back then, could be moved by sectarian hatred.

Grandfather Maidens was prominent in Masonry. When a young man he was initiated into the Norwood Lodge and then, at twenty-three he moved his family to Havelock and helped to initiate the Havelock Lodge, becoming its first Master. After moving to Belleville he very quickly joined the Lodge in that city and eventually became a life member. In the year 1931-1932 he was the honoured District Deputy of Prince Edward No 13. He obtained his thirty-second degree in the Scottish rite.

Grandfather received his education in Percy Township, but obviously he could not have gone far in school. Yet it is obvious that he was ambitious both for himself and his family. Being a commercial traveller, especially with a district that stretched right across Canada, must have been a hard and a lonely life. It was probably at this point that Grandfather, filling in the long evenings, began his self-education. He started reading his bible and studying theology, enough to eventually qualify as a lay preacher and reach high office in Masonry. He deserved a great deal of credit.

Life was quite different in those days on Victoria Avenue in Belleville. Life was much slower. Without the safety net we have today of social services, people looked after one another.

As a child I remember hearing the stories about Annie and Lizzy Morton. These were two older maiden sisters whose job was to look after the library in one of the churches, obviously not a very high paying position. They were literally, to quote an old-fashioned phrase, as poor as church mice. Once a week, on the same evening, they were asked to dinner at my Grandmother's. They ate a great deal and always afterwards they would go home with a large parcel of the "leftovers" from the meal. All the family treated them as honoured guests. These ladies were small and they twittered. Once Uncle Grant, who had just bought a new convertible, suggested that he would drive them home. The poor dear souls got into the car and sat up on the back of the seat with their feet on the seat proper; they had never before been in a car.

Uncle Foy, one of Mother's younger brothers, was a customs officer, and chiefly dealt with the products from the distillery at Corbyville. This was during the prohibition era in the United States when the smuggling of liquor was big business. Uncle Foy used to go down to the harbour and inspect the boats coming in and out. I remember as a

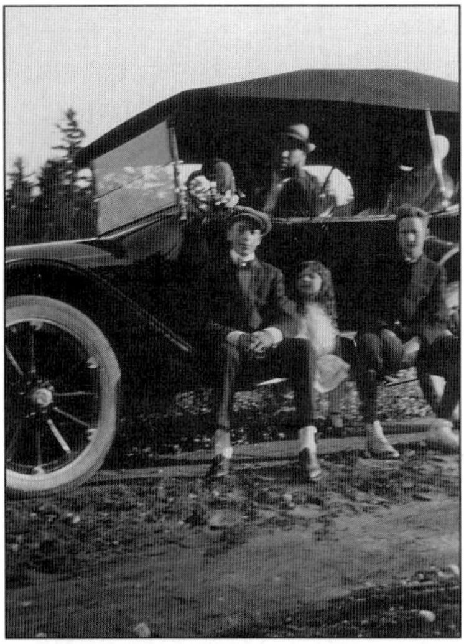

child driving down with him. He would drive to the end of the pier, which was long and narrow, and then turn around. I was terrified when he would back up to the edge of the pier in order to make the turn. I later found out that Uncle Foy would quite often find a mysterious bottle of booze sitting on the seat of his car after he had made his inspection!

Years later one of my cousins was getting married. It was wartime and he could not buy any liquor for the reception that was being held in Toronto. He asked Uncle Foy to help him. He came to Belleville with two empty suitcases and met Uncle Foy at home. Foy went down to the cellar, dug into one corner of the coal pile, and filled the suitcases with bottles of scotch that he had hidden away. It is grand that one can call on family in times of need.

Aunt Della married J. T. Warren. He was twenty years or more older than she was. I do not believe that she ever called him anything other than Mr. Warren. Warren had started an agency selling pump organs, but he moved with the times and turned to selling pianos. He used to take pump organs as trade-ins on new pianos and I have heard that his salesmen used to take axes and break up the old organs at the back of the sales building. Aunt Della was an excellent piano player and she met J.T. when she was hired to demonstrate the qualities of the pianos that were being sold. Later, once again, J.T. moved with the times and he opened the first new car agency in Belleville.

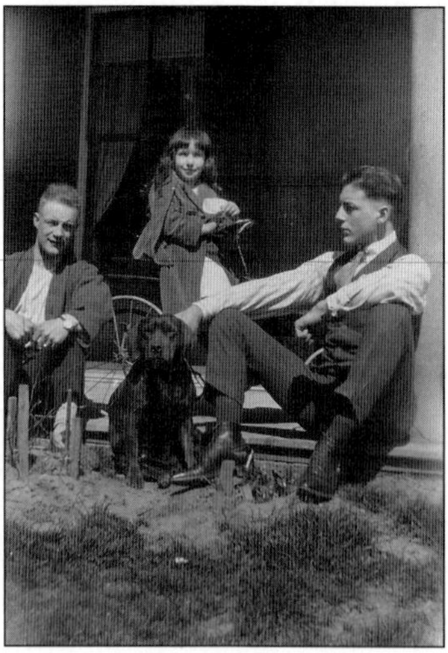

J.T. Warren's car dealership was a large stone building on the south end of Front Street in Belleville. It still stands to this day. Aunt Della was left a widow at an early age but the building seemed to be some sort of a status symbol to her; she never sold it until she was very elderly.

June, my cousin from this union, has told me a great deal about those early days. June is now ninety and I look after her in a retirement home close to where I live. June adored her father; he gave her a car when she was a teen-ager in High School (that must have been most impressive in those days) and she used to fill the car with her friends on a Saturday night and drive up the old Number Two Highway to Cobourg to go to dances at the Cobourg Pavilion down by the beach. When June was still quite young she used to drive to Oshawa with some of the salesmen and then drive a new car back to Belleville. How times have changed!

J.T. Warren built Aunt Della an impressive house with a large enclosed verandah further east along Victoria Avenue from my Grandfather's home. Warren would never give Aunt Della cash but allowed her to run accounts wherever she wished. Della loved cream puffs and regularly ran up bills at Ernie Dicken's Bakery on Front Street for cream puffs and butterscotch tarts. I remember those tarts from my childhood for they were absolutely delicious, and rich, and drippy. I think the recipe must have died with the company because I have never seen their equal since those days.

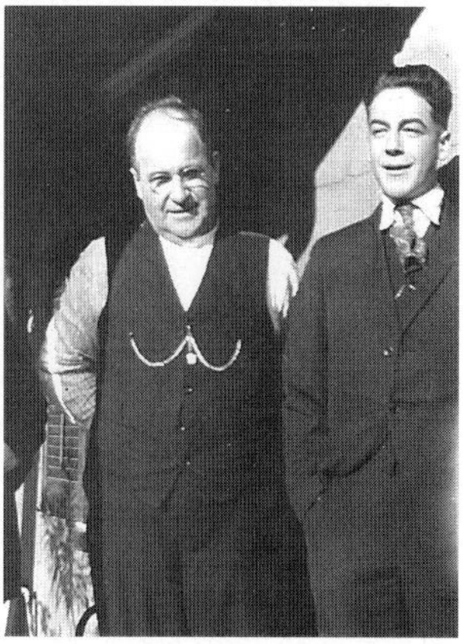

Back to Grandfather Maidens. He retired at sixty-seven with a bad heart condition and died at seventy-one. Mother always maintained that he strained his heart by carrying his heavy sample cases. I have a copy of the obituary that was run by the *Ontario Intelligencer* of Belleville. It is a glowing tribute to the man. The headline states, "Prominent Churchman, Mason and Business Man Passes." It tells of his work in the church, his status as a Mason and his prominence as a Conservative. It also mentions that he died suddenly of a heart attack while he was attending the furnace of his home at 167 Victoria Avenue. It is most inappropriate to say so but I wonder if he had dug into the wrong part of the coal pile!!

If my Grandfather Bennett was an eccentric, then my Grandfather Maidens was a model of convention. Both in their own ways were great successes.

Chapter Three

The Chinese Connection

The Chinese Boarding House

Jack Pollock was a well-known Toronto art dealer and artist in the sixties in Toronto. I was Art Advisor with the Community Programmes Branch of the Ontario Department of Education. It was my mandate to assist wherever possible in the development of the visual arts as a leisure-time pursuit. I travelled the province arranging workshops, giving speeches on design, advertising how to borrow professional exhibitions, and supplying information on where to locate supplies.

Once a year all the advisors attended a Leadership Course at Guelph along with some hundreds of community leaders. The mornings were devoted to leadership training and the afternoons were given over to training in the various media. Each year different disciplines were stressed: oil painting, weaving, portraiture, pottery and others. I hired Jack Pollock to be one of the professionals on staff.

As Jack says in his autobiography, *Letters from a Gentleman of Excess*, he was hired to teach teachers how to teach. Jack was charismatic and a great success. A year later I again hired him, this time to travel for six weeks giving painting workshops in small pulp and paper towns in Northern Ontario. He would teach two or three hours a day and would then be transported from one place to another, by plane when necessary, into remote communities. Jack relied more and more on these teaching assignments as income while he attempted to establish his small art gallery on Elizabeth Street in Toronto. It was on this six-week trip that a young man walked into one of his workshops and asked Jack to look at his paintings. That man was Norval Morrisseau; the rest is well known visual arts history. In two books, the one mentioned above and, many years later, the glossy coffee table book on Morrisseau by Lister Sinclair and Jack Pollock, I was given credit for pointing Jack towards Morrisseau.

At one time, when Jack was almost destitute, I visited him one evening. His gallery was a one-storey building on Elizabeth Street facing west toward the Sick Children's Hospital. Jack was sleeping in an alcove behind a curtain at the back. He told me that he was being evicted in a matter of days. He very much wanted to move next door to a three-storey brick building that had once been a Chinese boarding house.

Here is Jack's version of what followed: "That summer (1962) I met Morrisseau. Paul Bennett, who had hired me to teach up north, decided he would like to try la vie boheme, and rented the second floor of the gallery. Bernie and I moved to the third. Well, Paul, (later to be director of the Gallery Stratford, then the Ontario Craft Gallery, and now God knows what) loved the colours violet and blue, loved coloured glass and Victoriana, and loved organs (the musical kind). He was also totally opposite to B, and I, in that he was fastidious to the point of obsession. The gallery building was old, creaking and dust filled. His vacuum was on most of the time, and he quickly got tired of the happenstance, hand to mouth existence that was the old village. He moved out and on to bigger and better organs. B, and I were relieved when the vacuum finally stopped."

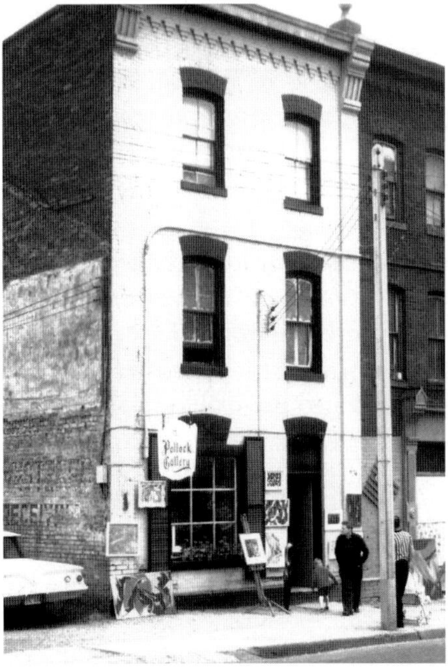

Here is my version of what followed: After Jack told me that he was going to be evicted from his gallery, I went home to bed. I was living in an apartment on Russell Hill Road at the corner of St. Clair Avenue. I woke up in the middle of the night with an idea. I jumped out of bed and went down to Jack's, knocked on the window of the gallery and woke him up. I suggested that I would give him a year's rent, six hundred dollars, and he could move into the deserted Chinese boarding house next door to his present gallery. The gallery could be on the ground floor, Jack could live on the second floor, and I would live on the top floor. He agreed. I went to the bank in the morning and borrowed the money.

The house was in bad shape. I redecorated the top floor. The kitchen was elementary. The bathroom was shared with Jack on the second floor; nothing was ever done to it and you had to cross rafters to get to the toilet. After I moved out a few months later I was told that when the contractors opened up one wall on the third floor they found the arm bones of a man inside it!

Jack and his lover Bernie lived on the second floor and it was never changed from its original condition. The gallery opened with fanfare and Jack held his very first successful Norval Morrisseau exhibition. I do remember that after the opening I went to bed and in the middle of the night I awoke to the smell of smoke and voices on the second floor. I went down and found Jack trying to pacify Norval who had built a small campfire in the middle of the room. He had been dancing around it, either thanking his gods or attempting to appease them for his trip to Toronto.

Bernie grew jealous of the fact that I had tried to help Jack, and one day he went to Budd Thomas, Supervisor at the Community Programmes Branch of the Department of Education and told him that I was hurting Jack's image at the gallery by inviting young boys up to my rooms — an utter falsehood. Budd, a good friend of mine, advised me to move out as quickly as possible. I did so and moved above a store at the corner of Avenue Road and Boswell. Jack never did thank me for helping him but he did eventually return to me the remainder of the money that I had paid him in rent.

Chinese Neighbours

Last year I returned from Cuba by a charter plane. I was seated on the aisle in a row of three seats near the front. The flight attendants tended to fall over me as the aisle did a bend around our row.

The lady in the seat beside me was returning with a group from six weeks of Christian work in a third world country. She was the wife of a minister, abrupt and abrasive and on a high from a successful adventure. She spoke to me, "What is wrong with your legs? Oh, you have two complete knee replacements. Do you know how long they last? Only five years." I, of course, found this news very gratifying as it had taken me about a year to get over each operation. She asked me about my work. "You were an art gallery director. I suppose you thought the Barnes Collection at the Art Gallery of Ontario just marvellous?" I told her that I had not seen it. "You are supposed to be an art gallery director and you did not see that show?" And so she went on and on, with me becoming quieter and quieter.

The flight attendant was a handsome young man. He was attentive and charming and looked good enough to eat. He was wearing a large diamond ring on his left hand. He stopped to speak to me. I said, "That is a very beautiful ring that you are wearing." "It was given to me by a friend." I answered, "I think your friend is a very lucky man." He blushed and went on with his work. The woman beside me hissed into my ear, "He is a homosexual." I answered, "So am I, madam."

You would have thought that I had announced that I was a terrorist. She scrunched over on her seat so that she was practically sitting on the armrest of her companion. She refused to speak to me and spent the last part of the trip talking indignantly about the terrible influx of Chinese into her North York neighbourhood.

Just before we got to Toronto this lady looked at me and said with great compassion, "I am going to pray for your soul. There is, of course, the possibility that you could be saved." I answered, "Thank you madam, I, too, will pray — for your Chinese neighbours. And oh, by the way, I did not go to the Barnes Exhibition because I had just had one of my knee operations and also I returned from Europe just a few years ago, where I was on a Canada Council grant and visited two hundred and forty galleries. Thank you for your concern."

The woman sniffed. The attendant came along and adjusted my seat belt and we landed in Toronto where I noticed my lady friend fall into the arms of her husband and two, tall, strapping sons. I was glad some people loved her.

Chinese Checkers

My Mother was a proud woman. She was proud of her three children, her family and her country. She was especially proud of her United Empire Loyalist background; one of her ancestors, Hans Waltimeyer, had founded the city of Belleville, originally called Meyers Creek. Mother and my younger sister, Jane, worked for many years on a family history. After Mother's death, Jane completed the work, a monumental task for which she deserves much credit. Mother would have been proud. Joan, my older sister, wrote a musical called *Loyalties* around the same theme. Jane assisted her, especially in the historic detail and the lyrics. Again, Mother would have been proud.

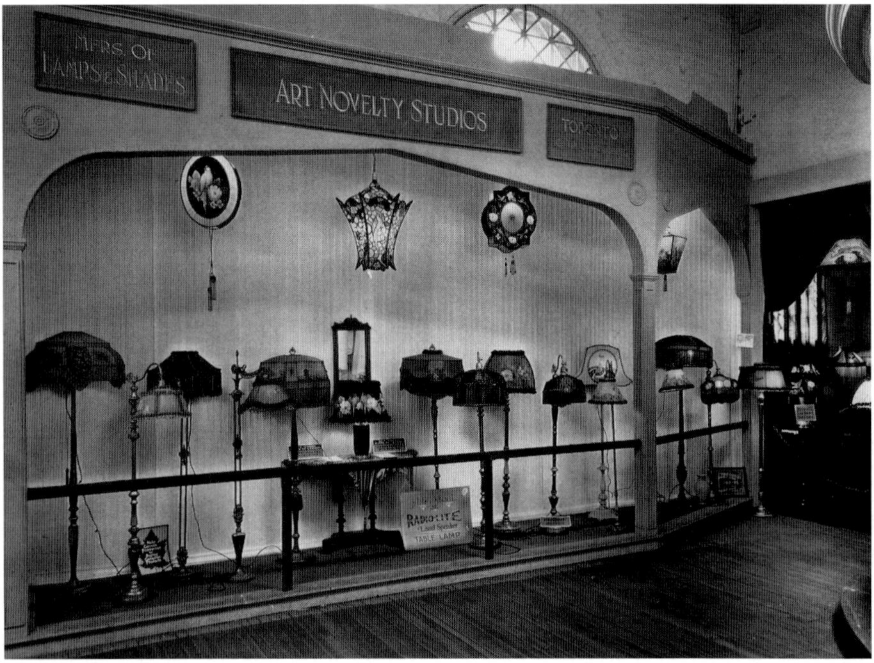

My Father was an artist. He was English. After returning to Canada from the First World War he had gone to Central Technical School and the College of Art in Toronto to complete his training. He and a friend started a company called, "Art Novelty Studios", which made lampshades, lamps and fancy furniture. Their first order was for Christmas decorations for Simpsons; they went on to paint a gross of silk stockings with butterflies at the top on one side, for Eaton's. Flappers were delighted. Next came the contract for the lighting and shades at the "Silver Slipper", a nightclub that stood down by the lake at Sunnyside. I have photographs of the Art Novelty Studios displays at the Canadian National Exhibition. These displays were huge and would bankrupt a small company today. The company at one point had a hundred and twenty employees. But all was lost in the 1920s crash, after which trade barriers came down and the American market swamped Canadian manufacturing.

With the crash, even though it had been a limited company, Dad lost our house and car but managed to hang on to all of our furniture at home. There was a wonderful three-section leather screen painted with floral decorations, which Mother had "fed" with lemon oil every month. I still have that screen in perfect condition after seventy years. I also have a wrought iron dining room fixture with rampant lions, a hanging lamp with a mica shade, stools, a tea table, and magazine

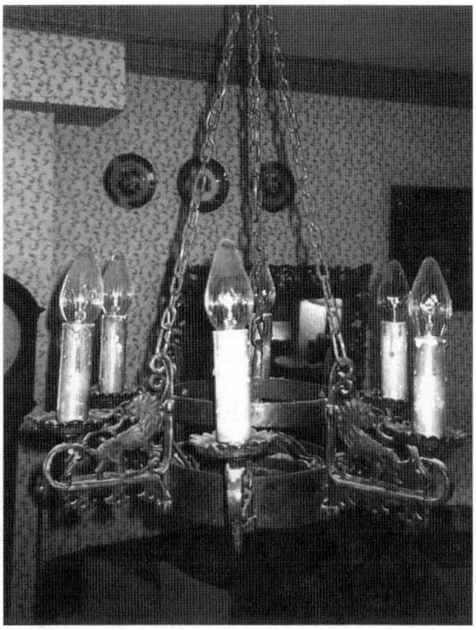

racks. Other luxury items that survived the crash included a hand-painted bedroom suite from my parent's bedroom and a miniaturized bedroom suite in robin's egg blue custom-made for my sister Joan. Two Persian carpets accompanied these. I was surrounded in my early days by beautiful objects.

My Father had two oil paintings accepted by the Ontario Society of Artists in 1929. Mother was equally creative in many ways. Her approach to my own upbringing certainly showed that she was ahead of her time. Mother made sure that we all liked the finer things in life. At Christmas, for example, there was no baseball glove or skates for me. It was the depression and money was very scarce, but I remember being overwhelmed with a beautiful cinnabar dresser box; next year came a sterling brush and comb, then a leather travelling case. The imprint was laid with certainty, and all my life I have attempted to surround myself with beautiful objects.

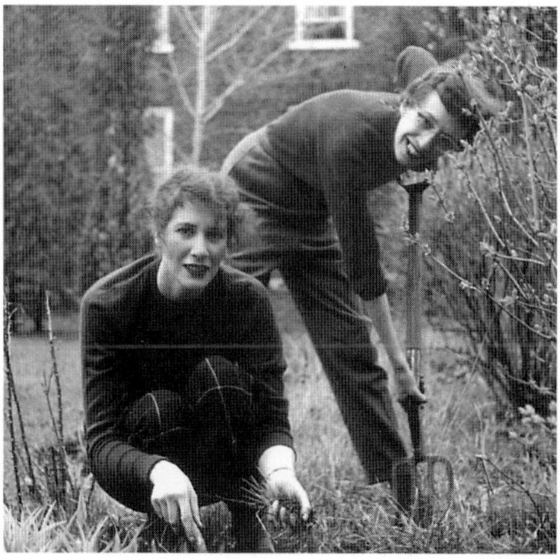

Joan and Jane each took degrees in music, Joan in piano and Jane in singing. I went to grade nine in piano. Joan and I both suffered the same problem: we were always too nervous to play in front of an audience. To this day music for me is a private thing. I have sung in church choirs for a good part of my life. I studied the piano, then classic guitar, then the Celtic harp. I have played them all, over the years, with a certain degree of proficiency. Almost no person has ever heard me play. Indeed I do think that some people think that I play very well because they have never heard me. I leave it like that. Now I have my clavichord and harpsichord. The clavichord especially is a very quiet, seductive instrument. One reads for one's own pleasure; why not play for the same reason? I play late at night; I am at peace and nobody hears me.

The amazing thing is that I made a career of giving speeches about the visual arts. I do not have a trace of nervousness there.

Back to Mother. Mother and Jane used to love to play Chinese checkers. I can still see them bent over the board in concentration. Each one would take thirty alleys, no ten alleys only for them. The board would become a confused mass of solid alleys in the middle of the game. Gradually it would sort itself out and one of them would be triumphant. They played this game for years. Joan and I left home to carve out careers for ourselves. But Jane, bless her, stayed at home with Mother, worked on family history, played Chinese checkers, gave piano lessons, took singing lessons and was Mother's companion until Morse Goddard came along when they fell in love and were married.

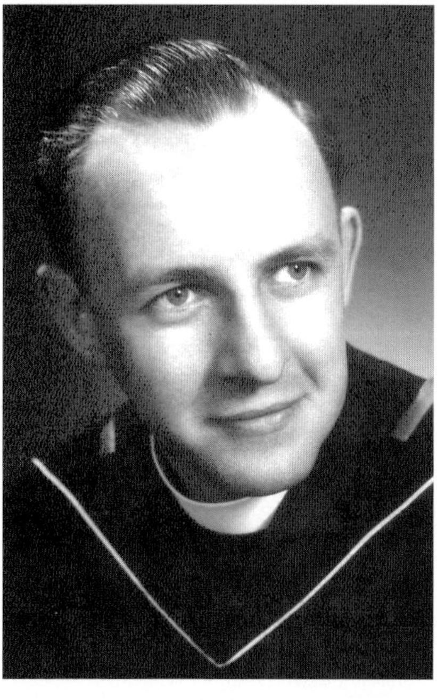

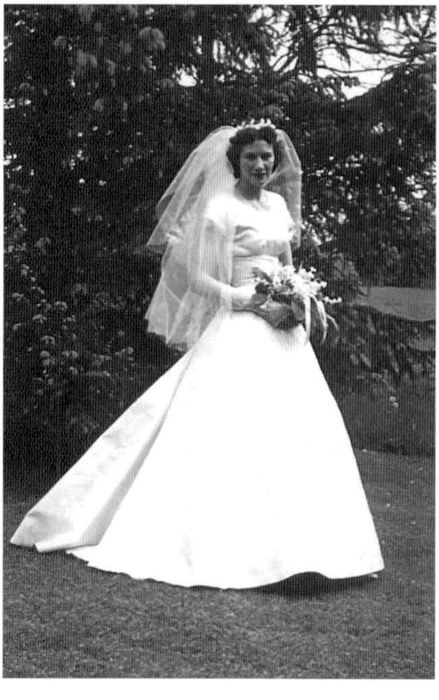

A Chinese Gentleman

One day in the eighties when I was living in Stratford I decided to drive to Toronto to do some Christmas shopping. I went into the parking garage at the Eaton's Centre and up the circular ramps to one of the floors that had a connecting bridge leading into the store. After the long drive I had to go to the washroom and I found one just inside the door.

I used one of the stalls and came out to wash my hands. A man spoke to me; he was Chinese. I was terrified. I am a gay man, an older and wiser one after the excesses of youth. I have two knee replacements and can no longer run with impunity. I want to keep out of trouble and I never speak to another individual in a public washroom. The man advanced toward me, gesturing with his hands, speaking his own language and pointing at the stall I had just vacated. I washed my hands, grabbed a paper towel and fled.

I finished my Christmas shopping and returned to my car to drive home to Stratford. I discovered I did not have my keys. Loaded down with parcels, I made my way across the store to the lost-and-found counter. The lady there was glad to see me. She said that a very kind, old, Chinese gentleman had brought my keys into the lost-and-found. He had explained to her that he had found them on the floor inside one of the stalls in a men's washroom. I thanked her and went back to my car, glad to leave a city of such frightening dimensions.

Chu Chin Chow

The title of the newspaper article reads, "Tabernacle Choir Triumphs in Musical Pageant of Nations". The paper is the *Ontario Intelligencer* in Belleville, an issue from the late 1930s. The sub-titles say, "Originality of Conception Marks the Presentation of Musical Numbers, Singing Brilliant, Wide Range of Music is Sung in Character and National Dress." For me, under ten years of age and impressionable, it was the opening of a magical world of music, dance, stage movement and colour. It was the choir concert presented by the choir of Tabernacle United Church in Belleville.

We had moved from Toronto to Belleville, my Mother's hometown and attended the family church, Tabernacle United. My chief joy in going to service was to hear the choir sing the anthem each Sunday morning. Then came the many practices associated with the giving of the concert. Dad and my Uncle Grant were baritones, Auntie May was a soprano soloist, my cousin Gertrude Bennett-Post who was taking ballet lessons was doing a dance and Dorothy Bradley, a family friend was the choir leader. She arranged the music and costume and directed the acting. Mrs. Duff played the piano off stage and her son Gardiner sang a number of solos. It was a close group of friends, and my family knew everybody.

A number of quotes from the newspaper reveals the florid exaggeration of language that was typical of those times in journalism, especially in small town newspapers.

—"The audience was one of the largest which ever gathered to attend a festival of music by a local choir, the performance of numbers were insistently applauded.

—"Not only was musical talent of a very high order revealed, but surprising gifts along histrionic lines were indicated by many who took part.

— "The pageant moved in a musico-dramatic atmosphere, the entire effect was such as to make every music lover present realize how much more effective song is when acted in character,

—"the costumes, the acting and the music combined to make one of the rarest events ever enjoyed in music."

There was a long list of scenes from many nations. Soldiers and Indians represented Canada; From China came my Father singing as the Mandarin Chu Chin Chow from a First World War musical in London. In his scene there was a Chinese girl and a Chinese coolie; an oriental rhythm was marked throughout this piece. Then came a French scene followed by an Irish one where my cousin danced as an Irish fairy to the air "Come Back To Erin". A Scotch scene followed with Auntie May, dressed as an old fish wife, singing "Caller Herrin" An Arabian story unfolded with my Father, this time singing the well known "Cobbler Song". Next came scenes from Italy, Japan and Romania with a gypsy encampment showing fifteen on stage at once. Uncle Grant was resplendent as a toreador and sang "The Toreador Song" from Carmen. Holland, Wales and the United States added scenes. Finally Britannia appeared on stage, the whole cast assembled, and "Rule Britannia" followed by "God Save The King" was sung.

My father did the lighting and was also highly complimented for the costume he had designed and worn as the cobbler in the Persian scene. It was considered a work of art.

What magic! No wonder I ended up in the arts. In my eyes it was the grandest thing I had ever watched. To this day I can tell you what various people sang in that performance. How can we talk about globalization in the face of such a memory coming at us from the past?

Chapter Four

Filling My Mind

My Education

I do not have many early memories. Some people can tell you about the first time their mother took them for a carriage ride, but I cannot. My first memory, strangely enough, is about my father's office. Some time after the crash he was once again in business, what kind I do not know. I was born in 1928.

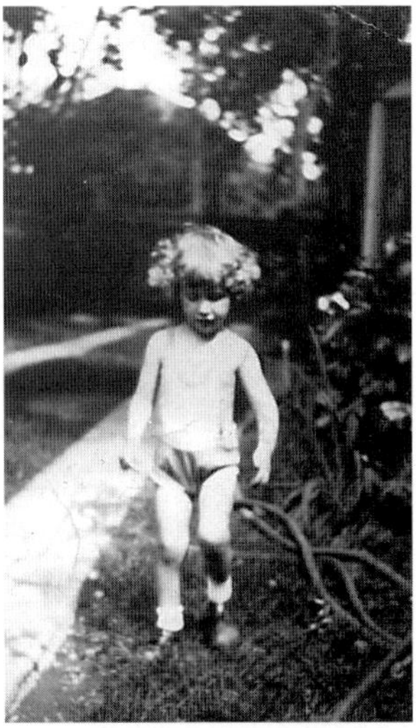

I visited his office and I remember that it was in Chinese red and black;, it had a modern look about it that I now recognize as Art Deco. There was a round window with a window seat and above the seat there was a shelf with an Encyclopaedia Brittanica. I was very impressed.

It is strange how the very act of writing seems to act on the subconscious and memories start to surface. I remember that Dad used to dress up formally on a Sunday morning in the cold weather and take the three of us, my two sisters and me, out for walks in and around Queen's Park. I have a picture of Joan, Jane and me hanging over the top of a cannon, all of us dressed in our best winter clothes. I was wearing a tam, a small black coat and knee socks. Dad impressed me as a very important man, for he was wearing a long black coat, a bowler hat, white gloves and a white handkerchief sticking out of his

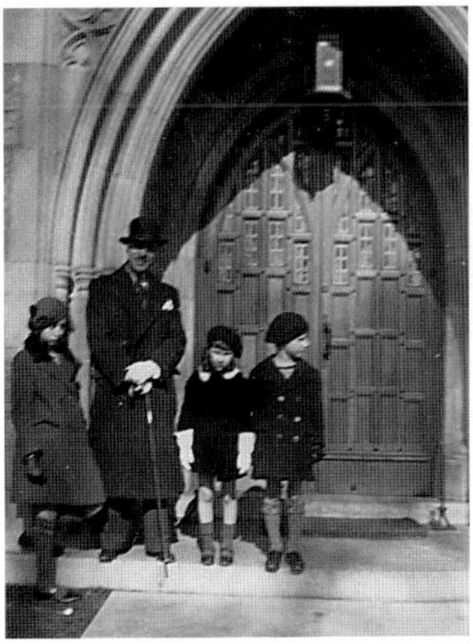

pocket. He was carrying the cane that Joan still has with an inscription on it in sterling silver, "Presented to Lieut. D.L. Bennett by Tommy's Club, Arden, Ontario, 1918". Dad had recruited his own platoon in Arden prior to going overseas. I have this memory because on this walk I became very frightened; I was dawdling along behind the others, when Dad turned, and (this was very unusual for him) threatened that they would go on and leave me to find my own way home. I rushed up and joined them, but the memory of fright remains.

My strongest memory is of my first day of school. We were living on the second floor of a large Victorian house on Bay St; across the road from us was a Catholic nunnery. My first school was on Bay St. a couple of blocks north of us. It must have been the winter term as we were wearing coats. My birthday was in January. I was duly deposited at the school and registered in a class. The very first day we had a fire drill. All the other students knew what to do. They formed up in lines inside each room and marched out into the school yard. I lingered behind my line; the school was on fire! What should I do! I had to save something, I ran into the narrow cloakroom at the back of my classroom and grabbed as many coats as I could and then struggled down the hall and out of the front door loaded down to the length of my arms and the strength of my body.

I still remember standing there in the sunlight at the top of a long set of steps and looking over the sea of juvenile faces. There was a roll of laughter that I have never forgotten — it was a giant wave that rolled over and over me. My memory ends at that point.

We moved from Bay Street and up onto Glen Road in Rosedale,

I have only two memories of my next school. I know that I walked west along a street and then went up a large flight of steps on a hill at the top of which was the school. In the spring all along the edge of the school yard boys would place rectangles of wood rather like very heavy window frames. They would be placed flat on the ground; at the front would be small doors with a number written above each one. The large doors had small numbers and the small doors had large numbers. The contestant would take an alley and roll it along the ground toward a door, if the aim was accurate and the alley rolled through a door he was rewarded with the number of alleys recorded above that door. If he missed the owner of the "trap" would keep the alley, I constantly lost all of my marbles. How I longed to win a bagful and go home triumphantly!!

We moved to Belleville and I went to Pine Street School; all I can remember about that school is the name and I could still walk the route to school today. I have no memory of my teachers or classes.

Then we moved out to Avondale just outside Belleville on the Trent Road. We rented a newly built Dutch style bungalow from a Mr. Bell. Behind the house was an old barn/driveshed from a previous generation. The corner and the street where we lived is now a mini-mall and both house and barn have disappeared. One field to the north was a one-room school where I finished my primary education. Here memories flood in, my first teacher was a Miss Hansler, followed by a Miss Murphy. Usually the teacher lived at the home of the chairman of the school board — so they could keep an eye on her moral behaviour I suppose.

Friday afternoon was the best time of the week for me. we had art for the first half of the afternoon and then Miss MacDonald, the music teacher arrived and we had music for the rest of the afternoon. Miss McDonald was a very glamorous person to me, she arrived in a big car, she was a big lady with a beautiful voice, she dressed very nicely. Christmas concerts were always very special and we started practising for them early in the fall. A stage with curtains would be rigged across the front of the room for the great event, when the parents would squeeze into the small desks and stand all around the sides. The concerts would go on forever as plays and music were performed. In one play I was Uncle Epitumus, I will never forget that name. At one point I had to fall backwards into somebody's arms, something cracked in my back and my back hurt for months. I was afraid to tell anybody about it, each night I would lay in my bed on my back as stiff as a ramrod, willing it to get better. It did for a while but in adult life I ended up with three disintegrating discs.

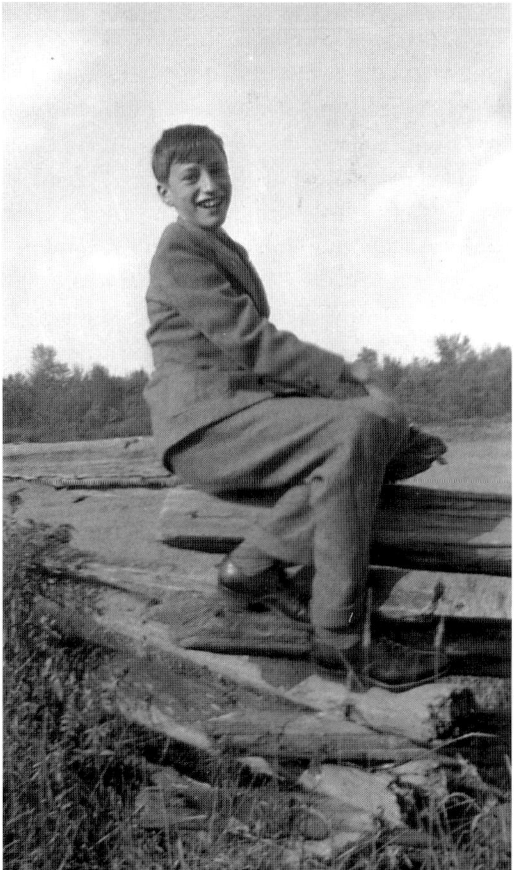

There was a large student enrolment of over forty students with only one

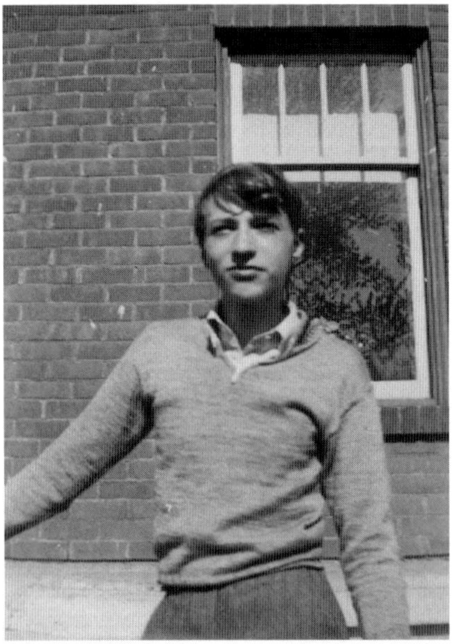

teacher. The teachers in those days must have been masters at the balancing act of teaching forty students eight different grades at the same time. One solution was to have the older students teach the younger ones at various times of the day. I managed to skip grade eight by listening to the lessons and trying the entrance examinations a year ahead of time. So on to High School in Belleville.

I took grade nine in the 1941-1942 school year at Belleville Collegiate Institute and Vocational School. My father was in the army and stationed at Camp Borden. Joan had just finished High School and was home for a year studying piano to complete her Associate of the Toronto Conservatory of Music degree. (That has now been replaced by the A.R.C.T — Associate of the Royal Conservatory of Toronto) She succeeded and the next year went on to University of Toronto. I remember only three things actually about that school. I remember being in a class on library rules and regulations. The teacher whose name I have forgotten became annoyed at the unruly noise of some of the boys and told us that we had better learn discipline as it was quite likely that we would all by in the army as soon as we left school. I remember Miss Saunders, the French teacher; who absolutely terrified me. She had a very sarcastic tongue. One day the class could not learn how to pronounce "Monsieur" properly, we had to repeat that word for most of the class,

I was never good in languages, and I credit that teacher for giving me a mental block that I could never entirely overcome. My third memory is of taking a bus home from school one day. An old man, perhaps a veteran of the First World War, came over to me in front of the busload of people and gave me a white feather as a sign of cowardice, I should be in the army, I was tall for my age and very thin but I was only thirteen/fourteen.

In the fall of 1942 we moved back to Toronto. Dad was stationed at Long Branch, he could get away for weekends much more easily with the reduced distance for travel. Joan was in Honours English at Victoria College at U. of T. If we lived in Toronto she could live at home and save the money of boarding out. Joan found us an apartment in an old

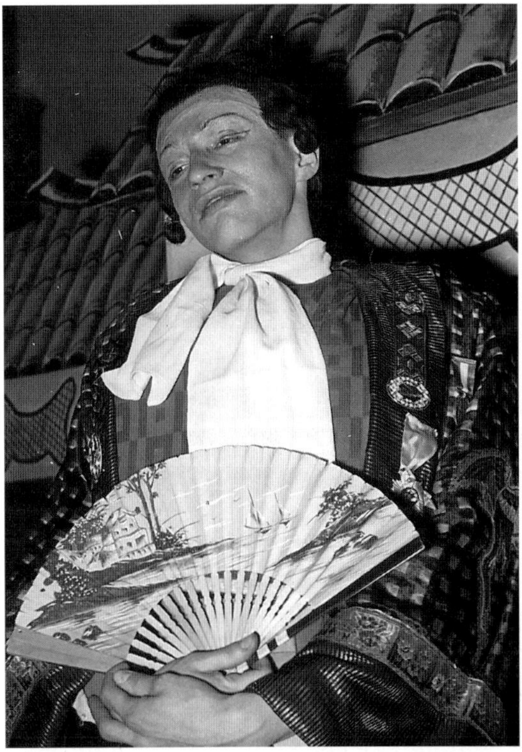

home on Palmerston Boulevard half a block below Bloor Street. I enrolled in Harbord Collegiate. I was well dressed and I had good manners. I was not especially bright in school. I really shone academically only when I went to University and was taking subjects that fascinated me. I had no aptitude for sports, I was fairly popular in a quiet sort of way.

I give Mr. Allister P, Haig, the music teacher, full credit for giving me confidence in myself. I enjoyed the music classes and in the fall of 1944 Mr. Haig asked if I would try out for the role of Pooh Bah in the Mikado. I did and won the part. My voice was beginning to mature. The fall and winter months were taken up with rehearsals. I kept a diary for that school year in which I never recorded any of my real thoughts or feelings but simply put down a stream of activities. I am amazed at how involved I was with other people. I was always going somewhere or doing something with other boys, I recorded all the tests and exams, mentioned French, Latin, Zoology, English, Geometry, History, Botany and Navigation, I became somebody in the school because of my performance in that production of the Mikado. I was called Pooh Bah in class and in the halls. My costume required me to wear pillows on my front and back. Mr. Haig told me sometime later that for him one of the funniest actions in the play was when turned to the front I was fat, with the stuffing of pillows, but when I turned around and had to bend over my tiny little backside was amusing.

The following year I was Lord Mountararat in Iolanthe. The performances took place on March 6,7,8, and 9, 1946. I will never forget the final evening, We had to wear a type of evening dress in black silk. The costume had black tights; I found mine somewhat close fitting and so switched with Lord Tolloller who was not quite as big as I was.

We had a dance in the second act with the Lord Chancellor. The three of us were dancing around; at one point Tollollер was in the centre and advancing up the stage when his trousers split from top to bottom right down the front, the black silk parted, and out tumbled the white lining!! I have never heard such laughing in my life, they had to ring down the curtain until the hilarity was subdued. After a period of time the damage was hastily remedied and the performance went on to much laughter the rest of the evening.

On May 7th, 1945 I went to school as usual. I was an officer in the Cadet Corps and we were outside practising our routines for the official inspection on May 9th. Suddenly we heard car horns honking out on the street and saw people starting to put flags out on the houses. We finished our drill and then Mr. Carlyle, the principal, called all the boys up in a crowd to the reviewing stand and told us that the war was over in Europe! We were given the rest of the day off. I dashed home and saw Jane and Joan rushing out to buy some groceries before all the stores were closed. I phoned a friend, Sid Eisen, and arranged to meet him. I wore gray flannels, a sports coat, pink shirt and a silk red polka dot tie (Wow).

Five of us gathered and gradually worked our way downtown along Queen Street and towards City Hall. There was a huge crowd there waving flags and noise makers. Ticker tape was hanging from all the poles and wires and confetti was everywhere. One truck went by carrying almost fifty people. I walked on the street car tracks so I could say I had done so on a busy day. We worked our way up close to the platform in frond of the city hall. A man was leading a singsong. Then a young lieutenant got up and asked why the people were so happy; he had seen friends die in his arms. He picked out six men in the crowd dressed in civilian clothes, yelled at them and asked why they were not in uniform. A young kilted piper went up and tried to drown him out with his pipes. A fat soft looking civilian with a quiet voice tried to say that we should all be friends now that the war was over and forget the war. An old veteran who had climbed a telephone pole yelled so hard that his teeth fell out. Somebody in the crowd threw them up to him and he caught them in his cap and put them back in his mouth. Up on the platform two drunk women and an airman were very belligerent with a civilian, asking why he had not joined up — let them see his discharge button, they had a father over in France, etcetera. The man moved away, he turned and looked at them with a scar on his face, balancing his one leg with a crutch.

I walked home and found Dad there, after he was transferred to the army camp at Longbranch he could come home quite often. Dad and I went over to Christie Pitts where there were bands, singing, a number of bonfires, and finally fireworks. We saw a soldier who was behaving quite normally until the fireworks started but then he went crazy with shell shock. It took a group of people to get him into a car and taken away.

The next day was anticlimactic; there was no zest and little flag-waving. Mother, Jane, Joan and I went down to the city hall for the memorial service. There were twenty thousand people there and the service was very impressive. I have a copy of the City of Toronto civic service programme for the day; the programme was long and solemn: We all went home about three p.m.

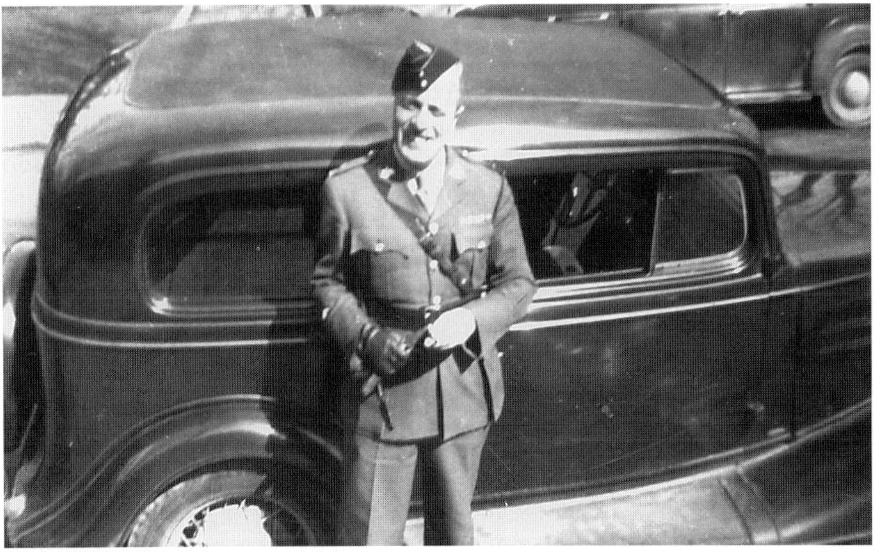

The next day, May 9th, was our cadet inspection at school. Dad was one of the reviewing officers. It was freezing cold. The regular cadets were .allowed to wear their suit jackets. The officers had to wear their sweaters only. Mine was light and I had never before been so cold: Dad took the second salute — the march past in columns of route. Then to our surprise we were ordered to go into the school auditorium and all the company drill, precision squad, P.T. drill, First Aid, Signals, etcetera were left undone — it was too cold. Dad said after that even in his battle dress he was frozen, and he was worried about me. Dad sat on the platform with the other dignitaries. He was a Major and I was very proud of him. The band played, there were speeches and we were dismissed until time for afternoon classes.

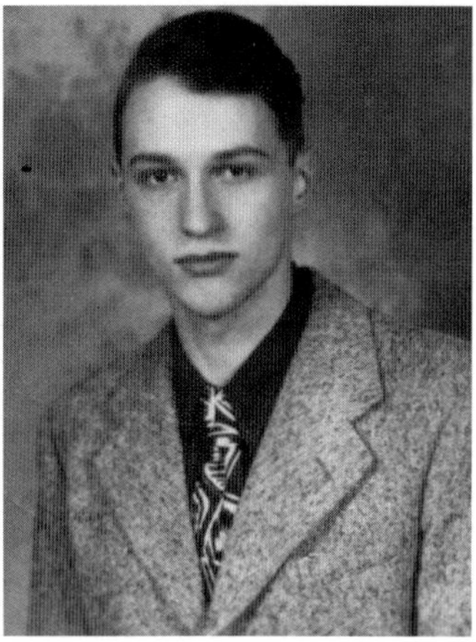

All through school I always had a job during the holidays. The first summer I had worked at Camp Borden, as recorded elsewhere. Then when Dad was at Longbranch I got a summer job there with another group of boys. During the previous winter a snow plow with its blade too low had taken a good part of the top layer of the pavement off the parade ground. Our first job was to level the resulting mess with shovels and rakes. We worked without shirts, I got too much sun and had to give up the job. Next I secured a good-paying job with Bordens delivering milk by three wheeled bicycles to the stores over on the islands. Each day I would go over by ferry boat and I enjoyed the experience very much. The following summer I worked at the Eclipse Pen and Pencil Company at a lathe cutting the ridges on the pens to allow the tops to be screwed on; it was the most boring job I had ever had. I swore that I would secure a good education to avoid ever having to settle permanently for a mind-numbing job. One other summer I stayed at my Aunt Ilah's home at Warings Corners in Prince Edward County and worked in a canning factory at Bloomfield stacking cartons of peas and then tomatoes in the warehouse. Aunt Ilah's lovely stone home is now a well known restaurant and conference centre in Prince Edward. It is not far from Picton.

I graduated from Harbord Collegiate in June of 1946. I had a first in History (I loved the subject) three thirds and four credits. Miss Saunders had come to haunt me — I failed French Composition.

In the fall of 1946 I considered returning to Harbord Collegiate and thought that I would repeat some subjects so that I could improve my marks. It was very tempting, the subject matter would surely be easier and I could once again shine in an operetta. Then my sister Joan started in on me — how dare I waste a year? I should at least try to get into University. I did try; I wanted Fine Arts but I knew that I did not have a chance.

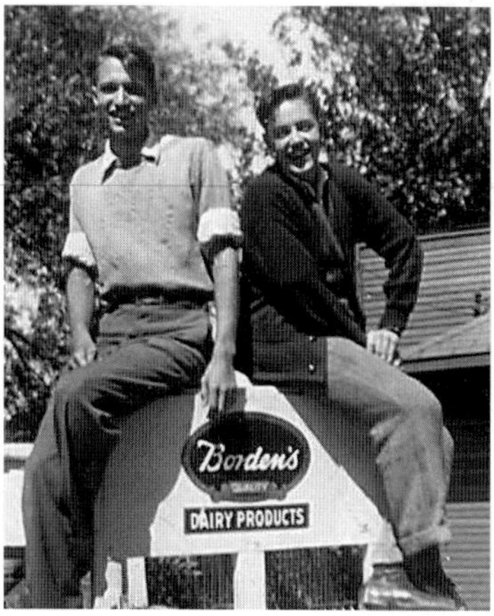

So I tried for the three year Pass Arts course, I was smart enough to consult the Art and Archaeology department, as Fine Arts was then known. I chose a series of courses in Pass Arts that would duplicate those in the first year of Fine Arts. In spite of the great influx of ex-service men into the University, I did manage to get into Pass Arts.

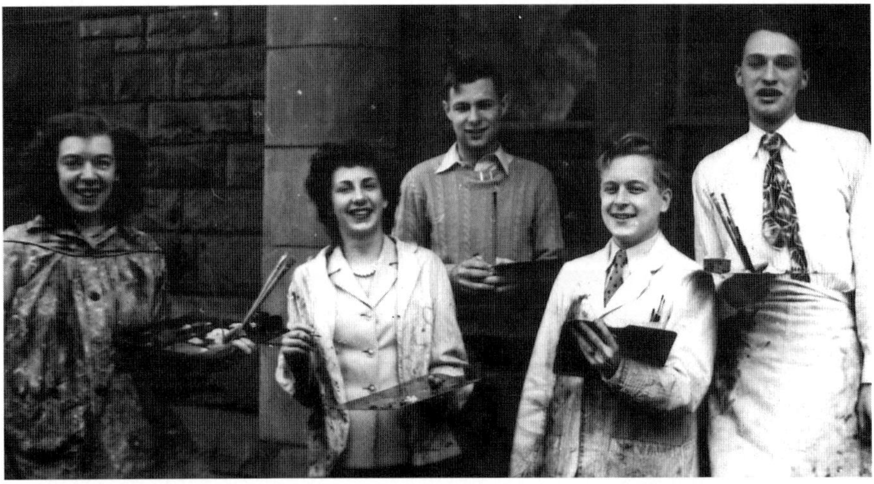

Eileen Roberts (nee Snyder), June Pemberton, Bill Withrow, Jim Chapman, Paul Bennett — Saturday morning painting class

As soon as I was into a subject that I liked, I blossomed. I earned a second class honours standing in first year Pass Arts and was able to transfer into the second year of the honours course in Art and Archaeology. I do not have a record of that year's marks but I have my marks for third and fourth years. In third year I received a second in Drawing and Design, Architectural Drafting and Analysis, History of Art and Italian History. In Philosophy a first, Religious Knowledge an A and English a B. In fourth year I received a first in Art and Archaeology 4i, and Philosophy, and an A in Anthropology, and seconds in Art and Archaeology 4j and History of Art and finally a third in Archaeology 41. Obviously I had some intelligence, I just had to have subjects that interested me.

We were very fortunate at that time to have Homer and Dorothy Thompson as professors. Unfortunately I only knew them in first year. They were both very important Greek scholars, who had met each other on a dig in Greece. Homer was a Canadian, born in Devlin, Ontario in 1906 and living until 1999. In the 1930s he spent his summers digging in Greece and in winter returned to Canada, where he was professor of classical archaeology at the University of Toronto and also curator of the classical collection at the Royal Ontario Museum.

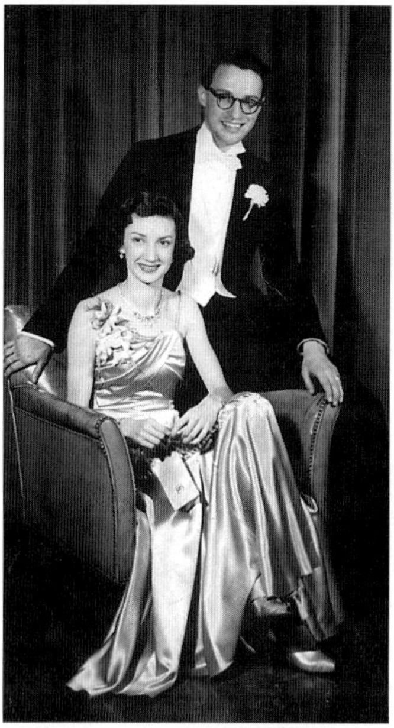

The South House Formal Dance, 1950. Victoria College. I escorted Mary Lou Dilworth

In 1947 he was appointed professor of classical archaeology at the Institute for Advanced Studies at Princeton, New Jersey. He was named director of the Agora excavations the same year. The agora was the old market area in Athens; Agora actually translates as, "the coming together place" — the civic centre of ancient Athens. For thirty-nine years he worked at this project, his chief work was the reconstruction of one of the buildings of the Agora, his team erected a two-storey stoa, a form of ancient Greek public building which now houses a museum.

One of my most pleasant memories of my Fine Arts period was the classes that I took with Dorothy Burr Thompson. She had published a book of translations of Greek poetry, *Swans and Amber.* She used to read some of these poems to us in the original Greek. Her voice was melodious and the sound was enchanting.

I also have an amusing story of the Thompsons. After the war our family moved down to the village of Newcastle, the Thompsons had a home in Orono, just to the north. They had planted reforestation on all of their land and the evergreen trees were nicely coming into maturity. One summer weekend in 1947 they kindly asked if our family would join them for tea on a Sunday afternoon. We all sat out on the porch of the old house, it was quiet and secluded surrounded by walls of trees. Dad, in his usual nonchalant English way, was smoking. I can see him now taking the cigarette from his lips, he flicked his ash over the railing of the porch as there were no ash trays in sight and swoosh —a complete decorative evergreen went up in flames. What a disaster, however the fire was very quickly put out.

I had just finished my first year in Pass Arts and been accepted in the Fine Arts honours course. We were never asked back.

I got along well with all of my classmates. I was in awe of some of them, especially those sophisticated worldly-wise women. There were twenty-six of us who graduated, only seven were men. The men were quite a closely knit group. I remember the day we walked across the campus in our gowns toward Convocation Hall for graduation. We

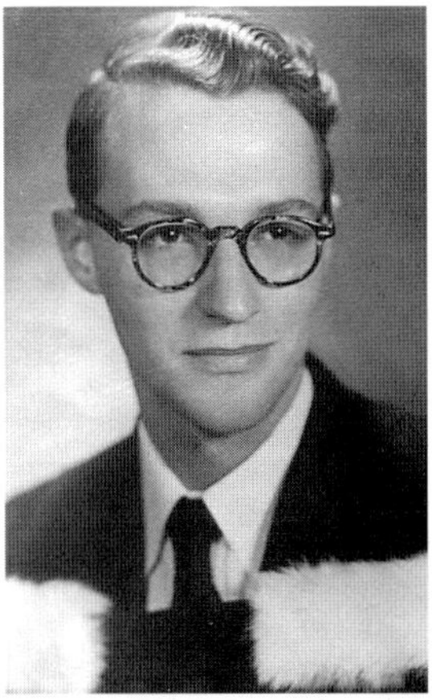

looked at each other and said, "Boy, are we cultured, now what?" It took years for that answer to fully appear.

A number went on to very successful teaching careers, I think of Eleanor Konkle nee Lever and Helen Gariepy nee Prendergast. Bill Withrow became the Director of the Art Gallery of Toronto, he navigated that institution through a period of growth for many years finally evolving into the Art Gallery of Ontario, it received the Henry Moore bequest and it grew to immense proportions physically. David Gardner had and still has a glowing career in theatre, film and T.V. He was also an administrator in Drama. Jim Chapman, one of our best scholars, died, soon after graduation, of cancer. Don Levitt, the happy-go-lucky clown of the class, had a brain operation and worked quietly for the rest of his life in commerce. Eileen Roberts nee Snider, the best scholar in our class, continued academically in the U.S.A. and ended in England where she married an architect, had two. children and lives in St. Albans, my father's home town. Eileen has written books about the architecture, the wall paintings and now the stained glass of the ancient St. Albans Abbey. Audrey Scott: nee Feasel, married Alan, a minister. Audrey, herself, also trained as a minister. They had two children of their own and also adopted a large number of disadvantaged children. They have loved and looked after the total number of their family through the years. They bought an old bus in order to take the whole family for outings. I could list the whole class, without exception we have all contributed to our families or to our communities. I believe that our University should be proud of producing such a productive class.

It is only recently, fifty years after graduation, that I have come to know better these friends from the past and appreciate their accomplishments and the different directions that a "cultural" education can lead one.

I am going to leave my education at this point. I worked for a year at the Training School for Boys at Bowmanville, then I worked for a time for the Big Brother Association in Hamilton: I returned to school and went to the Ontario College of Education in 1952-53. I received my Bachelor of Social Work, then the Bachelor and Masters of Education while working for the Community Programmes Branch of the Department of Education as mentioned elsewhere in this weighty tome.

Chapter Five

First Trip to Europe, 1956

In 1955 I attended a summer art course. I remember that I studied glass enamelling on copper and figure drawing. For some time after that I was involved in glass enamelling and enjoyed it very much. At the course I met two other teachers, Arn Bowers and Ladd Scube. One Sunday we three decided to go down to the Toronto waterfront and do some sketching. While there we started talking about Europe as Arn was just leaving for a two year stint of teaching in one of the schools set up at Soest, Germany, to teach the children of service men on duty in that country.

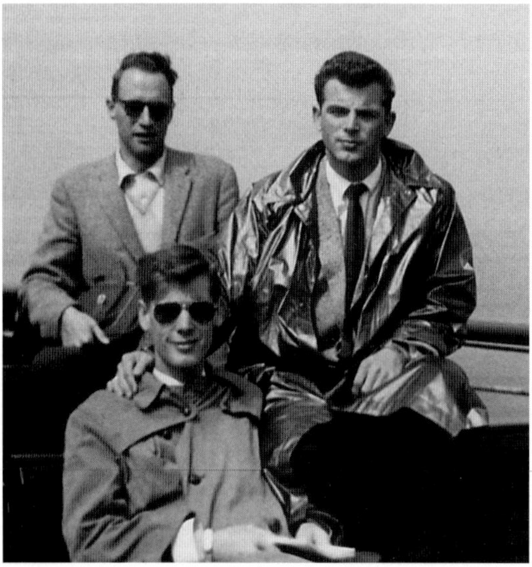

The more we talked about Europe the more excited we became and Ladd and I decided that we would join Arn the following summer for a tour of Europe, which in 1956 we did.

I kept a journal of that trip which became a one-hundred and seventy-eight page effort written on three-ring binder paper. The journal was never finished, our last stop was Paris and on the middle of the last day I was talking about Notre Dame Cathedral and suddenly the page is blank— something interrupted me. I know from pictures that we also visited the Eiffel Tower and that we took a plane home. The journal however is open-ended and perhaps that is how it should be for travel.

Although this trip filled only a two month period of my early life, I have read the journal twice in the last month, and I am amazed at the changes in myself, in travel, in Europe, that I witness now compared to 1956.

On the first page of the diary, I speak of travel costs. We went over by boat; the ticket was one hundred and eight-five dollars one way! The plane back was more in line with today's costs. It was three hundred and four dollars. Our train ticket, one way from Oshawa to Montreal, was eleven-fifty. Recently I traveled from Cobourg to Montreal return and the senior cost by Via Rail, return, was one hundred and forty-seven sixty-six. In Europe, I flew by plane from Portugal to Switzerland for ninety-two dollars. I left for my trip with six hundred and forty-two dollars in traveller's cheques and one hundred and forty dollars Canadian.

Arn and a friend of his, Ray Manson, met Ladd and me in Southampton. I have already indicated in these writings that I am gay, but none of the three friends I travelled with that summer is gay. In fact, I am not sure that I realized my homosexuality myself in those days. I know that on board ship I was attracted to the young men and spent time talking with them and playing games with them. Meanwhile, Ladd always had one of the female passengers on his arm. At times, for evenings in the lounge, we would form a foursome and Ladd's friend would bring along a girl friend and we would all go dancing. Nobody on the trip mentioned my non-interest in women. The situation was easier when the four of us were travelling together.

Another difference with the customs and manners of today was the fact that I had never been exposed to alcohol or beer. We were on a German ship and the younger passengers consumed much beer. I tried it a number of times but disliked it. In Germany, we were constantly offered wine; again I tried it but had no taste for it — at that time.

We travelled on a ship called "The Seven Seas". It had been an U.S. aircraft carrier, the Nellie, in the recent war.

It had been converted in the 1950s and made its first trip in 1954 as a passenger liner with only eighty passengers on it. One of our cabin mates was a former German submarine officer during the war. He told us that three times he had come after this very ship but it had always managed to elude him. He told us that he graduated in 1936 with a full class, and only two of his classmates were still alive.

The meals were very heavy on board ship. Finally toward the end of the trip I was eating only the soups, salads and rolls, and left the entrees of meat and potatoes alone. One interesting thing was that the

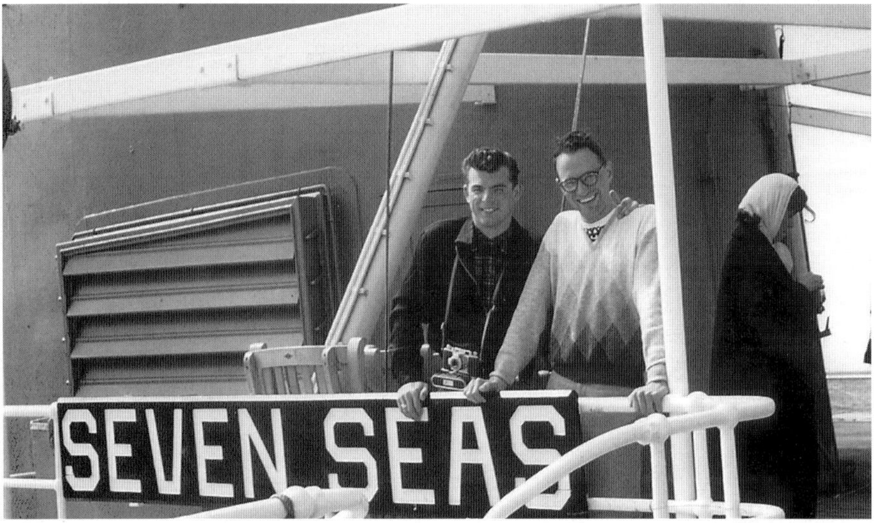

straws for soft drinks were real straws, not our manufactured type. The butter we ate was unsalted Danish butter.

It actually was a small liner; there was a very small swimming pool, a number of lounges and bars, some games rooms, a library and so on, but nothing on the scale of what we see today. We were four to a cabin and lucky to be on the top deck. We had a porthole. I went down to see one of the lower decks where the portholes seemed to look right out on the level of the big waves and they scared me to death.

As we sailed by the Isle of Wight, we saw hundreds of gulls, deep blue water and sailing craft playing tag with the liner. We turned around a red, white, and black light ship with lines full of gaily waving washing, and headed up Southampton Channel. All the friends we had made on board lined the rails with cameras clicking. Every sailboat with its crew dipping bared legs over the side waved at us, and eight hundred of us waved back. Tugs manoeuvred us into the dock. We gathered our bags from our stateroom and went down the white covered gangplank while a German brass band played a rousing military number. We had arrived in England. Arn and Ray Manson greeted us. Ray had a Volkswagen and we would travel in it through July and all of August.

Briefly, our itinerary took us through England, Wales, Ireland, Scotland, Belgium, Germany, and Switzerland. For a short time, we separated: I went to Portugal to visit friends, Ladd went to Yugoslavia to see some members of his family, and Arn and Ray went to Liechtenstein. We all met again in Switzerland and continued together on into Italy, Monaco, France, and so home.

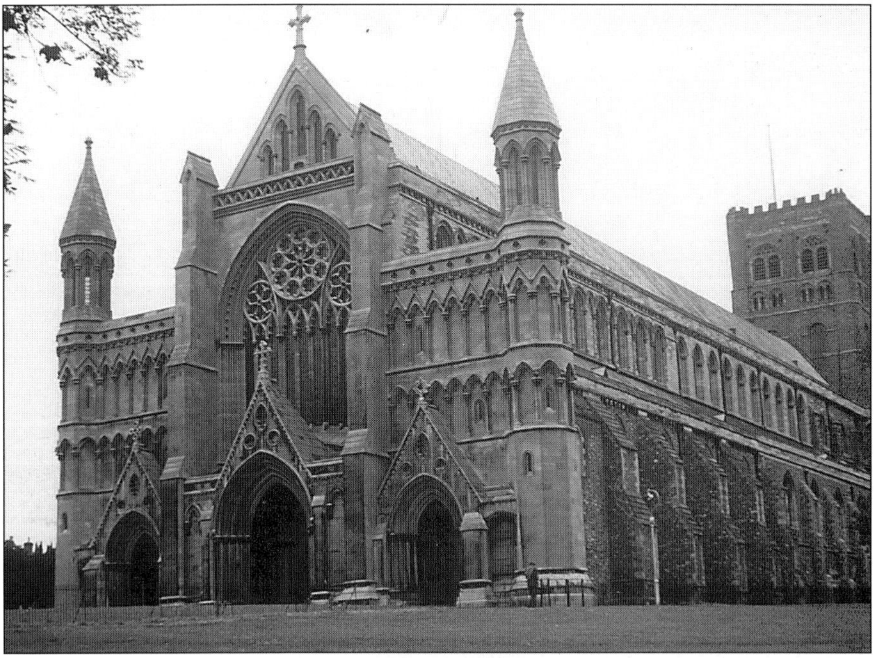

St. Alban's Abbey

In London I visited my Auntie Marge who was a nursing sister at St. Mary's Hospital. Then I travelled out to St. Albans to visit a large number of my father's relatives who had all gathered to meet me. We did all the tourist things, and saw all the tourist sites. We went to the theatre a number of times, Leslie Caron, starring in *Gigi,* gave Arn her autograph at the stage door of the New Theatre in London after a performance. London was lively but still bore the scars of the recent war; behind fences one could see the remains of bombed-out buildings.

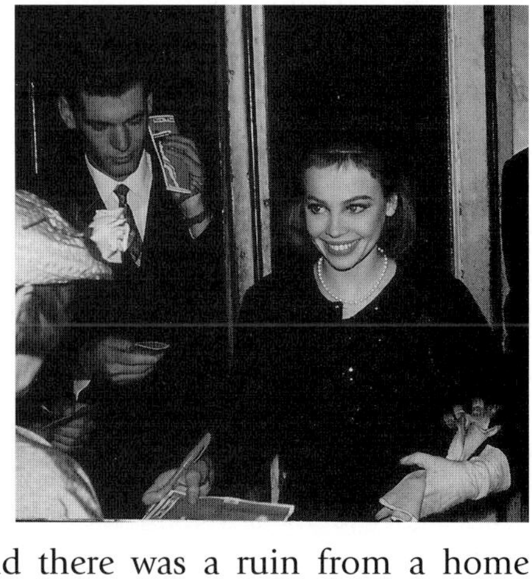

I remember going around the corner from the U.S. Embassy and there was a ruin from a home bombed during the war. Inside the burnt out shell was a three-quarter ruined graceful staircase turning in a lovely curve up and around as it ascended to the second floor. There had been a great deal of damage around St. Paul's Cathedral. It was damaged itself. A thousand homes and other buildings had been destroyed in the area around St. Paul's.

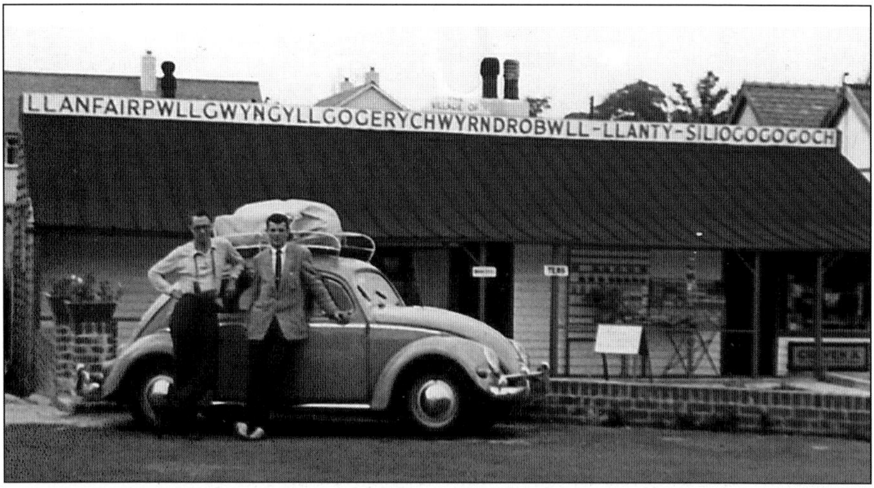

The war was physically evident to a great extent but also I sensed that the people had suffered considerable psychological damage and they would take a very long time to rebound. We met and talked to the average Englishman in the pubs and restaurants; there was a cynicism and apathy that was hard to overcome.

We were on limited budgets and could not patronize high priced establishments, perhaps in places more "posh" conditions might have been different. We did find the regular cafes and restaurants quite slovenly, seemed dirty and served poorly prepared food. All through my diary I criticized the food in England. An amusing point about this diary is that occasionally I wax rhapsodical about works of art but I was still a growing young adult and very concerned and mentioned the food we had for every meal.

The colours of Wales were unbelievable, soft greys, blues, greens, purples, — the country was like a poem. Ireland was the green that you imagine, people friendly, soft-spoken, girls lovely in Dublin, men badly dressed in many cases, parts of Ireland were under populated, fifty percent of the youth went to England.

We made the mistake in Scotland, of going to Glasgow first. It was one of the most uncomfortable cities that I had been in, the houses were all stone, huge areas of tenements with dark winding alleys and twisting staircases with stone steps worn down by countless feet. The buildings were black with dirt and scale was falling off the stone, the streetcars were old and ramshackle. However when we arrived in Edinburgh about noon one day we immediately fell in love with the city, we toured Princess Street, attended a ceremony of "Retreat" up at the castle involving thirty-two highlanders in full uniform, we met five girls and we all went dancing.

Back in England my diary mentions an interesting fact. We came to an airport and had to stop for a red light so that a jet could go by! The light said stop and suddenly a jet zoomed out of a nearby field just seemingly clearing the fences, then the light went green again.

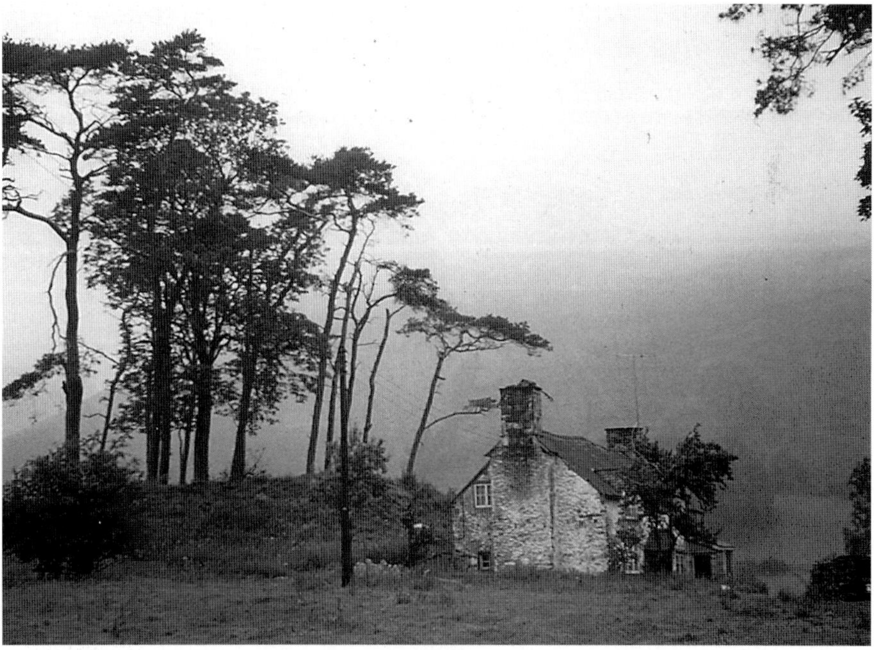

Wales

I would be remiss if I did not mention the historic buildings, Tudor cottages, old forts and ruined castles that we toured and looked at in England. Of course we visited the Victoria and Albert Museum, The National Gallery, The Tower of London and so on. We were having a look at our own history.

In Canterbury I finally found what I had been hoping to find during my visits to antique stores all along the route. I had constantly been asking about old lap writing desks. In a tiny little shop the attendant brought out a little desk of rosewood about eighteen inches high, a foot in depth and eighteen inches wide. It had an overall inlay of intricate ivory in a naturalistic pattern. Two ink bottles fitted in to the top and two doors opened to reveal two drawers and a fold down surface on which to write. It was magnificent. I bought it for six pounds and it sits on a table in my bedroom today. It was made between 1820 and 1850, probably in India on order from a European. The desk was tenderly placed in a box, wrapped well and I carried my treasure back to our vehicle where

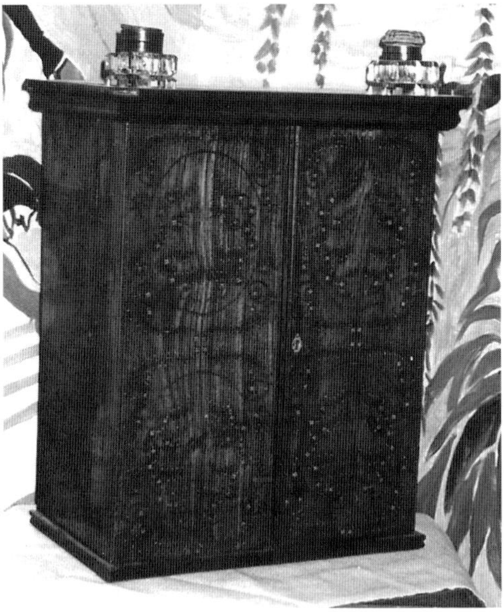

I placed it in the trunk after transferring my suitcase to the top of the car.

After various adventures we came to Dover, boarded the ferry and crossed to Ostend in Belgium. The country itself was very flat and the city seemed to emerge from the water as we approached it. Proceeding to Germany, we crossed the border at Aachen, where we were amazed not only at the war damage but also at the great amount of reconstruction going on. We saw the same thing in Essen and Dusseldorf.

Compared to Britain, there was a feeling of vitality in the air; the people were healthy, tall, blond and muscular. It was summer and a good percentage of the young people seemed to be on the move — on bicycles, on trips to see the rest of Europe. It gave me a strange feeling to cross the Rhine on a new bridge. Imagine what that would have meant only a few short years before? Now groups of people were picnicking, sunbathing, swimming and playing games with children along the riverbanks. We were told that every time a German cuts down a tree he must plant three trees in its place. We travelled the autobahns, the four-lane highways that Hitler had built in the 1930s to ease unemployment. Continuing across Germany, we reached the great European plain, a smiling land of rich earth, waving trees and rolling hills.

We visited Werl and Soest, the Canadian army centres of occupation. In Soest we took pictures of the crooked steeple; an architect was commissioned to design a church, near the end of the construction the city fathers decided to not pay him his full fee. The architect had his revenge; he put the steeple up at an angle. Soon people came flocking to see it; the revenge had worked in reverse. The architect then built twelve other churches in the district each with a crooked steeple.

We visited the city of Munster in West Germany. This city was seventy per cent destroyed during the war: The city now had the largest debt of any city in Germany, but it was rebuilt with a feeling of adventure in design. All the light standards stood free of wires in clean-cut design. In certain areas part of the old mediaeval town still stood. These people had not rebuilt it in pseudo Gothic in an attempt to blend with the old. They built in a modern style and the old beamed Gothic structures stood side by side with the clean-cut style of modern architecture. Both a good design and so they harmonized together.

In the same city a group of local architects were given the problem of building a new opera house. The lot was an odd shape and they had to incorporate the remains of the old opera house into the design. There was an old brick wall and a stone archway with Ionic columns. This old relic was featured in a courtyard at the front and the new opera house circled it. The new structure was in mauve, blue and grey tile with railings in silver and ebony. The bareness of the architectural features across the front was broken by a piece of sculpture of Picasso lightning. Down the side of the building the stairways to the various seat levels rose in rhythmic pattern ending with a circular stair well at the back of the building. The old redbrick stone columns covered in trailing vines should have jarred against the blue and mauve tile, yet the effect was overwhelming.

We went on to Switzerland. I left the others and took a train across France, Spain and Portugal. My problems with tickets, missed meals and seating, are worth a chapter in themselves but I shall leave it all to your imagination. In Lisbon I joined a married couple of friends of mine and enjoyed a week of being fed well, sleeping in a good bed, and being guided to all sorts of sights: John and Doris Hart were in Portugal learning the language so that they could go as missionaries to Angola where they would have to learn another language. They were taking special classes with other missionaries in Portuguese. John did more than attend conventional classes: he went out and talked to people, he bought a newspaper every day and translated it word for word, and he went out of his way to invite African students in Lisbon up to their apartment where they could spend an evening speaking Portuguese. He and Doris started going to Portuguese church services. The result? In a few months both John and Doris could speak the language fluently while the other students were afraid to open their mouths.

The final event I went to with John and Doris was a bullfight. It started at ten o'clock at night and we got home well after midnight. It was most enjoyable, they do not kill the bulls but drive cattle into the ring at the end of the fight, and the bull joins the animals and goes out with them.

I flew back to Switzerland, from the parched plains of brown dust with the odd cork tree a green dot on the landscape to a lush land of carefully cultivated small fields and neat houses. Ladd, Arn, Ray and I joined forces again and drove south over or through mountain passes and tunnels to Italy. We all started to worry about our finances. Ladd started to sleep in the car, and I had to join him to conserve my money. Sometimes we slept out on the ground; the first night in the open I could not shave in the morning because my face was covered with mosquito bites. We had adventures and misadventures. We took a gondola into Venice, the cost, two thousand, five hundred lira — four dollars. It was a fortune to us by that time. We took a motorboat back out of Venice. It cost us a total of three hundred lira.

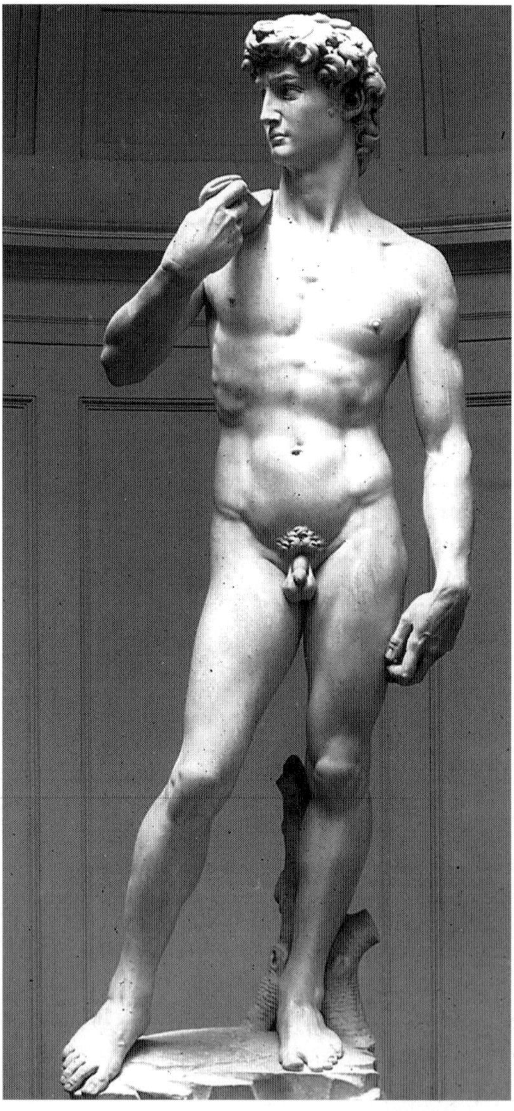

What can I say about the artistic treasures of Italy except that they were wonderful? Michelangelo's David in Florence I still consider the most beautiful piece of art that I have ever seen in my life. We climbed the Tower of Pisa; an odd sensation because of the lean. We saw the Sistine Chapel frescoes, the mosaics at Ravenna, Padua and Siena. We ate spaghetti day in and day out and drank coke because we were told that the water was not palatable or safe.

North to the Riviera, Monaco, north again to Paris, where Ray and Arn left us to return to their teaching posts in Germany and we took a train into the centre of Paris, had a day of sights and then flew home, broke, tired, dirty but elated after a wonderful adventure. I took hundreds of slides, showed them all over, gave talks, put them away. Two months ago I took them out, sorted them, and had the best of them made into colour photographs which I have incorporated in the right places into my journal.

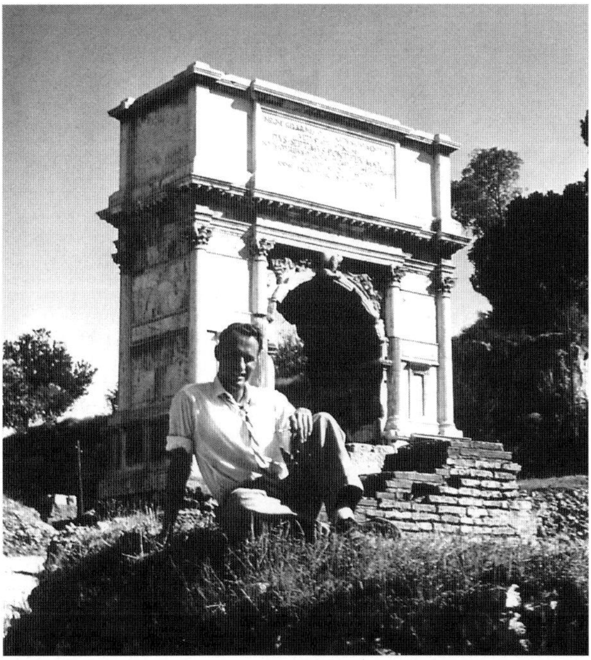

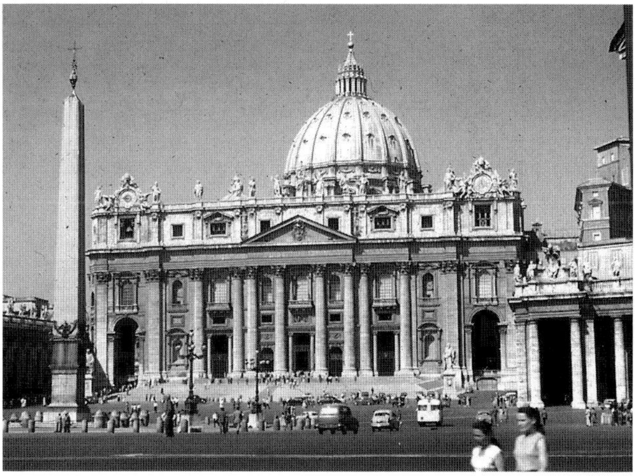

Chapter Six

Community Programmes, 1959-1964

From 1959 to 1964 I worked in Ontario for two organizations that became, in my case, closely linked together. In the spring of 1959 I graduated with the degree of Bachelor of Social Work at the School of Social Work, University of Toronto. I had specialized in group work methods, I already had an honours degree in Fine Arts, I was at dinner in Hart House at the U. of T. one evening and Alan Toff, the Undergraduate Secretary of Hart House sat across from me. He told me that he represented Hart House, because of its Art Gallery, on the Board of the Art Institute of Ontario. He mentioned that the A.I.O. had just received a grant and was looking for a Director to circulate its exhibitions and develop other programmes. I was interested, so I applied. Martin Baldwin and George Hulme interviewed me and I secured the position.

A short time later I saw a position, advertised in the *Globe and Mail,* for an Advisor in Art and Crafts for the Community Programmes Branch of the Ontario Department of Education. This position carried a much better salary, benefits, and a complete network organization throughout Ontario to help in its work.

I had an idea. I met with the C.P.B. people, explained about the A.I.O. and after a number of meetings involving the Executive of the A.I.O. and senior staff of C.P.B. I became the Art and Craft Advisor of C.P.B. in a full time position combined with Director of the A.I.O. as a volunteer. The combination worked perfectly. The mandate of the C.P.B. was to work in the leisure field through Recreation Committees and Adult Education. The A.I.O. supplied travelling art exhibitions, speakers, judges and demonstrators. As Art Advisor I had the network I needed: art clubs, art classes and associations; and through the A.I.O. I had the materials they could use.

own suggestion, to Advisor in Art. I was much more at home in the regular art field and the Branch already had a number of excellent craft advisors. Mary Eileen Muff, Bunty as she was known to all, later Mrs. Hogg, was the Advisor in Crafts with a strong emphasis on weaving. She set up the weaving guilds around the province; much later she was involved in the World Crafts Council and was awarded the Order of Canada for her work. Bunty knew where she was going, what she wanted and what she expected. She was jolly, enjoyed a good joke, and could, when the occasion warranted it, become very angry.

Henry Longstaff was Advisor in General Crafts. He was older and preferred to prepare how-to-do-it booklets in his office sanctum rather than face the rigours of the field. Henry disliked the modern move to fast meals and the sight of some marmalade inside a plastic straight jacket could set him off for the day. Henry was the Branch character and, I think, enjoyed playing the role. George Merten was the Advisor in Drama and Puppetry; he was well known in the field and respected as a puppeteer. Eleanor Syracuse was the Advisor in Rural Development. I did not see her very much as her work kept her apart from the rest of us. Budd Thomas, Supervisor of Special Services was our immediate superior; he was a rugged, thoughtful, deep thinking individual that everybody related to with ease.

What did I do? I worked closely with the amateur art movement in Ontario. A great deal of my work was organized through Recreation Committees. I worked directly with art leaders, executives, art classes, clubs and associations. The work consisted of leadership training for adult art groups: weekend workshops and seminars; executive meetings on programme planning, teaching techniques, group work and solving organizational problems. The second part of my work involved leadership training for children's groups, workshops on projects and skills, lectures on design, painting demonstrations, critiques of local art work, programme planning, arranging exhibitions and guest speakers, and writing articles for bulletins.

There was a strong provincial network of representatives and offices with whom we worked a great deal and had a good rapport. The representatives worked hard developing recreation in their districts. They were a great deal of fun. I remember stories told by Bob Secord about the Owen Sound area. He said that one night he was driving in a terrible snowstorm and going very slowly; suddenly a car roared around him at a very fast speed. Bob thought that this particular person must have amazing vision so he speeded up and followed right after the man. They got to the next town in no time at all and came to a stop-

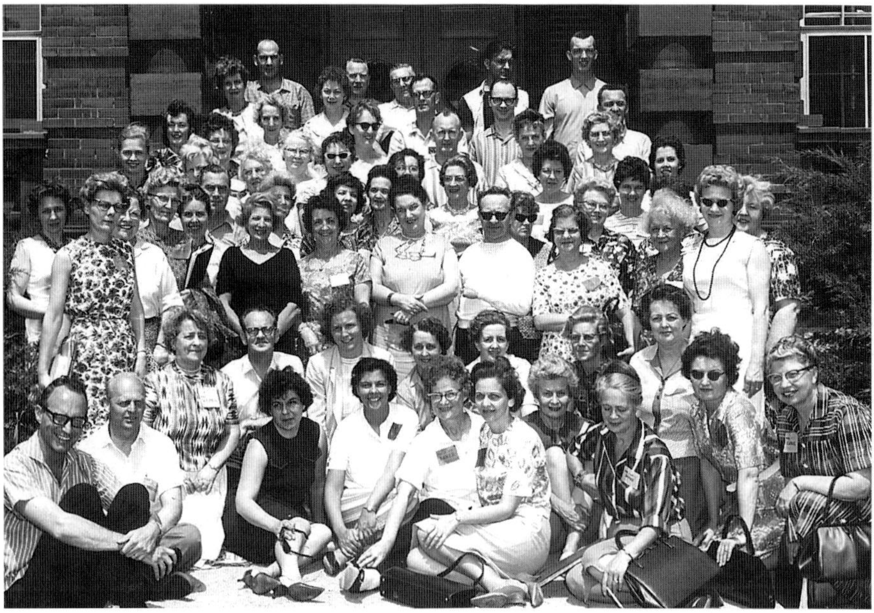

Provincial Leadership Institute. June, 1964. C.P.B.
Course Co-ordinator — P. Bennett

light. Bob hopped out and ran up to the car in front to thank the man for getting him home so quickly. The fellow rolled down the window and said, "I never tousch the stuffff." Another time in a bad storm Bob followed a man who turned along another road and Bob went right on following. Finally they came to a stop near a house. Bob jumped out and asked the man where they were and the man said, "I don't know where you are, mister; you just followed me up the lane to my house,"

Once Bob was in charge of a square dance and he lost his way to the hall. Finally he thought that he had located the right place and went in. There were people all around a large room. He organized them into squares, turned on the music that he had brought along and started to call a square dance. After a while he thought that something was wrong, as he could not find his contact person. He went over and asked a dignified man about it — he had interrupted a wedding reception.

After I joined the Branch I was in the office, at 559 Jarvis Street in Toronto, learning procedures. Then, one by one, I was called out to the various regions to learn about the amateur set-up.

The week of January 16th 1960, I drove from Toronto to Hanover on the Monday and met with Bob Secord in his office. I then drove to Chesley to the local high school where I met Miss Eleanor Lochead, the local high school art teacher. I was amazed when I walked through

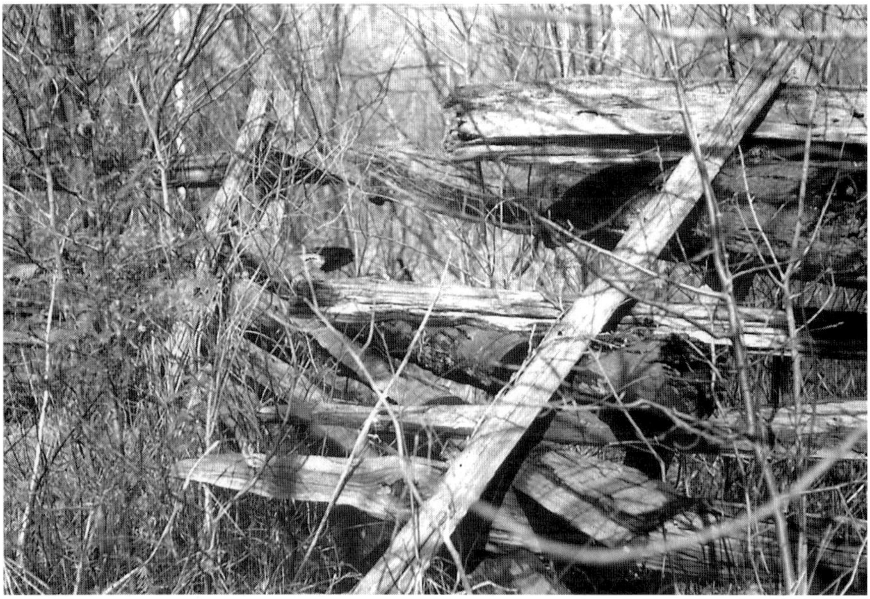

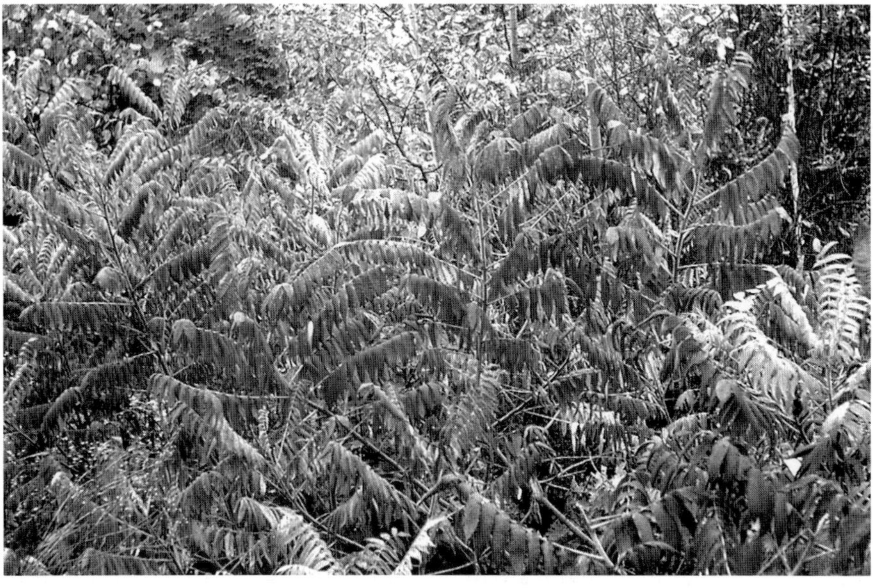

Slides used in lectures

the corridors of the school to find a dozen good paintings. At a later date I had a long talk with the school principal, Orville A. Kalbfleisch. He had started a policy some years earlier of using money from various school fines and the minimal profits from the selling of some text books to buy good paintings, including a middle-sized A.Y. Jackson, a George Thomson, a couple of Eleanor Locheads, and others.

There were fifty people present at the meeting that Eleanor had arranged for that evening. I gave a talk and showed my slides. Then the group moved from the auditorium to the art room and I gave a criticism of all the paintings that had been brought in; each person was allowed to bring in two paintings — all wanted a careful analysis and listened attentively. We broke the critique with coffee and a pleasant lunch. It was the longest critique that I had given to date. I left feeling that Eleanor Lochead was quite a remarkable person, sending her adult students out on assignments and giving them problems in perspective such as painting doors and windows of their own churches.

In 1962 I returned to Chesley and once again met with the local group; forty-five were present. Eleanor had asked me to give a felt board demonstration on colour relationships. I did this and then reinforced my points on colour by showing a set of slides on composition. A great deal of discussion followed. Finally I showed a couple of filmstrips, followed by a break and a buzz group on art programming.

I visited most of the districts. Each year I developed a new set of slides; often stopping along the road to take a particular view of an old house or scene that would demonstrate a point I wanted to make. There would be an evening programme for the club or class but really the important thing was to meet with the executive or the teacher and talk about programmes. I pushed the Art Institute of Ontario travelling exhibitions of professional paintings. I claimed that so much could be learned by studying original works of good art. I had a list of professional artists that could visit and give workshops or even one-evening lecture. I talked about the new films and filmstrips that were available and what good art books were on the market. This was almost forty years ago when the rural parts of Ontario did not have the masses of materials and opportunities that are available today.

I have copies of my weekly reports for the whole period of my time with the C.P.B. when I was on the road a great deal. When I look back over these reports on my work I am amazed at its scope and variety. For example, on a two-week trip across Northwestern Ontario I met people from fifteen communities at twenty-six meetings during forty-three hours of lectures and seven hours of consultation!! There were slides,

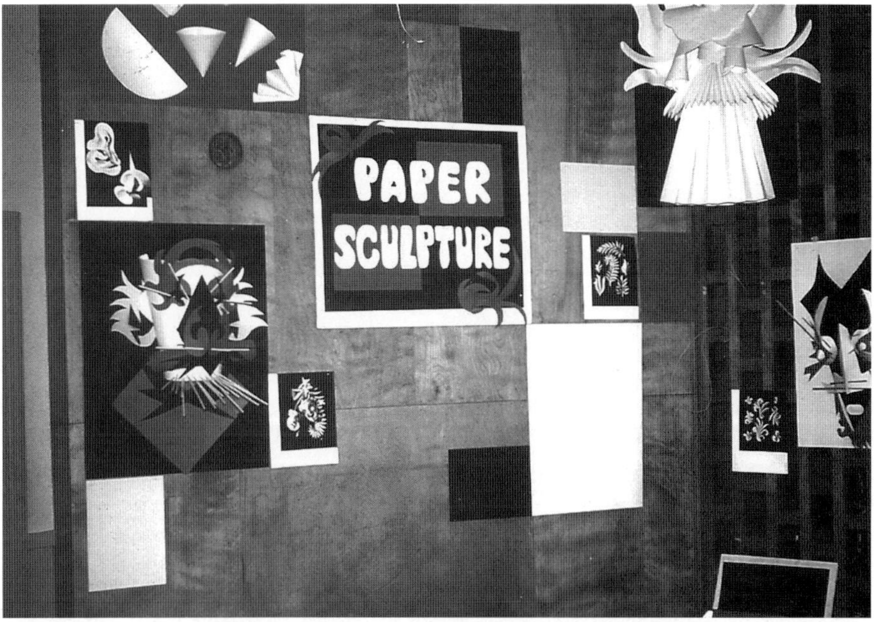

demonstrations of oil painting and paper sculpture, lectures on children's art and — very popular, teaching sessions on how to make interesting and dramatic decorations for dances and other celebrations.

One thing I greatly appreciated was that I was able to take my three week holiday in the summer and add three weeks of a leave of absence so that with a total of six weeks I could go to the University of Toronto to secure my Bachelor of Education degree in 1961 and my Master of Education degree in 1964. In the eight courses I took leading to the Master's degree I received four "A"s and four "B"s.

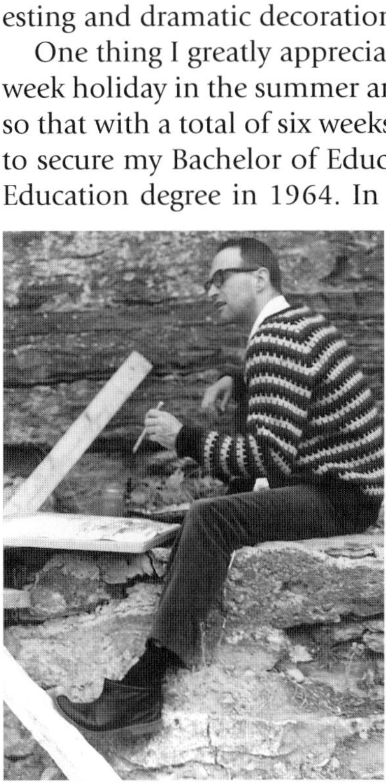

All through this period from 1959 to 1964 I was acting as Field Director of the Art Institute of Ontario. With Mrs. Nan Girard doing the office work and acting as exhibition booking agent I helped develop the Institute by seeking out exhibitions that could travel. The demand for shows grew at a wonderful rate. The new Ontario Arts Council was giving grants to assist in the development of the arts in this province. At a meeting of the general executive of the Art Institute of

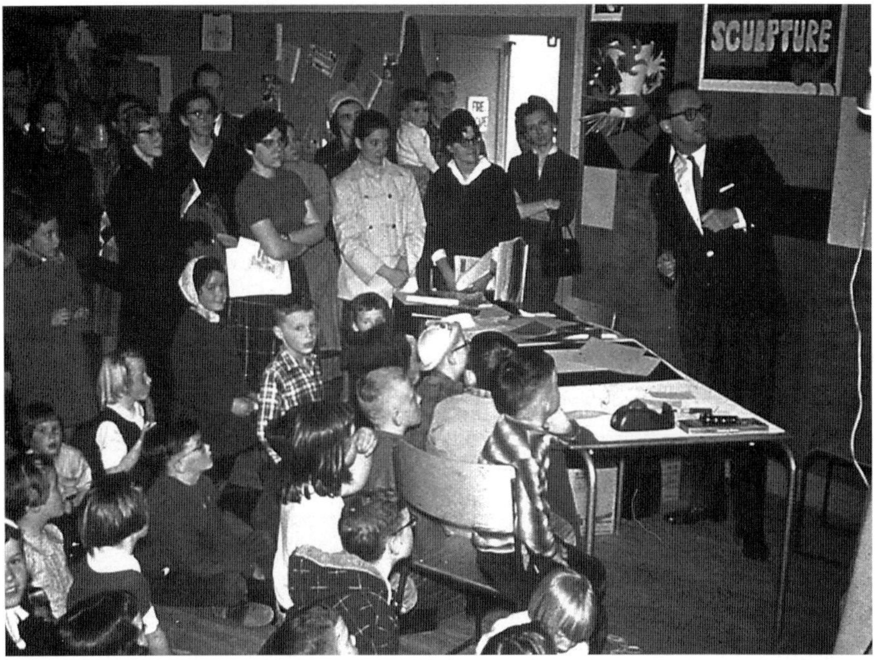

Ontario on February 21st, 1964, came a resolution to develop a petition asking the Arts Council for funding to hire a full time Director of the Art Institute of Ontario. Funding was secured and I decided to leave the Community Programmes Branch and become the first full time Director of the A.I.O.

I had received one honour while I was with the C.P.B. that I value highly. At one point I travelled to Northwestern Ontario to Quetico Conference and Training Centre. Bunty Muff asked me to accompany her on a weaving and design course that she had set up for Indian women, most of whom had to fly out by plane from isolated settlements. At the end of the course, which ran for a number of days, there was a ceremony that involved dancing and talking in the Cree language. At the end of it I was called forward and given an Indian name, "Wah-Say-A-Non, -"Bright Star".

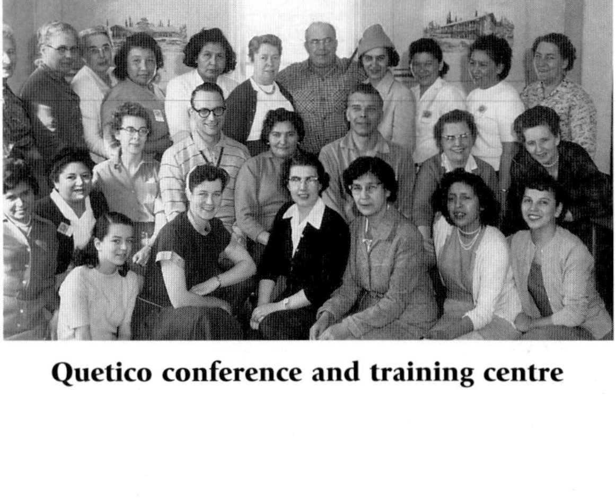

Quetico conference and training centre

Chapter Seven

Modus Operandi

Community Programmes

When I first started visiting groups, I thought that I was only going to give that group an entertaining, educational evening programme. I soon found out that as well as giving one programme, if I was able to talk to the teacher, leader or group executive, I could also give enough information to direct a group's programmes for a year or more. For example, members of a group might say that they were bored with painting still life. Actually there are many ways of painting still life and these had to be explained. The group could bring in an exhibition of good, original paintings; techniques, colour mixing, composition, all could be explored based on one professional painting. Films or filmstrips could explore design fundamentals, there was a wealth of material but the group had to be exposed to it.

At times these people were desperate for information. You sometimes felt that they were sucking your blood right out of you. The information and teaching material had to be constantly updated. In spite of the wealth of information available today on T.V., radio, and computer, I still think that a real life individual, who can interact, see problems and suggest personal solutions, is the best approach for dealing with isolated communities.

There were certain pitfalls that you had to watch for. Never agree to stay in somebody's house, if there was the slightest possibility of having a private motel room nearby. If you stay with someone you feel you have an obligation to be entertaining, to look at Grandmother's paintings that are pulled from the attic, or to give the children a lesson in perspective — all wonderful and exciting, but instead of projecting a dynamic image of great enthusiasm and energy for three hours in the evening to the whole group, you are working for ten or twelve hours. A high-powered image takes energy and you are not fair to the total group if you use up that energy on individuals.

Let us say you have been out on the road a couple of weeks. It reaches the point where you feel exhausted just setting up the equipment then you turn and face the expectant audience and you turn yourself on like a flashlight for three hours; afterwards you turn back again, totally drained.

For exactly the same reason I refused to have drinks with local politicians unless there was a special reason where it was obligatory to help a local arts group. Sometimes, most kindly, a Mayor or local bigwig felt it his or her duty to meet visiting "dignitaries". Perhaps that person was equally happy when I made an excuse.

I found the appraising and criticizing of art works a very valid part of my work. This was so right throughout my career with paintings and crafts. My background in design especially stood me in good stead here. My training in fine arts, social group work and education all came together in this aspect of my work. I would give a lecture and then often criticize two hundred paintings afterwards. I went into one company town where the group had been given a spare building for their art centre. Paintings were hanging in the basement, and on the first and second floor on every square inch of wall space and I had to criticize every painting that night.

What was my procedure? First I would ask the name of the teacher and rapidly walk around and find his or her pictures. Understandably these pictures were usually better than the students, and I would deliberately build them up somehow in the eyes of the local people. I was not there to destroy. I was there to be positive, not negative; always there is something positive you can say of advantage to the painter. Sometimes I've noticed the local teacher standing in the doorway afraid that I was going to destroy him. Up to that point he had been the expert but when I went in I was the expert and if I destroyed his work he had to stay and face the embarrassment. I just went on to my next town the following night. I would not destroy anyone's reputation.

If somebody brought up a painting (and very often they would bring up their own work at the end of the meeting and stand there while I criticized), if that person was over sixty years of age I would have to say positive things about it because that is all he or she wanted to hear. They were not likely to change their style because of a few comments on my part.

I used to take the approach of first saying what was good about a painting and would then try, with a number of valid remarks to help them to advance a little. Very often paintings were too small or the oil paint was not thick enough and the lovely oil painting quality had been lost. You could not go too far in your remarks because they might not be able to follow you. On the other hand, I had not travelled a thousand miles to say nothing useful. You had to hit a happy medium; never destroy, always encourage. The criticism became very important, and had to be given in a way that was acceptable. It was a very delicate business.

I have found that art gallery people, very often curators, become so involved in their subjects that, in a lordly way, they begin to talk down to other people. My theory is that if my car breaks down on the road, it could rust away beneath me before I would know how to get it started! A car mechanic could talk down to me but he does not. I may know something about art but that does not entitle me to belittle other people's knowledge and achievements. This is possibly one thing that comes from grass roots development — I know something about art and art appreciation through my training, but I have always been able to talk to people and not down to them. This egalitarian attitude is very important.

I have always thought that I made good use of my Bachelor of Social Work degree: I have been handling groups all my life. Once I went to a Women's Institute. The older small group wanted to enlarge and so they invited young mothers to come to a meeting and bring their children along. They had intended to provide a nursery but it did not materialize. When I went in there were sixty women sitting in a double circle all with their children — some asleep, some crying, some born, some not quite born. I proceeded to set up my things. A little boy ran out and started playing boat in one of my boxes. Every eye in the room was on him. I picked up the child and held him on my knee while I talked (he kicked me in the shins for the whole duration of my speech),

There was one superb potter there who had just moved to the area from Toronto. Later I found out that she had trained at the Royal Academy in England. At the end of my talk I had to discuss the possibilities of a craft show. I talked about this person's work. I held it up. It was absolutely beautiful. Suddenly I looked around the room and I realized that about half the women in the room had a look of envy, a look of dislike almost hate on their faces — this woman's work was so good. They could not possibly reach that level themselves if they wanted to do crafts. It suddenly dawned on me that here they were, tied down with all these children, doing their Christmas decorations or whatever it was they were making in crafts. Then, here came this expert who was so superb that they could not possibly equal her. I stopped talking about her work and moved to the next closest woman who had done some stitchery with a special name that I have forgotten. She was a Scottish lady and I said to her, "How many types of stitches do you have there?" She said she did not know. I said, "Well make up a number — we won't know the difference!" She said, "Oh, I couldn't do that, I'm Scotch". That broke the ice, and the women began to laugh. There was a woman there with a special machine for cutting the yarn for rug hooking to the right length. She demonstrated how it worked. I nodded to the potter who started to ask questions about rug-hooking and seeking advice from the others. I could feel the atmosphere melting. She showed a genuine interest and asked exactly the right questions. She gave the other women status again and the mood become happier.

I backed out, packed up, and left the potter in the middle of the group. She carried on organizing the exhibition.

I remember one group many years ago where a young College of Art graduate decided he wanted to be an artist but he also wanted to live in a small community. He started one of the most fabulous groups that I had ever seen. It was extremely exciting. The group wanted a local art club quarters. So often with things to do with the arts the people sit and moan, "Why doesn't the government help us?" but if sports are involved the people go out and do something practical, they raise money, float a bond, build the curling rink or whatever, and pay off the bond with exciting programmes. People so often concerned with the arts just sit and complain. This kind of apathy is one of the battles I had to contend with.

This particular group to which I am referring did not sit and moan. They wanted their art club quarters in an old school that was going to be torn down to make room for a new library. They planned a campaign very carefully, and even had the wife of the mayor on their committee. They went to the town council and said, "Don't pull down a great, solid old building because it seems a little too big. It could be renovated to accommodate both the library and rooms for other organizations, including the art club." After much discussion they got what they wanted and the results were spectacular, their rooms were in the basement of the building and they were "arty". They had an outdoor show for which they all dressed as beatniks and they drew flowers on the sidewalks and had flower baskets hanging on the main street. Everybody in the community came to see them. The Public had never heard of an outdoor show where you could sit at tables drinking, and watch women dressed like Parisian models (but with not quite the right shapes). This may sound tame today but do not forget that I am talking about forty years ago!

The art teacher in this group painted a portrait of everybody in town. When he ran out of commissions he painted a big mural in the local restaurant and received free meals for a year. This proves how exciting he was.

The next night I went to another town where there were eight people sitting and saying, "Why aren't we getting on?" I said you need some excitement and went through what I had seen the night before. I went back to Toronto. I was called into the office of the Director of the C.P.B. and shown a letter from an indignant woman who said, "How dare you send up a government official to tell me to put my paintings out on the sidewalk!" These show very different attitudes.

I have talked about being a grass roots developer, but not all the grass roots were in isolated areas. On October 16th 1961 I visited the Mental Hospital at 999 Queen St. West in Toronto. I will quote from my report. "I arrived at 9:30 a.m. and was met by a Mr. Frisby, a live wire, eighty year old, who is in charge of the English and Citizenship classes at the Mental Hospital. I was at the hospital until 2:30 p.m. I attended three meetings and spoke briefly on a slide set."

The second group came from the women's ward. After lunch I met the Philosophy group. This group had been studying the Renaissance. Mr. Frisby was to have a filmstrip projector for me but it did not materialize so I talked about my work and had a discussion on composition based on a few slides that I had with me. Mr. Frisby was delighted with this work. He liked the cultural aspect of the talk, linked as it was with an interest in life, experiment and adventure.

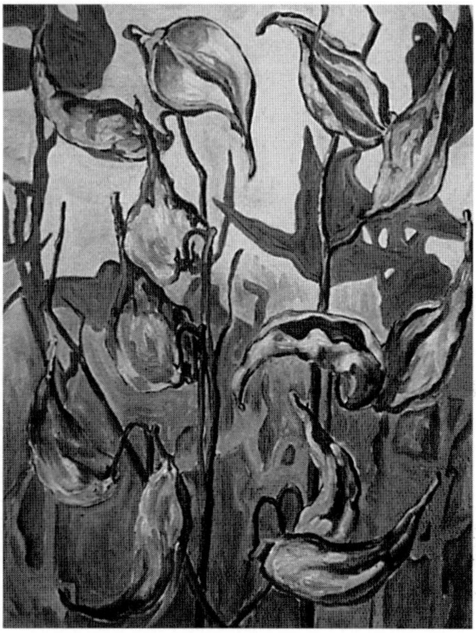

I was asked back three days later for the same three groups but much bigger attendance. In the morning sessions I gave painting demonstrations. I used milkweed as my subject and had a most appreciative audience. I found the men more analytical and the women more emotional in their criticisms. In each case I built my painting according to the comments from the audience. I was somewhat startled in the men's ward when one of the patients, just after my introduction, came up to my easel, took my brush from my hand, mixed some paint and did a large doodle across my canvas. He then sat down quietly and I was left to base my painting on his doodle. In each case the group asked to have my paintings as a decoration for their wards.

The afternoon group studying the Renaissance was another challenge. Mr. Frisby asked me to speak on Leonardo da Vinci. I pointed out that I had been away from the field for a long time and such a talk would involve considerable research on my part. Instead I gave a lesson on perspective, one of the great discoveries of the Renaissance. I did not teach it so much as lead the group to discover it for themselves. I spoke briefly, and then gave out scissors and construction paper, and the students, in pairs, had to cut a street scene in perspective. Whenever a mistake was made, a snip of the scissors could correct it. I noticed an amazing thing in this group: the doctors and staff were far more inhibited than the patients. The doctors produced very little, the patients; with great enthusiasm, produced a great deal.

Another aspect of my work was the conducting of workshops to train leaders in children's arts and crafts. I conducted a number of these sessions while with the C.P.B. During the Christmas holidays of 1962 I gave such a workshop in Kingston at the Agnes Etherington Art Centre at Queen's University for people from the Kingston Y.M.C.A. and various church groups in the area.

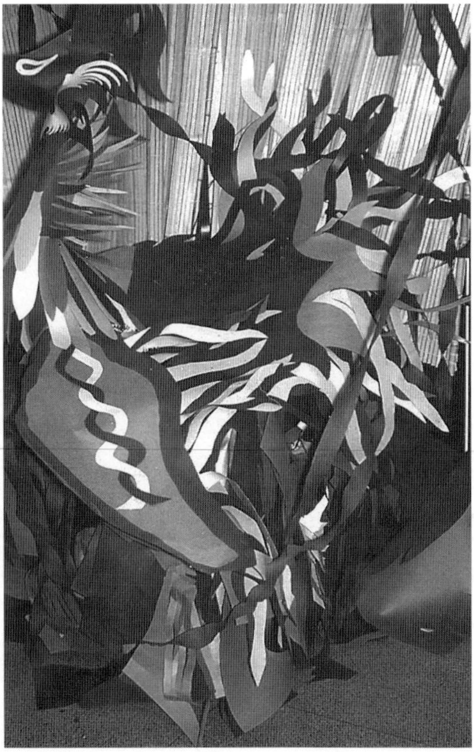

My course consisted of eight two-hour sessions covering the creative approach: paper sculpture and allied crafts, print making, scrap material construction, soap carving, mosaic work, papier mache, costumes, poster making, group projects, the locating of resources, teaching techniques, and programming.

I used twelve of the art and craft films owned by the C.P.B. I received a great deal of cooperation from the staff of the centre. The course was very successful, resulting in two more requests for similar courses in the area. In spite of the Christmas holidays the thirteen people who started the course came out to every session including the Saturday cleanup.

I also developed bulletins on art subjects. The first one I produced was "Decorations for Dances". In my career, I had had a great deal of experience in this area. I loved to think of a hall as a three-dimensional space; you only have to hang one streamer from the ceiling to the floor and you have cut that space. Walk around that streamer and you will realize that the whole area of the room is changing as you walk. Now, develop this idea, string fishing line back and forth across the hall for wall to wall; hang streamers from this invisible support in columns and they will appear to stand rather than hang.

String more fishing line at various levels across the ceiling and buy some adding machine paper rolls; cut them with a power saw into narrow coils and throw them over these lines, they will fall in coils from different heights. Open a door or have a couple of fans that give you a breeze and the columns will sway. Have a few spotlights and dreamy music and you will dance and not be sure what level you are on in the room. Isn't thinking in terms of three dimensions better that a few little scraggly decorations pinned up here and there around the walls?

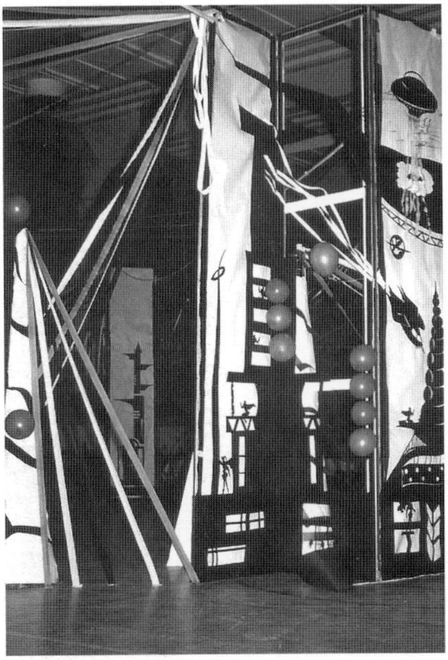

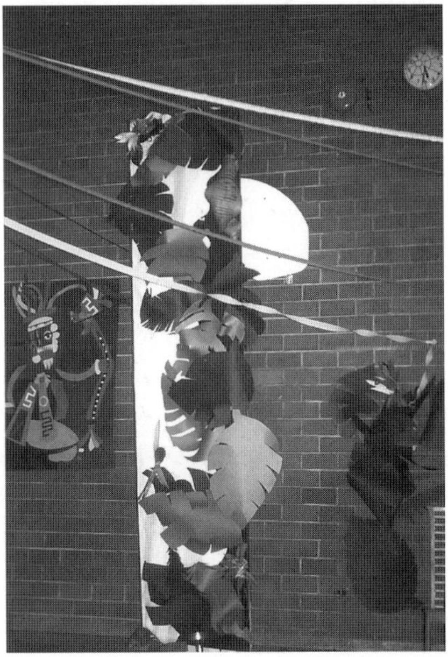

Chapter Eight

Sounds from the Past

We moved to Avondale, between Belleville and Trenton, in the late 1930s. There was an old barn/driveshed behind our house, a relic of earlier days, and in it was an old Bell Organ. It was massive, ornate, and covered in straw and dirt. The bellows were damaged. — Only one of the two foot pedals worked but if you pumped the one pedal fast enough and pressed you knees out against the two swell levers you could produce a musical sound.

I was twelve years old and fascinated. Here was a voice speaking to me from one hundred years ago. I was learning to play the piano, under the tuition of Bill Connor in Belleville. In 1941, I started Belleville Collegiate Institute. The war had started in 1939 and Dad was again in the army stationed at A10 Training Centre at Camp Borden. Joan had started at the University of Toronto in 1942. Obviously, it was better for all of us to move back to Toronto. I never really forgot that reed organ, however.

After the war the family relocated in Newcastle and there I acquired an old Dominion reed organ. In its best days the Dominion Organ and Piano Co. of Bowmanville exported organs to Australia, New Zealand and South Africa, even some to Russia. One was discovered by a traveller in 1957 in a church in Lapland. I have a manufacturer's certificate and warranty for style 174D, no44080, for five years from July 29th, 1905. I also own a "Dominion Organ and Piano First Method for the Piano book".

The book cover states, "the company manufactures highest grade pianos and organs and that 70,000 instruments have been sold". It states also that the company received international awards in Philadelphia and a medal in Chicago in 1893 and awards for both pianos and organs at Paris in 1900. Unfortunately records show that the company finally closed in 1936; tastes in popular culture were changing.

The piano was on the west wall of our living room and the huge organ spread its dominating influence from the north wall. I took the organ works apart, cleaned them, and in the process I realized that none of the vital works that made it play were above the keyboard. It

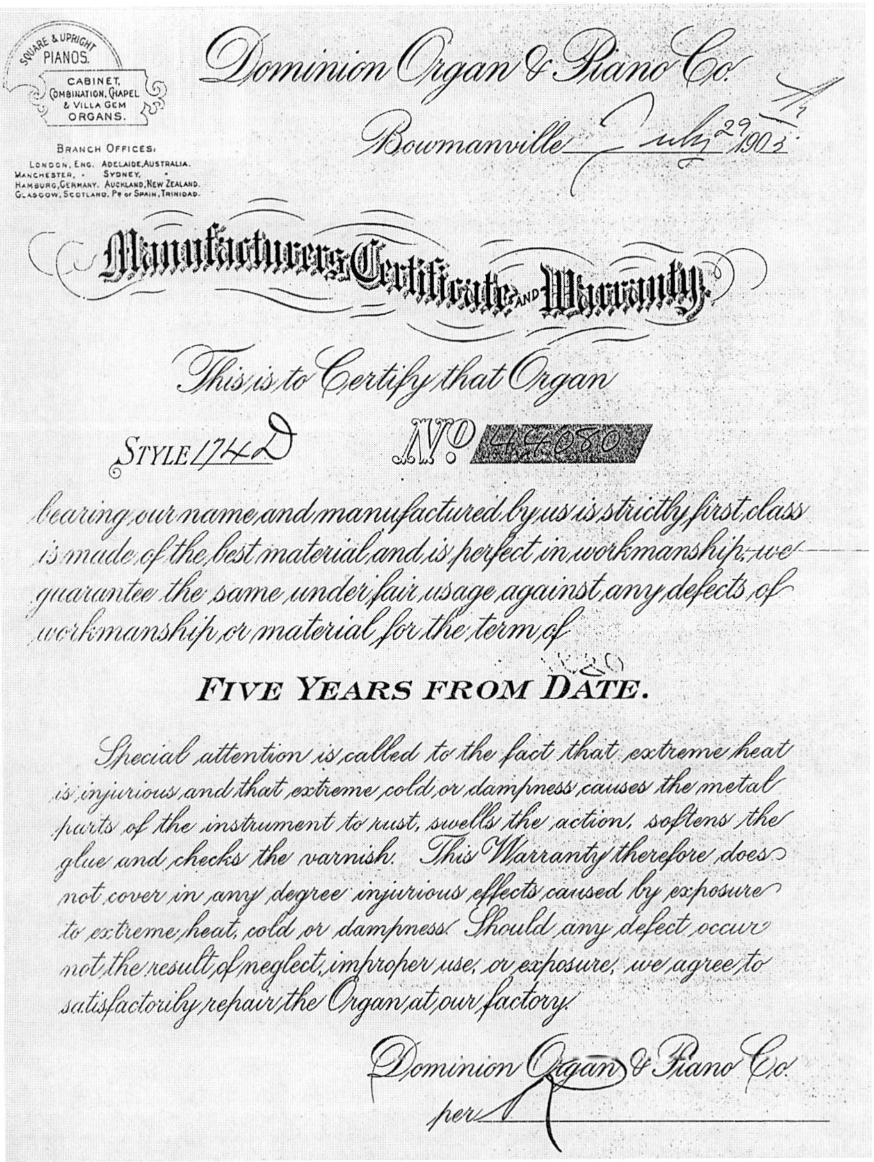

SQUARE & UPRIGHT PIANOS.
CABINET, COMBINATION, CHAPEL & VILLA GEM ORGANS.

BRANCH OFFICES:
LONDON, ENG. ADELAIDE, AUSTRALIA.
MANCHESTER, " SYDNEY, "
HAMBURG, GERMANY. AUCKLAND, NEW ZEALAND.
GLASGOW, SCOTLAND. PT OF SPAIN, TRINIDAD.

Dominion Organ & Piano Co.

Bowmanville July 29 1903

Manufacturers Certificate and Warranty.

This is to Certify that Organ

STYLE 174 D No. 44080

bearing our name and manufactured by us is strictly first class is made of the best material and is perfect in workmanship; we guarantee the same under fair usage against any defects of workmanship or material for the term of

FIVE YEARS FROM DATE.

Special attention is called to the fact that extreme heat is injurious and that extreme cold or dampness causes the metal parts of the instrument to rust, swells the action, softens the glue and checks the varnish. This Warranty therefore does not cover in any degree injurious effects caused by exposure to extreme heat, cold or dampness. Should any defect occur not the result of neglect, improper use, or exposure, we agree to satisfactorily repair the Organ at our factory.

Dominion Organ & Piano Co.
per

was all show. Perhaps in the old days it was a status symbol in the parlour for the ceilings were high and the Victorians loved ornate furniture with mirrors and side brackets to hold oil lamps. Now I must make a confession. I had never before or have never since destroyed the essence of a musical instrument in my whole life but I cut the top off and lowered the lid of that organ to just above the keyboard! It still played in its truncated size; the piano again assumed its rightful dominance in the room, and all was well.

I have wonderful memories of that living room in Newcastle. We were a musical family. At Christmas, after Mother had produced one of her miracles of Christmas dinners; our family plus uncles, aunts, cousins, strays, and what have you would sit in the living room and the music would begin. There was the piano and the organ and I went through a period of folk guitar. We had a number of good singers, — Dad, Uncle Grant, Jane (developing a glorious voice) and I would sing, Half a dozen of us would play the piano. We would go through all the old favourites. Dad sang, "Down the Vale'" while I accompanied him on the piano, Joan and Uncle Grant would play duets, Jane and friend Ethel would play duets, Uncle Grant would sing; We would keep switching around until all of us joined in the last item, a spirited rendition of the "Hallelujah Chorus". When we were young, before our move to Newcastle, Mother would play a lively song, and all the young children, led by a number of the adults, would join in a line and snake our way around the house, up the backstairs and down the front stairs until the house was rocking with laughter and fun. I miss it now.

When I finished the first part of my education and started working in Toronto a friend moved the organ to Toronto in the back seat of his convertible. I think that eventually I must have been ashamed of what I did to that organ because my memory is completely blocked out as to what eventually happened to it.

Some years later, in my role as Art Advisor for the Community Programmes, I had to give a lecture on Art to the local art association in Ridgetown. It was 1960. In my talk, I referred to old musical instruments. Afterwards a lady came to me and said that if I was interested in the old reed organs I should speak to the gentleman behind the counter of the hot dog stand. My talk had been given in the local arena. I spoke to Mr. Lee Simpson who was a man of many occupations: he ran the hot dog concession at the arena, he owned the Candy Kitchen store in Ridgetown where he and his helpers made all the candy that they sold, and he was the local

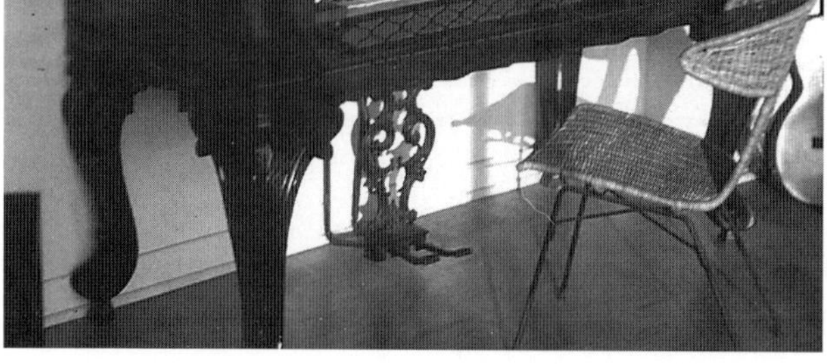

auctioneer. His store was full of antiques including an excellent collection of pressed glass.

I told Mr. Simpson of my interest in old reed organs and the smaller version of them, melodeons. He took me out to the barn behind his store. There in a corner covered by old round cheese boxes and bales of hay was the melodeon that now resides in the Canadiana Collection of the Royal Ontario Museum. When Mr. Simpson took me into the barn all I could see of the melodeon was one carved cabriole leg made of rosewood. I was extremely excited and I bought it on the spot for seventy-five dollars. I was also shown a smaller melodeon made in New York with lyre-shaped legs. I bought it a year later.

I do remember one incident in moving that melodeon. I had to buy a car rack for the top of my car. Then I took off the iron pedal section, as its removal was easy — a hammer simply knocked it out of its slots. By closing up the bellows, I was able to unscrew the four legs. I put these in the car and the main body of the melodeon went on the top. On the way home I went in for gas, the garage man looked up at the top of the car and told me that it was the smallest funeral he had seen that week. The rosewood body of the instrument certainly looked like a coffin.

One interesting thing about this instrument was that it played beautifully in the summer, but as soon as the central heat came on in the house in the fall it, and the other melodeons that I eventually collected, would hardly play at all. I believe that the old wood had become porous or else the bellows would dry out and leak air into the reservoirs. Even good humidifiers in the room would not correct this problem.

This Bell melodeon had been made in Guelph between 1865 and 1870. There are four stops, two controlling the reeds in the treble clef and two controlling the reeds in the bass clef. The melodeon principle is the same as in a mouth organ, and the reeds are very similar to mouth organ reeds. In some of my old instruments, I have found the hook that was used for pulling out the reeds in order to clean them. The hook is very similar to the old-fashioned buttonhook for shoes only a little more flattened at the hook end. Each reed has a catch where the hook can pull it out of its slot. If a note has a whining sound then it has likely caught some dust; pull the reed out and dust it and then replace it. A melodeon reed can be sharpened or flattened. If you file the free end it will vibrate faster and be sharper, if you file the heel or solid end the vibrations will slow and it will be flatter.

The design of this melodeon speaks most eloquently of an attempt at sophistication of design in Ontario in the later nineteenth century.

The rosewood is quite beautiful; the shape of the leg, however, is quite heavy in comparison to furniture design such as found in Europe at the time. The attempt at elegance is there however, even if the true proportion was not quite achieved.

In 1971, after some negotiations with Mrs. Helena Ignatieff, Assistant Curator of the Canadiana Department of the Royal Ontario Museum, I donated this beautiful instrument to the ROM. It was displayed at an exhibition titled, "Life Style of Our Forefathers, an exhibition of Canadian furniture and furnishings from 19th century Western Ontario" at the University of Guelph Arts Building during the Spring Festival of 1971.

This melodeon had been made by W. Bell and Co. of Guelph. This company by the end of the century was in a position of national leadership in the field. Organs were going off to Great Britain, Australia, and Africa. Agents were maintained abroad and the Bell Co even had a factory in England. Sadly, the company finally closed late in the 1920s.

I mentioned earlier that in 1962 I bought a second, smaller melodeon from Lee Simpson. It was beautiful in a plain rosewood case with two bands of egg and dart molding around the outer case. It stood on lyre-shaped legs. The body of the instrument measured one and a half feet by three feet by one foot. It was made by Prince and Company, was patented in 1846, and was probably made in Detroit. There was no place for a music rack at the top of the instrument. The two pedals, one for air and one for volume, were missing along with their stand and supports.

Lee Simpson had secured this instrument from the Steinhoff estate

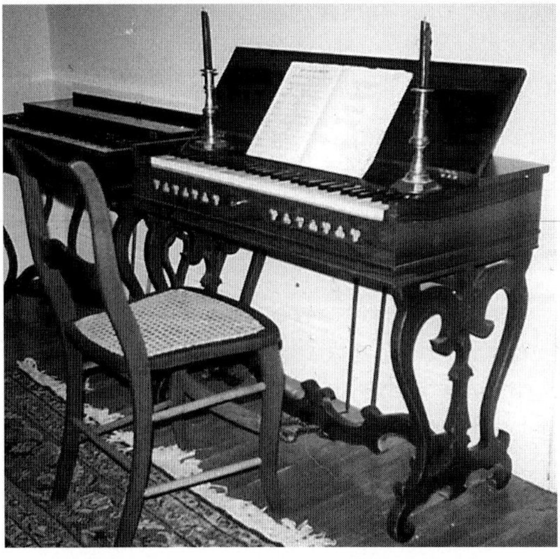

in Wallaceburg. He thought that the Hiram Walker Historical Museum in Windsor possessed a similar instrument. I wrote the curator, Alan Douglas; he wrote back and said that the melodeon was on loan from a Mrs. Macdonald of Windsor. In 1969, I again received a letter from Alan Douglas to say that his museum had finally received the melodeon from the estate of Mrs. George Macdonald. In the meantime I had had the case of mine refinished. I did the necessary work on the inside and I had obtained a set of pedals. I finally sold the Prince and Co instrument to a New York buyer, had it crated and shipped down to him. I moved on to other instruments.

R. S. Williams is a famous name at the Royal Ontario Museum. This man, Richard Sugden Williams was born in London, England in 1834, and at four, his family brought him to Hamilton, Ontario. In 1849, he began repairing musical instruments and in 1854, he started manufacturing them. At the same time, he started collecting antique instruments. In 1889, the business was moved to Oshawa. Then in 1902 the business was divided, the piano business stayed in Oshawa while R. S. Williams and Sons, Co. Ltd. carried on in Toronto.

Mrs. Ignatieff of the ROM told an interesting story about Williams senior. The ROM had received a small melodeon made by Williams from a Mrs. Jim Watson. The instrument had been built in Uxbridge and was the only one ever built there. Early in the 1860s Williams was visiting friends in that community when he fell and broke his leg. He could not leave town for eight weeks and he began to run out of funds. He went to the Bell Organ Co, branch office in Uxbridge and asked if he could make a melodeon there. They agreed. He built

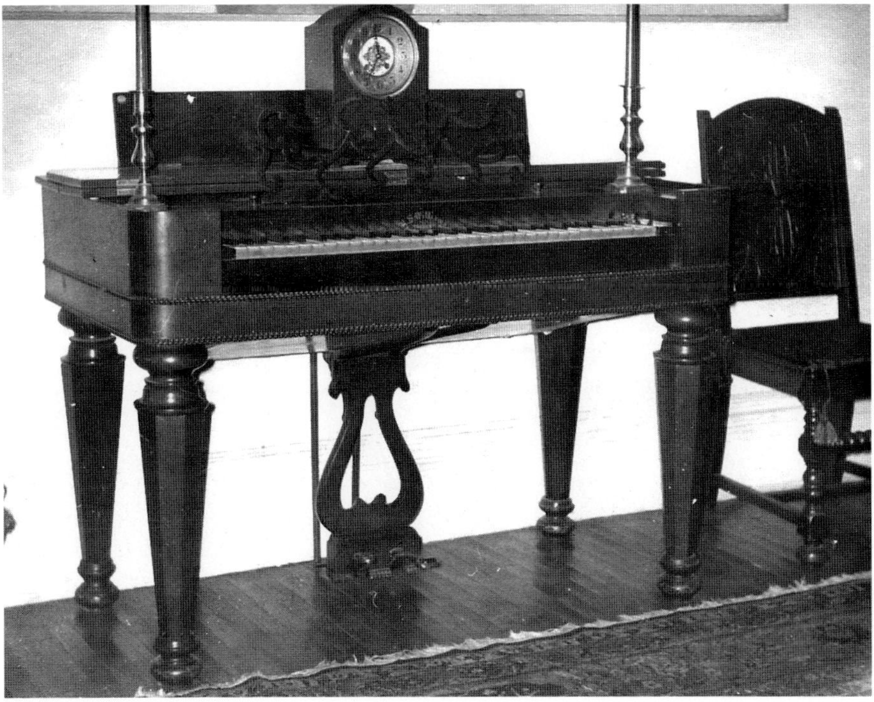

a small box of rosewood and put it on an ornamental iron stand. When the melodeon was finished he presented it to the small local church whose members had so kindly looked after him. That organ was used for fifty years until the congregation moved to a larger building and bought a new, large organ, giving the small melodeon to the grandson of the original organist, whose family presented it to the ROM

R. S. Williams Junior entered his father's business and became president on the death of his father in 1906. All through the years the collection of musical instruments had grown. In 1913 the son presented the complete collection to the ROM. For the rest of his life he continued to seek out rare instruments on his trips to Europe and continued to give them to the museum. In 1934 he rounded out his gift with the donation of more than 150 autographed letters and documents of famous musical personalities plus rare musical scores and books. The R. S. Williams Collection. of Musical Instruments now consists of around five hundred items.

One Saturday in the 1960s I was passing through the town of Brighton and I spotted a house auction. I stopped and was fortunate enough to buy an R. S. Williams melodeon made of oak for thirty-five

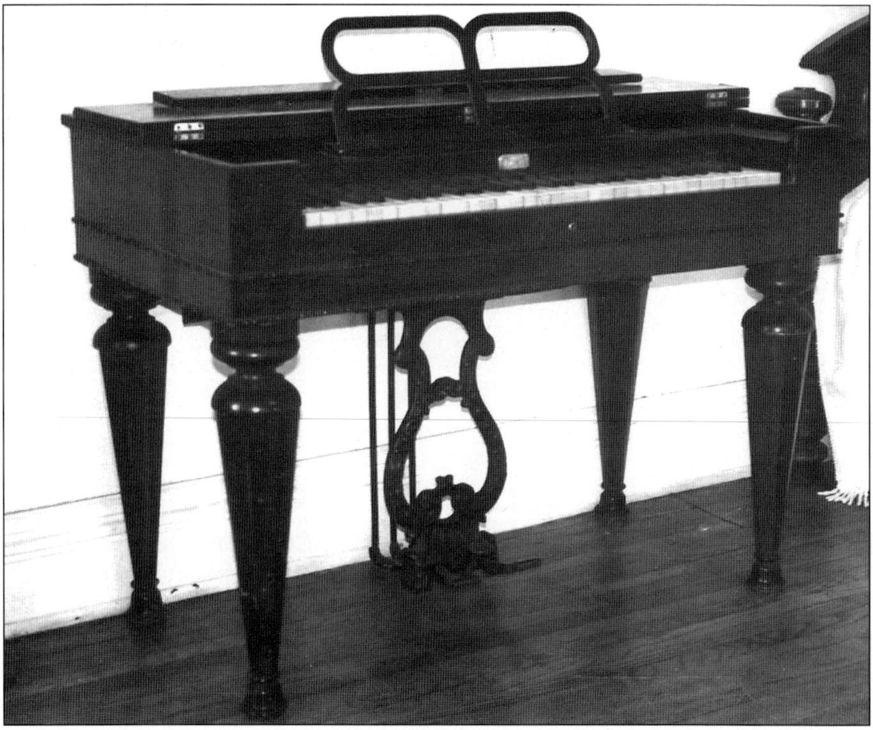

dollars. It was sturdy and somewhat simpler than some of the rosewood ones I already owned. When I was the Director of the Robert McLaughlin Gallery in Oshawa from 1970 to 1972. Jacquie Boughner was the education officer. This bright, pert, beautiful young lady was looking for the perfect gift for her sister and she bought this particular melodeon from me. I had a very nice letter from her sister telling me how nice it looked beside her fireplace and that it was giving her many hours of pleasure.

I bought another melodeon from a Miss Moody of Toronto. It was made by the Andrus Brothers of London, Canada West, between 1840 and 1867. I sold it to William Roberts, the artist. I own a number of his watercolours and admire his work greatly. At that time he was living — in Ayton, Ontario.

Mrs. Ignatieff in a couple of instances put me in touch with people who owned melodeons and wanted to sell them. One such was a Mrs. Dorothy Dingwall of Toronto who owned a beautiful walnut melodeon made in Connecticut by a company named Schoninger. She had received this instrument from an aunt in Rhode Island in 1940. I bought it and I later wrote to Helen Ignatieff that I did not have any place for it in my apartment except in the bathtub! I used to swim every day in the apartment pool and showered there. When I had a party I used to put two signs on the instrument; one said, "Don't laugh, it's not your bathtub" and the other said, "Please don't turn on the shower; bathtub is occupied."

In 1966 I wrote letters to the librarians of the public libraries in Bowmanville, Guelph and Clinton and also to the Chief Curator of the National Gallery of Canada. I was seeking information on the old organ factories in the various towns. I also knew that Robert Hubbard at the National Gallery was interested in this topic. I received courteous replies from all including a page or so of information, some of which I have quoted above,

Two years passed and suddenly I received a letter from a Mr. Murray Draper, Past Superintendent of Sherlock-Manning Pianos, Limited of Clinton, Ontario. Mr. Draper stated that he had found my letter in 1966 quite by accident when checking a file concerning organs. He wrote that he had been interested in organs, as he had worked on them for years. We exchanged a number of letters with me growing more and more excited about meeting this man. When he had started in the factory in 1936, there were between 130 and 150 employees at that time. He had actually worked with one of the original Doherty employees for a period of five years.

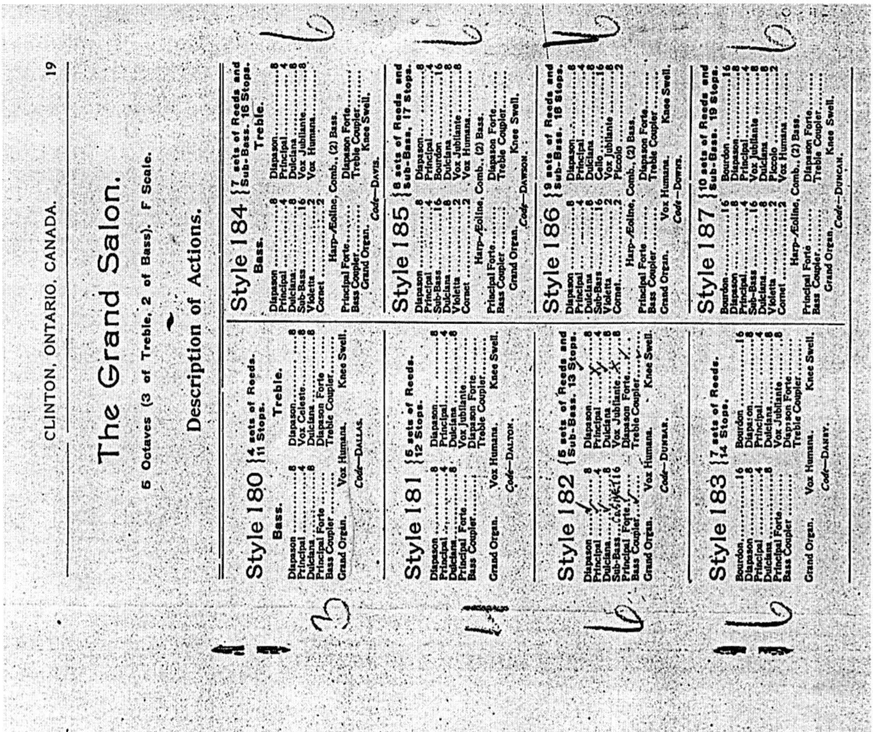

W. DOHERTY & CO.

The Grand Salon.

Height, 7 ft., 2 in. Depth, 2 ft. Width, 4 ft., 6 in.
Weight, boxed, 500 lbs. Cubic ft., boxed, 63 ft.

Our Grand Salon is one of the most elaborate designs we ever made, and is, we believe, without an equal as a parlor organ. Made in Walnut or Oak. The extension is furnished with a large incurved circular mirror. The whole case is adorned with raised carvings, panels and trimmings. It has carved music desk with music receptacle and drawer beneath, swing lamp-stands, handles, etc., and in every respect a most desirable Organ.

CLINTON, ONTARIO, CANADA. 19

The Grand Salon.

5 Octaves (3 of Treble, 2 of Bass). F Scale.

Description of Actions.

Style 180 {4 sets of Reeds. 11 Stops.

Bass.		Treble.	
Diapason	8	Diapason	8
Principal	4	Vox Celeste	8
Dulciana	8	Dulciana	8
Principal Forte		Diapason Forte	
Bass Coupler		Treble Coupler	

Grand Organ. Vox Humana. Knee Swell.
Code—DALLAS.

Style 181 {5 sets of Reeds. 12 Stops.

Diapason	8	Diapason	8
Principal	4	Principal	4
Dulciana	8	Dulciana	8
Principal Forte		Vox Jubilante	
Bass Coupler		Diapason Forte	
		Treble Coupler	

Grand Organ. Vox Humana. Knee Swell.
Code—DALTON.

Style 182 {5 sets of Reeds and Sub-Bass. 13 Stops.

Diapason	8	Diapason	8
Principal	4	Principal	4
Dulciana	8	Dulciana	8
Sub-Bass	16	Vox Jubilante	8
Principal Forte		Diapason Forte	
Bass Coupler		Treble Coupler	

Grand Organ. Vox Humana. Knee Swell.
Code—DUNBAR.

Style 183 {7 sets of Reeds. 14 Stops.

Bourdon	16	Bourdon	16
Diapason	8	Diapason	8
Principal	4	Principal	4
Dulciana	8	Dulciana	8
Principal Forte		Vox Jubilante	8
Bass Coupler		Diapason Forte	
		Treble Coupler	

Grand Organ. Vox Humana. Knee Swell.
Code—DANBY.

Style 184 {7 sets of Reeds and Sub-Bass. 16 Stops.

Bass.		Treble.	
Diapason	8	Diapason	8
Principal	4	Principal	4
Dulciana	8	Dulciana	8
Sub-Bass	16	Vox Jubilante	8
Violetta	2	Vox Humana	
Cornet	2		

Harp-Æoline, Comb., (2) Bass.
Principal Forte. Diapason Forte.
Bass Coupler. Treble Coupler.
Grand Organ. Knee Swell.
Code—DAVIS.

Style 185 {8 sets of Reeds and Sub-Bass, 17 Stops.

Diapason	8	Diapason	8
Principal	4	Principal	4
Sub-Bass	16	Bourdon	16
Dulciana	8	Dulciana	8
Violetta	2	Vox Jubilante	8
Cornet	2	Vox Humana	

Harp-Æoline, Comb., (2) Bass.
Principal Forte. Diapason Forte.
Bass Coupler. Treble Coupler.
Grand Organ. Knee Swell.
Code—DAWSON.

Style 186 {9 sets of Reeds and Sub-Bass. 18 Stops.

Diapason	8	Diapason	8
Principal	4	Principal	4
Dulciana	8	Dulciana	8
Sub-Bass	16	Cello	16
Violetta	2	Vox Jubilante	8
Cornet	2	Piccolo	2

Harp-Æoline, Comb., (2) Bass.
Principal Forte. Diapason Forte.
Bass Coupler. Treble Coupler.
Grand Organ. Vox Humana. Knee Swell.
Code—DOWNS.

Style 187 {10 sets of Reeds and Sub-Bass. 19 Stops.

Bourdon	16	Bourdon	16
Diapason	8	Diapason	8
Principal	4	Principal	4
Sub-Bass	16	Vox Jubilante	8
Dulciana	8	Dulciana	8
Violetta	2	Piccolo	2
Cornet	2	Vox Humana	

Harp-Æoline, Comb., (2) Bass.
Principal Forte. Diapason Forte.
Bass Coupler. Treble Coupler.
Grand Organ. Knee Swell.
Code—DUNCAN.

The original company, W. Doherty Co., began business in 1875. Capital was needed and so it became Doherty and Company as partners were added. Later the company became the Doherty Piano and Organ Co., as about 1900 it started making pianos as well as reed organs. In 1920 the Sherlock-Manning Piano Co purchased the active business and the businesses were merged.

Mr. Draper told me that Sherlock and Manning were two Doherty employees who learned their trade at the Doherty factory in Clinton and then moved to London and opened a factory of their own. They were successful and came back, as Mr. Doherty was growing old, wanted to retire, and sold the business to them.

In the summer holidays I drove to Clinton and met Murray Draper, who took me to the factory. It was summer and the factory was closed for a period of time so that the employees could have holidays. We went in and through the ghostly building, lit only by the daylight coming in through the large windows. Murray Draper took me to a good-sized private room of his own, where he was still making and repairing reed organs. The factory actually had not made reed organs since they were made in the Second World War to be placed on Canadian Corvettes for church services. It was like going through a time warp. Murray spoke with a love of his subject, and he understood the complete working of the instrument.

He also had another hobby: he collected old music boxes, mostly European. He sat me down in a chair. I was facing a large set of shelves covered with many, many music boxes. Sunlight was streaming in the windows and lighting the intricate detail of the boxes. Some of them elaborate in detail and decoration.

He went from one to another and played the same song for me on each. It was wonderful, — a trip into our musical past.

On a subsequent visit I taped a long interview with Murray. Most of the following information comes from that interview. The Doherty Co. was the biggest in Canada. Its main markets were in England. Trainloads of fifty organs were sent each week to Halifax to be shipped to Liverpool and for years one dealer only handled them in England. Other trainloads were shipped to Australia, Germany and other European countries. The company sent out elaborate catalogues. The biggest promotions were the trade fairs in London and Australia. It was very aggressive selling, with a wide use of the telegraph. The company had worked out a code in order to save words on telegraph fees.

The organs were each crated individually. The organs could have up to one thousand reeds. The reeds themselves came from Germany. They would arrive on a cell board or individually. On elaborate organs, cell blocks would be placed above each other. Voicing was a fine art, the bend or twist of a reed could give different sounds of clarinet, flutes, cellos, harps and so on. Diapason refers to ordinary pitch; it was an eight-foot frequency and was the foundation stop for which the other sets were tuned. Tone was full, round, pure, pipelike and smooth. A two foot frequency was the highest, such as the piccolo; the thirty-two foot frequency was the lowest, the stop called sub Bourbon. It was a solo stop with a rich, full tone.

The Doherty church organs had a set of foot pedals and two manuals. The church organs always had a bellows at the side and a boy to pump them. There was a dial at the side of the bellows and the boy had to keep the pressure within a certain range, too low and not enough air, too high and too much pressure. The bellows always had to be prepared to have a reserve for heavy chords. I was told that years ago one local family in Clinton, had a summer visitor who liked to come and pump the bellows in the Anglican church, that boy turned out to be Sir Ernest MacMillan

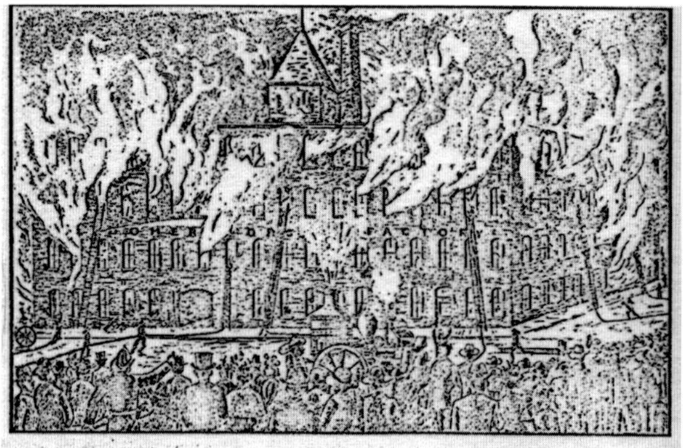

VIEW OF OUR OLD FACTORIES IN FLAMES.
Which were totally destroyed, February 1, 1898, and have been replaced by new factories, as shown on page 4, which were in operation by July 1, 1898.

The Company had two great fires. I only have information on one of them. The first factory had been above a store, uptown with one employee. With growing commercial success a large factory was built, four storeys high, and with a hundred workers. In February 1898, it with subsidiary buildings, all burnt to the ground. The present factory was then built and by July of that same year the company was shipping out its carloads of orders.

A factory like Doherty's spawned other industries in the local area. There was a sawmill, timber rights were owned for sections of bush. Local woods were always used, pine and spruce, some maple for the frames and inner parts. Most cases were made of walnut, which was very abundant at that time. Veneers came in later, first in panels and then in the main areas of the cabinets. Murray spoke wistfully of the wonders of working with walnut. Keys were cut locally, as early as 1886 they were made of celluloid. A very few were made from imported ivory.

A production line was organized, there was a department to make the bellows, the action parts, the stops, the cabinet shop was the largest, and there was a finishing room, assembly and shipping. Power was supplied by steam engine. The factory dried its own lumber; coal was used as well as scrap wood from the factory.

Murray remembered old men of eighty-five working in the factory. There was no retirement or pensions, no holidays. It was a sixty-hour week, workers started at seven a.m., had an hour for lunch, many of them would go home, work ended at six p.m., six days a week at ten hour days. Doherty was the one and only boss, he could fire or hire at will. There were a few women in the offices, no women in the factory.

The Doherty Company had a wonderful reputation for a good product. It is so easy to think that Canada exported only raw materials in it early pioneer days. Here is proof of a small town, literally in the wilderness, that produced a luxury product that it exported to important countries around the world. This cultural product created a payroll that kept this small town alive for over fifty years.

Sometimes I go to auctions today and along comes a small desk made of walnut or rosewood. I know at first glance that it once was a melodeon and I am sad. Melodeons were hardy instruments; if the bellows were broken they could be repaired. If you try just remember, do not use leather, it will be too stiff to pump the bellows, I know from personal experience, use rubberized cloth. I have always found that all the works are there and ready to work if cleaned and with a good bellows. To me they have always spoken of a pioneer past reaching for the good things and hardy enough to stand up and fight the bad things. A desk, bah, let it sing with its own voice.

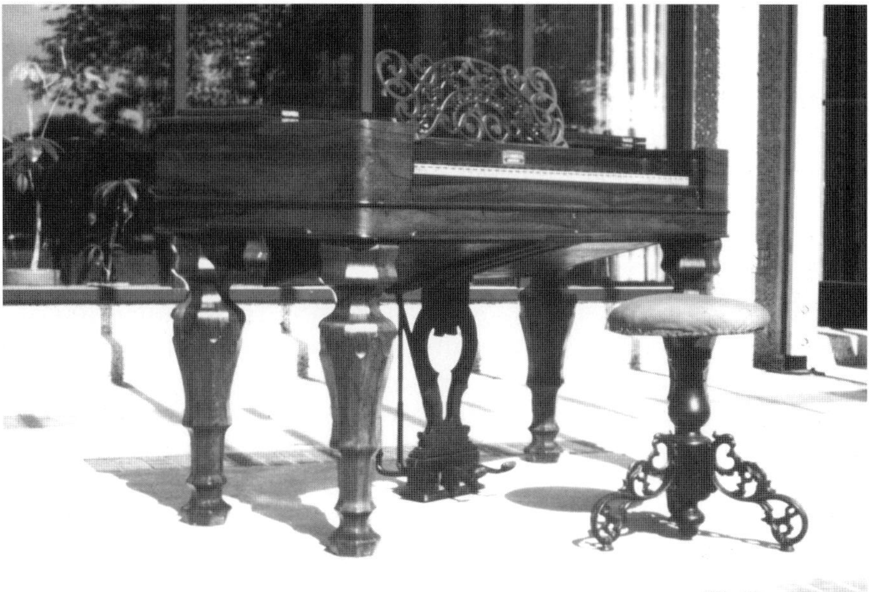

Chapter Nine

Gay Toronto

Many years ago I heard that there was a gay dance club in Toronto. I cannot pin down the year because although I kept extensive records about everything else in my life, my gay life was a hidden matter concealed from my family, my work place and my straight friends. I decided that I should write this chapter in order to balance out all other aspects of my life that I have been recording. I looked at my two shelves of carefully chronicled records and realized that I have very little material to draw on, so I shall use my memory alone. I do have one photograph album that bears the label, "Friends and Lovers".

It was the late 1950s or early 1960s. A friend told me that there actually was a club on Yonge Street that catered to gay people, where you could buy soft drinks and some food, listen to modern dance music, dance together and have a good time.

I did not believe that there could be that many gay people around. I decided to find out.

I heard that the club was called Maison du Lys, House of Lilies, and that it was on the east side of Yonge St. just above Wellesley. There was a laundromat on the ground floor. Perfect. On a Friday night I would take my laundry over and while my washing was taking care of itself I would watch what was going on. With great trepidation I did so. I settled down with a magazine and suddenly the door burst open and in came a very handsome young man carrying a bundle of what seemed to be bed sheets! He put them into the various machines and then talked to me. They turned out to be tablecloths. He told me about the club and suggested that I go upstairs and see what it was like. I finished my wash, put it away in the car, and did so.

There was a long stairway up to the door. I was greeted and told that I had to be recommended by a friend. At that point I heard a voice that I knew; an old school friend came over and told the owner that it was all right to let me in. I paid my fee, walked in and that evening was the first time in my life that I had actually been in a room with at least a hundred gay people. I could hardly believe that such a world existed. I made friends, I was invited to various tables, I danced — and returned time and time again.

The club was an amazing place: I do not remember there being any liquor or drugs; perhaps I was too innocent to recognize them or maybe it was before these items became so important. I do remember an owner named Rick, another owner named Sara. I am not sure if they were partners in the business. I do remember that in the early days there was a signal system. As the evening wore on and a crowd gathered there was an attendant at the bottom of the stairs to open the door. If he signaled that the police were coming in, plain clothes or in uniform, all the men would rush to the tables and try to look small, and then the few women present, maybe ten or more, would grab male partners and try to dance frantically all over the floor to fill it up and make it look like a heterosexual club. The police would walk around for a bit and then leave.

As time went on the club developed Saturday night stage programmes; these usually consisted of a series of drag queens performing, miming to the singing or acting of a favourite star — Judy Garland, Betty Davis and later on Bette Midler. Some of these drag stars were really very good. The younger they were the more easily they could look like women. The older ones tended to look bony, with shoulders too large or arm muscles too pronounced. Many became very good comedians; it was almost a must that they were all quick with the comeback so that they could throw an insult or a joke back after a comment from the audience.

Some of the costumes became too daring by the morality standards of that day. One evening the programme was moving along nicely and one performer stripped right down to a very small G-string, when suddenly whistles blew and we were in the middle of a police raid. The "girls" were all arrested and the names and addresses taken of all the people present. Identification was checked.

I remember going back the next night, on a Sunday, and only six people turned up.

A fund was started to help with the legal expenses of those arrested. I do not know how much was collected but I do remember that the one who collected it disappeared with the entire take and was not seen again in Toronto. It was not a large amount, fortunately.

I will always remember one incident that happened one night that bothered me greatly. There was an older waiter working at the club. He had had a wife and three children. He discovered that he was gay, his wife left him taking the children with her, and eventually he had lost his job. Now he was working in a gay club as a waiter to make ends meet. He was an educated man and well spoken. He became enamored of a young man who was quite new to the scene, but the young fellow was not the least interested in him. The young man was feeling pretty good; he was young and decent-looking although he had no job and very little education. The older man said something to him and our young man then, in a loud voice, started to sweep the floor with the waiter, calling him a chicken queen, an old man, and every swear word that would apply. The waiter just wilted and seemed to disappear into the floor. It was pitiful, and I felt ashamed for the sake of all gay people. I swore then that I would never sink so low as to allow myself to be placed in such a situation.

In spite of the above incident, on the whole I really enjoyed that club. For the first time in my life I felt surrounded by people who faced the same problems that I did. I still remember quite a number of the club habitués. One of the leaders of the pack was Murray, of indeterminate age, who was a professional clown in an ice show. He loved dressing in drag, wore outrageous costumes and had a tongue that could cut you in half. Cliff was a dancer, a milder man than Murray, always nice to me. Those two, and others, lived over on Jarvis Street in an old apartment building just below Bloor St., aptly named "The Queen's Court" The apartments were huge, and I visited there often. Usually somebody would rent one and then pay the rent by subletting to other gays. The combination of people in these situations was always changing as couples formed different allegiances. I remember Bob, once a ballet dancer, who was great with a sewing machine. A tailor, he once made me a pair of trousers. Bob also was a great dancer and taught me to dance the cha-cha. Bob went on to a great career in costuming. Johnny was always coming and going, he was a bank messenger and was very proud of having an older lover with a big car. They appeared to be genuinely fond of each other and stayed together as long as I knew them. Russell was a little mite of a thing, who rented a room from me after he arrived from up north. He tried to go to school and I tried unsuccessfully to act in the role of a foster parent. He enjoyed the setting I gave him in my home but eventually he became too undisciplined and erratic, and I asked him to leave.

Fred was another story. He worked in a bank, was Dutch, was gentle and I could have settled down with him for life. He also rented a room from me. He did not like Toronto. I never did "have an affair" with him as the quaint phrase puts it. I saw him off by plane to

Vancouver and a local gay newspaper wrote that I had cried buckets all the way home. Who was that anonymous gossip columnist?

All my life I have always created a pleasant setting in which to live. Even at university I had the aquarium that my Father made for me out of wrought iron when I was a child, standing at the back of my desk; I had posters on the walls, arty touches here and there — who says drag queens have all the talent? — in my residence room.

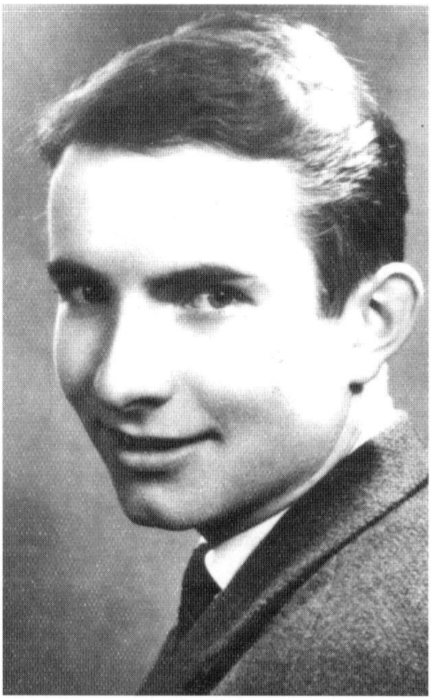

Fred

I had a very pleasant apartment on Avenue Road; I liked to give parties and people seemed to like to come. At that time the Sunday brunch was the "in thing", first of all, I remember with tuna casserole. How times have changed. At one of my parties I really wanted to do it up with style. I bought many bottles of gin, filled the refrigerator with them, unscrewed the tops and added just a little vermouth. My martinis were served in my collection of pressed glass goblets, rather large but I did not have any others. A helper went through the crowd of Sunday revelers filling the glasses as they were emptied. At the end of the party I was told there were three broken relationships, two car accidents and one divorce. The party was hailed as a great success.

Time moved on; clubs opened up in other locations. I was told that the new clubs often had the same ownership as earlier ones. The gay crowd was fickle and liked to move to a new location. The clubs upgraded their interior decors, lights were installed that made everything worn that was white glow in the dark. The baths multiplied and for many became the rage. I used to go to the baths occasionally but never on a regular basis. Then AIDS struck ———.

Once a male prostitute was arrested with a list of people's names on him. My name was on that list although I had never heard of the boy or knew him. Perhaps I looked affluent or gullible and he had spotted me as a possible client. I never found out why he named me, but a friend told me about this, and I decided to become more inconspicuous. I was holding down a good government job and did not want to jeopardize it. At the height of my Toronto gay period I was going to the clubs Friday, Saturday and Sunday evenings and dancing up a storm on most of those nights. Often, usually on a Saturday night after the club had closed at 2 a.m., I would either ask a group back to my place or go to somebody else's. It was a wild life and, like everything else frenetic, I tired of it eventually. It was 1967 and I had just met Jay. I left the club scene as so many do, and never returned.

Memories

Once, years ago, I was travelling by bus to Toronto. I sat down beside a handsome young soldier. We shared a magazine and made friends quite easily.

We arrived at the Dundas St. bus terminal. The soldier said that he did not have to be at Camp Borden until the following day and would like to stay overnight in Toronto. He had a pleasant open face and so I suggested that we stay over at the Ford Hotel.

I registered and we went up to our room. It soon became apparent to me, — "after a pleasant conversation",— that my new friend was clueless as to certain aspects of my life style. I climbed out of bed, wrapped myself in a bath towel, sat on the floor with my back to the wall, and proceeded to give him a lecture as to the pitfalls of what he was doing.

The soldier interrupted me. He said that he had brought me to the room to beat the s___ out of me and steal everything that I had. He said I was, after all, a decent sort, he told me to get dressed. We shook hands and left the hotel. I was carrying my suitcase but I decided to go for a walk in Winston Churchill Park before I went home.

Chapter Ten

The Art Institute of Ontario, 1959-1968

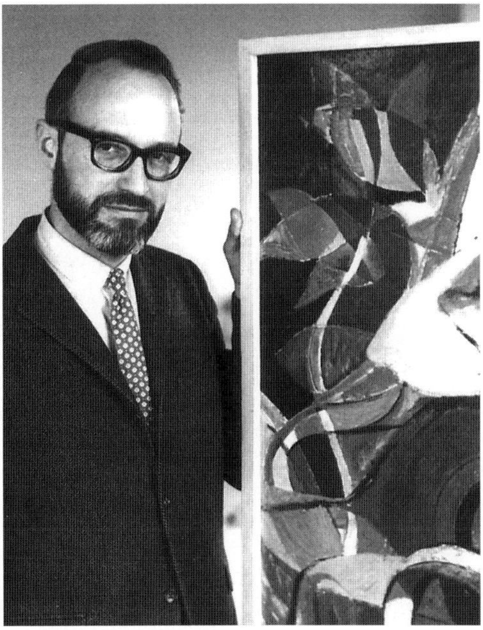

I have looked forward to writing this chapter. Looking back over my total work experience, this was the period that I enjoyed the most and in which I accomplished the most. One is expected in life, in a career, to gradually improve one's performance, to gain stature in one's profession and so end up at the top. The fact is, I peaked early. I believe that I did good work the rest of my life, but for personal satisfaction and a sense of accomplishment nothing ever equalled working for The Art Institute of Ontario.

The Art Institute of Ontario had a short history. In 1947 the art galleries of London, Hamilton, Windsor and Hart House met to consider ways in which they might cooperate in organizing exhibitions for circulation to the four centres. Its success attracted other centres until the group had grown to nine participating galleries; it became too unwieldy in terms of administration and in 1952 through the efforts of Martin Baldwin, then Director of the Art Gallery of Toronto, The Art Institute of Ontario was formed. Membership included The Art Gallery of Hamilton, the Art Gallery of Toronto, Hart House of the University of Toronto, The London Public Library and Art Museum, The National

Gallery of Canada, The Ontario Association of Architects, The Ontario Society of Artists, The Royal Ontario Museum and the Willistead Library and Art Gallery.

When I became Director of the Art Institute of Ontario I was a full-time paid employee. I had my office in my own home complete with a filing cabinet and a typewriter. At first I used my own Volkswagen van for carrying ten paintings around on my tours; later as more funds were available the A.I.O. leased me a station wagon. Nan Girard was the Information officer, and the only other paid employee. She handled all the bookings of the exhibitions, typed all reports and handled all correspondence. She too had her office in her own home and we spent a great deal of time on the 'phone. Nan learned to forge my signature convincingly. The exhibitions were stored at the Art Gallery of Toronto, especially during the summer months. As the exhibition programme became more popular few of the exhibitions spent much time in Toronto as they were constantly on the road going from one place to another.

Nan Girard performed miracles working with our exhibitors. Time and again when I was out on the road I would be told how she had helped somebody or an organization out at the last minute when a big building was opening or festival planned and something went wrong. She could always put her finger on a likely exhibition of merit and ship it quickly from one place to another. She had a kindly, motherly, "phone" voice.

The budget of the Art Institute was miniscule compared to that of exhibition programmes today, my salary was eight thousand, two hundred and fifty dollars a year. Nan was paid a straight forty dollars a week. These figures included the renting of office space in both our homes. The total budget for exhibition preparation in 1966 was just over six thousand dollars. Many exhibitions came from our founding members; others I personally sought from commercial galleries, individuals and art societies. In 1966 the total budget for the whole operation was thirty-seven thousand dollars. This covered fees to lecturers, my travel expenses, express charges for exhibitions, office expenses preparation of new shows, the refurbishing of old shows and crating and salaries.

Even as late as 1968 the fees for booking exhibitions were only ten, fifteen or twenty dollars, depending on the size of the show. The Institute paid all the express charges. There is an interesting point here. Originally the shows were supplied free of charge and the exhibitor had to pay the express charges. However I found on a couple of occasions that the shows arrived, for example at schools, were not even opened because people were too busy with other work! The shows were free; the School Board paid the express and so who cared? We seldom value what is free. We reversed our approach and instituted a fee structure and the A.I.O. paid the express. When somebody had to personally pay a fee that person made sure that the exhibition was hung and shown to the public.

Each year the A.I.O. would produce a catalogue of one hundred and twenty pages. It was mailed to the complete list of exhibitors plus, of course, other important individuals and institutions. In the 1967-1968 catalogue the table of contents was broken into different sections, each one describing the type of exhibition. These were: Originals, The Student Professional, Prints, Sculpture, Crafts, Design, Centennial, Religious, European Reproductions and Film Programmes, and Film Descriptions. The shows varied greatly. There were sixty exhibitions offered, many from the most prestigious institutions in Canada.

I must mention the Ontario Society of Artists teaching shows. The most famous of these was, "Chair and Variations", prepared for inclusion in the 81st Annual Exhibitions of the Ontario Society of 1953; this exhibition consisted of eighteen original paintings, each prepared by a different artist, including R. York Wilson, Cleeve Horse, Andre Bieler and Sydney Watson. The artists were each given the same subject, a pioneer chair from a museum near Niagara-on-the-Lake. Each painted his own interpretation of the chair. This was the most popular

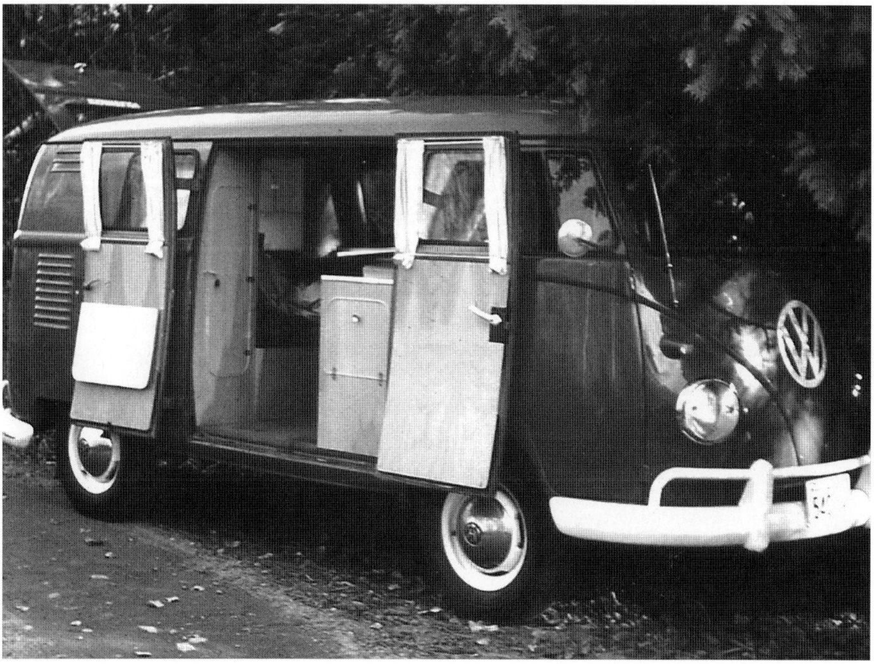

of all the A.I.O. shows. It was on the road constantly over all the years of the Institute's life. We had it updated twice by having the works rematted and reframed.

I was fortunate to have a piece of very good publicity in *Weekend Magazine* in 1965. Bruce Moss, a feature writer for the magazine, travelled with me on one of my trips. I was driving my old, red Volkswagen van with its top speed of forty-five miles an hour. Bruce travelled with me for two days, could not stand the slow pace, and then flew the rest of the way in his private plane, waiting for me to turn up at each stop. The complete trip was ten days.

I was carrying, individually crated, ten marvellous paintings that today would never be allowed out of their temperature controlled, humidity controlled environments in art galleries. The most valuable one was "Abstract in Blue" by Borduas, owned by the Art Gallery of Toronto, valued at four thousand dollars then and would be worth a small fortune now. Imperial Oil had loaned a painting by Harold

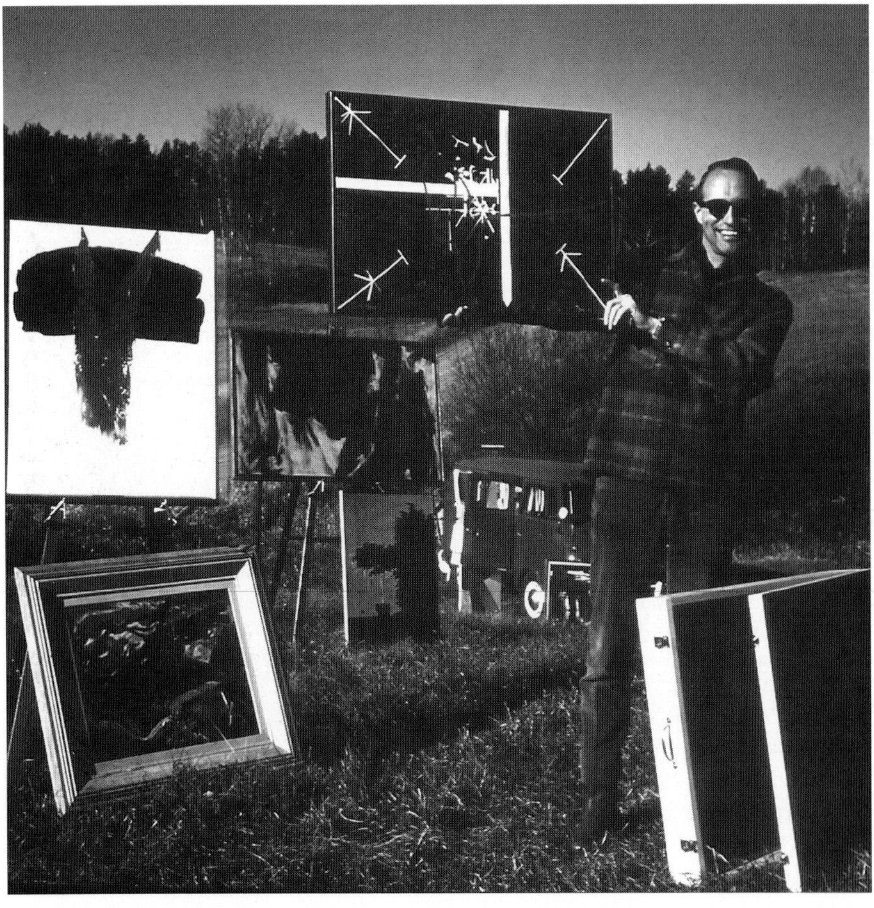

Town; it was one of his "Tyranny of the Corner" series and had been painted on plastic. Town had warned that the painting might split in half at some point. I was delighted that it did not do so on this trip. Others painting were by Jock Macdonald, A.J. Casson, J.E.H. MacDonald, Greg Curnoe, Kazuo Nakamura, R. York Wilson and Charles W. Jefferys.

Moss asked me to stop one day, take out a painting and show it to a group of Indian children that were walking along our road. I refused. I did not want that type of a phony story, and I suggested that I had not come along to illustrate his story but he was there to record mine.

On this trip I travelled by way of Canada to the Lakehead, then dipped into Minnesota to shorten the distance to my first stop, Fort Francis. Then I went north to Kenora, up to Red Lake, over a winding gravel road most of the way, back to Dryden and over to Atikokan, then back to Fort William and Port Arthur, Red Rock, Beardmore and Terrace Bay. In three weeks I had travelled more than three thousand miles, seen and talked to approximately two thousand, six hundred and thirty people.

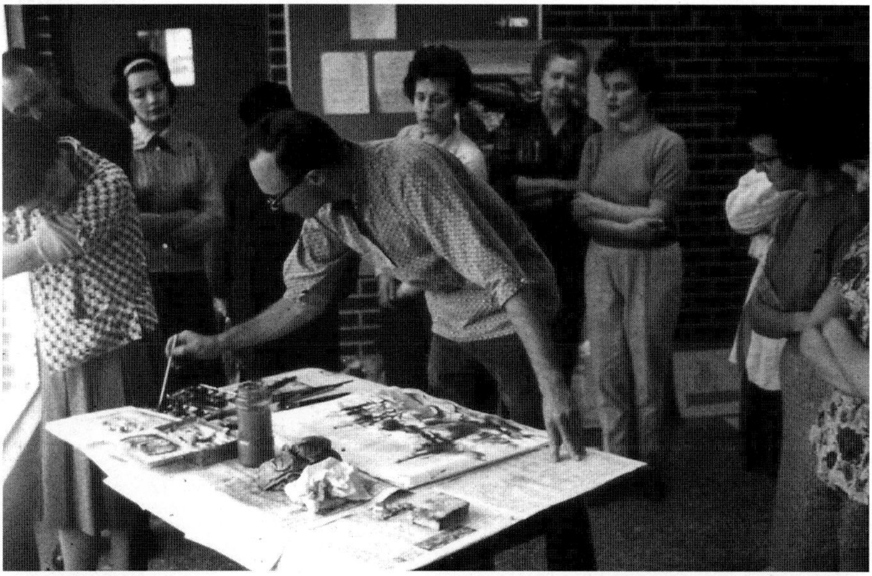

Moss picked up remarks from the audience such as, "I'll give you three dollars for that", referring to the four-thousand-dollar Borduas, or a suggestion from a lady who thought that Town's work would make a nice design for an evening dress!

Bruce had started his article with reporting a small announcement he had seen in a local paper about my talk in the auditorium in Red Lake. It read, "While watching pink elephants I remembered; guess I'll sober

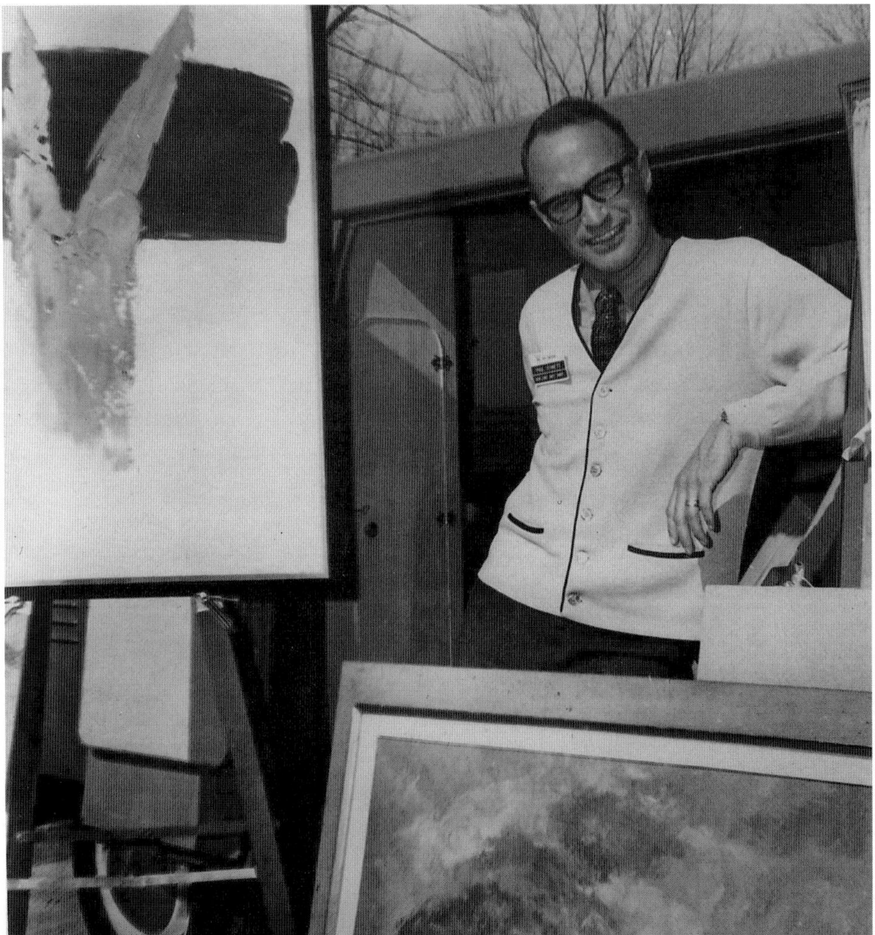

up an' take the Missus to the High School Tuesday evening, sure must take a lot of paint to make those paintings worth ten thousand dollars."

His rather flippant attitude made me wonder whether I had made a mistake in bringing such costly art to the north. However he reported later in the article that four hundred adults and students jammed the auditorium; members of the drama club had flooded the stage with lights and rigged a microphone and nobody seemed to think the exhibition the least bit highbrow.

I continued to do a great deal of touring. After a while I was forced to curtail it somewhat because of the increasing demands on my time for administration work. I did take one other tour in the north that brought some publicity. I drove to Beardmore and transferred my boxes of paintings to the "Polar Bear Express" and went by train to Moosonee. At Moose Factory there was a tuberculosis sanatorium. I still think that it was somewhat ridiculous to show that set of completely irrelevant paintings to Eskimo women, but it was great fun. The women were happy, rosy-cheeked and giggled a great deal. Before I left Moose Factory I was taken by dog sled out on the river. I was well wrapped and sat up on the sled, while the driver either ran along side or on the runners. I clearly remember that I had never been so cold in all my life. I also remember that there were huge piles of coal at Moose Factory, brought across the river by truck in the winter on the ice and stockpiled for the rest of the year to keep the sanatorium warm.

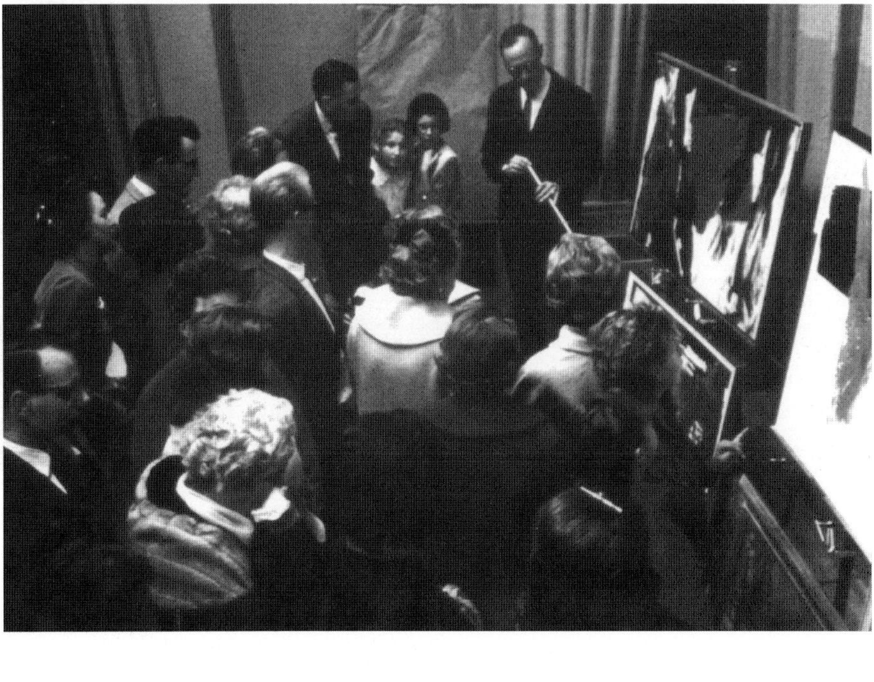

The Centennial was coming. I was working a great deal with the Ontario Arts Council, with the Director, Milton Carman, especially. Milton told me one day that the Council had a Centennial visual arts project but was not too happy with it. The following morning I was shaving and I came up with another idea for a centennial project that had a large number of positive benefits. Why not buy a large number of paintings from Ontario and Quebec artists, circulate the big show, break it up into small units for travel to smaller galleries and then give the works to the permanent collections of the art galleries of Ontario? The positive benefits? It would mean money to artists (who always needed it), it would create goodwill between Ontario and Quebec, it would create a first-class contemporary exhibition for the big galleries, with a spin- off of smaller shows for the smaller galleries; and it would place contemporary Canadian works of art in the permanent collections of Ontario galleries.

The project took off; one hundred and fifty thousand dollars was raised from three different sources: The Ontario Council for the Arts gave fifty thousand, the Art Advisory Committee of the Ontario Centennial Planning Branch gave fifty thousand, and another fifty thousand was raised from another government agency for the ancillary costs of the project — the jurying, packing, shipping, storing and insuring of the exhibition. The headline on a complete two-page spread in the *Toronto Telegram* read, "A Spectacular $150.000 Gift for Ontario Art Galleries".

Across the bottom of the page were pictures of Milton Carman of P.O.C.A., myself from the A.I.O., and Charles Tisdall from the Centennial Planning Branch of the Department of Tourism and Information. The administration of the project was left in the hands of the Art Institute of Ontario.

The juror selected was Bryan Robertson, the very successful Director of the Whitechapel Gallery in London, England. Robertson was famous for his "New Generation Exhibitions". He also was a newspaper critic and the writer of books on contemporary art. He was the author of a widely regarded book on the American abstract expressionist, Jackson Pollock. Robertson came to Canada in May of 1967. It was a whirlwind adjudication with a week in Toronto, a day or two in London, Kingston, Ottawa, Sudbury and the Lakehead and a week in Montreal and Quebec City. Unfortunately I had arranged too fast a tour. I much regretted it, for Bryan Robertson was not a well man, he suffered from asthma. I remember my frustration when he was too slow getting to the Toronto airport and the plane was actually held up so that we could catch it. Once in my seat I was gasping for air. However Bryan lived up to our expectations. He was asked to pick approximately one hundred works; hopefully there would not be too lop-sided a split between Ontario and Quebec. Approximately a total of eight thousand works were submitted for the jurying. Robertson did such an outstanding job in choosing the winners that the Arts Council flew him back from England so that he could attend the grand opening of the show he had juried, at the Art Gallery of Ontario.

The show created much publicity and interest. especially in the choosing of the works. It was wonderful that works were chosen from Northern and Northwestern Ontario. Quebec was pleased with the works that were bought for the exhibition in that province. I must have copies of dozens of newspaper clippings covering The Ontario Centennial Art Exhibition. *The Telegram* critic reported, "it surprised and delighted almost everyone who saw it. The gallery tingled with excitement as a crowd of one thousand three hundred and sixty-seven people pondered the collection of paintings and sculpture created in the last five years by ninety-two Ontario and Quebec artists." The Honourable James Auld opened the exhibition (in the absence of Premier John Robarts involved in election duties in London, Ontario).

The art scene in Canada impressed Bryan Robertson. A year or so later he had an exhibition of sculpture by Robert Downing, a Canadian, at the Whitechapel Gallery in London.

Changes were in the wind. The Art Institute of Ontario had reached the limit of what it could do with its resources and staff, the demand had grown huge. The Art Gallery of Toronto had just become The Art Gallery of Ontario; as such it had a mandate to cover the whole province of Ontario. In June of 1967 Martin Baldwin, President of the Art Institute of Ontario received a letter from the Council for the Arts, awarding the Institute a grant of thirty thousand dollars. The letter went on to stipulate that the Council would withhold payment of the full grant until such time as the A.I.O and the A.G.O. had resolved the problems of duplicating services within the province;, in other words, merge or no money. On June 30th 1968, Mr. George Hulme, treasurer of the A.I.O. turned over the charter of the Art Institute of Ontario to the government of the Province of Ontario. Ironically the very success of the A.I.O. had rendered it redundant.

I was given a small sketch by the Group of Seven member, J.E.H. MacDonald, as a thank you for my past services to the Art Institute, the gift was a unanimous vote of the Board.

I am attaching a letter from a Mrs. Margaret Frazer to the Art Institute on June 4th 1966. I think that it is a reflection of the interest of our public.

At the end of the summer in 1968 I left for Europe on a Canada Council grant.

I look back now in amazement when I think that in 1963-1964 the A.I.O. offered 50 exhibitions, there were 137 bookings and 177,118 viewers, in 1966-1967 there were 69 exhibitions offered with 715 bookings and 2,000,000 viewers. There were two full time staff. The following was a letter received from a grateful citizen.

Box 1262, Parry Sound,
June 4th/66.

The Art Institute of Ontario,
11 Roosevelt Drive,
Thornhill, Ont.

Dear Madam/Sir:

We folk of Parry Sound who are interested in Art wish to extend to you a great word of thanks and attempt to express our appreciation for that wonderful opportunity one recent evening (in May) to have your Mr. Paul Bennett B.A., B.S.W., M.Ed., lecture to us on art at the Parry Sound Library. Some of us were a bit reluctant to attend that night because sometimes a speaker has little to offer and, or else cannot portray his real thoughts on the subject. But happily, this one no sooner began than we knew we were in for a real treat with lots of humour and the very best of instruction to boot.

I wondered if Mr. Bennett has written any books on art that one might purchase? Instead of asking him about this I slipped away home after the meeting. At that time I had inflammation of the inner ear, was more deaf than usual and because I live alone didn't realize how deaf I was 'till I got there. However, I phoned Mrs. Anna Jalava the Parry Sound art instructor of night school asking her about this. She didn't know. I told her what a great pleasure it had been to hear Mr. Bennett. She suggested I write you and tender our thanks. She gave me your address for this purpose. I felt quite honoured to have this privilege but afraid very inadequate to express so much for everyone - I truly hope that others have written too.

As for me, though my deafness kept me from hearing but little of his words, it did not deprive me of what Mr. Bennett had to impart in the interests of art. I am deeply grateful for what I learned for somehow he has that rare gift of being able to transmit his thoughts to my understanding without the use of words.

How I wished that I could have brought the three landscapes to have them criticised even they were wet and not finished. One chap left the meeting and went home for his paintings. He wasn't gone long. I live 6 miles away from the library.

But here again, I was enabled to measure my work by the kind yet matter of fact manner with which Mr. Bennett showed the strong or weak points of other people's work.

In closing, may I only mention that I had never had before any lessons from a human teacher, but have learned from God and His wonderful nature all around us. Have had my oils about ten years, but started back there during those depression years with floor paint and watercolours. The family having grown, married and gone and my husband passed away nearly 20 years ago, I find this gift so comforting, helpful and financially good, and I took the woodshed to convert into a studio.

If ever anyone comes to Parry Sound and cares to come out highway 518 I shall be most happy to chat and fellowship in the language of art. Thank you for sending Mr. Bennett.

Sincerely,
"Margaret A. Frazer"

Chapter Eleven

Modus Operandi

The Art Institute of Ontario

I use the term grass roots developer proudly. Back in the days of my travel with a van of paintings I was a breath from a new world for many people living in a cultural wilderness in the far reaches of Ontario. I believe that I was suited for the work. I was young, intelligent — I think, not too bad looking, and very energetic. I was educated and perhaps, best of all, I had an attitude that said I might know something about art but I could not change a tire or drive a tractor if I had to. I could look at an amateur painting with evident interest, analyze it and tell the artist what was good and then advance my criticism two steps beyond that person and give some direction for future development. I never went too far. I had come a hundred miles to assist that artist, not destroy his interest in the subject.

Criticism is an art in its own right; I usually watched the artist's face as well as the painting when I was talking about a particular work, as the face often reflected on how far I could go. Some I could jolly along, others were fearful and had only with great difficulty been persuaded by friends or relatives to bring their paintings for the critique.

Some critics only like one kind or style of work. I was trained in art but I was not a great painter and this helped me. I did not favour this or that period or style. I could tell a good painting regardless of the style or school that it reflected.

I think being gay helped me in this work. I belonged to a hidden minority of society, maybe not so hidden now but it was in those days. I could recognize the underdog and sympathize with him or her. Actually in almost every amateur artist there was an underdog because most were sure that their work would not stand up to comparison, that they had very little talent. I was there to say this is a creative thing, it is good for you, it reflects a different part of your life, be proud of it.

Being gay helped in another way. I am sure that women on the whole felt safer with me; they did not know why perhaps, but they did not have the feeling that I was coming on to them. There were a few extreme cases where they came on to me; in one instance I actually changed my motel room in order to hide. I considered it a compliment; obviously I was not considered an effeminate or arty type.

Body language and watching for other signs were so very important. In the early days my lectures and evening programmes often took place in schoolrooms with fixed desks. This was before the time that large, important recreation centres became the small town places of meeting. If you wanted to see a miserable husband look for the one who had come to a lecture on art because he wanted to please his wife (he actually hated the idea of coming but maybe she would let him watch hockey in peace for the next month) There he sits in a desk that is too small for him, it makes him think of his own primary school when he hated his teacher. As soon as I stood up in rooms crowded like that, — in fact anywhere — I always loosened my tie, you could see the husbands visibly relax. I would take off my jacket; even that would help.

As I became more experienced I would try to change the room somehow, if the chairs were in rows, I would ruffle them up, move them into groups. I was not there in an authoritative role. If it were in an auditorium I would never speak from the platform. I was not God speaking from on high. I stood at the front on the level with my audience. If I had paintings along, they were on their easels at eye level also. I asked the people as they were coming in to come up and see them that helped to loosen up the whole room.

After my formal talk I would ask that we have the coffee period, if there was to be one, before I gave my criticism of the local work. People were nervous and getting up and moving around the room helped to relieve the tension.

In spite of all my homemade psychology some times things went terribly wrong. All I could do was pass the embarrassing situation off with a laugh. Once I had criticized a work, a painting of a bowl of flowers. It was good and I explained that even in that small subject you could give a three dimensional affect, or perspective, by using bright colours and sharper lines on the leaves of the flowers at the front and then having darker colours or softer blended colours with blended lines on the objects at the back. Then I had to say something negative or else the man standing holding his work in front of himself would think he was Picasso. I did say that the frame was completely unsuitable for the work, it did not isolate the picture so that you would see it for itself, it competed with it, the carving and bright gold fought with the picture so that you did not know what to look at. There was a gasp from the audience, I looked at the man, and he smiled a serene smile and said, " I am the local frame maker."

I had another rule I used to follow to some degree. If there was a local millionaire who might buy the art club a home of its own, I wanted to know his name so that if his paintings came up for criticism I could praise them lavishly. (Of course I am exaggerating) but I must admit that sometimes I was more careful in criticizing particularly the work of the elderly. They would never change their style regardless of what I said, they had brought their works in order to have some praise, and I obliged them.

I remember once that after I had given a talk on creativity a dear old lady brought up a small, water colour about ten inches wide by five inches deep. The subject was a river emptying into a lake with trees on both sides on the banks. There was stillness in the room and I knew that this was something special. I admired the painting profusely and then the dear soul said, and this was after I had talked about creativity. "Do you know what I copied it from? I already knew that she had sold four works on the same subject. I said no, she said, "The back of the five dollar bill" (Note, I just checked all of my bills and money and the picture is no longer used it must have been an old bill) I felt like ordering a painting from her myself.

I always asked if I could arrive early so that I could set up my equipment in the meeting room and check the electrical outlets. I hated doing this sort of thing while people were coming in. Once I did make a terrible mistake. I had been on the road for a number of days. I arrived in Owen Sound and went directly to my motel where I stretched out for a sleep. The phone rang and it was the principle from the High School. I had arranged to go and speak at the school assembly and I had pinned the note on the back of my last night's notes. I told the principal to keep the students, literally hundreds of them, singing the school song and to send twelve older students out to the street curb. I was there in five minutes, the students carried in my easels and boxes of paintings. Each painting was individually crated. I started talking as I was putting the paintings on the easels in the auditorium, a somewhat harrowing experience.

Speaking of equipment, I always used to carry a large flashlight with me because, in the early days in the small one room schools especially, just before I ended my talk, often all the lights would blow out. The ladies had slipped out to make tea and set up the lunch and two or three electric kettles would overload the wires and blow out the fuses. I would take my flashlight and ask somebody in the front row to hold the light on me and I would finish my talk. Soon the lights would be back on and we would have our tea or coffee and I could proceed with my criticism.

THE ART INSTITUTE OF ONTARIO

Director's Report
May, 1965

Note: As the Director's last lecture tour overlapped the month from April into May and was not mentioned in the last report, this report will deal with that tour from April 24th to May 14th and will also list the new exhibitions in preparation for next year's programme.

Between April 24th and May 14th, the Director:

1. Visited fourteen towns and cities for lecture purposes.
2. Lectured for 32½ hours.
3. Spoke to a total audience of 3,006. This was made up of 1,046 adults at evening meetings and 1,960 students at school meetings.

Attendance and hours

Apr. 23-4-5	Attended Craft Conference at Lake Couchiching			
Apr. 26th	Orillia	- High school	½ hour	720
		Evening meeting	2 hours	91
Apr. 28th	Sault Ste. Marie	- High school	1 hour	90
		Evening meeting	2 hours	20
Apr. 29th	Wawa	- Evening meeting	2 hours	50
Apr. 30th	Thessalon	- Evening meeting	2 hours	15
May 2nd	Elliot Lake	- Afternoon meeting	3 hours	200
May 3rd	Sudbury	- High school	½ hour	410
		High school	½ hour	400
		Evening meeting	2 hours	120
May 4th	North Bay	- Evening meeting	2 hours	150
May 5th	Englehart	- Evening meeting	2 hours	35
May 6th	Timmins	- Evening meeting	2 hours	60
May 7th	Kapuskasing	- Evening meeting	2 hours	30
May 10th	Val d'Or	- Evening meeting	2 hours	85
May 11th	Noranda	- High school	½ hour	310
		Evening meeting	2 hours	85
May 12th	Kirkland Lake	- High school art club	½ hour	30
		Evening meeting	2 hours	60
May 13th	Burks Falls	- Evening meeting	2 hours	45
		Totals -	32½ hours	3,006

Totals of Four Lecture Tours: The Director visited 54 towns and cities and lectured to 10,479 people.

New Exhibitions for 1965-66 Season:

1. "The Medium is the Message" - Prepared by the Ontario Society of Artists in which each panel explores a different medium. The emphasis is on the newer types of media such as acrylics. Parts "A" and "B".
2. "Water Colours/65" - Prepared by the Canadian Society of Painters in Water Colour.
3. "Ontario Society of Artists--Individual Members Show" - Eight members of the O.S.A. have each lent five paintings in water colours and oils, fairly modern in interpretation.
4. Ron York Wilson Mural - The cartoons, sketches, and a small section of actual mosaic of the mural by Mr. Wilson for the outside of the Bell Telephone Building in Toronto.

. . .

The Art Institute of Ontario
Director's Report - May, 1965 - 2

New Exhibitions for 1965-66 Season (continued)

5. "Four Winnipeg Artists" - 20 paintings by one woman and three men, young artists of Winnipeg - Warkov, Head, Tascona, and Mikuska.
6. "Seven Painters from Vancouver" - Seven paintings typifying the newer west coast development.
7. "Western Landscape as History" - 25 water colours from the Glenbow Foundation.
8. "Carl Rungius" - Oil sketches of the four seasons in landscape from the Glenbow Foundation.
9. "Goodridge Roberts War Sketches" - In water colour.
10. "Bergman Woodcuts" - Sensitive woodcuts by the late Winnipeg painter.
11. "Canadian Graphic Society Exhibition" - Graphics from across Canada - purchased outright by the Community Programmes Division.
12. "New Dimensions in Printmaking : Winston Leathers and J. K. Esler" - Mr. Esler states he will attempt to print anything that will go through the press.
13. "CBC Television Set Design" - Visuals or sketches in various media on television programmes.
14. "Royal Canadian Academy Architectural Section" - The photographic exhibition prepared by the architects on current Canadian trends in building, for the Royal Canadian Academy Annual Exhibition.
15. An exhibition of photographs of public buildings featuring excellence in brick and tile work.
16. "Commemorative Medals by Dora de Pedery Hunt" - Bronze medals - an art form being revitalised in Canada.
17. "Twelve Canadian Sculptors" - Small pieces in bronze, welded steel, wood and metal, cast stone, and granite, by twelve well known Canadian sculptors.
18. "Ontario Sculptors" - Ten pieces of sculpture in bronze and stone.
19. "Polish Handicrafts" - Ceramics and weaving secured from the Polish Embassy.
20. "Texture and Colour Handweaving, 1965" - From the Ontario Handweavers and Spinners featuring rugs, draperies and upholstery fabrics.
21. "Canadian Guild of Potters" - 80-odd pieces of pottery - purchased outright by the Community Programmes Division.
22. "Canada at the Triennale" - A free standing exhibition of photographs plus a model of the Canadian pavilion at the Triennale in Milan.
23. "The World through One Eye" - 28 photographs by Philip Pocock.
24. A photographic exhibition by Michael Lambeth of Toronto.
25. "The Architectural Student looks for Design from Nature" - In which the sensitive eye of the would-be architect looks for design fundamentals in nature.
26. "The Architectural Student looks at the Village" - Drawings, water colours and ink sketches in which the would-be architect explores an old Ontario village.
27. "Learning from Prints" - A show of graphics from the Ontario College of Art.

The Institute plans to withdraw approximately 21 exhibitions from last year's programme. A number of the older shows are being revitalised, for example, the exhibition "Early Ontario Architecture" is being reproduced with a more up-to-date layout, and the "Group of Seven" sketches are being reframed.

PAUL BENNETT,
Director.

THE ART INSTITUTE OF ONTARIO

DIRECTOR'S REPORT

- January 1st to February 15th, 1967 -

Publicity for A.I.O.

(1) T.V. - On January 12th at 12:00 noon I appeared on the Elwood Glover T.V. interview show for a 14 minute discussion on A.I.O. program, my tours - especially to the north, and the Ontario Centennial Art Program.

(2) T.V. - On January 27th at 2 p.m. I appeared on an interview program in Port Arthur - 14 minute discussion on A.I.O. program, my tour and Ontario Centennial Art Program.

Lecture Tours

January 5: Orangeville, evening meeting, 70 people present. I was introduced by Recreation Director, who stayed for complete meeting and assisted in clean up afterwards. Well over half of the audience had heard me speak there 2 years ago.

January 14: I left Toronto for North Western Ontario tour. On the way out of the city I passed one of the Centennial Truck Caravans - about 10 very large transports. I had for a brief moment a feeling of pride that the A.I.O. was also contributing to Ontario's growth through its program. (My mother's U.E.I. ancestors might have been proud). Drove to Kirkland Lake on 1st day (370 miles).

January 15: Drove from Kirkland Lake to Cochrane (90 miles). Evening meeting, 50 people present. First visit to this town.

January 16: Train from Cochrane to Moosonee (186 miles). Took from 9:30 a.m. to 6 p.m. - 2 hours late departure. Snowmobile from Moosonee to Moose Factory (continually inhabited by Europeans since 1670).

January 17 & 18: Paintings set up at hospital, seen by some hospital staff (30), a tour by Eskimo patients in T.B. wards (50), an evening lecture (1½ hours) to audience of 70 (many Indian students from residence school), a ½ hr. talk in a school assembly (grades 7 & 8) - 200 present, a two hour figure drawing class to 10 art enthusiasts.

Highlight of visit: I was dressed in sheepskin troussers and coat, buffalo robe, and taken for a dog sled ride on the Moose River behind nine huskies. It was 30 below zero.

January 19: Train back from Moosonee to Cochrane. Dug car out of a snow drift.

- 2 -

January 20: In a.m. 40 below zero - hard time getting car to start, doors would not close, windows would not clear, and the brakes were frozen.

Drove the 140 miles to Hearst. Evening meeting at Hearst (Catholic) College - new amphitheatre auditorium, tiered seats - 250 present, mostly students from college plus some townspeople, 1st visit by myself.

January 21: Drove 150 miles to Geraldton.

January 23: A very interesting situation developed in Geraldton which points up the necessity of having a good contact in a community. I originally wrote two letters to the Chairman of the Recreation Committee - no reply. I then phoned from Toronto - very non-committed response, no action. When I arrived in town, I had an extra day to put in as the rest of my schedule was set, I called on the high school principal, a Mr. L.D. Holland - immediate enthusiasm. Mr. Holland arranged for a school assembly on Monday morning - 60 interested students attended and stayed almost an hour discussing the paintings, asking questions, etc. Mr. Holland was very impressed and asked my permission to call a meeting that evening in the school library. He announced this to his students over the P.A. system, made some phone calls to art interested persons. 30 people came out on a few hours notice. About 20 others stayed for part of the time until they had to go off to night class.

January 24: In the a.m. before I left for Beardmore I visited the hospital on the suggestion of the Ladies Auxiliary and made suggestions re the purchase of two paintings as a Centennial project for the lounge. Then drove to Beardmore (56 miles).

Meeting in Beardmore Public School - at 7:30 p.m. - 28 Cubs and masters, 8 p.m. - 50 in audience. Last time here there was a small audience with a lot of young children; this time adults - men and women and some teen-agers who had heard me in the assembly at Geraldton. Increase in audience - good publicity on part of the local contact - sent mimeographed information home with all the school children.

January 25: Drove from Beardmore to Red Rock - 2 hours to go 60 miles. 6 inches of snow during night, most of the road unploughed, blowing.

Set up display at 1 p.m. at Red Rock Recreation Centre. At 2 p.m. - gave a ½ hr. talk to 200 school children grades 6, 7 & 8 from public and separate schools, high school students. Man stayed on duty - young people in all afternoon. Evening meeting - 60 present, from Red Rock and Nipigon. My third visit - most successful, people friendly, greeted as an old friend.

January 26: Clear day - drove from Red Rock to Fort Arthur, 65 miles. Contacted C.P.D. and art interested people.

- 4 -

February 4: Phoned Sioux Lookout - my contact was away in California - left planning to others, nothing done, therefore no meeting. I was sorry for local group, glad for myself - exhausted after 5 nights - 5 towns and driving. Drove 230 miles to Lakehead - saw two wild moose at side of road.

February 5 & 6: In Lakehead. On Monday a.m. visited Community Programs Office. Discussed art situation in North West with C.P.P. representative. Phoned a number of local art contacts.

February 7: Drove to Schreiber - 120 miles. School assembly at 3 p.m. 200 students. Evening meeting 60 present. Car load came from Terrace Bay where I had visited previously. First visit to Schreiber.

February 8: Drove to Marathon - 53 miles. Made very welcome by local group and the Recreation Director. First time for this type of program in Marathon - evening meeting - 55 present.

February 9: Drove to Manitouwadge - 57 miles. Made very welcome - first visit. Magnificent (1½ million dollar) recreation centre with beautiful library, curling, arena, club rooms, etc. Welcomed by Mrs. Bray - librarian and long time user of the A.I.O. exhbibitions. High school assembly - 175. Evening meeting - 70 present. Very lively discussion Manitouwadge is a company town - mining, 3000 population.

February 10: Drove to Wawa - 120 miles. Terrible driving - snow storm, trip took four hours. Very bad storm in evening - in spite of it 45 present; auditorium of Separate School, local art group has fallen apart, evening organized by one local enthusiast.

February 11: Left Wawa at 8 a.m. Drove all day. Accident: at 4;50 I was 25 miles south of Sudbury at Rock Lake. Travelling 60 m.p.h. A green '65 Rambler came around a corner and down a hill on my side of the road. He hit my car. Result, the complete left side of the car smashed the door beside me off, three wheels wrecked, a door and fender on the right side pushed in. My car took off four guard rails. The engine and side of the Rambler wrecked. Injury: minor cuts on arm and leg, whiplash. I feel the safety belt saved my life - no windows were broken. The other driver admitted it was his fault, wrote a statement saying the light was in his eyes. He was not injured. The police charged him with being on my side of the road. The eight crates of paintings were not damaged. Weather 17 below zero. I finally reached a motel in Sudbury, after a hospital check-up at 11:30 p.m.

February 12: Spent part of morning at Memorial Hospital, Sudbury, having X rays to neck. Friends from Toronto drove to Sudbury and brought me home.

- 5 -

Conclusions on Trip

(1) These trips were originally started to publicize the travelling exhibition program of the A.I.O. In view of our present capacity-bookings, this is no longer necessary. The program, in interest and attendance, is valid in its own right.

(2) The North West, for a number of years, has had many tid-bits of the visual arts - - never a full course meal. There are courses at Quetico - (Roberts, Bayefsky, Millar, Bennett), workshops at the Lakehead (Weisman, Griffith), Community Programs Division started 3 day workshops (in the last 2 years Page (8), Christie (8), Cosgrove (8)), the C.P.D. art adviser, Walter Sunahara, and my own trip for 8 years now.

I strongly recommended at the Lakehead that they try to engage a full time professional artist. Such a person might be a part time resident artist at the University. This person might become part of the University extension and travel, as the professors do, out to Red Rock, etc.

(3) In six towns where I had a very good contact person, there was an excellent coverage of publicity - newspapers, radio, T.V., phoning committees, mimeographed handouts at schools. In such places I had larger audiences than before - Orangeville, Red Rock, the Lakehead, Atikokan, Fort Frances, Beardmore.

(4) In three towns the audiences were smaller. Lack of a good contact, changing executives, curling bonspiels, etc. - Kenora, Red Lake, Dryden. One has occasion to wonder if the over abundance of hors d'oeuvres is becoming a monotonous diet. Should the A.I.O. tie in with the C.P.D. to produce a "total environment" - that is a C.P.D. workshop, set up a good exhibition and combine a skill course with sensitivity lectures.

(5) From my own personal point of view - on further tours I am going to have to play down the criticism of local works. After eight years on the road I am reaching the point where I have no more to say. At the Lakehead I attempted a constructive criticism of 100 paintings on a Saturday afternoon. Part way through I called for a break - I could no longer function critically. The amateur painting is now reaching the point where all I can say is "Paint more".

(6) Of the seventeen communities visited during this period, seven of them were new to this program...Cochrane, Moose Factory, Hearst, Geraldton, Schreiber, Marathon and Manitouwadge. These did produce good sized audiences.

(7) Speedometer readings. On leaving Toronto - 12,820, at Sudbury before accident 15,664 = 2,844 + 242 (Sudbury to Toronto). Also travelled 370 miles by train.

- 6 -

Attendance Summary: Lectures January 1st to February 15th, 1967

	Adults	Students
Orangeville	70	
Cochrane	50	
Moose Factory	30 50 70 10	200
Hearst		250
Geraldton	30	60
Beardmore	50	30
Red Rock	60	200
Lakehead	235 50	
Atikokan	65	500
Fort Frances	75	
Kenora	35	
Red Lake	30	
Dryden	30	
Schreiber	60	200
Marathon	55	
Manitouwadge	70	175
Wawa	45	
Adults	1,170	Students 1,615

I lectured in 8 schools (45 minutes) to 1,615 students, in 17 communities 20 times (2 hours) to 1,170 adults. Total attendance 2,785. I travelled 3,456 miles.

- 7 -

Ontario Centennial Art Program:

Mr. Summerskill has worked most diligently on this project during my absence. A full statement will be in the next report.

Eaton Foundation Grant:

Mr. Baldwin approached the T. Eaton Co. for a grant toward exhibition preparation. A letter dated January 13th advises the A.I.O. that the foundation will pay $500.00 a year forthe next three years, a total of $1,500, first payment November, 1967.

Paintings of a Province:

This exhibition has been very well received. It is now completely booked for the year and a half it is with the A.I.O. Mrs. Girard has had to refu more than 100 requests for bookings of this show. Considered in two par it has 49 bookings.

Exhibition Program:

There are 447 bookings of exhibitions through February, with 628 through June. This may be compared with last year at this time when there were 316 through February and 413 through June. In addition, there are already many bookings for next Fall and Winter.

PAUL BENNETT,

Director.

February 24th, 1967.

Memories

Years ago I used to drive north on a Friday evening to spend the weekend at a friend's farm. One such night half way along the two hour drive I picked up a hitch hiker. The young man was in his last year at university, in his early twenties, muscular and charming. He said that he was on his way home to his family farm. The family had gone away for a rare weekend to visit a married daughter and he had agreed to be home by late Friday evening to look after the chores.

We came to the cross road where he turned east. I suggested that I would drive him the rest of the way. He was very grateful. As we drove along the boy suggested a short cut down back roads. We went on and every short cut seemed to become wilder and wilder. Finally we were driving along a track in scrub bush. A sixth sense told me that I was getting into trouble.

Finally we came to the long lane leading up to a substantial farm house. We stopped before the deserted house — and much to my relief — we had a "pleasant half hour of conversation".

The young man went to get out of the car. He put his hand on the door handle and turned to me and said, "Oh, I almost forgot about the money". Suddenly my fears rose again, his size frightened me, farm boys are rough and strong. I had never been robbed before. A chill ran up my spine.

He continued, "You have been so kind to me driving out of your way to bring me home, I would like to give you two dollars toward the gas."

Chapter Twelve

Jay

I was living in Toronto on Bedford Road. A university friend of mine, John C., was teaching in a northern community. He used to come to Toronto on a Friday night, go to the theatre or a movie, stay at my place and then travel down to Peterborough on Saturday morning to visit his mother. One very late evening in the spring of 1967 I had gone to bed and was sound asleep when the doorbell rang and woke me up. I stumbled down the stairs and let John and a friend in. I showed them to the guest room and then promptly fell asleep again.

The following morning John came into my room and said, "Come and meet Jay." I did so; there he was, in my eyes the most beautiful person that I had ever known, sitting up in bed and smiling shyly at me. Jay had been a student of John's and now he was in his last year of a science course at Western University. The three of us had breakfast together and then they were on their way to visit John's mother. Jay and I exchanged phone numbers before they left.

We talked on the phone and then went our separate ways for the summer. Jay was travelling to the east coast with a school friend; I drove to Mexico with my sister in my car with her trailer. In the fall Jay came to visit and we connected. The relationship lasted ten years according to Jay, and twenty-three years according to me. He was twenty-one and I was thirty-nine when we met. At the end of ten years he told me that he wanted more space; he had met a ballet dancer/antique dealer and wanted to get to know him better. Regardless, I visited Jay's century farm for the next thirteen years at least once a month.

Jay had grown up early. His father died when he was in his teens and he inherited the family century farm. There were relatives on farms in all directions, but he had the original family farm. He sold off by auction his father's prize herd of cattle as he could not look after them and pursue his chosen career of teaching. Jay wanted to rent out the land, at least temporarily and upgrade the home and the barns.

Jay's mother remarried a few years later. Jay lived on alone in the house and I would visit weekends. Part of the house was turned into an income apartment. In a way, I was the weekend helper, aiding in building fences, helping bring saplings from the bush for planting around the house and doing other chores. Of course, being city bred, I was useless in many farm matters.

We had wonderful times together. For example, we went to auctions, I remember once at an auction that Jay wanted an old pioneer quilt that had been woven locally. Being an old hand at auctions I said that I would bid for it. I got the quilt at a very inflated price. The next day when walking in the local village an old timer asked me why I wanted to take that quilt to Toronto. When I said that I had bid for Jay, he swore and said that he had bid it up because he did not want to see the quilt leave the county! So much for my helpfulness at auctions.

We visited antique stores looking for old pieces to match some of the original ones in Jay's home; we played bridge with his mother and stepfather; we visited friends and relatives.

Soon after we met I received a Canada Council grant and left for ten months in England and Europe. Our relationship survived that separation. We bought identical tape recorders and sent cassettes back and forth to each other almost every week. I described my travels and work: Jay told me about his training to be a teacher, the finding of a job, and the work on the farm.

Looking back one often realizes what stupid things one has done in life. In this case we used the same tapes over and over instead of saving them and buying new ones. So I lost the complete verbal record of my trip. We had arranged a code, if my tape started Dear Jay and his mother's name Anne, he could safely play it in front of her. If the tape said only Dear Jay, it was for his ears only . I still have a few bits and pieces of these tapes and wish I had the whole set.

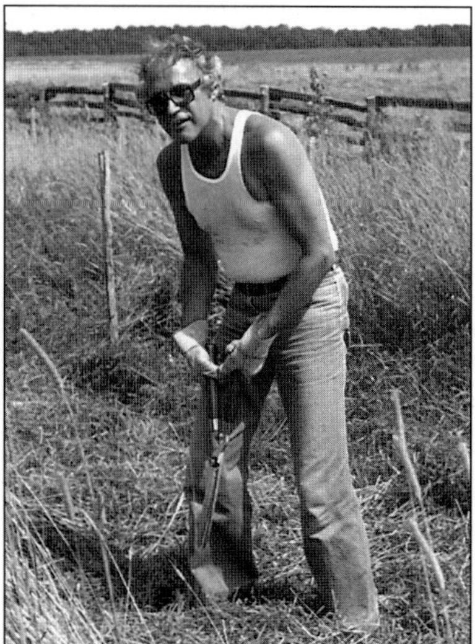

Digging a perennial bed

Jay loved horses. He had two and hoped someday to upgrade and breed them. I bought a thoroughbred hunter named Emsuma who was in foal (Jenny, 1972) and learned to ride — not very well. I had a bad back from a childhood fall and was always careful of my balance, and the horse sensed my insecurity I am sure. Jay went to horse shows; sometimes I accompanied him.

We travelled. Jay bought a small British sports car. I do believe it was to spite his family and show his independence. We had a wonderful summer trip to Cape Cod. We bought antiques wherever we went until Jay, literally, had to unpack me so that I could get out of the car. I do remember one incident where we knew we were short of gas. We kept on going hoping to find a gas station. We finally ran out of gas at the top of a hill; the car coasted down the hill and right into the front of the pumps at a station.

We spent a holiday in England where we visited my English relatives. Another time, 1975, we went to Dubrovnik, Yugoslavia. I will always remember a bus tour we took on that holiday.

We sat at the back of a bus, the windows were open and the gasoline fumes gave me a terrible headache. We stopped for lunch at a worker's vacation resort. Whenever I travelled in my work and did not know what to eat, I used to order bacon and eggs as it was a safe meal. I did so in this case. They brought me a tin plate filled with grease; in that grease were two pieces of fat and two eggs like bullets. I rushed from the room and was sick to my stomach.

Eventually, after twenty-three years, came the day that Jay told me he was going to be married. He had met a bright, beautiful, poised nurse. She was an excellent horsewoman. I was sent an invitation but I did not go to the wedding. I do remember one thing; on the last weekend I spent on the farm before the wedding, I was driving down to Toronto the Monday morning and not watching my speed, I will not mention how fast I was driving but I was stopped by a policeman and given a ticket for two hundred and thirty dollars: A woman friend of mine was going the same speed a little later. She cried and was given a ticket for one hundred and ten dollars. So much for the battle of the sexes.

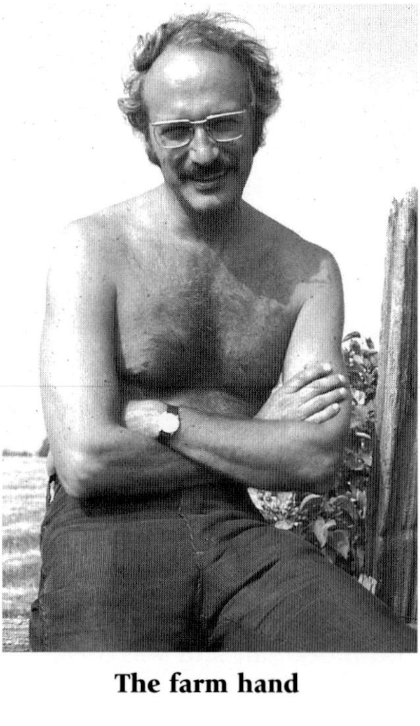

The farm hand

Now it is over ten years. I was never invited back to the house in all of that time. Finally came the death of Jay's mother, and my sister and I went to the funeral. We had travelled a great distance and Jay and his wife Barbara graciously invited us back to the house afterwards. We saw all the improvements to the farm — the training ring, the rebuilt horse stalls, the better draining of the yard. The house looked inviting and warm, with many feminine touches. We had a wonderful meal. Barbara told Jay later that she wished that they had invited me years ago.

Now that time has softened my outlook on the affair I look back in wonder at how long Jay and I were together. There 'was a wide difference in our ages; he was a scientist and a farmer and I was an arty type. On the whole I was not much use around the farm. I tried, but I do think I was more of a liability than an asset. Now he can go to church with his wife on his arm and all is well. We could never do that. I wondered the last few years why our activities were so limited. But now I understand. Perhaps if I had been able to ride properly that could have made a difference, but why bother dwelling on that? Jay was so beautiful both inside and out that he used to take my breath away. I remember the good things, even the silly things — imagine waking on a summer night with a gentle rain pouring down and rushing outside in the nude to dance wildly on the lawn, and me a grown man!!!

I will end this chapter by inserting a small article I did some years ago for a local gay magazine. My series was called "Memories". This was one of my grand moments and present memories.

Memories

I was city bred. My partner operated a century farm. I do not remember if the following incident concerned straw or hay. I just remember the fact that it was a perfect day, one of my strongest memories of a very long relationship It was an October day. The sky was that deep bright cerulean blue that only appears in Ontario at that time of year. The sun was brilliant. We were in a field of rolling land; there were no buildings in sight. The only sign of human occupancy were the old fences of cedar rails. The hedgerows were filled with brilliant golden rod and purple asters. The air was filled with the humming of bees rushing to secure the honey before the cold weather set in. There was the city boy proudly driving the new tractor. The tractor pulled a farm wagon and Jay was heaving the bales up and arranging them in neat rows for transport to the barn. He was stripped to the waist and had a golden tan from working outside all summer.

There I was actually doing a regular farm job rather than just mending a fence or cleaning a stable. I was so proud. I had arrived and was actually doing some worthwhile work with my partner: as his partner on his family farm. It was the most perfect day that I remember in a more than twenty-year relationship. I do not even remember if we had a pleasant conversation that night after lights out. I just remember that I felt worthwhile, I felt valuable, and I felt a real partner.

Chapter Thirteen

The Canada Council Grant, 1968-1969

When I started to prepare for writing this chapter I got out my album on the Canada Council. In it I have a copy of my application for the grant, the Council's reply, my reports to the Council every three months listing my day-to-day progress, the list of museums and galleries I visited, the famous people I met, the list of the theatres I attended, the movies I went to, the objects I collected, my final report and catalogues and booklets I collected. Then I got out the complete set of coloured slides that I brought back, each carefully labeled, thank God. I still have a half dozen partial tapes that I dictated and sent to Jay; I have previously stated how we sent tapes back and forth and just taped over used ones to send our weekly news — thus I lost my complete verbal record of the trip!! As I went over all this material I was gradually absorbed into that period; it was a wonderful year, full of adventure, colour, new information and friends, In retrospect I do not think that it could have been any better.

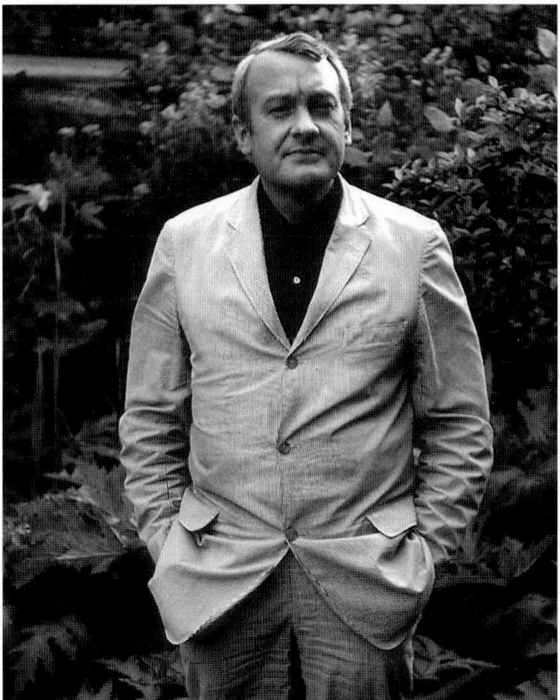

I was thirty-nine years of age when I applied to the Canada Council. My work with the Art Institute of Ontario was completed. It had merged into the Art Gallery of Ontario. I was tired from my frequent lecture tours and the work on the Ontario Centennial Art Exhibition. I was ready for a change. I prepared an application to the Canada Council and sent it off on October 14th, 1967; the award was granted on February 20th 1968.

I wished to visit Europe and New York: from October, 1968 to May, 1969 in London and outlying areas of England; in June and July, 1969, in New York, U.S.A. My plan was to study the administration, training schemes and extension services of art galleries and museums intending at the same time to visit commercial galleries and artists and immerse myself in both the contemporary and historic art scenes, I stated that I would like to make possible contacts for travelling exhibitions for Canada, and while in Europe visit Paris, Florence and Rome on gallery tours and Greece for a short holiday. In August and September 1969 I would prepare a report on the information garnered during the trip and distribute it to the art galleries and museums of Ontario. I did all of the above and a great deal more.

I was granted the full amount of my request for money, seven thousand dollars plus four hundred and forty-four for travel. The Council gave me a letter of introduction signed by Jules Pelletier, Chief of the Awards Section.

I could not have been more fortunate. I had met Bryan Robertson, the Director of the Whitechapel Art Gallery, when he came to Canada to jury the Ontario Centennial Art Exhibition. We had some weeks together, touring Ontario, jurying and seeing the works of art submitted by the professional and otherwise artists. We had become good friends and respected one another's work.

Bryan asked me to stay at his home and make it my headquarters while I was in London and I did so. He was a giant in the Visual Arts scene in London. In the early fifties he had become the Director of the Whitechapel Art Gallery located in a run down part of eastern London. He had a wonderful eye for new talent, and he introduced a completely new generation of artists to the London scene. His series of New Generation Exhibitions were an annual event at the Whitechapel Gallery from 1963 to 1968. Artists such as David Hockney, Bridget Riley, Philip King, Paul Huxley and John Hoyland were first featured in these shows and soon after started establishing important reputations for themselves. Bryan also had a New York connection; he was friends with, and had written about, among others, Helen

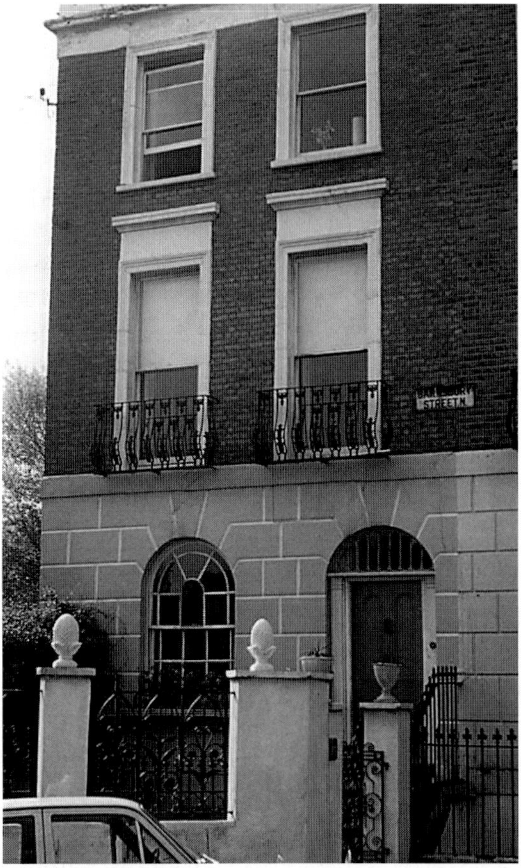

Frankenthaler, Robert Motherwell and Jackson Pollock.

Bryan Robertson was also an art critic for one of London's newspapers, *The Spectator*. I remember going with him to view an important exhibition on the Bauhaus style. He seemed to simply walk through it; then a few days later I read his review in the paper and it was scholarly, precise and piercing in its analysis.

Bryan Robertson, together with John Russell and Lord Snowdon published the definitive book on the contemporary visual arts scene in England, *Private View*, in 1965. This book investigated the immediate past, Henry Moore, Barbara Hepworth, John Piper, and so on and then moved on to people like Bacon, Chadwick and Armitage in the 1950s; then it launched into the new generation that was current at the time. It examined the total scene, the commercial galleries, public galleries, schools, art associations and patrons.

So I moved into the home of a celebrity. It was a small, Georgian townhouse in Islington, 73 Barnsbury Street. One of the first things I found out, and I already suspected, was that Bryan Robertson was an eccentric, and the British do this best. He was not in good health; he had a bad case of asthma, and was quite out of condition physically. He tended to stay up late at night and then sleep late in the morning. I will always remember one morning when I got up and looked out the back window and saw Bryan (still in his dinner jacket — he had been writing a review of an exhibition all night) arguing with the dustman, or garbage collector, as we would call him. Evidently something had happened to Bryan's favourite garbage tin and he was annoyed.

I was told (this happened before I arrived) that the phone rang one evening quite late, and it was Princess Margaret; Bryan had been asked to dinner and had forgotten to turn up. Lord Snowdon, husband of Princess Margaret, had been the photographer for *Private View*.

Bryan did two wonderful things for me. He wrote to more than a dozen important people in the visual arts and arranged for me to visit them. I went to St. Ives in Cornwall and spent a wonderful three hours late one afternoon with Barbara Hepworth. We had "tea" — in crystal goblets. At the end of the interview she gave me, signing each one of them, two books about her own work. The one is in a plastic sleeve and was in honour of the conferment of the Honorary Freedom of the Borough of St. Ives, Cornwall on Bernard Leach (the potter) and Barbara Hepworth in recognition of their international contribution to the arts. Dated September 23rd, 1968.

I had many such meetings with important people: for example, Mr. John Pope-Hennessey, Director of the Victoria and Albert Museum, Mr. Norman Reid, Director of the Tate Gallery, Sir Anthony Blunt, Director of the Courtault Institute and Mr. Martin Davies, Director of the National Gallery. Many times I was taken to lunch; a few times doors swung open in offices to reveal a lunch had been prepared and was waiting.

The other wonderful thing was that Bryan Robertson gave me a magical "feeling" about London. He took me to exhibitions. I met artists such as Paul Huxley who was staying at Bryan's house for a period, and Bridget Riley. I bought two prints of hers from a set of four. I could not afford the whole set. It was the "Nineteen Greys" series; they still hang in a place of honour in my home. He directed me to almost every museum in London. He showed me Camden Passage, Petticoat Lane and Portobello Road where I bought Georgian air twist goblets, Chinese ivory calling card cases, and opal rings.

Last but not least, he taught me something about the art of eating; he treated me to at least a dozen of the better restaurants in London. We would go to the Cafe Royale for a wonderful lunch. One evening, along with Paul Huxley, the three of us went to L'Etoile. I was thinking that we would go out and eat, I would be home early, and be able to go to bed in good time. On a tape to Jay I described this meal. We started with a martini at home, and then went to the restaurant arriving about nine p.m. We had a gin and tonic first, two types of wine during the meal and a pear liqueur afterward. The waiters were in tails, the tables set with white linen with gleaming silver and crystal, All the head waiters seen to know Bryan and always conducted us to a table with a deep flourish. At the end of a meal Bryan always took the bill and turned it over and signed his name and address — and we walked out.

That night I had a filet mignon and Bryan and Paul split a wild duck. My filet was three inches high and then covered in pate de foie gras. A brazier was rolled up to the table and our plates were all heated and then placed in front of us with a flourish. The salads arrived and even the dressings were mixed to our specifications. The menu, of course, was in French and Bryan, sensing my ignorance, consulted with me in the ordering. Bryan knows wines and would speak with the wine steward about a '52 or a '62 with complete nonchalance. For dessert I had a meringue with roasted chestnuts, Bryan had new apricots with oranges and Paul had a pineapple with thick sweet syrup.

We left the restaurant about midnight. — and I woke up at four a.m. and could no longer sleep because of the rich food. To Bryan, both eating and conversation were an art. As I said to Jay on my tape, if I were to stay too long at Bryan Robertson's I would have to develop a new order of living, and also have a much larger budget, — only once or twice I paid for lunch. As I have seen Bryan leave a tip of two pounds, ten shillings. From that you can figure the cost of the meals, and that was in 1968.

Bryan also liked to entertain at home. He would have a maximum of four people. At that particular time when I was visiting he was serving a supper, which consisted of an oven egg dish. The following was the recipe that he wrote down for me: To be cooked in fire proof, white oven dishes or soufflé dishes. Ten to twenty minutes in a hot oven. (400 degrees). Allow to stand for ten minutes before serving. For four persons if half sloshed — so as to not see what was hitting them.

Cut up with scissors four or five bacon rashers and grill. Leave to cool, not necessary to keep hot. Place in the bottom of each bowl one-third of a carton of thin cream (One carton needed for each greedy visitor.) Add some bacon to each pot. Scatter large amounts of dried or fresh tarragon and black pepper from a mill. Place small pieces of Gruyere or mild cheese in each pot. Cover with cream. Break one or two eggs into each pot and cover with black pepper, tarragon and cream.

Bryan also had a special salad, which he called his "Exquisite Salad" and he made it for four people. The recipe is as follows:

Four heads of endive or chicory, 2 ripe avocado pears, 2 bunches of watercress. Can be done with unpeeled cucumber slices and chopped fresh mint instead of watercress. Remove half stalk of watercress, slice endive into 1 or 2 inch lengths. scoop avocado out with a teaspoon.

Place all together in large bowl. Have a stiff drink and then add the dressing. The dressing consisted of 2 teaspoons of sugar, 1 teaspoon salt, ground black pepper from a mill, 4 to 5 tablespoons of olive oil, 1 tablespoon of tarragon or wine vinegar, juice from half a lemon. Stir and apply.

His late evening suppers were a great success. I have duplicated these recipes, a number of times and I have two warnings to those who wish to try them. First of all make sure that you wait at least ten minutes before serving after the white bowls are taken out of the oven (if not you will have a liquid and not a solid dish) Second this combination is fabulous but just about the richest dish I have ever attempted. Those with cholesterol problems beware.

Bryan Robertson did me a great favour in introducing me to important people at every level of the visual arts community. My reports back to the Canada Council read like a who's who of the British visual arts establishment. The fact is, basically I am a shy person and I am frightened of pushing myself forward into unknown situations. I am amazed now that I had the nerve to even apply to the Canada Council for a grant to go to Europe.

I know that I had spent years giving lectures and talks to people all over Ontario and I was good at it, for I was constantly asked back to give a repeat programme, and often my audience would have doubled when I returned. Likely I had a native talent, which was sharpened with practice and a certain outlook on life, which said "I can do this but there are many things that you can do better than I can". With this outlook I never talked down to people and people found they could relate to me.

The fact is I was role-playing the outgoing individual who gave those talks. Often I had the feeling that I could withdraw from that individual talking at the front of the hall and sit up in a corner near the ceiling and listen and look down from my secret self at that stranger down there. Bryan gave me the push that I needed to meet people with confidence. It was as if he implied I was important enough to talk fearlessly to other important people. I remember conversing with a young artist who had gone to see Bernard Leach, the famous potter, in St. Ives. He looked around the room and saw a number of film canisters on a shelf. He asked what they were and was told that they were films taken in the 1930s when Leach was in Japan working with Japanese potters. The Japanese still regard Leach as one of the finest potters ever. This artist actually asked Leach if he could bring those films back to Canada and have them reproduced. Leech agreed and we were probably saved some priceless records of a master potter, I could never have done that. I would have thought of it but never asked the question. I fell partly back in my old ways when I returned to Canada but not altogether; my year away did give me a new vision that I never forgot. I have Bryan Robertson to thank for a great deal of that change on my part. I think now that I never did properly thank him. I do not know if he is even alive, he was not a well man and that was many years ago. Hopefully writing about him now at such length in this memoir can be construed as gratitude.

As I have stated a number of times through these writings, I am gay, and so, of course there was another aspect of London that I had to explore. First of all I went to a number of gay pubs or bars, they were friendly and relaxing and I could enjoy a pint of beer (for which I had now developed a taste) or have something to eat. I was nervous about meeting people. The amazing thing is although I recorded all my movements related to my exploration of the arts, I did not even mention the name of a pub in my records. Gradually I became bolder and discovered Germane Street and the Turkish baths located there. I think I could still find my way there after thirty-five years. The baths were old and elaborate, I seem to remember their ornate decor, and there were dressing rooms and a large dormitory with beds surrounded by curtains. There were the steam rooms themselves at different levels of heat. I do remember one was called the "tepidarium", a couple of the halls had small pools where you could cool off.

I made two friends there. One was Patrick Maury, a young Frenchman who was studying at Oxford. I remember him telling me that his parents owned the apartment that they lived in in Paris. It was the first time I had ever heard of that possibility. It was 1972 when I finally bought a condominium of my own that the possibility became a reality. Patrick was dark, slight, pleasant smile and handsome. I met him at the baths on February 10th. We saw quite a bit of each other. We spent the afternoon of February 17th at the British Museum, spent the evening of February 23rd together and went to Covent Garden to see the Royal Ballet perform "Olympiad" and "Song of the Earth" on February 24th, I have notes in my diary where I had sent him letters, I also noted that Pat arrived from Southampton at 9:30 p.m. on March 2nd. Obviously he had been home to see his parents. On March 21st we visited Bath together and toured the Pump Room, Bath Abbey, and then we went on to Stonehenge and Salisbury. I have a note that we attended a church service at Salisbury Cathedral and then we took a train back to Southampton where Pat took the liner Normandy to

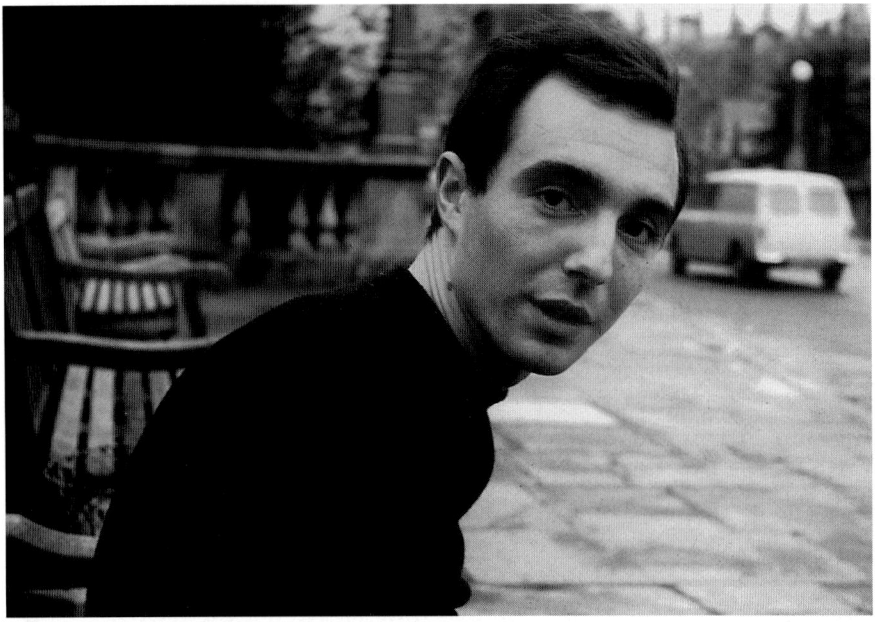

France and I went back to London. My final note on Patrick Maury was on May 15th where I met him at Paddington station and we took a train down to Oxford and walked around the city. Pat was very tired from his examinations and I returned early to London.

In 1971 I had a letter from Patrick. He told me that he had finished his contract with London University and gone back to France. He was now in the air force and had been appointed a lecturer in English in an air force school not far from Grenoble He said he was bored to tears and had no friends there. Evidently he had to spend a year in the forces as a French citizen, he said he would be finished six months from that time in August.

I made another friend in London; his name was Simon Kent, and he was a minor star in the musical, *Ann Veronica* based on a novel by H.G. Wells. I still have the original cast album of *Ann Veronica* signed by all the members of the cast. Simon had just completed a round the world trip on a cruise ship where he had been part of the troupe that provided entertainment each night in the ship's theatre. Simon was clean cut, handsome, cheery and a great deal of fun. He, also, was a very cultured individual and we went to many museums, galleries and theatres together. When I was in Italy he sent me a long tape in which he spent at least ten minutes rhapsodizing over the "Frescoes from Florence" exhibition that was then in London. I saw *Ann Veronica* twice and had supper with Simon after each performance. I visited Canterbury with

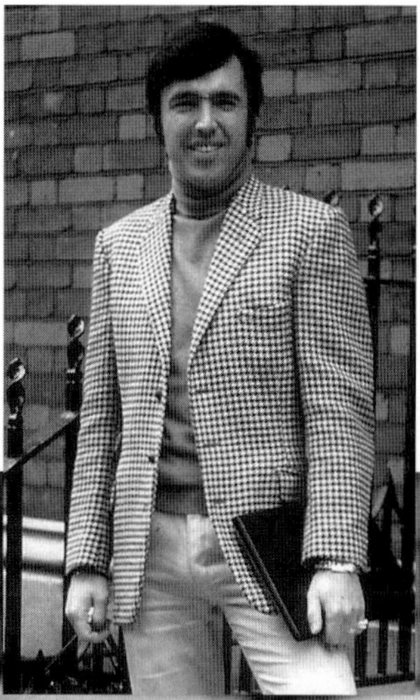

Simon and saw the cathedral and town. In London we visited the Victoria and Albert Museum, St. Bartholomew the Great church, the oldest Norman church in London, in fact the note in my diary two days before I left London reads, "Card to Jay, night letter to Neil, large parcel of clothes to Joan. Met Simon Kent at noon; we visited the National Gallery to see

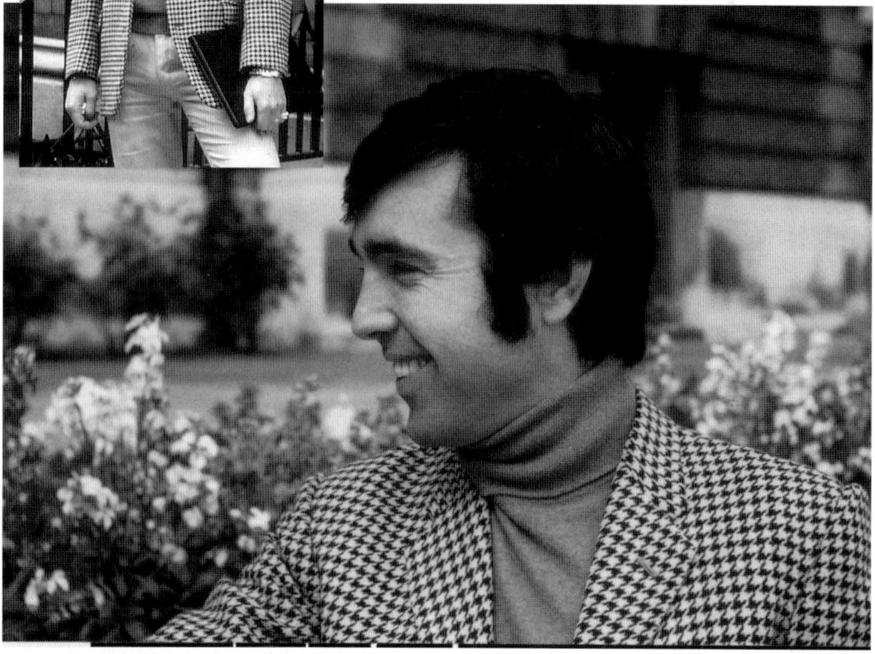

Stubbs painting, The Cheetah, then visited Temple Church and Mid Temple Hall, walked embankment, and went to top of Shell Building. Tea in Festival Hall. In evening I went to see *She Stoops to Conquer* with Tom Courtney at the Garrick Theatre,"

On Sunday, May 25th I left London for home at 3:15 and before that had lunch with Simon at 12:30. We kept in touch until 1974. Actually Simon took a trip to New York and flew to Canada for a few days when we went up to meet Jay at his farm. By that time Simon had shed his clean-cut look and grown a large mustache and had long somewhat shaggy hair, very becoming and still the cheery individual.

I have written above at length about some of the people I met on this wonderful trip. Now a summary of where else I went and what I did.

I had extended my activities considerably from those listed on my original Canada Council application. Before I was through I had visited eighteen countries, spending anything from three days to a month. I flew to New York and then on to Iceland on September 2nd, 1968 where I stayed for three days and toured the island. The musical *Hair* was very popular at that time. I saw it five times in different countries but in Iceland it was the most interesting; it had all the beads and hippy clothes that one saw elsewhere, but all the cast was blond.

On September 6th I flew on to England and that very evening I went with Bryan Robertson to attend the opening of an exhibition, "The St. Ives Group". On Sept. 7th I saw a Matisse exhibition and on Sept. 8th a Henry Moore exhibition. and I was on my way.

From October 7th to 10th I visited Scotland, by train, stopped off at Norwich on the way to visit some relatives. I met administrators, heard about programmes and saw exhibitions.

I went back to London briefly and then on to Wales for two days. In Wales there were two projects that impressed me very much. In August, 1967 two silk screen designs, ten feet by six feet and ten feet by twenty feet, by professional artists, appeared on two hundred and fifty sites (billboards) all over Wales. It was a plan to introduce the art experience into everyday life. This was to be followed with three-dimensional works in resins or fibreglass.

The National Museum of Wales had a school service. It had ten thousand portable exhibits that were loaned out each term. These were small, glass fronted exhibition cases, boxes of specimens, works of art, framed pictures, mounted illustrations, models, fabric, slides and filmstrips. The service had been in operation for twenty years; it had a staff of twenty-three and produced one thousand new exhibits each year. For example, an English teacher could borrow a model of the Globe theatre, a model of an Elizabethan home, filmstrips on English costume, mediaeval buildings, Cathedrals, all to illustrate Elizabethan literature. A wonderful idea that I introduced, on a small scale by comparison, at the Gallery Stratford some years later.

From November 4th to 8th I visited Holland. I still have the list of museums, galleries, sites, canal boat rides and bars that Bryan gave me to visit. I saw the Stedelijk Museum, the Rijksmuseum, Boymans's Museum; I visited and walked Amsterdam and Rotterdam, attended the Ballet. I heard of a wonderful plan to assist artists. Every person in Holland is entitled to support if he does not have a job and is over twenty-five years of age. If an artist is out of work, he asks for assistance. A social worker looks into his case and if he agrees that assistance is needed he calls in a committee of artists, art historians and administrators. If that committee agrees that the artist's work has merit, then that person can sell his/her work to the government. Seventy-five percent of the money comes from the central government the rest from the municipality. Assistance can go on indefinitely. The pictures go to the Ministry of Social Affairs, to offices, to hospitals and some are saved for museums. The Dutch painter, Karel Appel, at one time received assistance in this manner.

I also heard of an interesting practice in Belgium. In that country there is legislation concerned with the selling of works of art during an artist's lifetime. If a work is later resold, at a higher price, the artist receives a percentage. For example, an artist's work may go up a great deal in value: he may have sold a work originally for fifty dollars; later, if it is resold for five hundred dollars, the artist will receive a percentage of that resale value — a most interesting concept.

I visited Sweden from November 16th to 21st. In Stockholm I spent four hours at the Wasa Museum, a fascinating look at an ancient ship, The Wasa. In Europe during the Thirty Years War, Gustavus II Adolphus was one of the most powerful leaders in Europe. He ordered a large vessel to be built in 1625; in 1628 the Wasa cast off on her maiden voyage, capsized, and sank in Stockholm harbour. The Baltic is unique in the fact that the minute termites that normally eats wooden wrecks dislike the lack of salt in the Baltic. The Wasa was left undisturbed. In 1956 it was discovered once again and after much difficulty it was raised and broke the surface on April 24 in 1961. It was then moved after further salvage work, and is now in its own dockyard incorporated with the National Maritime Museum. Divers have also raised three thousand five hundred objects from the site of the wreck. I saw the ship in the early stages of its preservation; today it surely must be a wonderful thing to see.

My biggest interest in Sweden was the National Scheme for Travelling Exhibitions. The scheme was just developing and consisted of travelling exhibitions of art, artifacts and natural objects. Among the experimental exhibits was "Multiart' which featured mass produced art and opened simultaneously in one hundred locations. Works were sold from all locations and a national contest was held to see which centre would sell the most. Another show was called, "To the Land in the West". In the nineteenth century one-fifth of the population of Sweden emigrated to the U.S.A. The show was a replica of an emigrant's trunk filled with related material.

Earlier I have talked of my fear of venturing into the unknown or in attempting to meet important people. Now I must admit to my biggest folly in that regard and tell how I was forced to go out on my own. So far my foreign travel had always been to countries where I knew that I would find people who could speak English — Holland and Sweden for example. I finally decided after Christmas to take a holiday from my research and go to a country just for the pleasure of experiencing it. I chose Morocco. One night in a pub I met a young man who had just returned from that country and he was wishing very much that he could return. He spoke French fluently and had travelled all around Morocco, We talked at great length and I thought how nice it would be to have a guide. I finally suggested that I would pay his ticket by air if he would accompany me in that capacity. He said he had money enough of his own to survive in that country. He agreed after we had had a couple of meetings and ironed out details. I went and bought the tickets. He asked if he could show his to his family and so I gave it to him.

When next I saw him he was wearing a new winter coat and admitted to me that he had decided not to go and had turned the ticket in and bought himself a coat with the money! So I learned the hard way the stupidity of my own fears and that I should trust myself to survive. It is amazing how this exercise has brought back my memories. I had buried that incident deep in my subconscious and only while writing this chapter this evening has it surfaced again.

Finally I was off on January 7th, 1969, to a really foreign country, quite different from anything I had seen in my life. I was going to Morocco. I flew to Gibraltar, stayed overnight at the Queen's Hotel for twenty-five shillings and took a boat the next morning to Tangier.

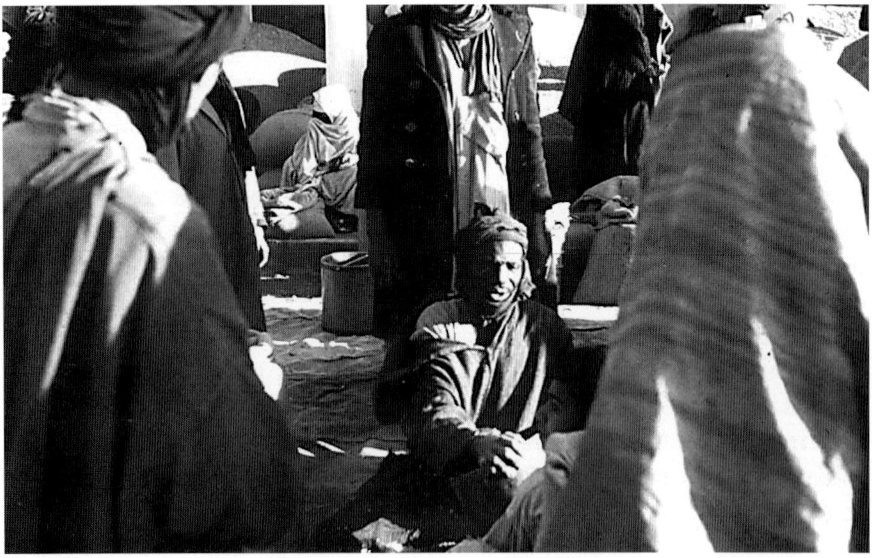

From there I went by plane to Casablanca, and then to Agadir. There I happened to meet Sheila Melton, a newspaper woman from New York, and a friend of hers, Leo. Sheila had rented a Fiat and on January 10th we drove south one hundred and fifty miles to Goulimine, a town on the edge of the desert, where we saw "Les Gens Bleus", the blue people. These desert people dyed many of their clothes various shades of blue. We checked into the only hotel in town and were up early the next morning to attend the camel market. There we saw the desert people in their long flowing robes in various shades of blue and sand to brown. The market was full of groups of standing camels interspersed with goats, the males with long curling horns. A snake charmer held his cobra (?) high in the air, its broad flat head staring out at us. We left around eleven a.m., drove to Tiznit, then back to Agadir. The three of us stayed at Agadir for a couple of days. There were only two incidents worth repeating. I went in the Atlantic and found the undertow very strong, I had to gradually work my way some way down the beach before I could safely get back to shore.

Also the three of us decided to walk the beach some distance beyond the commercial hotels. We then went up to the top of a sand dune and stretched out in the sun. Suddenly a shadow crossed my line of vision and I saw a youth standing over me. There were two other boys with him. I looked around and saw other boys coming up the dune from the other side. They were all smiling and polite but all I could think of was Montgomery Clift and Elizabeth Taylor in the movie, *Suddenly Last Summer*. I spoke to Sheila and Leo and we quickly grabbed our towels and moved away down to the beach and along the water's edge back to the inhabited areas.

From Agadir we drove to Essouira, roamed the city and took photos of early fortifications, markets and the fishing boats in the harbour. I said goodbye to my new friends and took the bus to Marrakesh. I certainly do not want to take the reader through a day-by-day accounting of this trip. But I will mention some of the highlights. Marrakesh is one of the four Imperial cities of Morocco; it has a huge square that is busy day and night with milling people — snake charmers, beggars, entertainers and tourists. I stayed in the Hotel Tazi right on the edge of the square.

One day I was sitting on the roof of my hotel reading *The Lord of the Rings*. It was long and the only book that I took on the trip; once I got into it I thoroughly enjoyed it. A young Englishman came up to the roof to sunbathe. His name was Gordon Smith and he was a sax player in a London Jazz group, "The Ends". He had come to Morocco to

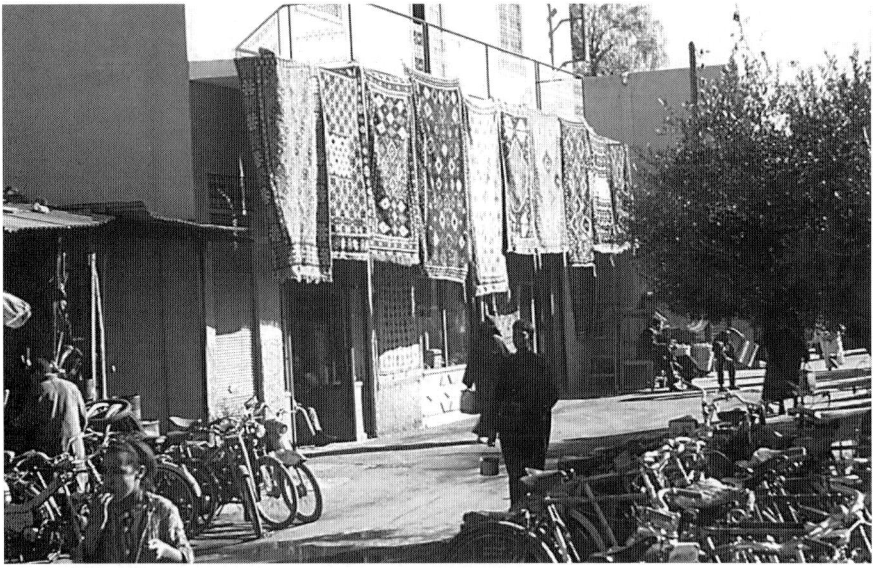

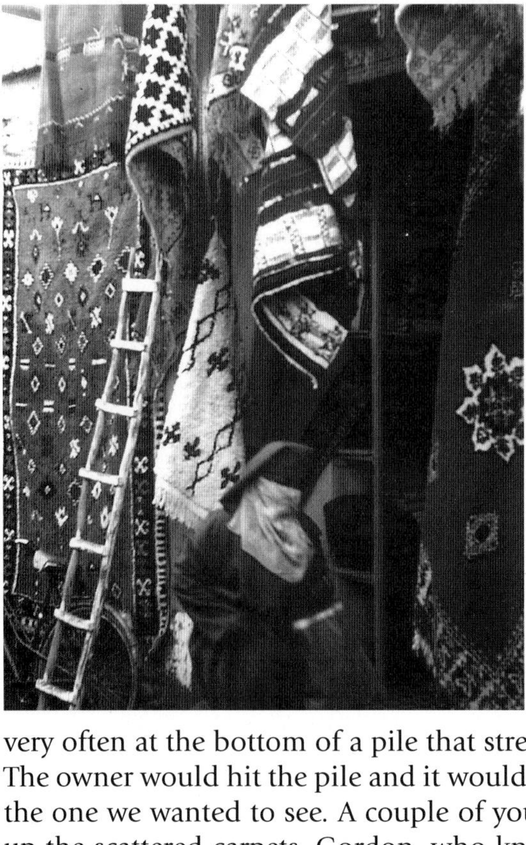

recuperate; his girl friend, who had been the double for Elizabeth Taylor in the movies, had committed suicide and he was very upset. When he wasn't playing in the band he used to go home and follow his trade as a carpet installer. He knew a great deal about rugs. Obviously he was not gay but we became friends and ended up travelling together for two weeks.

I was hoping to buy a Moroccan carpet to take or have sent home. We would go into a carpet store and Gordon would ask to see a certain carpet, very often at the bottom of a pile that stretched almost to the ceiling. The owner would hit the pile and it would fall over, he would pull out the one we wanted to see. A couple of young boys would start piling up the scattered carpets. Gordon, who knew his carpets would reach

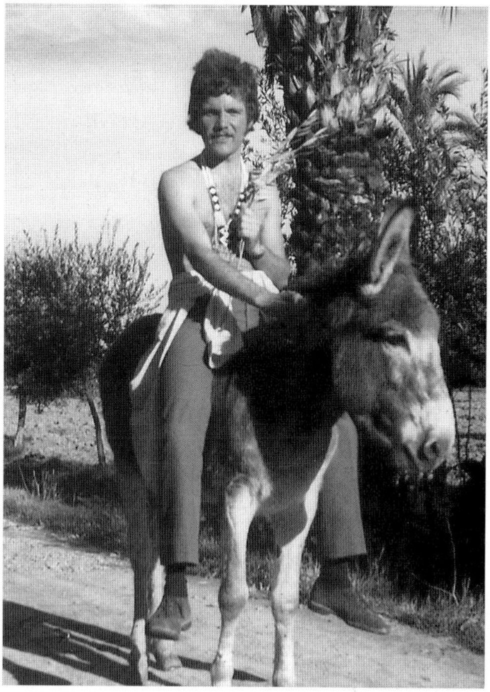

into the pile and expertly pull out a few wool threads — much to the surprise of the shop owner. Then the bargaining would begin. Moroccans are not allowed to smoke tobacco or drink alcohol but they do smoke pot. Some would be produced (I never indulged) Gordon and the owner would smoke, and in the end we would leave without having bought anything because Gordon firmly believed that the quality was not good enough.

Marrakesh was a beautiful city; far to the east you could look and see the looming Atlas Mountains. The Saadiens Tombs were jewels of architecture with carved cedar doors and geometric tiling. In the Medina, the old city, one could roam along many narrow crooked streets. The markets were full of colour, especially on the wool dyers' street where the hanks of bright orange and blue wool were hanging on lines to dry stretched across the street high above. There were streets for pottery stalls, brass and copper stores, basket sellers, and rug sellers. Everywhere there were water sellers carrying skins full of water and little pannikins for drinking.

Memories

One evening in Marrakesh I went to a French sub-titled American movie. I sat beside a handsome man of about thirty his parents were sitting on his far side. He told me that they did not speak French. We arranged to have dinner at his home the following night. I went off to this date with some trepidation as well as interest as I had never been inside a Moroccan home.

As soon as I arrived at the home my host asked for money to buy a bottle of wine. He reached out and took all the money I had in my hand I had been smart enough not to take a large amount with me. A young boy was sent off to secure the wine. I remember that we had a Moroccan style meal although

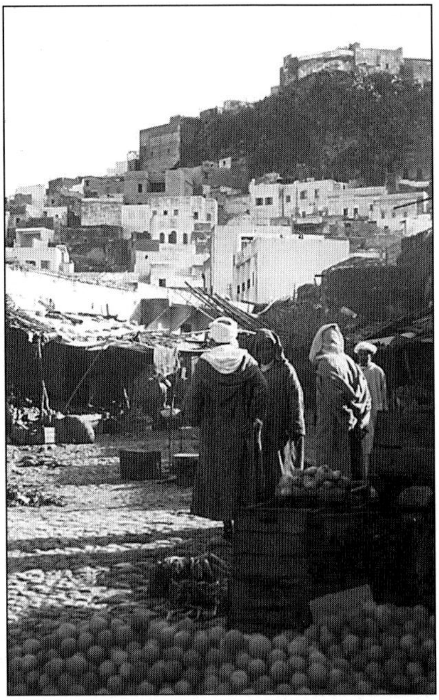

I cannot remember what we ate. We finished the wine. When my host closed his bedroom door I noticed two policeman's uniforms hanging on the back of it!! Needless to say that discovery did not exactly excite me. But my host was skilled and we had "a very pleasant conversation".

Later that evening my new friend hailed a taxi and paid for it out of the money that he had taken from me. He then gave the taxi driver instructions to take me back to the Hotel Tazi thanked me for visiting his home and bade me a friendly and courteous farewell.

We saw the Koutoubia or high tower, the Mamounia Gardens and the Bhia Palace. All decoration was geometric as the Moslem religion does not allow the portraying of natural figures. In the morning when you went out of your hotel young boys wanting to act as your guide would besiege you. Usually such children were bribed to steer you to certain stores specializing in goods intended for tourists. They could become a nuisance; I discovered that if you went out of your hotel and walked quickly as if you knew exactly where you were going the young guides would think that you were not tourists and leave you alone. This worked about four out of five times.

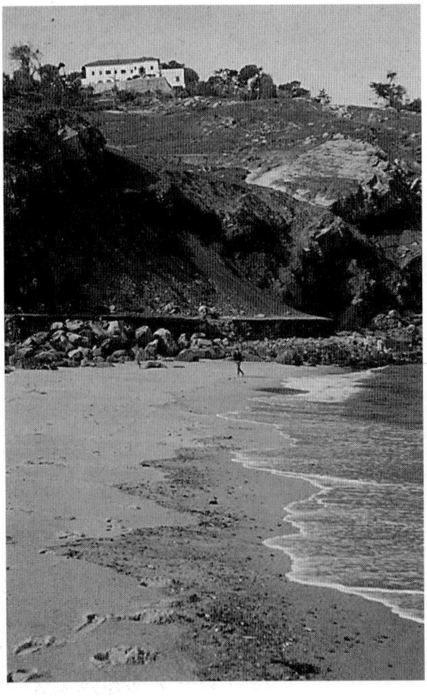

Bryan Robertson had written to a friend of his who lived just outside of Marrakesh, and we went to visit him. Ed Wolfe was charming. He owned a donkey and both Gordon and I rode on it. That was the first time I ever saw poinsettias growing six feet tall. The house was lovely, Moroccan in style. There was no electricity; an extremely deep well supplied water. Men were singing as they picked olives. We sat on the roof with our two hosts, Ed Wolfe and Jim O'Connor, for refreshments.

We finally took a wonderful, modern train to Rabat. Here we visited an Artisan Ferronnier, a craftsman in iron. I bought a large praying mantis and six small bugs and shipped them home to various friends. Then we proceeded to Meknis by train, where we stayed in the Hotel Majestic. I never did stay at any time in my travels at one of the "American chain hotels" (they were too expensive) and, besides why travel all the way to a foreign country to have a hotel exactly like one you would have at home? Usually if I arrived by train I would enquire after a small hotel that was within walking distance (with my bag) from the station. Usually I found a place interesting and related to the country where I was visiting. In Meknis there was a goldsmith's street behind a closed gate. We visited it and I bought a heavy gold ring with a black stone for one hundred and twenty dirham, twenty-four dollars, for Jay. The ring was hallmarked.

On January 29th Gordon and I took a taxi from Meknis to Moulay Idress, the holy city, and then on to Volubilis, a city of Roman ruins. It was wonderful country with the Atlas Mountains in the distance, cherry trees and rows of orange and olive trees. Volubilis especially impressed me with its Roman ruins dating back two thousand years. The city sat on the top of a hill and there were arches left and paved streets still showing the ruts of the chariot wheels. You could look through a doorway and see wonderful mosaics with walls still standing three feet high around them. On by train to Fez, the last of the four Imperial cities. Here the beautiful tiled fountains and city gates especially impressed me.

Finally back in Tangier, and I knew the trip was nearing its end. Bryan Robertson had arranged for us to stay at the home of Mr. Rex Nan Kavell, the owner of the Redfern Gallery in London. The house was magnificent, large with wings going in different directions; it stood on the top of a cliff and faced north looking across the Straits of Gibraltar toward Spain. It was the only time that I have slept in a bedroom with an original Picasso painting hanging on the wall across from my bed. My floors were marble in black and white tiles, covered with wonderful oriental rugs; there was an ornate armoire in my room of bird's eye maple. The curtains were Indian covered in hand embroidery and looking like altar cloths. The house had seven bathrooms. An artist and his wife were staying there at the same time. There was an attendant looking after the house. Guests were expected to take in their own food and prepare it. The artist and his wife prepared curry and we had it one night for supper. The gatekeeper gave us couscous.

A path led down the cliff to the beach, and Gordon and I left the terrace and went down there to sun bathe; as happened so often we had groups of young boys watching us. Two dogs from the house accompanied us, almost like guard dogs.

The house, called "El Farah" was on Old Mountain Road. There was an old Volkswagen in which we went into Tangier to shop on two different days. Finally I found art items that had not been mass-produced for the tourists. I went into an old shop, something like an antique store, where I found three bride's belts, hand woven in geometric patterns and embroidered in gold thread. I was told that they were made by the young women of certain tribes to show their skills in weaving and embroidery and then worn as part of their bridal outfits.

The belts were about seven inches wide and eight feet long with tassels at the ends. I bought the three of them, two for the equivalent of ten dollars each and one for six dollars. I gave one to Bryan Robertson when I returned home, the other two are hanging in my home today.

Finally we took the boat from Tangier across to Gibraltar, thirty-five miles, and stayed at the Victoria Hotel. It was a pleasure to hear English again after a month of French. I must admit that once I got started speaking my school French in Morocco I could not be stopped, it just flowed out, mistakes and all, especially in restaurants.

I spotted three old fans in a window of a store: a Chinese one in ivory, and Indian one in sandalwood and a French one in wood and paper. I ate street vendor food for twenty-four hours. I was almost broke, and went to the store just before my plane took off and bought the fans for three pounds. We had saved money by walking all over Gibraltar and thoroughly enjoyed it.

My plane arrived at Gatwick at midnight, I was back at Bryan's by two a.m. and we talked until 4:30 a.m.

Once I had caught my breath back in London, caught up with the current exhibitions, written up some of my notes, and obtained more money from Canada, I was ready to tackle more countries in Europe. I had met Simon by this time and I enjoyed having his company on many of my gallery and museum outings in London. Now I planned a trip to Vienna and Paris.

On March 5th I left by train for Vienna. I took the train from London to Dover and boarded the boat for the three-and-a-half hour trip to Ostend, then on by train through Belgium and Germany to

Austria. In Vienna I visited all the museums, attended the opera a number of times — heard the Vienna State Opera present the *Tales of Hoffman* and *Cosi Fan Tutti* and the Vienna People's Opera present *Madame Butterfly*. I took an afternoon tour to the Vienna Woods and the Klosterneuburg Monastery.

On March 10th I went by train to Paris. One amusing thing happened on the train. I was reading a copy of Bulwer-Lytton's book, *The Last Days of Pompeii* on the train. It was a ragged copy that I had picked up at an old book store in London. Each time I would finish a chapter I would carefully tear off the pages read and deposit them in the garbage can. I had no intention of carrying the book once it was read. At one point I looked up as I was doing this and saw the look of horror on the faces of my companions in the carriage who were obviously watching me, the rich tourist, who had so little regard for a book.

I had a wonderful time in Paris. There was a general strike on at the time: no post, no electricity, and no tubes. I walked from 10 a.m. to 4 p.m. I visited all the famous places: the Arc de Triomphe, the Tour Eiffel, and the Aquarium du Trocadero, Notre Dame. With no lights on the stained glass was doubly beautiful in Notre Dame. I walked around outside the Louvre,

Le Jardin des Tuileries and the Orangerie. All museums and galleries were closed because of there being no power. I spent a day at Chartres travelling by train. I toured the Cathedral and walked all around the town. There I took the best slides of any that I took during the whole

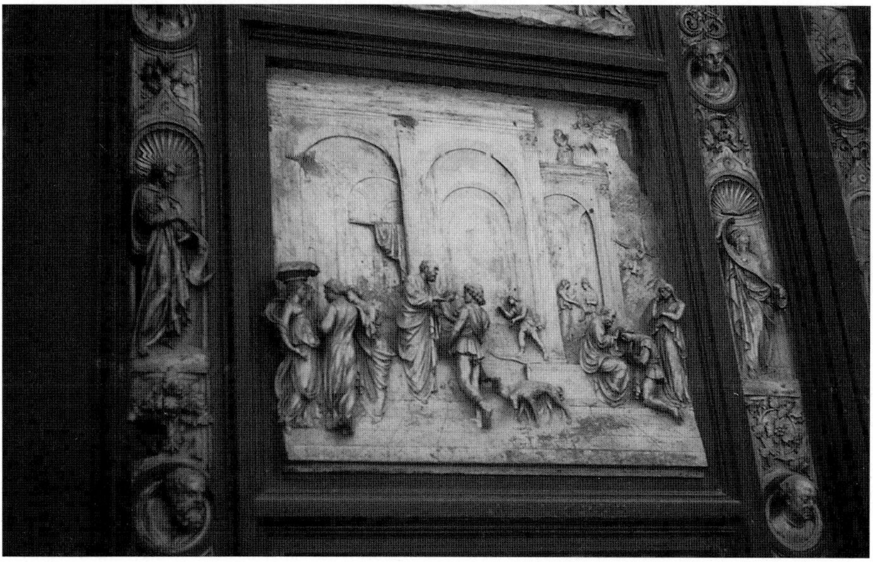

trip: By March 13th the lights were on again, I visited the Louvre for five hours. On March 14th I took a train out to Versailles. I returned in time to go and see Sainte-Chapelle with its spectacular glass. On my last day I visited more museums, and saw the Opera House. March 16th I returned to London.

My trip was winding down. I made one last (my longest) trip to the continent. I left London on March 26th and finally returned on May 1st. Then on home to Canada on May 25th. I spent from June 8th to June 23rd in New York finishing the research for my project.

I must confess that my last trip in Europe was purely for my own personal enjoyment and development. I did not seek out museum directors and ask questions about the training of personnel or security or travelling exhibitions. I did absorb the museum atmosphere , saw

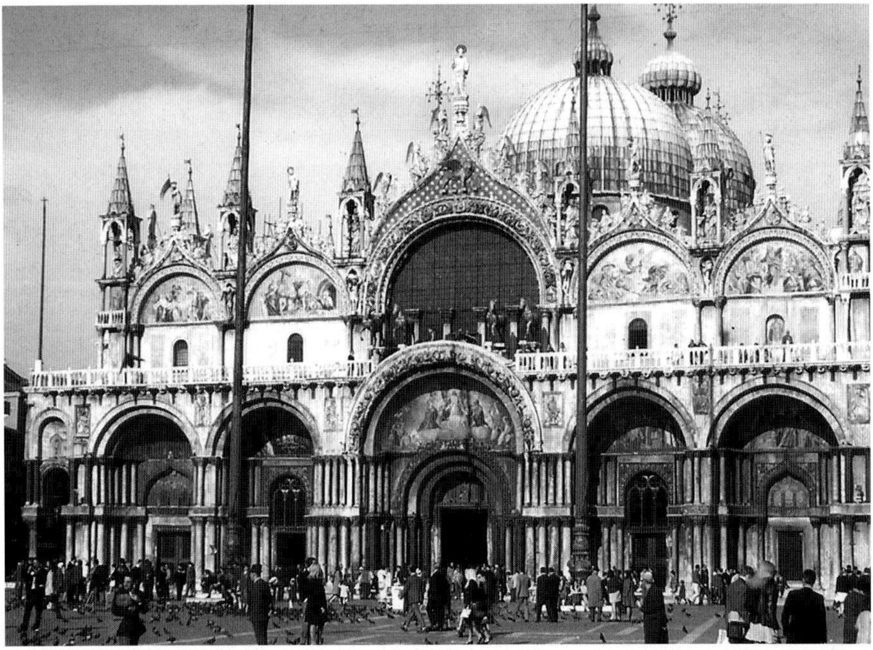

the wonderful artifacts, gathered just how the public viewed their own institutions. Perhaps I needed to know that in order to complete my education.

I left London by the Victoria Station on March 26th, and took the boat to Calais and a train, a couchette, through France and Switzerland to Italy. I changed trains at Milan and again at Rome and arrived in Naples the evening of March 27th. I found a pensione for three dollars a night, had supper there (two forty) went to bed exhausted and then read until 10 p.m. One comment about Naples: in all my travels I had never heard more horns or seen more reckless driving by cars, bicycles, or scooters than in that city. I left Naples by 10:30 the next morning and returned by 8:30 that evening after spending the day at Pompeii. Next day I wandered Naples, walked to the National Museum and saw the opera, "Tosca", at the San Carlo Theatre in the evening. On March 30th. I took a boat to Capri, did all the tourist things: went by boat to see the Blue Grotto, and so on.

April 1st, I travelled on to Rome where I visited St. Peter's Basilica and saw the Pope at a special student's service, saw the sites and sounds of that ancient city and thoroughly enjoyed myself. I continued on to Florence by train, my favourite city in Italy, where I again stood in front of "David" in awe and marvelled at the Cathedral, Giotto's Tower, and the bronze doors of the baptistery. I bought presents for friends in leather, three splendid wallets for ten dollars (what a change today) Next day I went on to Siena and then back to Florence. I made a change of plans there. I had meant to go to Venice and then fly to Athens. However in a shop on the Ponte Vecchio in Florence I saw a ring and a pair of cuff links, both in gold. The ring was massive and had four white opals in a row across the top; the cuff links had a slice of Australian opal across each, surrounded by a black band of enamel. I bought them. They were expensive and so I decided to go to Athens by train. I gave the ring to my niece, Beth, who still wears it a great deal. I still have the cuff links. I do not regret changing my plans.

In Venice I revisited the famous sites that I had seen in 1956. This time I stayed at Alberge Gobbo, again near the station. It was a small hotel on the second floor of a building. I walked St. Mark's Square and every time I went near a jewelry store I could swear a handsome boy would lean seductively near me and describe the wonders that could be bought in that particular store. I am sure that my memory does not deceive me in this; I did not see any girls behaving in the same way. I wondered if I was so obvious? I always beat a hasty retreat.

Two things I did enjoy in Venice. I visited the Island of Murano and went to the Museo d'Arte Vetravia, the glass museum. There I saw glass blowing and the exhibits of Venetian glass through the ages. Also, my favourite painter of the Renaissance in Venice was Carpaccio, dates about 1472 to 1525. I sought out his paintings wherever I could find them.

On the afternoon of April 14th I took the train for Greece. The next morning I was in Belgrade and then spent all day travelling through Yugoslavia; we arrived at the Greek border at eight p.m. By 10:30 am, the next day I was in Athens, went directly to the Athens House Hotel, where I found room and breakfast. I visited the National Archaeological Museum and then went on to the Acropolis, the ancient citadel of Athens, where I viewed the Parthenon in wonder, the Erechtheion, the portico of the Caryatides, the Propylaia — the Tower of Wingless Victory. Then I went down to the old agora or market place and saw the Theseion and the Stoa of Atticus that had been reconstructed under the direction of my old Fine Arts professor, Dr. Homer Thompson. That day I met Don Cockerton from Calgary at my hotel and Tom Mullaney from San Francisco. I spent time with both sightseeing for the next two days.

On April 18th I went to the airport and met Fred Pattje, an old friend of mine who was now living in Vancouver. Fred had brought along a friend of his that I had met before, Bob Boettcher. We travelled together for the next nine days. First we "did" Athens again and I was

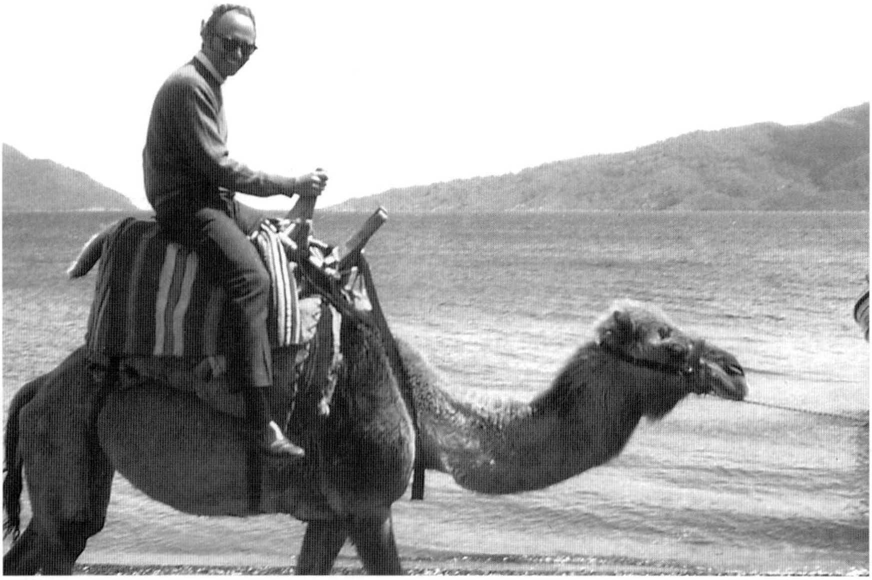

quite happy to see the Parthenon one more time. On April 20th we took a boat for the four-and-a-half hour trip to the island of Mykonos. It was gorgeous with brilliant white houses in the sun against an azure sea. We swam and sunbathed and ate and drank. We bought wonderful hand knit sweaters and had then sent directly to Canada, I bought six altogether, sending two to my nieces. They averaged ten dollars each and I considered them a wonderful bargain compared to the poor quality of the handcrafted items in Morocco.

At 9 p.m. on April 21st we took a boat for Rhodes. We had no stateroom and tried to sleep on the deck, not very successfully. We arrived in Rhodes at 9 a.m. and checked into our hotel, three to a room, sleeping until 1:30 p.m. We walked the walled city and marvelled at this stronghold of the Crusaders. The following day we rented three scooters and took off for Lindos. Bob had two breakdowns that held us up. I had never driven a scooter before and found I had trouble with my balance; in fact when we went around a curve with Fred and Bob ahead and me trying to catch up, and I went straight over a ten-foot drop. I called it a cliff but Fred laughed at me, I know that when finally Fred and Bob came back they had to reach over and stretch out their arms while I reached up high to them, and they pulled me up. I had an arm burnt a bit by the slide along the pavement. We returned to Rhodes, riding our scooters slowly. The next day we took a bus at 9 a.m. and reached Lindos and climbed to the Acropolis, the road up was lined with old ladies trying to sell us souvenirs of one sort or another. Back in Rhodes that evening we went to see a sound and light show on the history of Rhodes. It was in the grounds of the old castle.

The next day Bob left early to return to Canada and Fred and I took a boat across to the town of Marmaris in Turkey. We had a wonderful day, lovely old shops with beautiful carpets for sale hanging from the balconies and store fronts, unfortunately I could not carry anything else and also I was beginning to count my money much more carefully. We each had a ride on a camel. I did buy an ancient Roman glass bottle from the man who had dug it up. I still have it in my showcase. I am sure that with the iridescence and scaling, it is genuine. I paid eight dollars for it. We had a good lunch and then left at three p.m. to return to Rhodes., the sea was heavy and some of the passengers were sea sick.

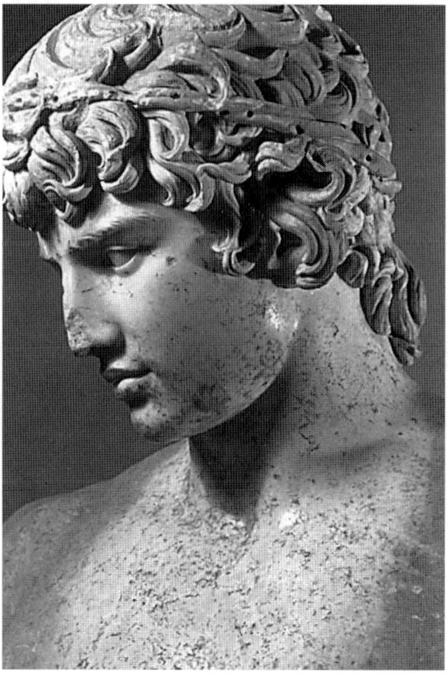

April 26th we flew to Crete and took a hotel at Heraklion. We visited the Palace of Knossos, toured museums, sat in the sun.

I bought a number of small cushion covers, they were easy to carry and you could put a cushion in them later. They were hand-woven and embroidered in peasant designs, and I have them today piled on the bed in my spare room. On April 29th, Fred and I flew back to Athens, Fred then went on to Holland to see his family before flying back to Canada. I stayed in Athens one more day; taking a tour bus up to Delphi, saw the wonderful statue, "The Charioteer". Toured site of shrine and temples, the spring flowers were everywhere and very beautiful. The bus drove to the Monastery of Ossios Loukas of the Byzantine Church and back to Athens.

I took a train back to London. It was an adventure. Before we got to the Yugoslav border we were in a station. The train only had a few people on it. Then I heard a dull roar, which suddenly grew louder as people appeared from all directions. They were migrant workers going north to Germany to work for the summer. They invaded the train, sat ten to an apartment for eight, brought their own food with them, offered me bread, cheese and wine when they ate. They were boisterous, cheery, singing, children crying, old people sitting stony faced all dressed in black. Very quickly the bathrooms were unapproachable. The passageways were filled with people and luggage. I sat up all night in a complete daze. We got to Germany, I do not remember the city, suddenly with a great roar everybody left the train and they all disappeared.

The train went through Austria and Germany, We reached Cologne and I had a couple of hours before my next train left. I put my luggage in a locker and went to see Cologne Cathedral, then on to Ostend, boat across the channel, I slept on a bench, and it arrived at 5 a.m., took a train to London and finally got to Bryan's home about 9:3o a.m.

I must not leave Europe without mentioning that a number of times I was able to see my father's English relatives. I visited Bournemouth and saw my father's twin sister, Auntie Chris. She was tiny and seemed to only come up a bit above my elbow. She had had a sad life, she had lost four children, and then she spent twenty-two years looking after her mother-in-law. The old lady died and then Chris's husband ran off with a younger woman and deserted Chris. She lived quietly in a nicely furnished upper apartment in Bournemouth. When I was leaving she gave me a beautiful Victorian Indian sandalwood calling card case from her collection. Also, I visited my Auntie Marge at Ewelme in December of 1968 as mentioned earlier in this narrative. I had visited Uncle Don and Aunt Marjory in Norwich when I was travelling by train to Scotland early in my tour. I also spent Christmas with them. I visited Uncle Lionel and Aunt Freda over New Years at Seven Oaks in

Kent. Then I spent a weekend or two with various cousins.

Finally I must say that I learned a great deal and collected a large amount of material related to my project. I brought it all back and wrote a thirty-page report to Canada Council with copies to every art gallery director in Ontario.

Many of the projects that I especially admired I have already mentioned in the earlier text of this manuscript. Everything else I have on file, but the information is at least thirty-five years old now, and I doubt that my readers would be at all interested in such facts as the Art Council of Great Britain having a budget of six million pounds in 1968-1969, etcetera, etcetera, So I will leave out the details.

After fond farewells and regrets I left London. I gave Bryan Robertson my typewriter that I had bought in London and, as mentioned already, one of my bride's belts that I had bought in Morocco. It took me years to realize just how much he had done for me in Britain.

On May 24th I flew back to Canada; the next day I went to Newcastle to see all of my family.

On June 8th I flew to New York for the last research for my Canada Council project. I found New York very expensive and was not able to stay there as long as I would have liked. I visited the Metropolitan Museum of Art, the Museum of Modern Art, the Guggenheim Museum, the Whitney Museum, The Cloisters, the Frick Collection, the Gallery of Modern Art, the Hayden Planetarium, the Museum of Natural History, the New York Historical Society and many commercial galleries. I went to the theatre almost every night, met with officials related to museums and galleries and flew back to Toronto on June 23rd.

The Metropolitan Museum of Art had an exhibition service for schools. It was preparing exhibitions on a grand scale. It had designed, researched and organized a series of six exhibitions in an edition of one thousand each. One thousand secondary schools in the U.S.A. were able to buy subscriptions to the year's services for about one thousand dollars. The six show subjects were Rembrandt, African Art, Mediaeval Culture, Ways of Seeing, King Tut, Protest and Hope. Each exhibition was to be accompanied with slide lectures, art notes, questions for teachers to ask, annotated study material on panels for the teachers, specialized teaching material for the library and material for allied subjects. Wow ——

The Metropolitan Museum of Art, in cooperation with New York University, Institute of Fine Art, for twelve years had been collaborating in the training of young curators in a two-year programme leading to a Master's degree in art history and certificate in museum training granted jointly by both institutions.

To sum it all up, in the 1968/69 year in England I made 177 visits to 72 institutions. I also had 77 interviews with various artists, and gallery and museum officials. These meeting varied from a full half-day with up to four people to a luncheon with one person. In New York I made 14 visits to 11 institutions; I visited 13 commercial galleries and had interviews with five people. I saw 54 stage productions in the ten months and attended cinema 45 times.

It was a good year.

Memories

Many years ago I spent some time in Greece. I was visiting Athens and I decided to take a bus tour up to see the famous ruins of Delphi. The bus was full of tourists and we stopped for lunch before we got to the shrine. It was May, the hillsides were filled with masses of wild flowers, the restaurant was crowded with our group. There were two waiters.

One waiter was a charming Greek, handsome and athletic. I kept noticing him and then I realized that he was glancing my way whenever possible. The two waiters rushed to bring out the main course. There was a pause before a sweet appeared, I noticed my waiter standing against the wall waiting for the slow eaters to finish. I left my table and went over to him and asked him the way to the washroom. He pointed, I went down to it and he followed. I realized that that left one waiter to handle desserts and coffee for the bus load of people!!!

I had a very pleasant, and inexpensive, conversation with my new friend. He went back to the restaurant to finish his duties. I was too embarrassed to face the bus crowd at that moment and so I went back to the bus and sat in a back seat. The laughing and talking crowd came out shortly, I really do not think that they had noticed my absence. There was however one older man, he must have been over forty, who seemed very attentive to me for the rest of the trip. "We had a nice conversation."

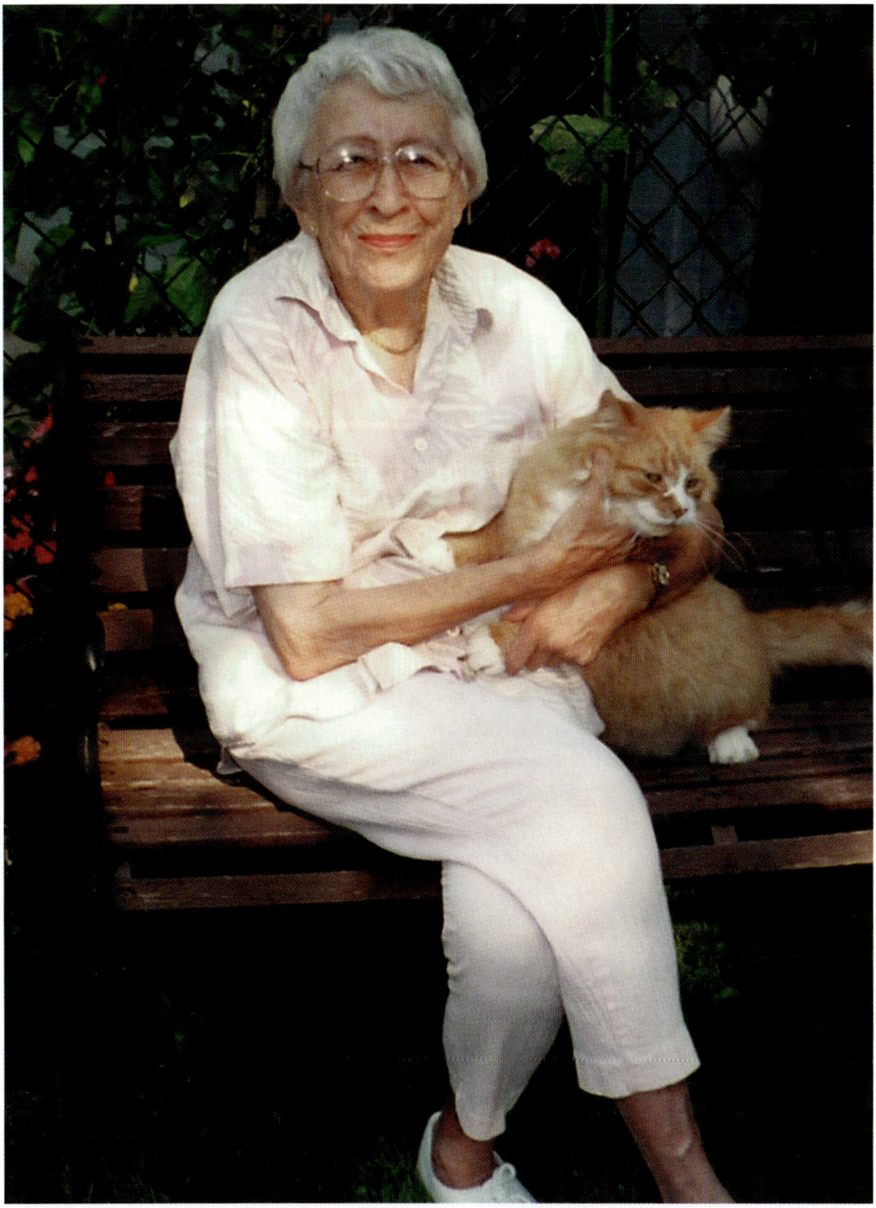

Joan St. Albans Bennett

This book is dedicated to my sister, Joan. She guided me in many ways through my life. She never did remember but when I finished High School I wanted to go back and repeat grade 13 to improve my marks for university entrance. Joan challenged me on this idea and instead I applied to U. of T. and was accepted. With this book she edited it, advised me on it, and in her will financed publishing of the book.

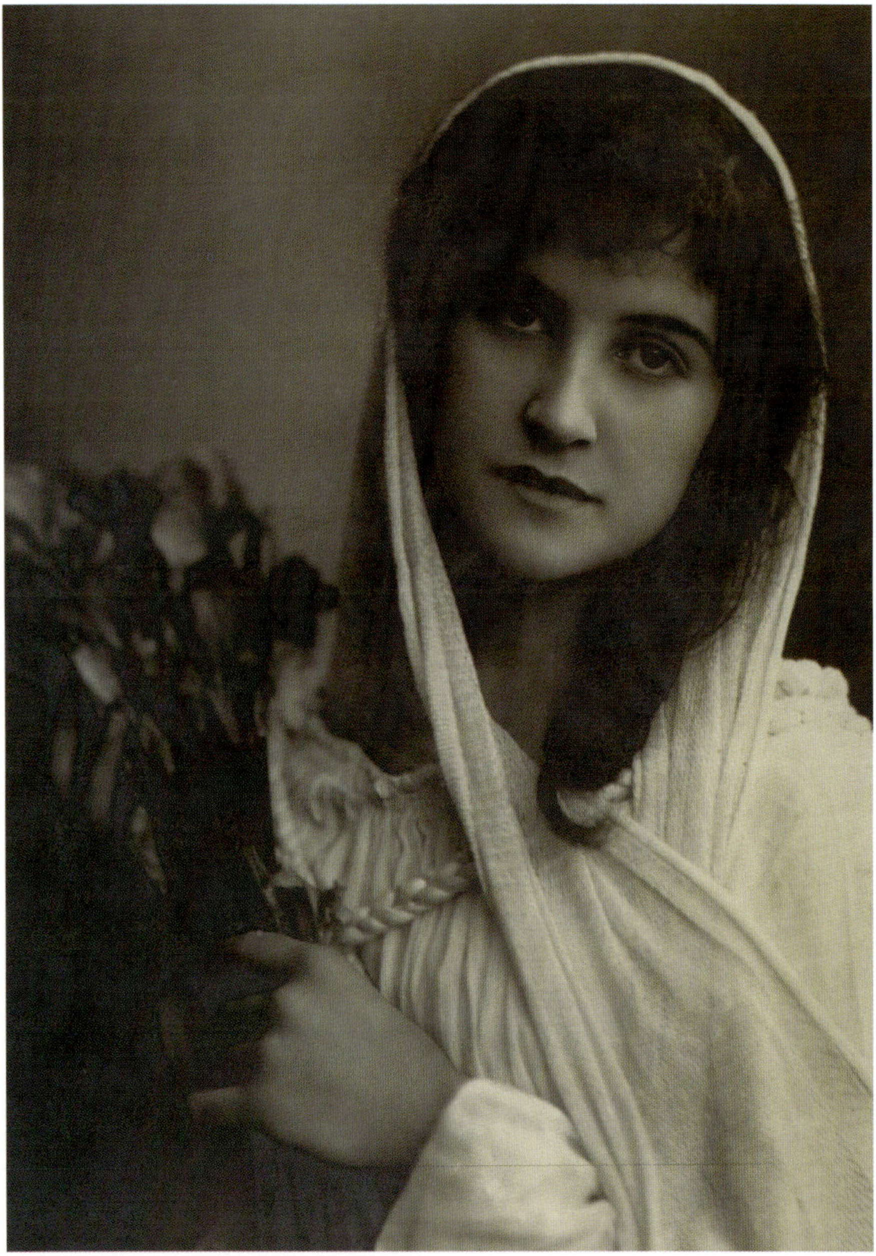

My Mother
Grace Winnifred Maidens, 1893-1963.
My Father was carrying a copy of this picture when he went over the top at Vimy Ridge at Easter, 1917. I believe the picture was taken when Mother was dressed for a religious pageant at church.

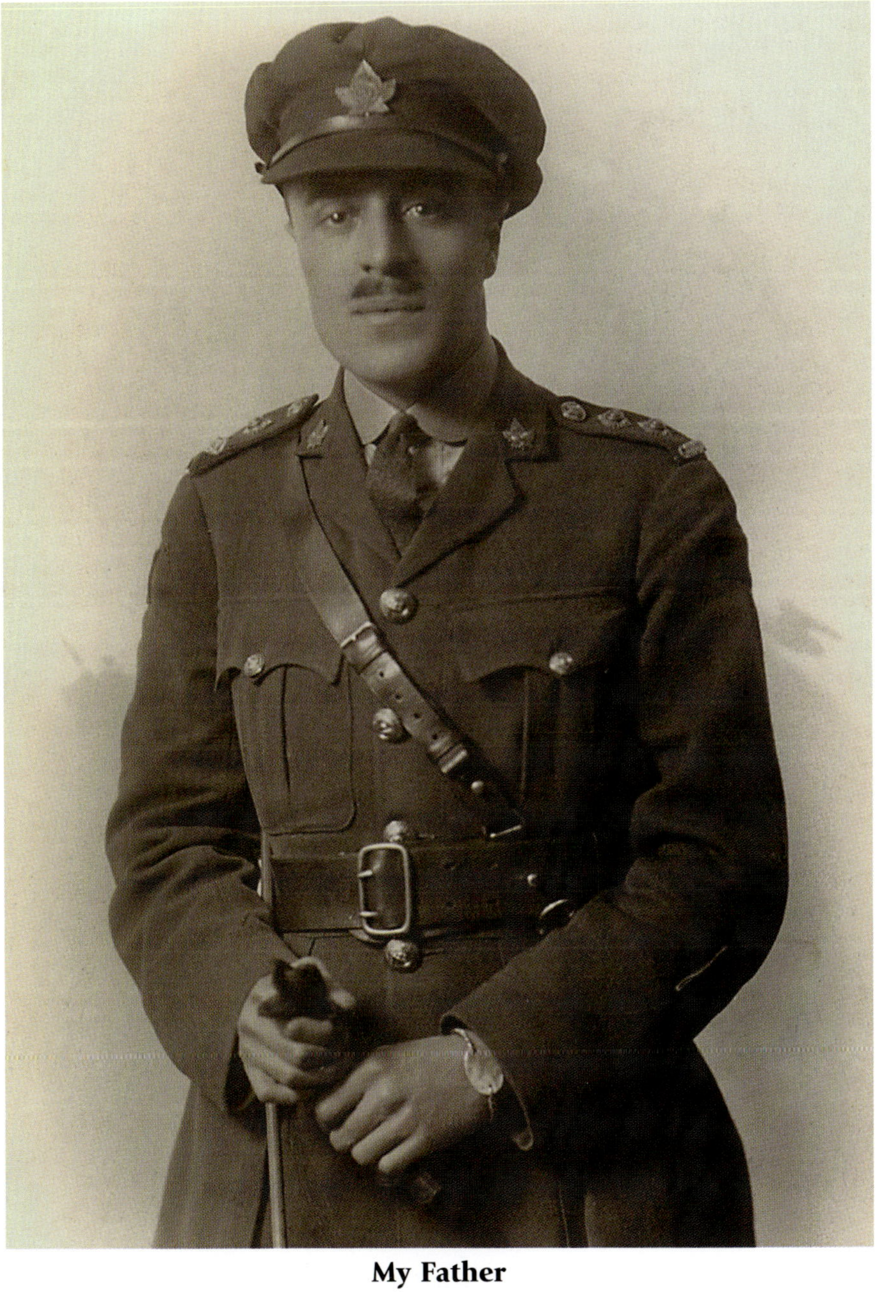

My Father
Lieutenant David Leonard Bennett, 1894-1965.
My Father became an officer in the land forces of his Majesty George V on September 25, 1916. He was twenty years of age. All the young officers were commanded to grow mustaches so that they would look older. Dad never shaved his off

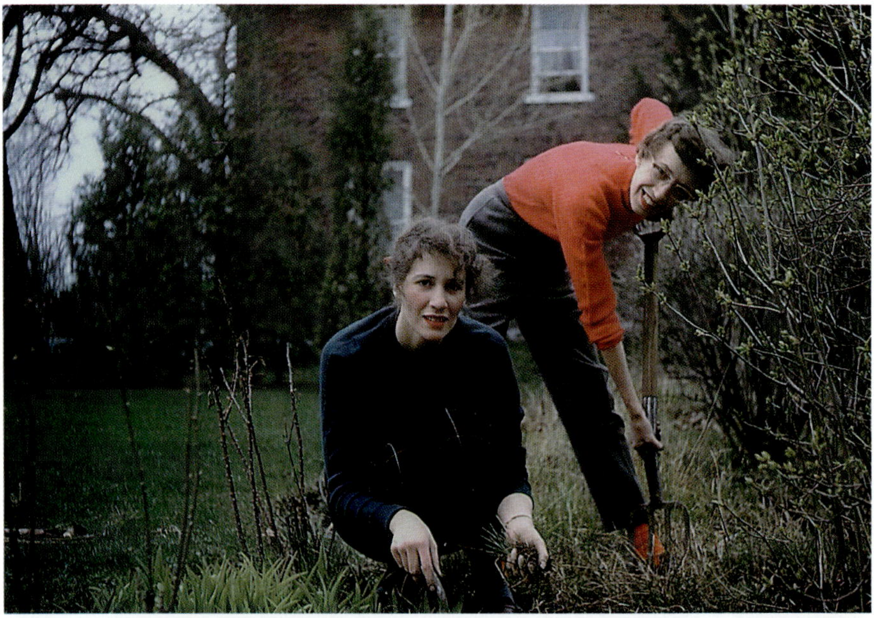

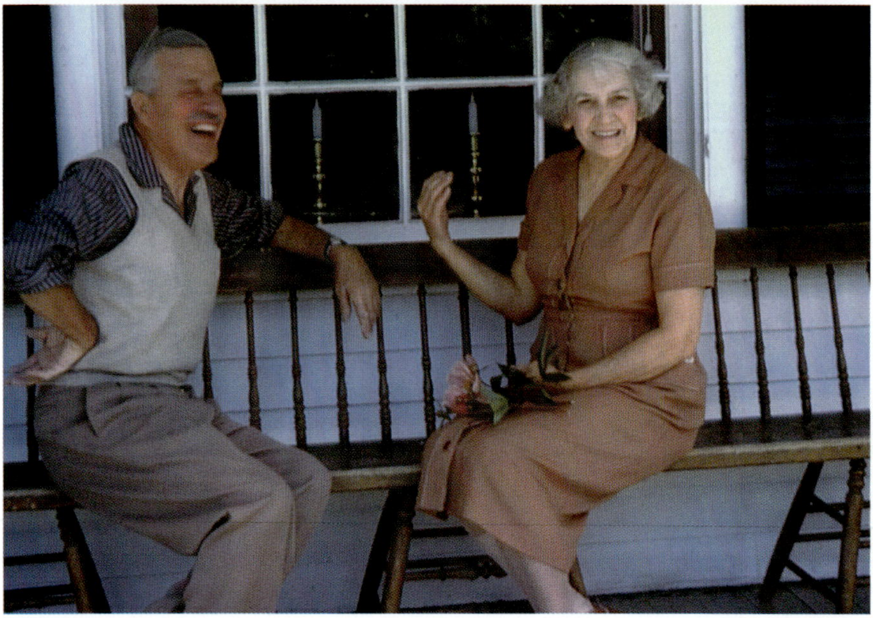

Jane and Joan, May, 1956, Mother and Dad, Summer, 1958
After the World War II my family bought a home in Newcastle, Ont. We called it "The Hollows" after Dad's home in England. Jane and Joan worked on spring flower beds. Mother and Dad sat on the front porch.

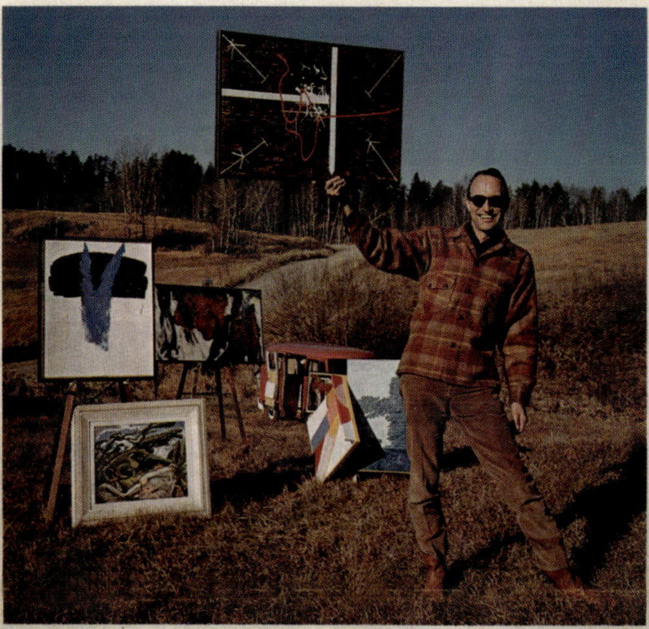

The art safari was made by Paul Bennett, director of the Art Institute of Ontario. He holds a painting by Harold Town. On the left is Borduas' Abstract In Blue valued at $4,000. Also seen are a Lismer and a Jock Macdonald.

Art That Gets Around

Original Canadian paintings go on a 3,000-mile tour of Ontario

Photostory by Bruce Moss
Weekend Magazine

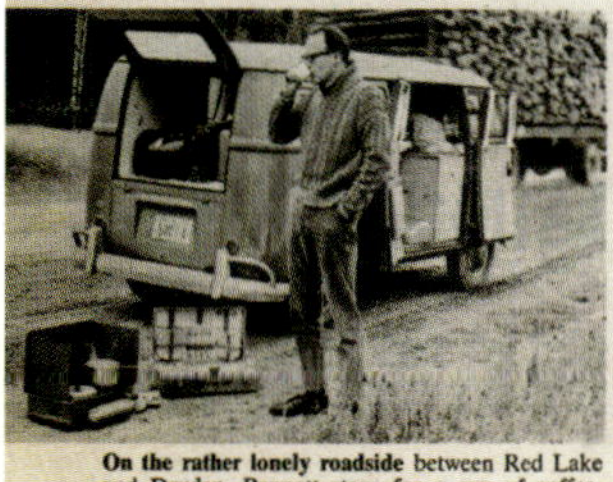

On the rather lonely roadside between Red Lake and Dryden, Bennett stops for a cup of coffee. The $10,000 art show waits in the Volkswagen.

LATE LAST FALL in Red Lake, Ont., the following announcement appeared in the stencilled local weekly District News under the heading "Uncle Charlie Says":

"While watching pink elephants I remembered: 'Guess I'll have to sober up an' take the Missus to the High School Tuesday evening. Sure must take a lot of paint to make those paintings worth $10,000.' "

Reading this somewhat frivolous comment in his hotel room, Paul Bennett, newly-appointed director of the Art Institute of Ontario, began to wonder if perhaps he had not been a trifle rash in bringing an assortment of top-quality Canadian art to the supposedly raw, uncultured shores of Red Lake, a picturesque mining town with a population of about 2,000 in northwestern Ontario. Certainly no one had ever attempted anything quite like it before.

Bennett, a lean, intense bachelor of 35 with a raft of university degrees, was more perturbed than amused by the item. The more he thought about the lecture he was to give that evening, the more apprehensive he became. What if the Red Lake District High School auditorium was empty when he arrived? Or worse still, supposing his sparse audience failed to appreciate the costly paintings he had brought with him and what if it made fun of them?

As Uncle Charlie had truthfully pointed out, the visiting art show — numbering 10 paintings — did have a total value of $10,000. But not because of the quantity of paint used. It was the first time in Canada, Bennett believed, that original paintings of such value had been part of a travelling exhibit outside the larger centres.

The collection included a Borduas abstract valued at $4,000; a bleak winter landscape worth $2,000 by J. E. H. MacDonald (a member of Canada's celebrated Group of Seven) as well as major works by such notable artists as Charles W. Jefferys, Arthur Lismer (another member of the Group of Seven), A. J. Casson, Jock Macdonald and Toronto's talkative Harold Town.

Also represented were R. York Wilson, well known for his mammoth curved mural depicting the Seven Lively Arts in Toronto's O'Keefe Centre; Greg Curnoe, a young Eastern exponent of pop art, and a Japanese-Canadian, Kazuo Nakamura, from Vancouver.

32 - Weekend Magazine No. 8, 1965

Art Institute of Ontario

Bruce Moss, a photo/writer for *Weekend Magazine* travelled with me for ten days in the fall of 1964 and published an article in 1965 titled, "Art That Gets Around" It created a great deal of interest in the A.I.O. work.

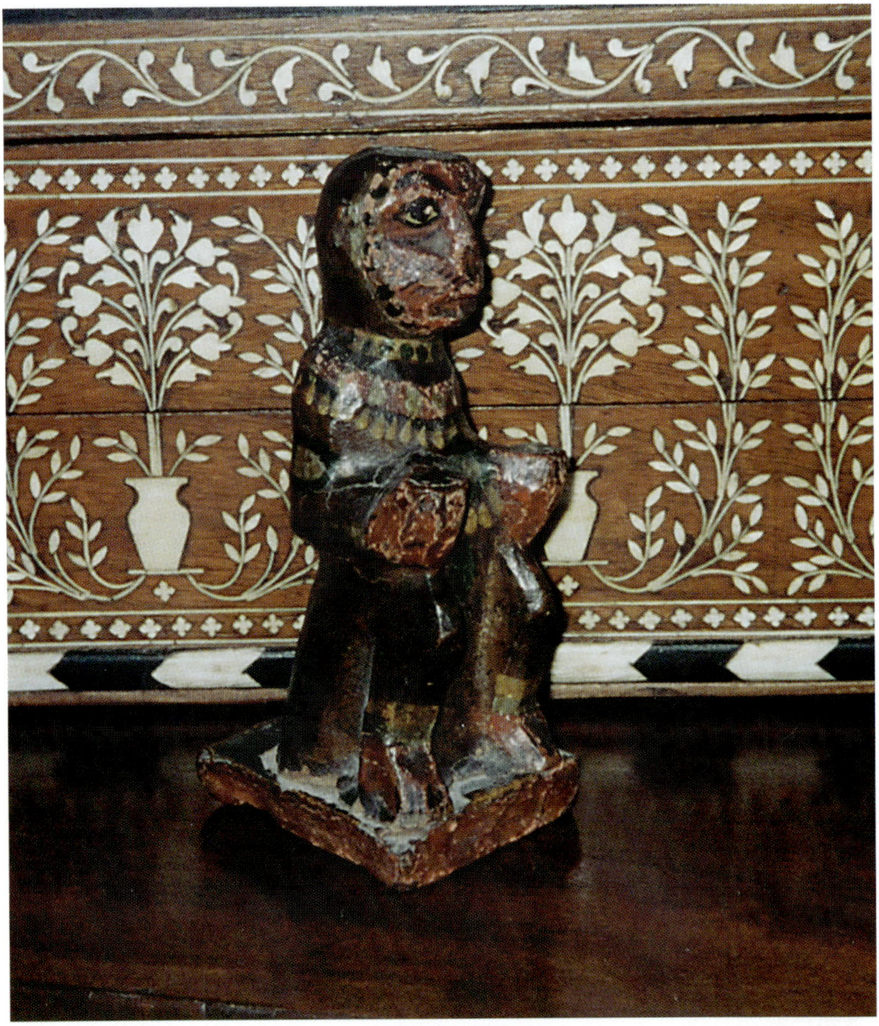

My House God

About 1875 an English officer returning home from India by way of Ceylon gave my Grandfather a small, primitive, wooden figure of a Monkey God that he had obtained in Ceylon, now Sri Lanka. He claimed that it was a House God. My Father brought this figure with him to Canada. It has guarded my home ever since my Father's death in 1965.

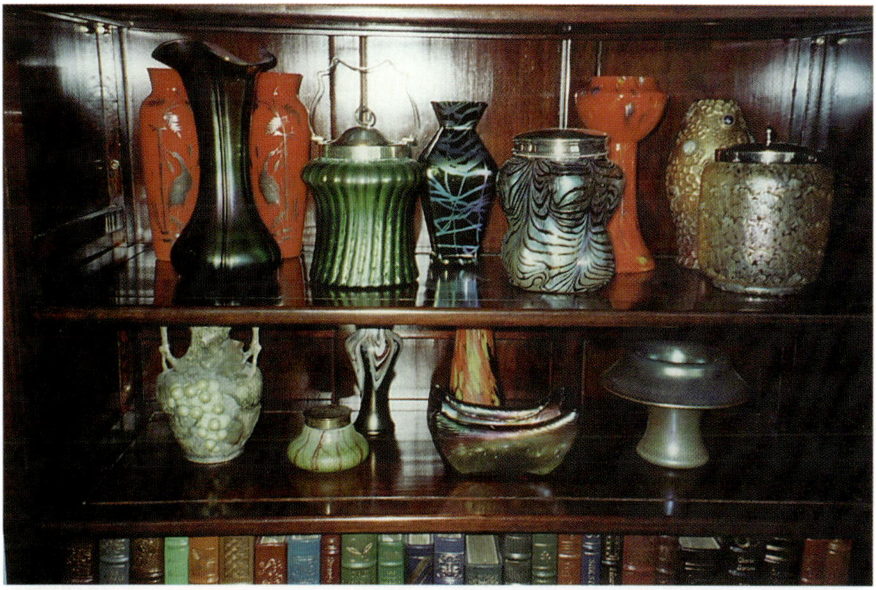

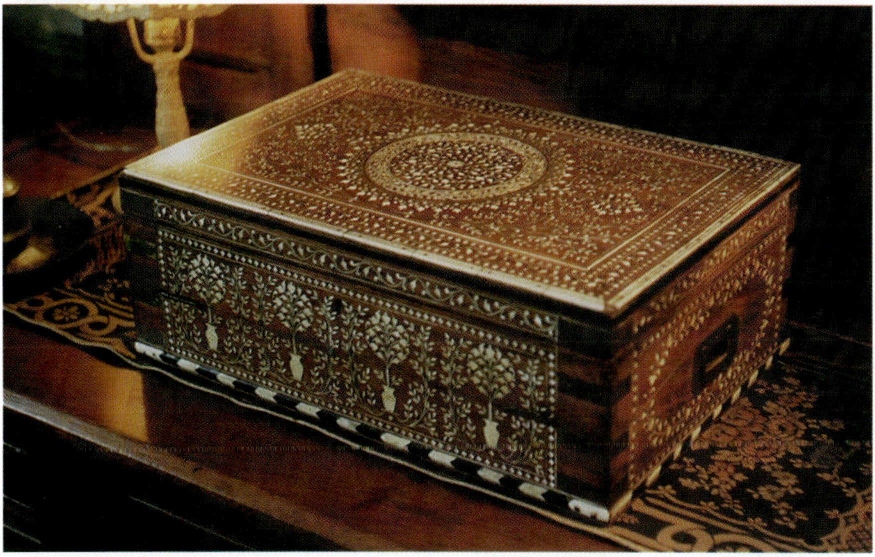

Bohemian Glass and an Indian inlaid table top desk

The glass pictured is all Bohemian dated from 1880 to 1918. Austria lost Bohemia as a result of World War 1 and it became part of Czechoslovakia. I love the opalescence and iridescence of the glass of that period. Also pictured is a writing case made in India with an elaborate inlay of ivory. Joan bought this in Edinburgh as a gift for my Mother.

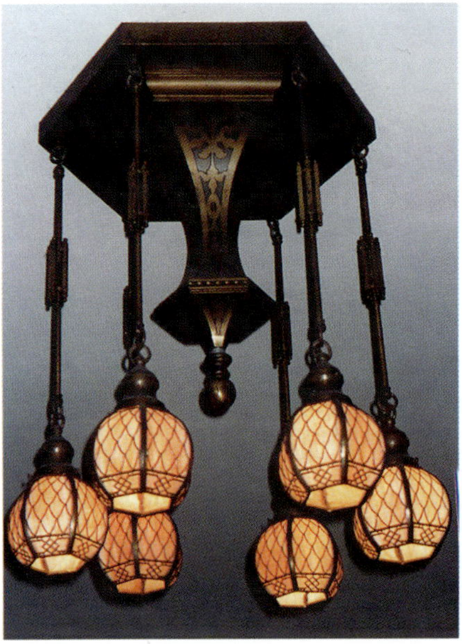

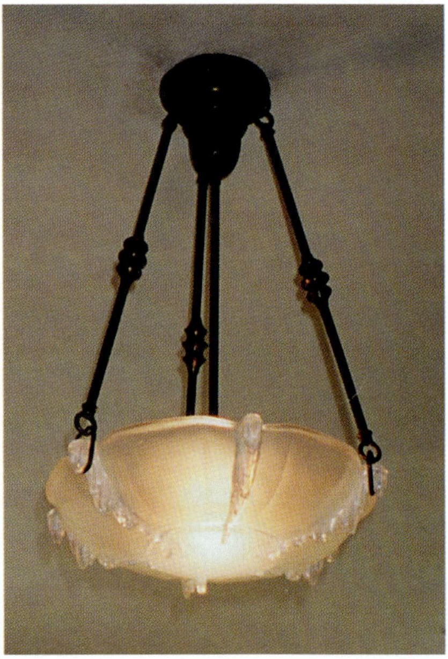

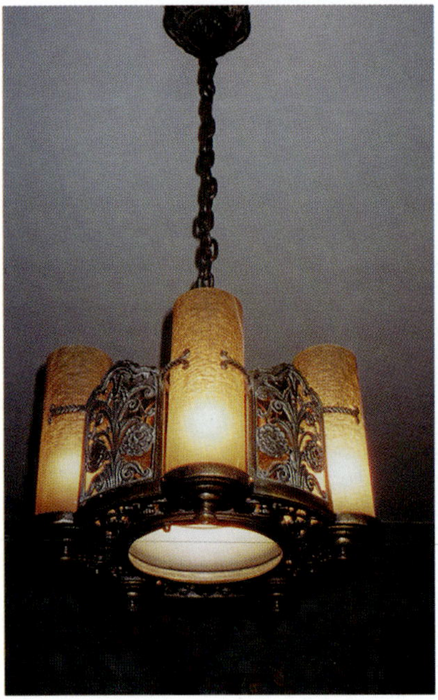

Three Ceiling Fixtures

My father and a partner owned "The Art Novelty Studios" in Toronto in the 1920s. The firm's major production was lamps and lampshades. I inherited a love of these lights and much of the lighting in my home is from that era. The three ceiling fixtures pictured are my favourites. The six light fixture is a signed "Handel" from Connecticut, circa 1910, the five light Deco one is from the 1930's, the opalescent French one, signed "Verleys" is 1930s.

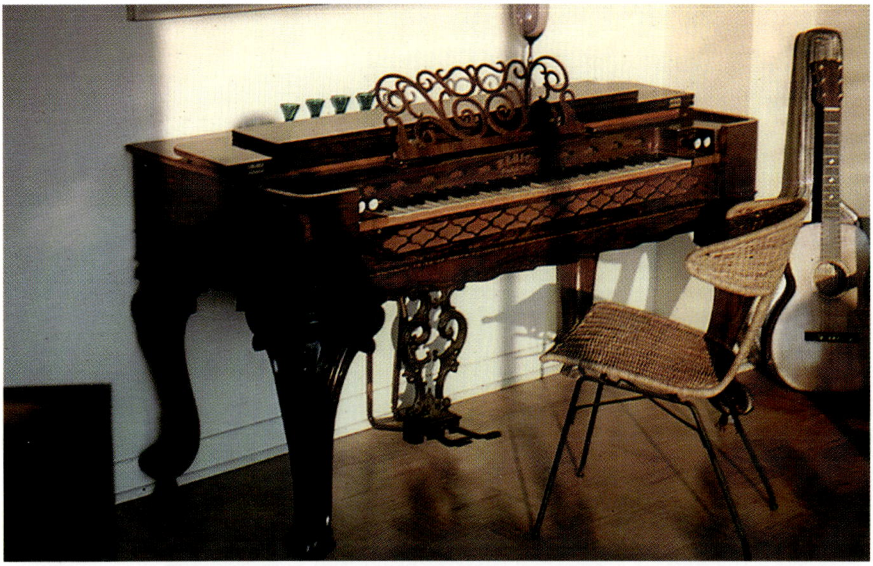

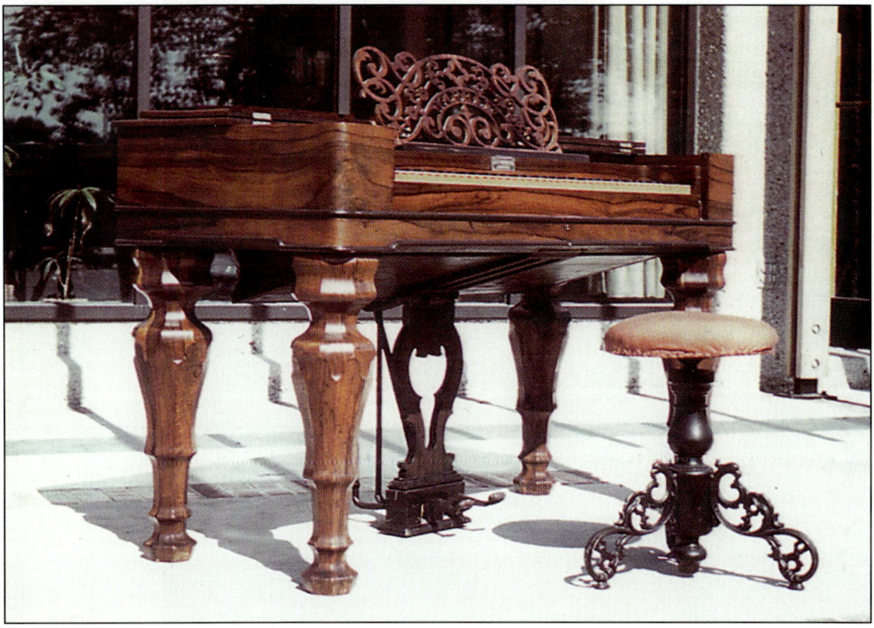

Melodeons

Through the '60s and '70s I collected 19th century reed organs called melodeons. The top picture is a W. Bell and Co. rosewood one made about 1860. I donated this instrument to the Canadiana Collection of the Royal Ontario Museum. The bottom picture is of a melodeon made of rosewood by Warren of Montreal.

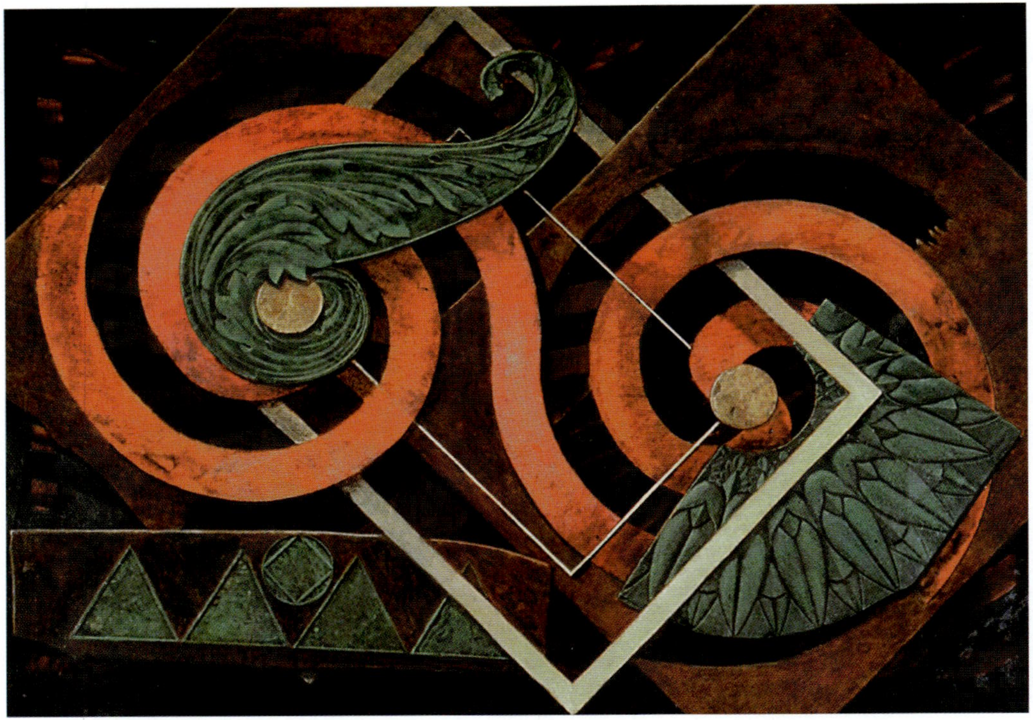

Persepolis III

1993, acrylic on paper on panel, 82.5 x 120 c.m by Ken Nutt, collection of Paul Bennett. Ken Nutt goes by his own name for his fine art painting. His pen name is Eric Beddows for his children's book illustrations. Persepolis is one of a series of paintings inspired by painted fragments of tiles from the ancient city of Persepolis built by the Persian King Darius.

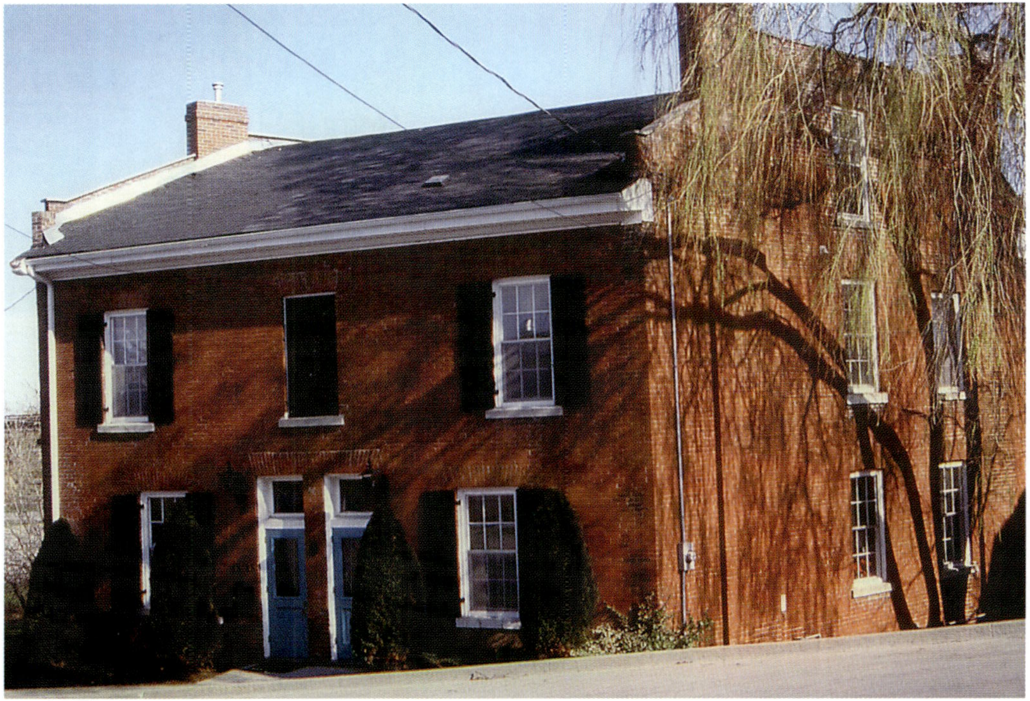

43 Dorset St. West, Port Hope.
In the spring of 1998 I bought this Georgian building built as a tavern about 1860, converted into a duplex after a fire about 1900 and joined into one home by Joan and myself in 2000. This photograph, by Daphne Svenningson of Port Hope, aptly pictures the bulk, design and solid qualifies of this home.

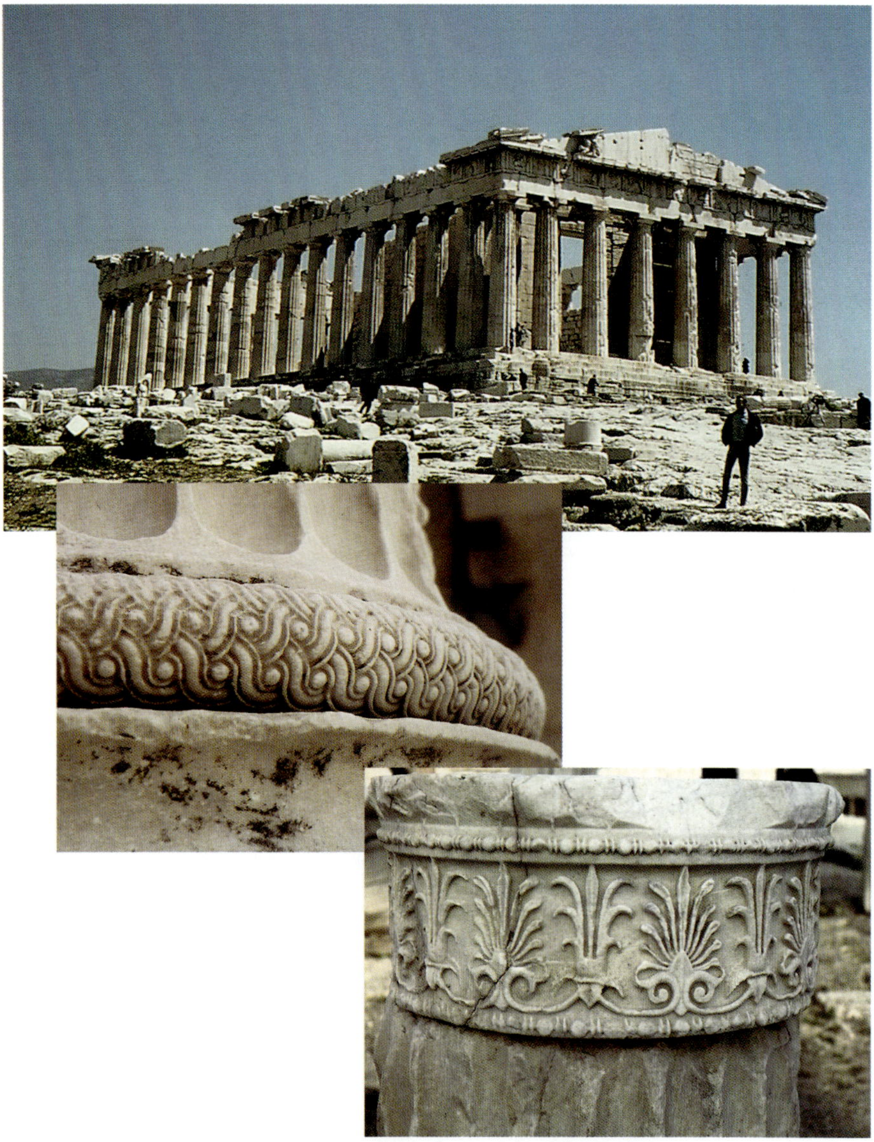

The Parthenon, Athens, Greece,

The Parthenon stands on the Acropolis in Athens, Greece with its entasis or slight convexity of a column shaft to correct a viewers optical illusion of concavity, it represents a perfection of detail in architecture that makes modern man stand in awe of the skill of our ancients. Even after two thousand five hundred years the decorative detail of broken columns on the Acropolis witnesses a concept of beauty and design that is still a standard in our own day. Photos taken in 1968.

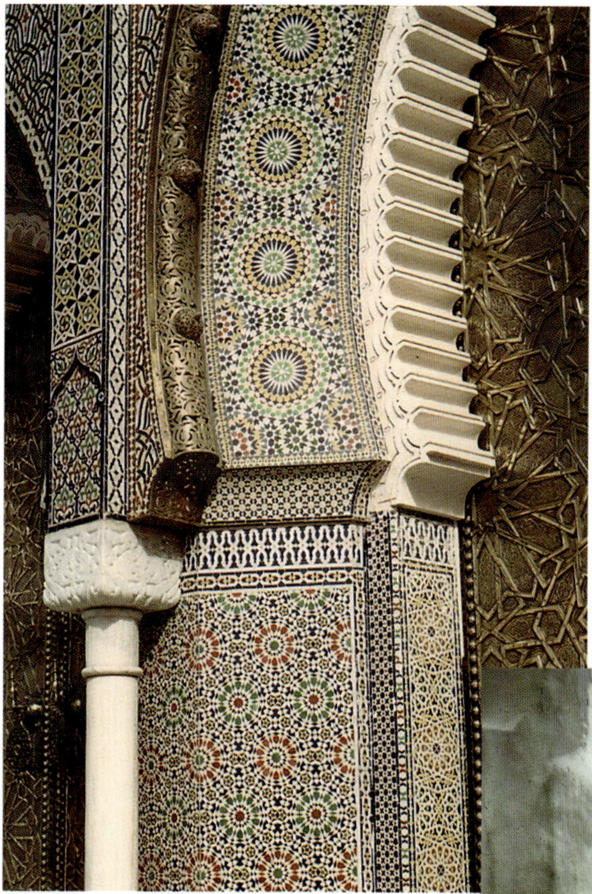

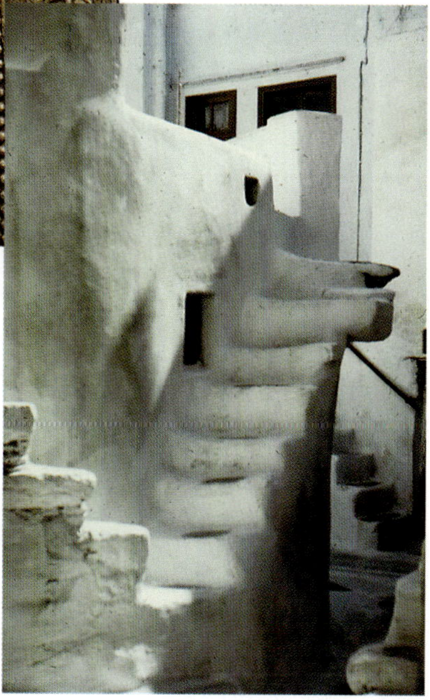

Morocco and Greece

The gates to a mosque at Fez in Morocco. The Koran forbade idols of any form including the image of man. Consequently most Islamic design is derived from floral motifs, so stylized that the natural forms are lost in the purely all-over pattern. This gate superbly demonstrates this fact. In comparison the architectural form of this outside stairway on the Greek island of Mykonos has been so worn over the years and white washed so many times that is has lost most of its architectural geometric quality and seems to be natural free form rock. Photos taken 1969.

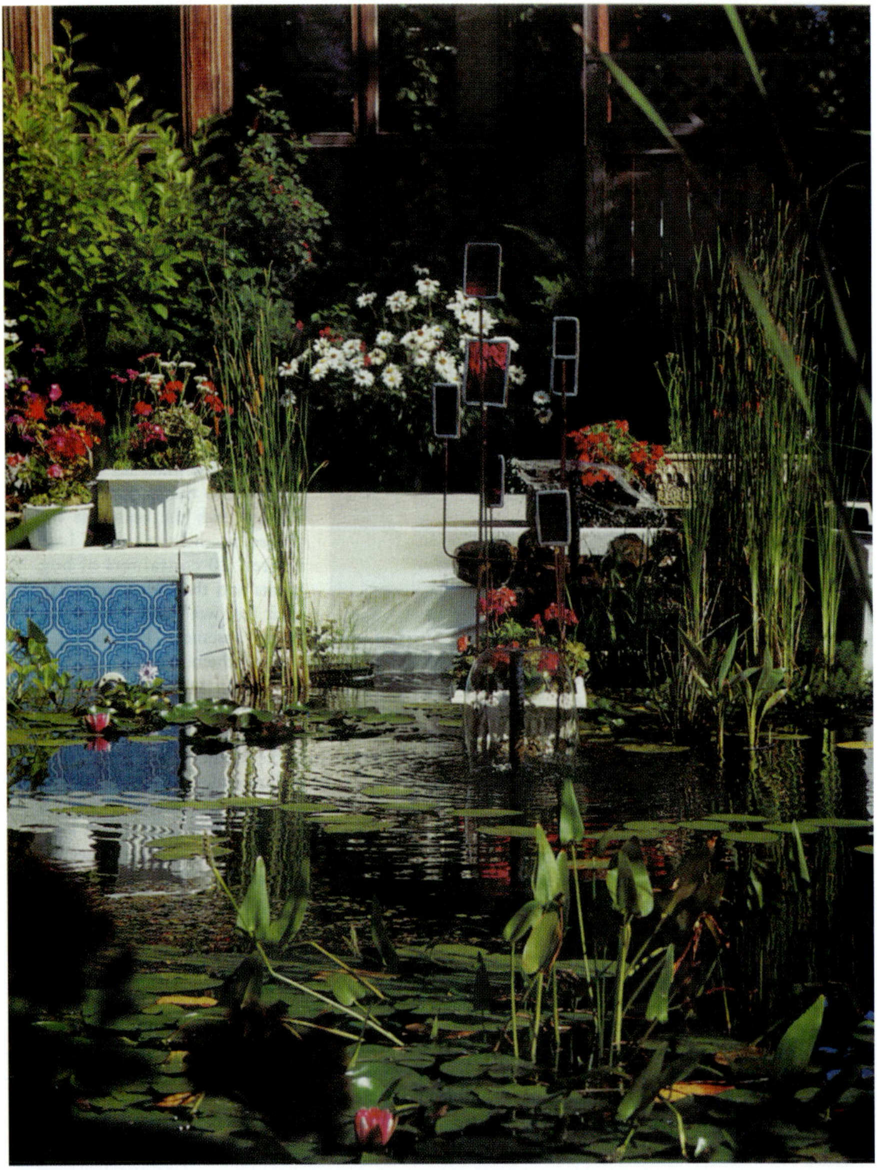

Swimming Pool to Water Garden

Chatelaine Gardens, a special interest publication of *Chatelaine Magazine,* published a feature article written by myself and with wonderful photographs by free lance photographer, Nir Bareket, in its spring/summer volume in 1997. In spite of the fact that the photos were taken in the fall when the vegetation was much diminished, Nir Bareket made the water garden look very luxurious.

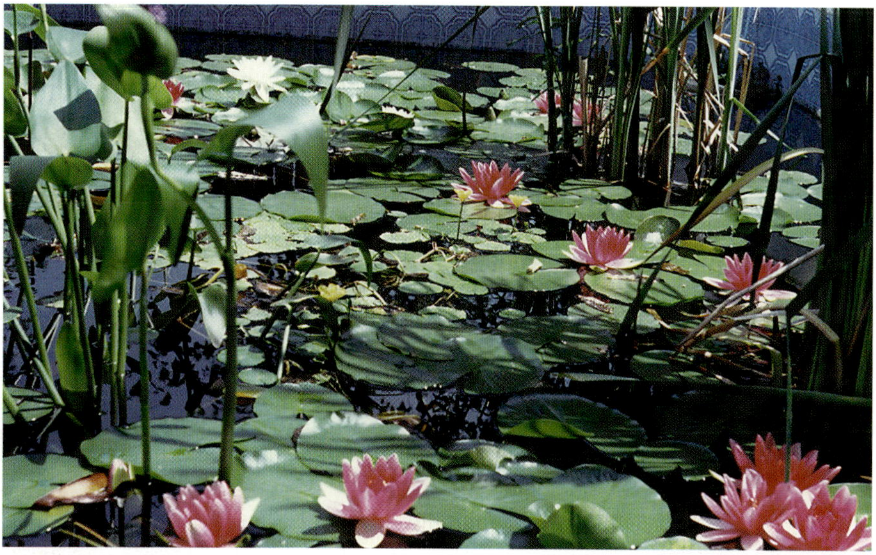

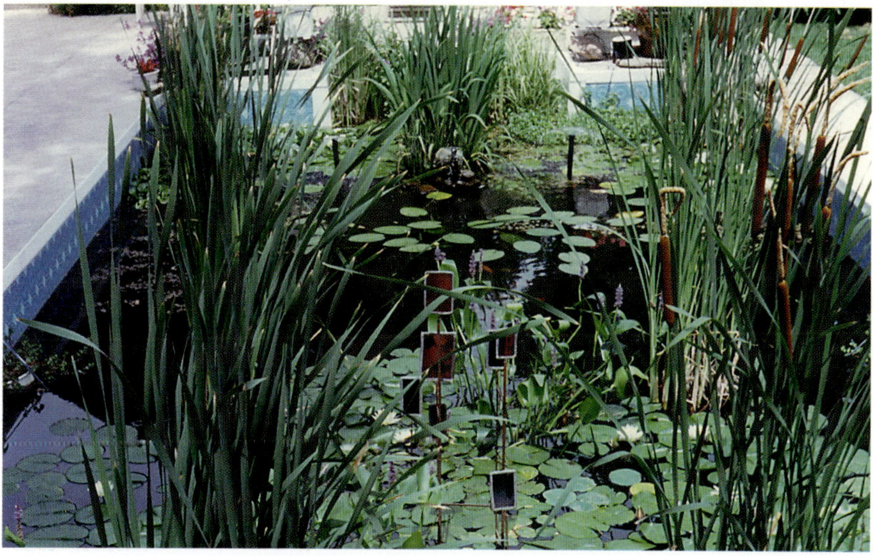

The Cobourg Water Garden

In its third year this pond was a mass of vegetation and other waterlife, - fish fry by the hundreds, dragon flies, frogs and toads in the spring, wild ducks, adult fish, bird life, different species below and above the water. Joan suggested that I could continue the cycle indefinitely; I had made a swimming pool into a water garden, next I could make the water garden into a sunken rockery and then eventually make the rockery into a swimming pool again.

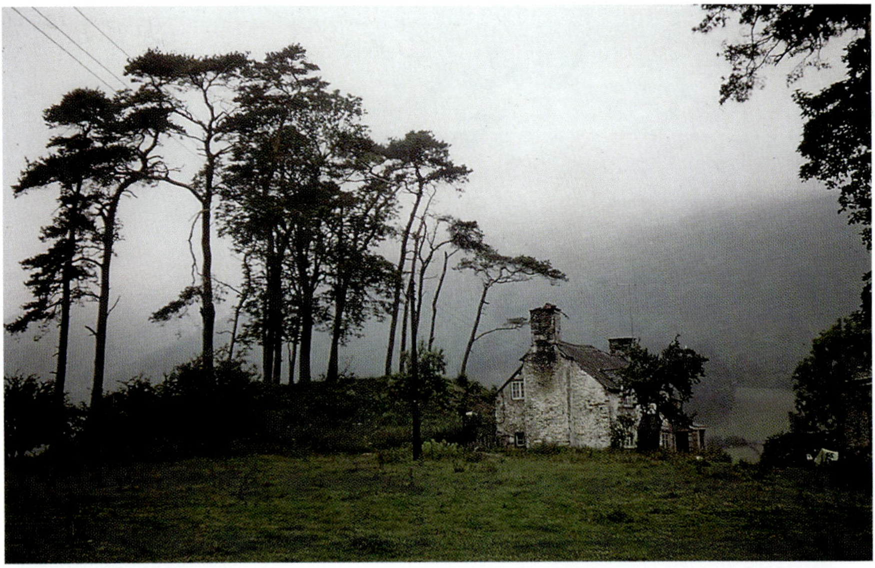

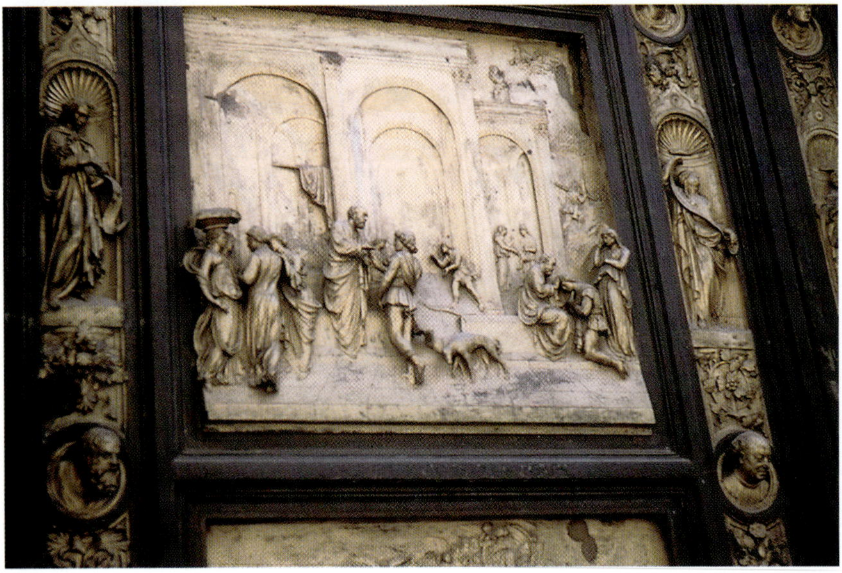

Wales and Italy

In the summer of 1956 I made my first trip to Europe. These two of my favourite photographs were made at that time. The Welsh countryside was filled with mist that suited the lush greens and greys of the ancient cottage and silhouettes of trees. The baptistery of the cathedral framed Ghiberti's magnificent bronze "Gates of Paradise" placed in the eastern doorway, the most important entrance.

Chapter Fourteen

The Robert McLaughlin Art Gallery, 1970-1972

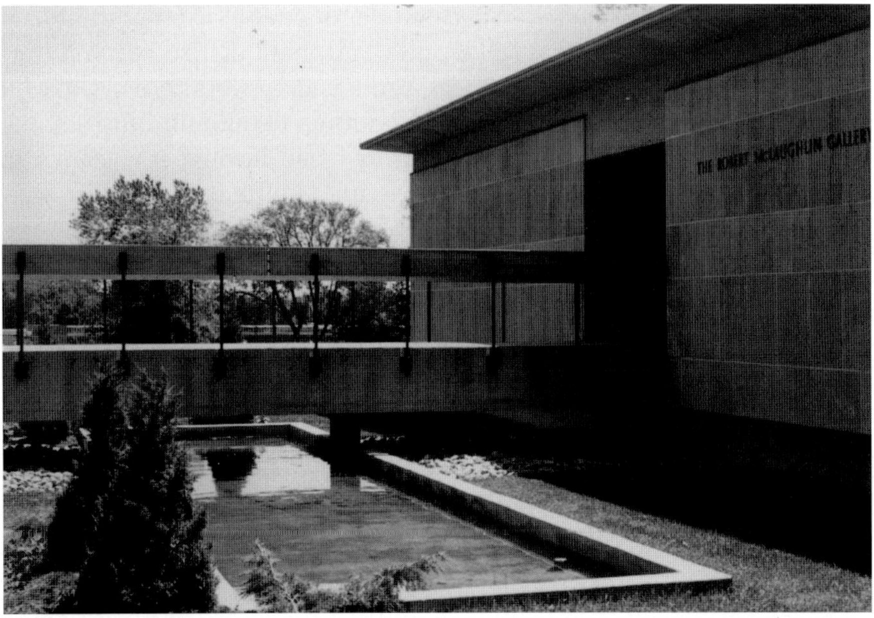

After I returned to Canada from my travels in Europe and New York, courtesy of the Canada Council, I went to see Peter Swann, then Director of the Royal Ontario Museum concerning a possible position for me that we had discussed before I went away. Dr. Swann had wanted to set up a graduate studies programme at the ROM that would lead to a graduate degree in Museology. He had suggested that I head it up, and consequently I had studied such programmes in England, especially at the University of Leicester. However on my return Dr. Swann told me that he had not been able to raise the necessary funds for the project, and so it had been shelved. Only recently it has dawned on me that perhaps he had been disappointed in the report of my studies while away and had somebody else in mind to fill the position. The programme was set up some time later.

On August 23rd, 1969, Kay Kritzwiser, the art critic for the *Globe and Mail*, wrote a Saturday feature on my return and the material in my report to the Canada Council. The article had three large photographs and took up most of three columns of newsprint. I was very pleased. It did impress Mr. Jack Wildridge, the owner of Roberts Gallery, 643 Yonge Street, Toronto. On the Saturday afternoon of the day that the article appeared Jack phoned me and offered me a job as Curator at his gallery. This was an important position in one of Toronto's leading commercial art galleries. I was flattered and accepted.

Unfortunately, I was not suited temperamentally for a commercial job at that time. I could not sell works of art that I disliked even if they were most competent and had been produced by well-known artists. I had been a grass roots developer for too long. I could and did sell the work of people like Peter Harris whom I had known for years and whose every work I thought was wonderful. I still have a small bronze medallion framed in my bedroom, the gift of a talented sculptor, whose work I promoted at the gallery and was part of a two-man sculpture exhibition. The medallion showed two young men, naked, and with arms around each other. The artist gave it to me shyly saying that the work was from his Renaissance period. I stayed at the Roberts Gallery for only a few months.

One day Dr. Barry Woods and Kay Woods came into the Roberts Gallery and asked if they could speak to me for a few minutes. Barry was president of the Robert McLaughlin Gallery in Oshawa. They offered me the position of Director of that Gallery. I knew that the public gallery rather than the commercial gallery was my field and I soon agreed.

McLaughlin Gallery was donated to the City of Oshawa by C. Ewart McLaughlin. It was named after the founder's grandfather Robert McLaughlin (1863-1921), founder of the carriage business that was the forerunner of General Motors of Canada. The sod turning ceremony took place on June 6th, 1968. The site, beside the new city hall complex and the library, was made available by the City of Oshawa. There was a great deal of room for future expansion. The core of the gallery's collection was thirty-seven paintings willed to the city of Oshawa by Alexandra Luke, the wife of Ewart McLaughlin, and herself a wonderful artist and a member of Painters Eleven. Luke's collection included a work by each member of that group. The gallery opened in the spring of 1969 with a display of Alexandra Luke's work and her collection. Jeremy Watney was the Director for a few months.

The gallery was small. It consisted of a large gallery, a small one, a sculpture court, a vestibule, a foyer, an information area and a small office on the main floor. There was a meeting room, a vault, preparation area, coatroom and washrooms below. Access to the gallery from the upper level was by means of a ramp leading from the street across a reflecting pool. There was parking at the back and side with entry through a lower lobby.

I became Director in early 1970 and immediately launched into an ambitious programme of events and exhibitions. I was most fortunate in finding an excellent staff: Heather Peel worked part time as secretary and accountant; Jacquie Boughner was Education and Extension officer; Brian Allard worked as guard and John McDonald was replaced by Ches Taylor as General Assistant. Mrs. Kay Woods, volunteer Chairperson of Acquisitions, became the volunteer Curator as the Painters Eleven project developed. There were a large number of teachers, leaders, classes and clubs developed.

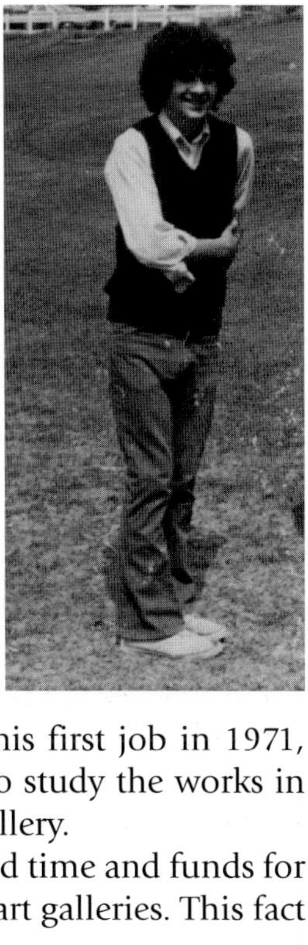

Garfield Ferguson, was a gifted artist. He joined the Teen Art Club. Later he came to work at the gallery as an art instructor and assistant to the preparator in 1971. He was always interested in art, taking courses and painting. He studied the Painters Eleven works in the collection. In 1975 he studied at the Ontario College of Art, after which he returned to Oshawa and the gallery. He continued his experiments and the development of his painting for twenty years, and in 1991 produced a one-man exhibition for the Robert McLaughlin Gallery. This exhibition travelled, I viewed it at the Northumberland Art Gallery in Cobourg. I was amazed and flattered when I saw his catalogue. In the acknowledgements he thanked me for having hired him for his first job in 1971, and he said that it gave him a rare opportunity to study the works in the permanent collection. He still works at the gallery.

In February 1970, the Board of Trustees provided time and funds for me to travel across Canada and visit twelve other art galleries. This fact alone shows the attitude of the Board toward having the best gallery possible. I had built a reputation of grass roots development, I had never been a gallery Director before and I deeply appreciated this chance to expand my experience and information base.

The fall programme of the gallery was publicized in the *Oshawa Times* in September 1970. It listed eleven exhibitions on view from Sept. 11th to Jan. 3rd, including Medals, a Polish Exhibition of Arts, a William Roberts Retrospective, a London Group of Five show, Fernand Leduc, and Wall Hangings. There were six Wednesday night programmes with speakers such as David Mirvish and Av. Isaacs, a Wednesday night art film programme, Gallery Guide Training Programme, a Young People's Art Club, a Young Mothers' Figure Drawing Club, Children's Art Classes, Sunday Afternoon Music Recitals, a Travelling Exhibition Programme, the Oshawa Film Society, an Amateur Film Festival, and the Oshawa and District Art Association offering of four classes.

I had known and respected Alan Collier as a friend and painter for many years. I organised a retrospective of his paintings in 1971. It opened at the McLaughlin Gallery and then travelled for a year to ten other locations in Ontario. Alan was very pleased with the result and donated a large painting, "Nude Back", to the permanent collection in 1973.

I always believed that one of the best ways to publicize an art gallery was for the Director to be visible. I accepted personal commitments, with the Board's approval. In 1970 I was Vice-Chairman of the Oshawa and District Council for the Arts, on Advisory Committees for both George Brown College of Applied Arts for its art courses and Sir Sandford Fleming College instituting a Fine Arts Programme. I acted on the Advisory Art Committee at the Ontario Institute for Studies in Education along with Doris McCarthy and Jack Pollock on the purchases of works of art. I was on the Fine Art Committee for the Canadian National Exhibition and actually hung the C.N.E. art show during one week of my holidays. I was a member of the Board of Whitby Arts Incorporated. Later I represented the gallery at the Ontario Association of Art Galleries. I was on the Mayor's Committee in setting up Colonel Sam McLaughlin's home as a public building, and a Visual Arts Consultant for the Province of Ontario Council for the Arts.

There was a very active Women's Committee involved in the gallery. Members of that committee staffed the Gift Shop, acted as docents for the school and other gallery tours and provided a large number of fund raising events from a June Art Mart to out-of-town bus tours and luncheons. In 1970 this Committee under the capable chairmanship of Mrs. Jean Mercer gave the Acquisition Committee five thousand dollars toward buying works of art for the Permanent Collection.

The McLaughlin Gallery received a great deal of free publicity both in Oshawa and in Ontario. I wrote a weekly art column for the Oshawa Times. The paper never limited my space and I had a free choice of subject: Often I would write up a new exhibition or a visiting artist. I took a trip to England and wrote two half-page articles on the sights and art of that country, I was fortunate in that I could dictate quickly and clearly; I had learned this while with the A.I.O. while doing so much work by 'phone with my secretary.

Mrs. Kay Woods was the wife of the gallery's president, Dr. Barry Woods. She was a wonderful hostess and often entertained at their beautiful home in the name of the gallery. She had a good eye and was developing a marvellous personal collection, She was very active in the gallery, first as a member of the women's committee and then as Chairperson of the Acquisition Committee. One day we met in my office and discussed what the collection guidelines should be. The Board was looking for an official policy. I was eager to have something that would set the gallery apart. We had the McMichael Collection as a model of what could be done with a single vision.

From this discussion emerged the Painters Eleven concept that has since made the McLaughlin Gallery famous. As stated above, the gallery had a close connection with this groundbreaking group of artists interested in abstract art in Ontario. Alexandra Luke, one of the Eleven, had been the wife of the founder of the gallery. Indeed the first meeting of the group had taken place in Luke's lakeside studio in Oshawa in 1953. Seven of the artists had participated in an exhibition at the Robert Simpson Company in Toronto. This had been arranged by William Ronald who was doing design work there. This show of non-objective and abstract painting went under the title of "Abstracts at Home" and the idea was to persuade the general public to consider that art could be used in everyday living.

The seven artists were Jack Bush, Alexandra Luke, Ray Mead, Kazuo Nakamura, William Ronald, Tom Hodgson and Oscar Cohen. After the Simpson's show this group of seven artists decided to meet to explore the possibility of showing their work as a group. They met in Oshawa and also invited Jock Macdonald, Harold Town, Walter Yarwood and Hortense Gordon. History was made that night. Jack Bush was the only one represented at a commercial gallery, Roberts, and so he agreed to speak to Jack Wildridge, the owner of Roberts Gallery, to see if they,

Painters Eleven, could have a show. Jack Wildridge agreed and the Painters Eleven went on to eight years of groundbreaking history in the Visual Arts of Ontario.

Now I must break the flow of this narrative to say that I am in a quandary here. Kay Woods and I met in my office and the idea of collecting Painters Eleven was born. I cannot remember the conversation; I really do not know who said the magic words first. I do remember that in the short history of Painters Eleven Kay published in 1971 I gave her credit for the thought. I also remember that at that time I was basking in the success of my work with the Art Institute of Ontario and Kay was just starting out. I would like to think that we thought of the idea together. Kay went on to develop the project while I went on running the gallery. Sometimes accompanied by me, Kay visited the artists and persuaded them to join in the Painters Eleven project. I remember going to William Ronald's, and Kay and I both bought watercolours from him for us. I presented the idea to the Board and spoke eloquently enough to have the Board accept our new permanent collection policy. We also persuaded the Board to use our limited acquisition funds to buy from these artists. I do know that I was the Director and I consider that there were three things in my career that I was especially proud of; one of them was the Painters Eleven project at the Robert McLaughlin Gallery. I will always be indebted to Kay Woods for her enthusiasm, for loving to have a purpose for meeting these artists. The gallery upgraded her stature from Chairman of the Acquisitions Committee to Curator of the Gallery. She accepted it as an unpaid position. She held the position proudly and was the chief influence in launching a major Canadian Collection on the visual arts scene.

I must elaborate on the collection policy. The gallery decided to collect letters, photographs, catalogues, and all pertinent material on each member of the group. It hoped to obtain a substantial number of works by the eleven during their years together, 1953 to 1960, and then acquire works up to the present. the gallery was to become the centre of research on Painters Eleven.

The policy received a great deal of publicity and many donations of works by the members. The gift list of 1970 was large: two charcoal sketches by Alexandra Luke came from Mrs. Gordon Hare of Oshawa, William Ronald donated nine watercolours and drawings;, four oil paintings of Hortense Gordon came from Chatham; thirty illustrations of Oscar Cahen were the gift of W.J. Gage of Toronto; three drawings by Ray Mead were donated by T. MacDonald, Director of the Hamilton Art Gallery, besides other works by other artists.

The Painters Eleven Collection brought Joan Murray to Oshawa. In the spring of 1972 Joan Chalmers and Mary Eleven Hogg, both Board members of the Canadian Guild of Crafts (Ontario) came to see me and offered me the new position of Director of the Guild. It was opening a new gallery and offices on Prince Arthur Avenue in Toronto. The craft field was expanding rapidly into a new professionalism. I could once again be in Toronto. I accepted the new challenge and moved on.

Before I leave Oshawa however I wish to explain one action suggested by myself and acted on by the Board of Trustees that caused great distress to the new Director, Joan Murray. In her biography, *Confessions of a Curator, Adventures in Art* she stated that the Robert McLaughlin Gallery mortgaged the income from its endowment fund by, in the first year of the new acquisition policy, buying paintings on time from the Painters Eleven members. That is the paintings were bought and then paid for over a period of five years. Unfortunately because of lower interest rates this turned out to be eight years. She did state that the paintings secured this way were, for the most part, very good ones and became the cornerstones for the collection. She said it should not have been done as it hampered the gallery's future.

I beg to disagree with her. Joan Murray came from a very cultured family in New York; she was surrounded by art, by artists and museum administrators from a very early age. She spent much time as a child inside art galleries and museums. She came to Toronto after finishing her art training and worked at the Art Gallery of Ontario, a very large organization. Before coming to Oshawa she had never worked in a small art gallery.

By comparison I came from a cultured family surrounded by music and art but never of the quality that graced Joan's early days. I worked at a grass roots level of the visual arts after finishing my art training. I came to Oshawa when it was an unknown entity; it was new, there had been an enquiry into the work of its first Director, the gallery had no direction. I gave it that direction. First of all it had multiple layers of programming and that gave the gallery a purpose. It became people-oriented, but to the professional artist it was still an unknown. Kay Woods and I came up with the Painters Eleven idea. I do not believe that artists like Harold Town and William Ronald would have looked twice at it if the gallery had not bought major works at that crucial point. Buying their art tied them to the project. Many times the original cost of that art came back to the gallery in donations from the artists themselves, their friends, families and patrons. Most small galleries do not even have an acquisition fund based on an endowment;

that endowment came from the McLaughlin family, the family of Alexandra Luke.

It was because of the Painters Eleven project that Joan Murray herself went to Oshawa. She was a remarkable Director. She wrote many books on art and Painters Eleven, she enthused Isabel McLaughlin, herself an artist of note, to spearhead the raising of funds with a huge donation for an expansion of the overcrowded facility. The enlarged gallery has a huge vault to hold its massive collection. There is a wonderful gallery of Isabel's own collection, also there is a first class restaurant, suitable office space and so on.

I heard Joan expounding on her theory about mortgaging acquisition funds when talking to other gallery directors. I read about it in her biography. I wrote her a letter explaining my view but she did not reply to it.

Chapter Fifteen

The Ontario Crafts Council, 1972-1978

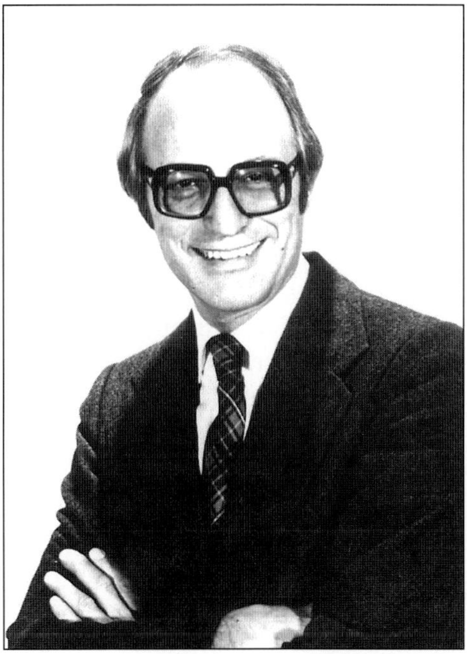

In the spring of 1972, Joan Chalmers and Mary Eileen Hogg offered me the newly created position of Executive Director of the Canadian Guild of Crafts (Ontario). The Guild had just secured premises for a new Craft Gallery and offices at 29 Prince Arthur Avenue in Toronto. They wanted me to expand the Guild's programmes and bring a new professionalism to the Crafts movement. I had enjoyed my work at. the Robert McLaughlin Gallery but I was ready for a new challenge and my home was in Toronto.

The history of organized crafts in Canada goes back to about 1900. At that time a Handicraft Guild was formed in Quebec to reawaken pride in the old skills and a shop was established to sell the products of the country artisans, later Indian crafts were included and it was expanded to include Eskimo crafts in the 1940s. Similarly, in Toronto in 1931 a group formed the Handicrafts Association; later changed to the Canadian Handicraft Guild, with a shop in Eaton's College St. store. The Quebec Guild exhibited at the Canadian National Exhibition in 1932. The Ontario Guild assumed this responsibility and administered craft exhibitions at the C.N.E. right into the 1970s.

The Women's Committee of the Guild was responsible for a very special show at the Royal Ontario Museum in 1961,"The Salvador Dali Collection of Art In Jewels", bringing record-breaking attendance.

In 1967 the Guild was re-named the Canadian Guild of Crafts (Ontario). In 1968 the Guild bought 140 Cumberland Street, where a very successful shop is still located, renowned, particularly, for its Eskimo art.

The Guild had many programmes: the craft gallery would have group shows, student exhibitions and one-man exhibitions and we had a growing mailing list for invitations to our openings. The Craft Gallery allowed the professional craftsman to have the same type of exposure that other commercial galleries gave to painters, print-makers and sculptors. Ten percent of the budget went to bursaries and awards for students to help them receive professional training in crafts. The guild had a close link with the Ontario College of Art and the community colleges that were now teaching crafts.

The Canadian National Exhibition Show each year, sponsored by the Guild, was the only annual, juried craft show in Canada; each year out of five or six hundred entries, professional craftsmen would choose one hundred and fifty to two hundred works of art for the show, based on craftsmanship, quality and design. Prizes were awarded for various categories. Also, the Guild ran three biennial exhibitions, "Craft Dimensions" in 1969, "Make" in 1971 and "Entr'acte" at the O'Keefe Centre in 1973, costing fifteen thousand dollars and sponsored by Benson and Hedges.

At that time the Guild had a membership of 1,350 people. All members received the bi-monthly, bilingual magazine called *Craft Dimensions* edited by the very competent Gwen Sands.

The Guild was steadily building up a small permanent collection. Mrs. Jean A. Chalmers donated funds on a regular basis toward this objective; for example, in 1975 she donated twenty-five thousand dollars to buy all fifty-nine objects that represented Canada in the judging for the international craft exhibition called "In Praise of Hands".

For years Mary Eileen Hogg had wanted a Craft Resource Centre. In 1975 the Junior League of Toronto funded such a centre which was designed to provide among other things, files on professional craftspeople, a reference library, a continuing directory on things of interest to craftspeople, reference files on supplies, markets, etcetera. It was located on the third floor at 29 Prince Arthur Avenue (my office had been on the second floor, I was banished to the basement and secured a spot in the old coal bin, they had removed the coal) Mary Eileen

Hogg had been instrumental in bringing the World Crafts Conference to Canada; In June, 1974, twelve hundred craftspeople from fifty-seven countries gathered for a week at York University in Toronto, at the same time as the international exhibition, "In Praise of Hands" was on view at the Ontario Science Centre. I was on the Canadian Coordinating Committee for the conference. There were weeks of planning for all the activities, I made two trips, one to eastern Canada and the other to western Canada publicizing both the conference and the exhibition. I especially sought craftspeople who might demonstrate at the exhibition. I opened a Guild exhibition, "Master Craftsmen" at the Confederation Gallery in Charlottetown. I also enjoyed visiting Fannin Park in Charlottetown, the home of the first Governor, General Edmund Fanning, an ancestor on my mother's side.

On arrival at the conference each delegate was given a white T-shirt to decorate and wear on North American Day. I decided to do something a little different with mine: I created a setting for it. I decorated it by wearing a 1920s-style orange, white and red bathing suit over the T-shirt. It had shoulder straps to which I attached WCC pennants. I wore a long string of wooden beads, and I wore a third pennant as a modesty panel. The cameras kept clicking all day!

In July 1974 I saw advertised in the *Globe and Mail,* a building for sale, an absolutely ideal building for 'the Guild. It was situated at 340 Dundas St. West and right across from the main door of the Art Gallery of Ontario. We went through viewings, conferences, arguments, inquiries, estimates, consultations, requests for government funding, disappointments, successes, charitable donations (Joan Chalmers) and finally success: the building was ours.

The new headquarters on Dundas St. featured many works commissioned from Ontario Craftspeople. Ruth Gowdy McKinley designed a series of hanging planters that were hung in an open well from the first to the second floor. Don McKinley designed a desk for the gallery space. Robert Jekyll hung stained glass panels. Robin Hopper added a three foot coffee urn and a set of mugs. Haaken Bakken designed a large brass door handle and Velta Vilson made hand-woven window blinds, to mention only a few.

Through the 1970s there was a growing concern that there was a duplication of services with the multicraft organizations serving the craftspeople of Ontario. Eight meetings took place over a period of three years between the Guild and the Ontario Craft Foundation. There were many problems, the Guild was self funded, mainly through its shop profits, the Foundation was government funded. the Guild emphasized professional crafts and quality, the Foundation was interested in a regional network of organizations that helped all craftspeople, amateur and professional, the problems and safeguards were all ironed out .

One new organization was founded and named the Ontario Crafts Council. This was in keeping along with the Canadian Crafts Council and the World Crafts Council. Twelve Board members came from each organization (one from each of the twelve Foundation regional organizations) plus a president for a total of twenty-five. The founding president was Joan Chalmers. Letters patent were received in August of 1976. I was Executive Director of the new organization and Beth Dingman, former Director of the Foundation, became Regional Development Director and Editor of Publications (Beth's previous career had been as a journalist especially with the *Toronto Telegram*).

In my role as Executive director I continued moving about the province helping develop a professional outlook for crafts with both the craftspeople themselves and the general public. My background in design was of great assistance in this. As well I believe my general attitude helped, I could still relate to people, in fact it was a craftsman who visited my office that suggested that I stop wearing a shirt, tie and suit and start dressing more casually, more in fact like the visitors that came to see me. I did as he suggested. I was also accepted as an authority and I carried that attitude with me. I said believe in yourself and the world will believe in you and by reflection, your work. I did not say it, but my own attitude was that I was an important person in their world and I would not be visiting them if I did not think that they too were important. Below is an example of my work.

I was invited to be the sole juror for an important crafts show presented by the London Art Gallery in September of 1977. In the Acknowledgements in the catalogue, Paddy O'Brien, the curator, stated

> The first three Major London Survey exhibitions were entirely selected and assembled by London Art Gallery staff members, but when it came to organizing the fourth we found that we were lacking the very special expertise required to do proper justice to the craftsmen of London. Consequently we were delighted when Paul Bennett accepted our invitation to act as Curator in the Field, and give us the benefit of his profound feeling for, and knowledge of, contemporary crafts in Ontario. To Paul, and to the Board of the Ontario Crafts Council who readily agreed to let us borrow his skills, I would like to express our warmest gratitude and comradeship. I would also like to express our sincerest

thanks to both the Canada Council and the Ontario Arts Council, without whose financial support and encouragement the London Art Gallery would not have been able to give the citizens of London this opportunity to view some of the fine work being produced by our community's craftsmen.

Paddy O'Brien

The following is my *Juror's Statement* from the catalogue -

The "Major London Survey — Crafts" exhibition gives the public an opportunity to view the variety and quality of crafts that are being produced in the London area. The craft disciplines of textiles and ceramics are well represented. Jewellery and wood have token representation. Other crafts such as holloware, glass and leather are absent. This is possibly a reflection of the training opportunities available in London.

Today's definition of crafts is far reaching. It takes in both traditional and contemporary concepts and designs. It takes in production work as well as one-of-a-kind pieces. It takes in the use of time honoured materials side by side with the products of new technology. The present exhibition provides a variety that ranges from a most sophisticated ceramic wall piece to a little girl's granny dress with smocking. Both examples, within the dictates of their particular techniques and materials, show originality and great technical skill.

The London scene in crafts is a smaller version of the total Ontario scene. The province's practising craftsmen break into five distinct groups with, of course, some overlapping.

At the top I would place a small number of professional craftsmen who reflect a suitable period of training, creative ability and lengthy experience. These craftsmen, on their own endeavours, have been accepted throughout the Ontario visual arts scene and are exhibiting in art galleries and receiving commissions.

The second group represents a North American phenomenon. These are women whose children have reached a stage of independence, freeing them to develop skills through continuing education programs and, in some cases, a full return to school. They have been interested in crafts for three to ten years and are steadily producing work of higher and higher quality.

The third group is a younger generation. It is in essence the young professionals who have attended community colleges or the Ontario College of Art and secured full time craft training. No doubt some who have flare, imagination and ability will with more training and experience move into the first group as time goes on.

The fourth group represents a different type of young person. This is the self taught individual who has developed an interest in a craft and pursued it for periods of one month to a year or more. These craftsmen show an amazing self confidence. Their crafts are rugged and utilitarian, and do not have great quality. No doubt, after a brief period of commercialization, some of these young people will realize that the public is looking for a higher quality and will seek suitable training or will leave the field.

The fifth group, by no means the least important, is the craftsman who is pursuing a hobby, in this case crafts, simply for the love of creative effort. This group studies through adult education systems including summer schools, and produces a wide variety of crafts with a wide variety of quality. Some of these craftsmen sell their works, others simply produce works for relatives and friends. Their endeavour is noble. I compliment them on their very keen interest.

For the sake of the Major London Survey — Crafts, my choice of works came mainly from the first three groups.

No doubt the London craft scene reflects the total Ontario scene because it has the same educational opportunities available to people interested in crafts throughout the province. One may secure full craft training, part time craft training, leisure time craft training. In the total visual arts scene, the craftsman has the same inspiration as the painter and the sculptor — all these visual artists are exposed to the visual stimulus of London, the sense of cultural excitement, encouragement and, indeed, opposition, all exciting facets of this major Ontario city.

As a juror for this exhibition, I was asked to select quality works. I was told there could be twenty or three hundred works in the exhibition. While visiting more than fifty craftsmen in their studios and homes I kept the word quality in the back of my mind. I was aware, however, that this was to be a survey exhibition. My procedure was to pick one or two works from each craftsmen, take suitable notes; then, at the end of my two weeks of visits, I had an interview, which enabled me to select the works presented in the exhibition.

I would like to thank the London Gallery for this interest in the craft field. The Canada Council is also to be congratulated for providing funding for this survey exhibition. The crafts scene is relatively new in Ontario. Crafts need documentation. I am happy therefore to see a suitable catalogue reflecting this exhibition for it assists the total crafts movement.

Lastly I must thank the London craftsmen. I appreciated the fact that they recognized the importance of this exhibition. I appreciated their acceptance of me as a juror.

I considered it an honour to act as a juror for this exhibition.

PAUL BENNETT, Executive Director
Ontario Crafts Council
Juror, Major London Survey Number Four — Crafts

The first cloud on the horizon, although I did not recognize it as such, was a request from the Executive for a record of my work schedule for one week. The Executive wished to study the administration time devoted to each programme. The resulting report was a two-page letter accompanied by nine pages of details on my activities. In five working days I received or made 54 'phone calls, received 29 letters, wrote 9 letters, gave 3 lectures and was away from the office for a day and a half on a trip to Timmins/South Porcupine. I also gave a lecture in Georgetown; I attended 4 full meetings and met with one or two people 27 times. I ate meals with five different individuals or groups and worked fifteen hours overtime.

In my analysis I stated that there was little time left to write reports or prepare slide talks, lectures or presentations. Almost everything was done "off the cuff". I added that it was ridiculous to be able to write only nine letters in one week.

I had written my report at the Oakville Go-Train station. I also questioned the necessity for a Chubb alarm system for our new building. There had been fourteen false alarms in a little over a month, which staff members had had to answer.

The above was requested in February 1976. In April I was asked to do a position analysis of my job. In this I gave a personal assessment, described the lines of authority, talked about task orientation and analyzed my workload. In my considered opinion I spent 50% of my time on the public relations aspect of Council work — by individual contact (person to person), group and audience, by phone and letter; 40% of my time on Board, staff and programme business; and 10% of my time on fund-raising.

In retrospect I realize that I considered myself a programme in my own right. Originally I had been hired to help in giving the craft movement a professional look. I continued to do this as the organization enlarged. There were twenty-five Board members, many of them from right across the province, many of them craftsmen, a few of them amateurs. Obviously they did not realize what I was doing. I thought I was on top of my work. There was an office manager to look after the inner details of the Council work. I met almost every day with all of the main staff. I attended all the committees that I was supposed to attend. I had direct input in raising funds from more than a dozen government sources in 1977. I took three years to secure a $78.000 grant from the Ontario-Quebec Commission for a two-province exhibition. One Board member complained that I had not raised any corporate funds. I had always understood that it was an important duty of the Board to raise corporate funds while the staff wrote the briefs for government funding.

On July 19th, 1978, Doug Mantegna, the President, asked me to go out with him for coffee across at the Art Gallery of Ontario. I did so and he handed me a letter and informed me that both Beth Dingman and myself would not have our contracts renewed, my employment with the Council was to cease as of November 1st, 1978. It was a great blow to me. I was told that a business manager and the President and the Vice-President would assume my workload on a voluntary basis!!

In September I wrote a report to the Board. I pointed out that the Council would need an Executive-Director. There had to be a working figurehead who could relate to other organizations. One government official put it succinctly when I asked him about my involvement with other Boards, committees and arts councils. He said, "The other arts do it; either the crafts field takes its place within the total arts scene or it becomes third rate". I ended my letter by stating that I did not believe that I had served the Crafts Council to the best of my ability in the last year. I did not believe that this was my fault. It was a year of indecision and non-direction from the Board. It was a holding year, a year that I found especially frustrating as, for example, brochures ran out and could not be reprinted. I was involved in four Boards and twenty other committees. I asked that the Board of Trustees of the O.C.C. specifically appoint people to represent the O.C.C. on these Boards. Ultimately I sensed that certain Board members saw my reading of my job definition as non-direction on my part.

I received letters of regret from three of the four community colleges with which I was working. Letters came from Visual Arts Ontario, the

Art gallery of Ontario, the Artisans Guild of Hamilton, Page Publications, the Canadian Society for Education through Art, the Peel Board of Education and crafts people such as Ruth Gowdy McKinley, Helen Francis Gregor; Lois Etherington, Stephen Harris, Donald Stuart, Ann Suzuki, Gail Bradshaw, Steven Levy, Jean Burke and Hart Massey. I am enclosing a copy of the letter from Hart Massey as I feel it was particularly eloquent.

I had gone to the World Crafts Council Conference in Mexico in 1976. I also attended the World Crafts Council Conference in Japan in the late summer of 1978. I enjoyed being with the Canadian group of crafts people on this trip. I did not attend any of the business meetings. I enjoyed myself and immersed myself in the culture of Japan. I was finished with the Ontario Crafts Council and waiting to begin my work at the Gallery Stratford.

The following letter was one of those received defending me:

hart massey + durham house rr 1 port hope ontario L1A 3V5 + 416 885 5038

Dear Mr. Mantegna,

I have recently learned, with some surprise, of the decision by the Ontario Crafts Council to terminate the employment of Paul Bennett. As a member of the Ontario Crafts Council and as one who has followed the evolution of craft organisations in Ontario with much interest this decision comes as a great shock and one I can only view with misgivings.

As Executive Director of the Ontario Crafts Council Paul Bennett has brought to the position a degree of professional competence which has contributed in great measure to the position the official crafts organisation of Ontario now holds, both with those organisations concerned with the arts generally and in government circles. This has no doubt contributed to the credibility of the Ontario Crafts Council as a truly professional body, competent to look after its own affairs and, therefore, to the obtaining of funds from various sources to further its goals.

It seems to me that if it is necessary to reduce the budget of the O.C.C. that there must be other ways this could be accomplished without causing so much damage to the good name of your organisation and its ability to function competently at a professional level. If the crafts in Ontario are to achieve the status they deserve they must be served by people of high calibre such as Paul Bennett. A return to the amateurism which plagued the craft organisations in the past is, surely, unthinkable. I would,

cont'd...

hart massey + durham house rr 1 port hope ontario L1A 3V5 + 416 885 5038

therefore, like by this letter to protest,most strongly, a desision which I feel is wrong and possibly disastrous.   It is to be hoped very much that the directors of the Council may have the wisdom to reconsider their decision before its consequences are felt.

For your information I am also sending this letter to Joan Chalmers and Stephen Hogbin.

Yours sincerely,

Hart Massey

Hart Massey.

Chapter Sixteen

Fur and Feathers

The Cat House

Until recently I have only had a fleeting acquaintance over the years with cats. My first knowledge of them came when I bought my guesthouse, "Crackers" in Stratford. I made friends with Mrs. Emma Schade, the dear lady who owned this Edwardian house. In fact we were good friends until her death at the age of ninety-eight in 1994. Emma sold me her house at a reduction far below the original price because I had agreed to keep and look after her two cats, she was going into an apartment and could not take them with her. I also agreed to take good care of the flower gardens and open up the five ponds that had been closed for many years - we were both hoping I could bring back to the garden some of its former beauty.

I really did not get to know those two cats very well. One simply took off and we could never recover it. I believe that she was missing Emma Schade. The other missed the first cat and with Emma's approval, her old cleaning lady, who loved animals, took the cat. My only real memory of this last black cat was of waking up one night and finding the animal sitting on the bedpost of my old Victorian bed and staring intently at me with large luminous eyes. It frightened me almost to death. I was not familiar with the habits of cats then and I had heard tales of old Egypt where cats would lie on top on people, children especially, and smother their breathing

The next time I experienced cats was quite recently. My sister Joan's companion had died and I suggested that Joan move in with me in Port Hope. At that time she was living alone in a very large house out in the country at the bottom of a hill that was difficult to negotiate in the winter. We had to renovate my house considerably converting a duplex into a single dwelling and so I packed up my furniture and moved in with her for six months while the work was being done.

Joan had a cat named Amanda, Mandy, for short. It had a history. Mandy had been a stray in the Florida neighbourhood where Joan and

Joan's partner, also named Joan, and a friend Ethel had owned a winter home for many years under which three stray cats were living, including Mandy. Of course the girls were feeding them over the winter, and leaving food with a permanent resident in the park to be doled out in the summer. The cats were very wary and skittish, as several attempts had been made to capture and remove them! However one day Mandy came up to Joan who was filling the water bowl, allowed Joan to pet her and decided to belong. For a couple of years Mandy travelled back and forth between Ontario and Florida until the girls sold their Florida home and brought Mandy back to Canada permanently.

Mandy was very shy, it slipped around almost: like a ghost. Joan Frith was an invalid by this time often sleeping in the daytime and staying awake all night long. Mandy was her cat at night; they would play games together as Mandy raced around the living room. One night a friendly mouse came out of its hole and Mandy jumped up on the coffee table to escape this monster. Mandy then became my sister Joan's cat during the day, when it lived a more sedate life.

I moved up to Rice Lake and slept in Joan Frith's bedroom. I would get up at night and find the cat sitting on the chesterfield in the living room right across from my door. It too, was watching me with large luminous eyes. Unfortunately by this time it was becoming quite old; we were finally moving down to our renovated house, the cat developed cancer and much to Joan's distress, had to be put to sleep.

Joan has never bought a cat, but for many decades, she has had several Siamese and other cats, all of which in one way or another arrived by chance at her door. This time a neighbour knew of Joan's affinity for these animals and told us of a stray that he had been feeding every morning. It obviously needed a home. A very old man in a very old house under a railway bridge had had a house full of cats and we did not know what had happened to them after his death. Perhaps this was one that had not been rounded up by the Humane Society. Of course we adopted Marmalade, Marmy for short. It was scrawny, with matted ginger fur, and the vet told us that it had the feline equivalent of AIDS. The vet suggested that we

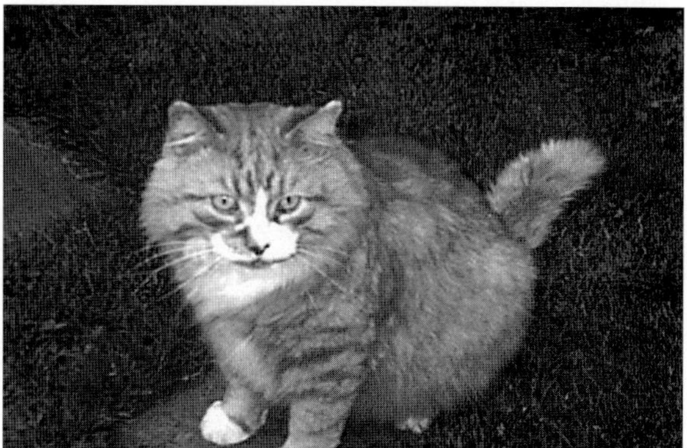

should not allow it to wander the neighbourhood because it might get into a fight and spread this disease.

Joan started to feed Marmy and I started to groom him every morning just after breakfast. She fed him and fed him, as he would not stop eating. When he reached eighteen pounds Joan checked some cat books and discovered that Marmy just might be a Maine Coon cat, all his characteristics suggested it, they go up to thirty pounds in weight! He is the most loving cat that Joan has ever owned, he will sleep on her chest, something I cannot stand, then move after a while to the side of her bed. Sometimes he will grace one corner of my bed (and banish Andy to the floor). Marmy loves everybody: people, other cats, even dogs.

Let us turn to Andy, my part-Dalmatian dog, he has always chased cats because they always run away from him. He attempted to chase Marm. Marmy turned on him and there was a great show of shadow boxing mixed with barking and large hisses. Marmy finally chased Andy four times around the island in the kitchen until the poor animal was dissolved into a cowering mass of dog flesh.

He went around the perimeter of every room that the cat was in for two weeks until Marmy decided it was time to make friends. Marmy went over and sat across Andy's front paws with Andy looking slightly wild-eyed. I took a picture of this event.

Now they are great friends and sit close together quite often. I nicknamed Marmy "Attila" because of his fighting prowess. Now I call him "Pumpkin" for obvious reasons.

Then along came Moggy, another phone call for help. Some people said a neighbour up the street had said that we were looking for a cat! These people were leaving town the next day and were going to have

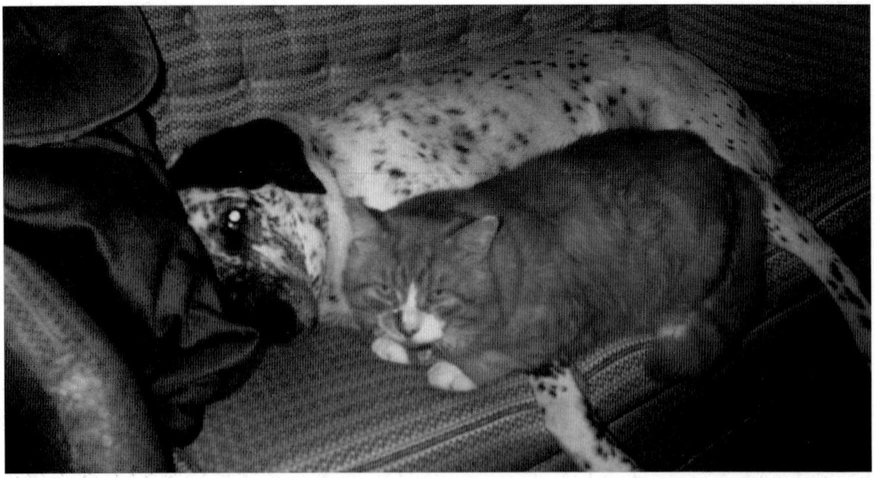

to take their cat to the shelter. Joan and I went to see it and of course fell in love with a beautiful longhaired white and tan cat. We brought it home. The name Moggy, evidently, is an old English term for cat. It .had some peculiar habits that we had to adapt to. It did not drink for three days. Then Joan noticed that it climbed up on her bathtub and reached over and lapped water from the drip coming from the faucet. It would only drink from moving water! I went out and bought a serenity pool complete with a fountain and a small mountain of pebbles. Moggy immediately took to this addition to the kitchen and went over and drank greedily from the fountain when it was turned on. Some of his other habits I will not discuss. I have been told that if you want to add suspense to a story just leave some parts of it a mystery.

Moggy had to cope with Andy. He did it a different way. He disappeared and lived in the attic for a few days on a windowsill. He would come down when Andy was not round. Then we put a child's gate across a stairway. Moggy, complete with a dish of food and a dish of water, could come and go through a crack that Andy could not negotiate. That went on for a while. Finally familiarity bred acceptance and the two actually began to pass each other without fear. Now all is well.

We have a neighbour who has a number of indoor cats. He also has a small, old mother cat that had had a number of litters and lived in an old driveshed on his property. The whole brood of mother and five siblings, all which survived from three different litters, would go to his kitchen each morning, actually go into the house, eat and flee without being touched.

I was worried about these cats in the winter. Last winter, I took a dog pen, put a dog heater in the bottom of it — I had this left from when I went to Cuba, a few years ago and had to leave my two dogs in a friend's barn for two weeks during February — added blankets and insulation and made a warm house for the strays. All was well, the cats moved in. Then one night something, likely a raccoon, found this haven. I found some blood the next morning although I do not think that any cat was killed, but they never returned. I realized that what they had lacked in their shelter was an escape hatch.

This winter I built with more skill. My first attempt at floor level on the deck did not work, everything got wet in the rain. Then I opened out a wooden chaise lounge, covered it with a plastic base, placed the heater which measured three feet by eighteen inches on a blanket, filled in the sides with an old sleeping bag, a pillow and some blankets, covered the whole contraption over with a large piece of liner that I had left from my pool construction, made two doors for pur-

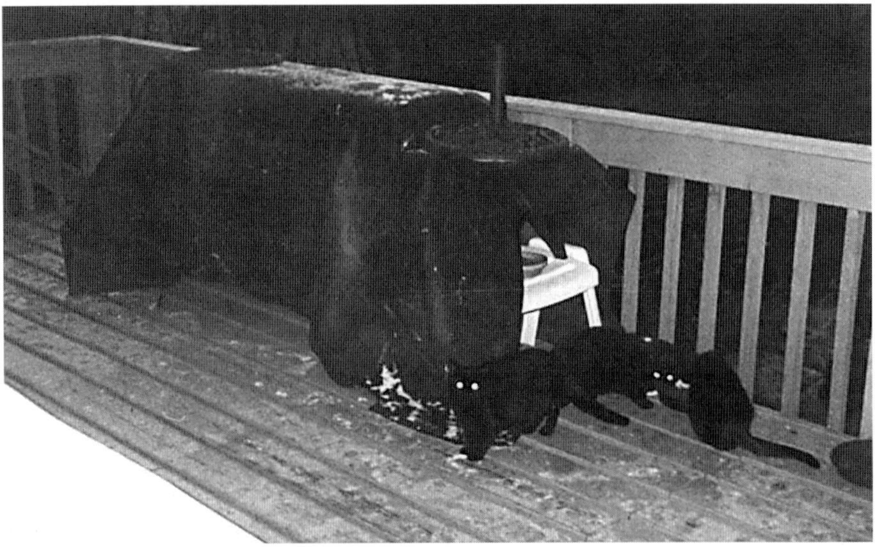

poses of escape, weighed everything down with two iron lawn umbrella stands, added a porch at each end, extended the top cover to keep the porches out of the wind and rain, added a double flap of towels as doors to keep out the cold winter wind and turned on the heater. I placed a bowl of water nearby that we change twice a day as it freezes over — we actually add boiling water and that melts the ice that has formed — we finally added two bowls for food that we fill twice a day. We put in two bowls because Marmie has decided to act as host and joins the strays quite often at mealtime. Marmie has developed a delightful relation ship with the mother cat: When he goes out on the deck she immediately runs over and greets him, lavishing kisses (licks) on his head which he returns. Then they sit companionably side by side staring out over the garden.

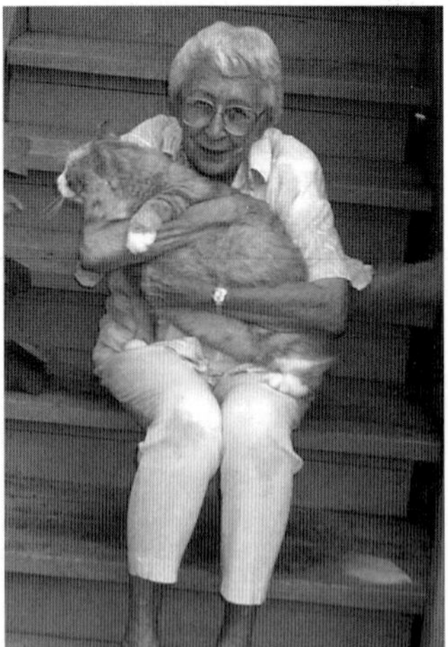

My sister Joan has named our cat house tenants: the kittens (all black but one) are named Midnight Green, Yellow and Blue; according to their eye colour; then there is Midnight Mama and also Checkers — in comparison to his siblings, a startling black and white. The sixth member of this feline family, a somewhat elusive cat, is a very dark and lustrous brown. He is a loner who comes and goes and seldom socializes with his siblings. What else could we call him but Sable? Occasionally the cats are joined by a large black and white that, we think, must have fathered Checkers. Other strays appear from time to time for a meal but they do not stay long. Midnight Mama keeps an eye on all of her brood; often they are eating when I take Andy out to the dog run, she will leave the food and run over to the steps to act as scout, watching Andy carefully so that when he comes up the steps she can tell the other busy ones when to duck into the cat house. I have become a dog and cat person.

Birds — Zebra Finches, Canaries and Budgies

For a number of years I would visit my sister Joan, the other Joan and Ethel at their Florida home in Vero Beach for a period during each winter. Once I stayed for almost a month, but usually it was for only two weeks, Twice Jay went down with me and we had a very pleasant time.

The girls were antique dealers and, every Saturday morning Joan would love to go out garage saleing. I would join her. She would check the papers; she had a grid system whereby she could list the sales in such an order that not too much time would be wasted driving from one to another. She had a special style of driving on a Saturday morning that was quite different from her usual driving; it was quite daring and reckless with amazing turns and spurts of speed that amazed me. Once I remember that she spotted a garage sale sign pointing down a street just as we entered an intersection, she wheeled to the right and immediately the siren of a police car came on right behind us.

We stopped and Joan played the little old lady act, she scrunched down, and (she is quite small already and looked as if she could not see over the windshield) she answered the officer's questions with a sprightly style agreeing with everything he said. She agreed that she should have turned on her directional signal half way down the last block; she thanked him for his vigilance and — did not receive a ticket.

One Saturday we came to a house that offered a pair of Zebra finches for sale; one of these finches looked out of its little nest and cocked its head at me as much as to say," I would like to live in Canada." I was hooked. I did not buy the pair but for the next hour I talked about them until Joan turned her car around, a great sacrifice for her on her Saturday rounds, and we went back to that particular sale. The pair had been sold. I went into mourning. A friend of Joan's heard of my disappointment and a few days later turned up with a beautiful pair of these little birds complete with a cage and food. She gave them to me. I was delighted.

I went to the authorities and secured the right papers to import the birds into Canada. We loaded the car for our return home. The birds were perched on the back seat and properly covered to keep them from too much stress on the trip. We arrived safely back in Stratford. I went into the business of being a bird fancier; the birds went into the business of breeding — and they never stopped. I bought a huge cage 18 inches by 18 inches and three and a half feet high. In fact I ended up with three of these cages. I started giving birds to friends, then to anybody. I swear that people started crossing the street when they saw me especially if they had their children with them because I did get rid of some birds by appealing to the children first and letting them work on their parents. Finally, some people actually believe that I left Stratford because I had run out of friends. That is not true; I left for family reasons.

I decided to diversify. I bought a pair of canaries. They were a lovely colour and for a while I enjoyed the joyous song of the male as he serenaded his mate. I had moved to Cobourg and bought an old house with a large sunroom across the back facing south. It was a lovely spot to place my cages of birds and I did enjoy them. Unfortunately the first female canary died. I could not find a female canary in Cobourg and so I tried in a pet stare in Stratford where I was attending a play. There was a pair of them, a beautiful white in colour'. Unthinking, and now that I think of it, very callously, I; bought the female and broke up the pair. She arrived in Cobourg, and two weeks later she died, I am sure of a broken heart.

Finally, I found a matching female in Cobourg. I bought her and much to my delight she presented the male with a clutch of eggs soon after. But they were infertile and did not hatch. Finally, I removed them. She did this three times. Finally I watched as she left the nest, hopped down from perch to perch to the bottom of the cage, lay down and died. I was broken-hearted and gave the male away.

I still had the finches and they had slowed down in their activities. I had a neighbour who was moving and asked if I would like a pair of budgies that she had given to her two young daughters. She said that the girls had been fond of them for a period but, typical of children, had lost interest. I went in to the home where everything was packed up. There were the two birds in a small cage placed in a corner of a bare room with no seed or water. Of course I took them and budgies have been a joy to me ever since.

The pair turned out to be two females. First I bought one male and then a second. After two years a female died as she had become egg bound. One feels so helpless with birds; there are very few vets that have the knowledge to look after them. Birds lose their energy so quickly and then are gone: One has to have a heart of stone and look to the positive to have birds for any length of time. I bought another female and finally I seemed to have made the right balance.

Breeders tell me that you should have three pairs of budgies in a large cage in order to have them start breeding. Well I had two pairs. I placed two breeding stations, across the top of the cage and I was recompensed for all my heartbreak in the past.

At first the two boxes were deserted for a long period of time, then one of the females started to go in and out of both of them. I had placed wood shavings inside each but she started to throw it out of one side. Her mate started to feed her and make a great fuss over her. There came a time when the male mounted her, there was a great fluttering of wings and a balancing act equal to the Cirque du Soleil. The female started to lay an egg every other day until six eggs were in the nesting box. She incubated them immediately. I could watch what was going on through a window in the side of the box. Often canary breeders will take the eggs away from the female birds and replace them with false eggs until all the eggs have been laid. Then they return the real ones to the nest, they are incubated all at once, and all are born on the same day. I did not do that.

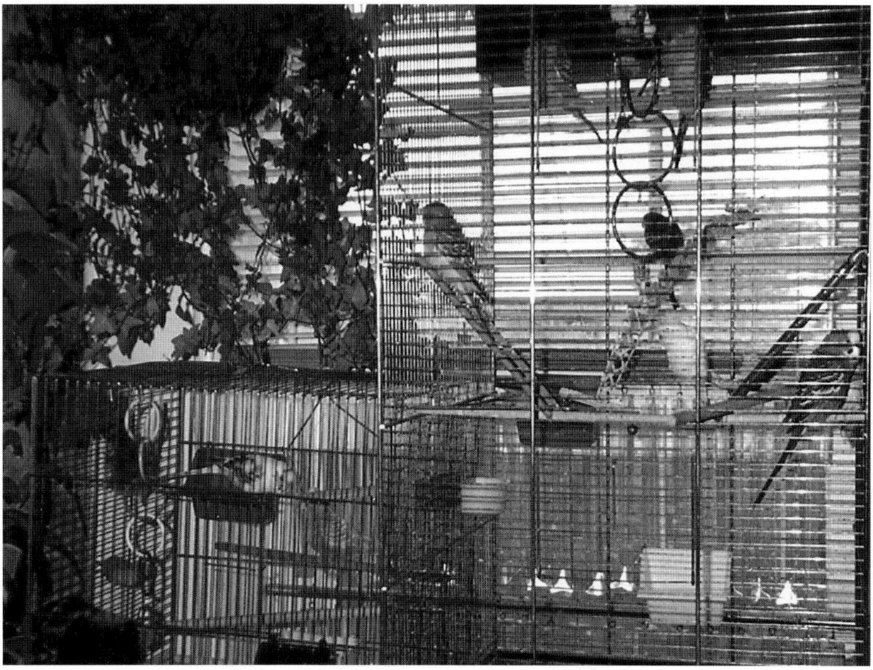

My female incubated as she went along and consequently the chicks started hatching at two day intervals after the regulation eighteen days of incubation; this meant that the first hatched were quite a size by the time the youngest were born. Five chicks were born from the six eggs.

Each morning I would sit in my whirlpool in the bathroom and watch the antics of the birds. Suddenly I realized the meaning of the passage in the bible, Matthew 10, verses 29 to 31, which tells us that not one sparrow shall fall to the ground without God knowing. My world enlarged in terms of the birds and became very important. I watched a family and community effort of the little beings that amazed me. Was it instinct or did they actually communicate together. They certainly made enough noise as they looked at each other. The father fed the mother through the front door and through a small window at one side. The chicks grew with amazing speed. The oldest appeared almost the size of the mother before the youngest, a scrawny little thing the size of your fingernail, was out of its shell.

The chicks were voracious and now the community of four adult birds came into action. First there was the occasional giving of food to the mother but as the days went on and the chicks got larger and larger they started to appear at the door of the box and the other birds started to feed them directly.

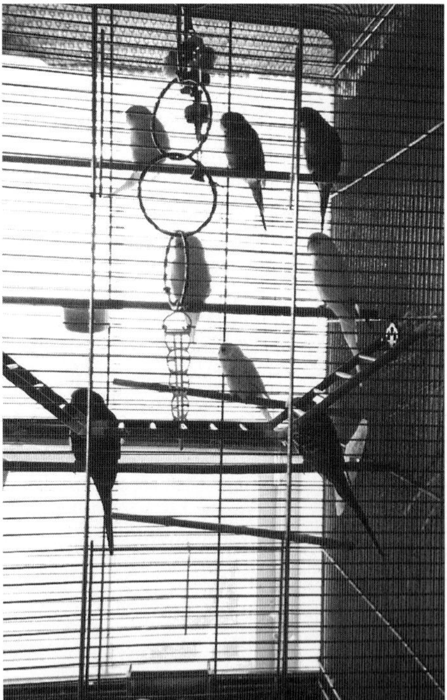

Then came the day when the oldest lingered in the door sticking its head out over the others. Then it stood on the edge and swayed back and forth. Finally it actually stood on the perch on the outside and when I returned to watch it was flying with great awkwardness from perch to perch. I watched the birds, one by one, as they repeated this procedure every two days. When the final moment came to fly the four adults always had their backs to the chicks so as not to embarrass them in their first fragile flights. Obviously, I am not an ornithologist, I do not use the right scientific terms, and I have taken too long in describing this phenomenon. Somehow it widened the world for me at a time, just after September 9th in New York when I saw men, the creators of great wonders in this world, falling like ants from the windows of one of their own greatest creations.

The five young were a variety of colours. The oldest appeared to be an albino; it is pure white and quite beautiful. Then came one with a yellow head and yellow streaking in its back feathers. Its tail is black with dark brown and it has white wing feathers; the other three are all blue on their bodies with black and white wings. They are a motley crew.

I now have only one cage of five budgies. I gave away my finches some time ago. People often ask me if I have taught my birds to talk. The answer is a resounding no. I like them in a natural state. I hate it when man, in his conceit has to imprint his own stamp on another being. That is why, when I receive a phone call from a policeman asking me to support the police effort to send children to a circus that is coming to town, I say no. I refuse to support children seeing an animal being forced to do tricks for their masters, man seemingly the superior being. But is he?

The Dog House

I was in my 30s before I owned my first dog. I had rented apartments for many years. Then I was able to rent a large house on Bedford Road in Toronto and I decided to get a dog. I bought a German Shepherd pup, an Alsatian to give it its other name. I was visiting my parents in Newcastle when the opportunity came along.

I named the puppy after a friend of mine who had just left Toronto and moved to Vancouver. He was Dutch and in Dutch his first name was Jannes, meaning John. Jannes was as adorable as all puppies are; he was black, white and silver and grew into a magnificent animal, a perfect German Shepherd. I trained him well and he went everywhere with me. I even took him one weekend to Rochester when I visited the art gallery there with a friend.

Then came the sad part. I was given a Canada Council grant to spend almost a year in Europe. I had applied for it. I was to study the training of museum personnel and extension services for galleries and museums. I had to leave Jannes when he was only two years old

I arranged for my sister and brother-in-law to look after him. In retrospect I know now that they really were not keen on the prospect. I

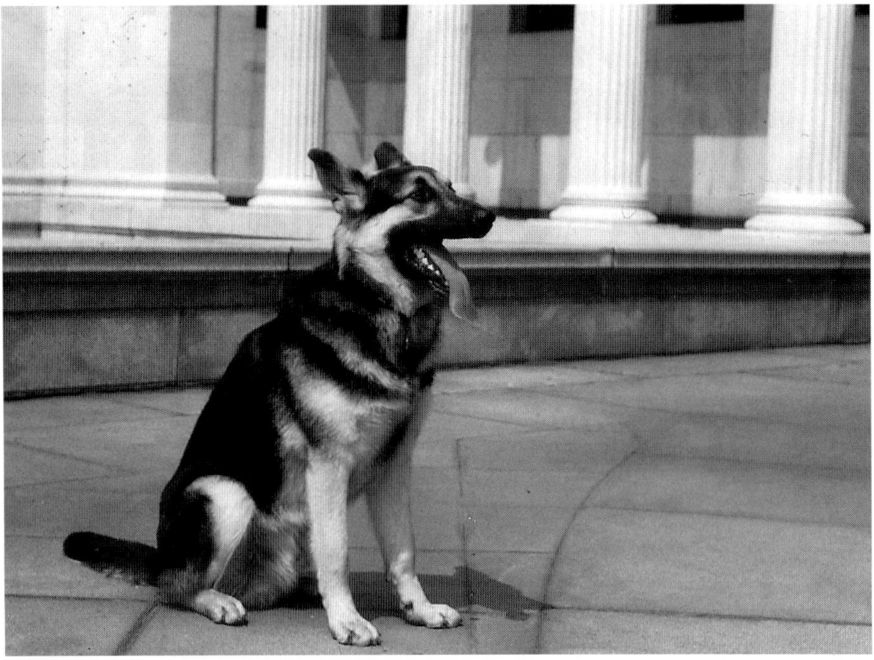

almost forced Jannes on them because I had no other place to leave him. I went overseas and had a frantic letter from my friend, Neil MacVicar, who had been sharing part of the house with me. Jannes had run away from my sister's and Neil immediately drove down to my sister's home in Grafton. Jannes had been found wandering miles away on a side road. Neil very kindly took him away, drove up to his father's farm just outside Ottawa, and left him there where he was very well treated. Mr. MacVicar was a widower living alone who had grandchildren frequently visiting him, and Jannes became a regular farm dog. When I returned to Canada I had to go to Ottawa and went out to the farm with Neil. Jannes did not recognize me; as Neil said, dogs get revenge also.

Some years later in 1971 I bought an Irish Setter for Jay, He had had an old farm dog when I first met him, but the dog had died. I remember finding a breeder in Western Ontario and driving there where I picked up the puppy and then drove up to Jay's farm. That night, in spite of having an alarm clock ticking away beside him, he howled away because he missed his mother.

I went down the lovely winding stairs in the front hall, brought the pup up from the basement and when Jay's mother came down the stairs in the morning, she found me curled up on the rug in the front hall asleep with the puppy nestled on my chest. Jess, the dog, grew into a fine red dog with a beautiful coat and was with Jay for many years.

When I went to Stratford I wanted a dog again. I now had a home and a place for a dog run. I had become interested in English setters and especially liked what were called orange beltons, the brown and white dogs. I had come to know Les and Gail Harrison in nearby Mitchell: they raised these dogs. Gail belonged to a group of breeders who looked out for English setters who, for one reason or another, had lost their homes. They placed these dogs. She arranged for me to have Andy, an orange belton, whose real name was Brandyrun's Special K.

He had a certificate of registration from the Canadian Kennel Club and had been born in Brantford. He was a beautiful dog and we took to each other immediately.

I moved from Water Street to Crackers on Erie Street in Stratford and opened my bed and breakfast place with an antique store attached. By this time I had left the Gallery Stratford and decided to be my own boss. One day a man came into my shop and said, "Oh, you have an English setter". I agreed, it was obvious. He then added, "I have a blue belton female English setter and I am going to have to put her down because we are moving to Australia at the end of the week and nobody will take her." I immediately asked about her. She was four years old, had never been fixed, her name was Saskia — named after Rembrandt's famous model because when she was a puppy she used to do little "Rembrandt's" all over the kitchen floor! The man said she had a nice head. I knew immediately that she must be overweight, whenever anybody says that about a dog I realize the reason. Anyway I said that I would take her. The man was delighted, the next day I drove to London and picked her up. She was a delightful dog and just jumped into the car and came away with me, tail wagging.

They had had her on a pill, I did not know there were such things for a dog. Anyway, two weeks after she arrived she went into heat, she had never had puppies before this time. Andy did the gentlemanly thing out in the dog run and after the requisite amount of time, Sally — I had changed her name — presented Andy and myself with four puppies. They were adorable, two blue

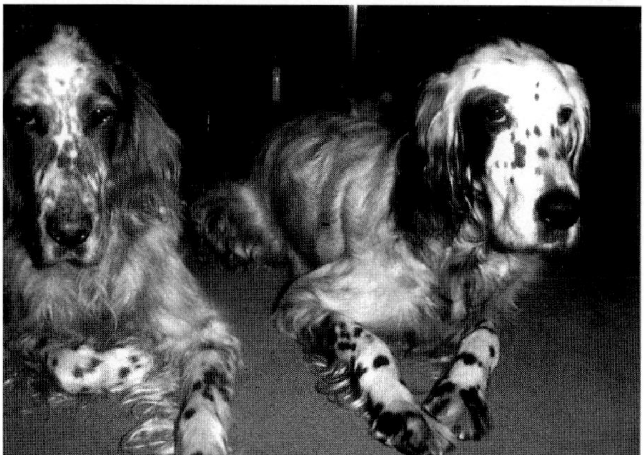

belton, two orange belton, two male and two female. Each sex with one of each colour, a perfect combination.

I had built Sally a birthing box in the basement. This was a large area of plywood about four feet across surrounded by a wall about six inches high with a ridge all around it so that a puppy could seek protection under the overhang and the mother could not roll on it. Sally was a good mother and fed the puppies all they needed. I have pictures of her standing in the dog run a few weeks later and all the puppies are reaching up under her for a meal.

I registered the pups (1986) and advertised for potential owners. They came eagerly. One was sold to Diana Graham of Durham, a friend of Jay's. She bought the one I had named "Orphan Annie" for some reason I can no longer remember. She renamed the dog "Chelsea" and I still keep in touch with her after all these years. She would send me an occasional picture of Chelsea; he was the blue belton male, lolling in grandeur on a rolling lawn. The orange belton male went to a gay United Church minister in Quebec. He and his partner came to Crackers to pick up "Zack" as they had decided to call him.

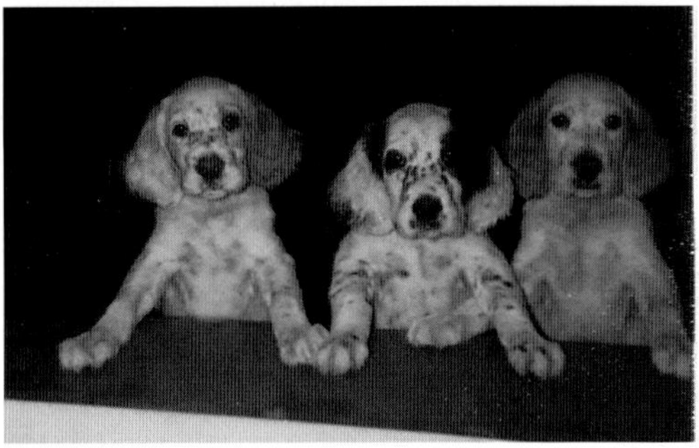

I visited them in Montreal when I was in that city a year later. Another pup went to a young lad in London who returned a year later and bought a second puppy from the next litter. The first pup had slipped through a fence and been killed on the street by a car. The last puppy went to a lighting man and his wife from the Stratford Theatre.

Sally had three puppies the next year, and then the following year something went wrong; she turned her back on two of the new pups and would not feed them. I gave them to my vet. His wife used an eyedropper to bring them through the early stages, and they survived. One other also survived but I felt it was time to stop the birthing and so I had her spayed.

The excitement and pleasure of those pups was one of the highlights of my life. Andy and Sally both lived to a good age for large dogs. When the time came I held each one in my arms and let each one know that it was surrounded by love as the vet gave it a needle and it quietly put its head down on my arm. It is so sad that a beloved pet lives for such a short time compared to man's own life. Let us hope

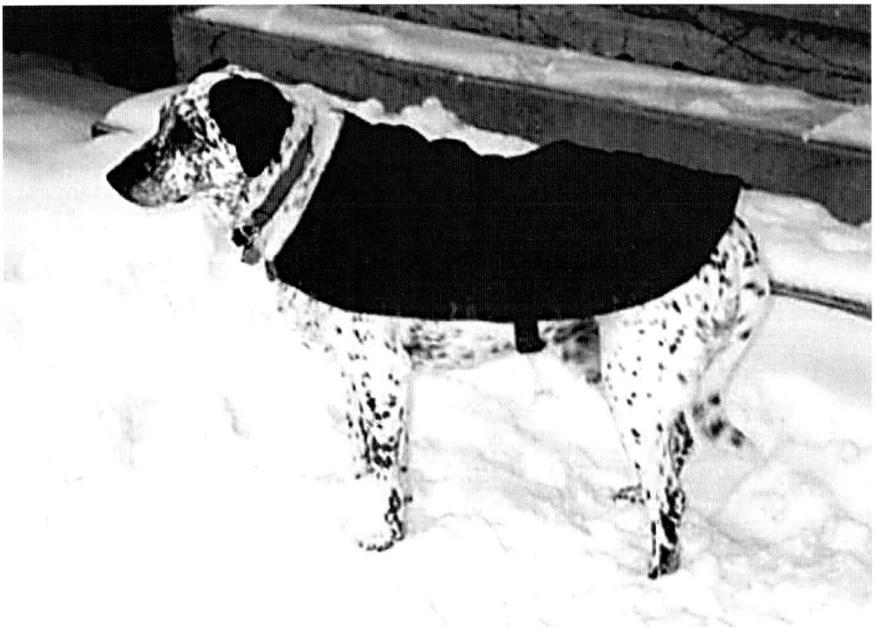

that the vision of all one's pets waiting for one in the beyond and then running up and surrounding one with love, eagerness and energy, is a true one.

My next dog is still with me at this date of writing. He must know that I am talking about him because he just got up from under the table where I am writing on my word processor and moved over to a large floor pillow. Andy is old now; he is half Dalmatian; as for the other half, who knows? Andy came to me through a friend, Pat Wilson of Stratford. I went for a while without a dog but I kept looking, One day I was visiting Pat, who at that time lived out in the country, and she mentioned that there was a stray dog running around from a nearby farm.

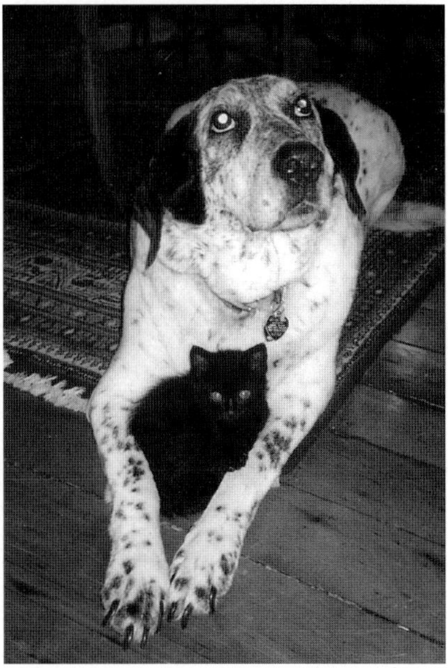

I saw it, liked it and brought it home. It also, had been named Andy. Andy's mother was a purebred Dalmatian and all her other pups looked like Dalmatians except Andy. The mother lived on a farm and evidently when she was in heat more than one male dog had visited her. I did not know that this was possible but Andy is proof. He is somewhat chunky with black ears and nose and a white body covered with a scattering of black spots of all sizes over the rest of his body. He follows me from room to room in spite of arthritis for which I am now paying one hundred and thirty dollars a month for pills for the disease and liquid for the pain, He laboriously follows me up and down stairs each time I change floors.

Andy has only one fault and he will never change. If he sees a dog his own size or smaller while he is out driving in the car, he will bark furiously at it until it is out of sight. A bigger dog and he is sensible and does not bark. All the time he creates this racket, he is wagging his tail. Now, if we see the same dog and he is not in the car, he will not bark; after all he is no longer protected and he might get into a fight. The same rule applies for wearing a lead or running free. He is a very smart dog. As Andy is now getting old and a little near-sighted, we are having more peace in the car.

One other dog deserves mention. She was an orange belton English setter and she came to me the same way through Mrs. Gail Harrison. She was with me at the same time as my present Andy, but she did not live so long. Her name was Jenny. Jenny actually was the name of my Grandmother. When I had my colt up at Jay's I named her after my Grandmother, Mother always told me that Grandmother loved horse

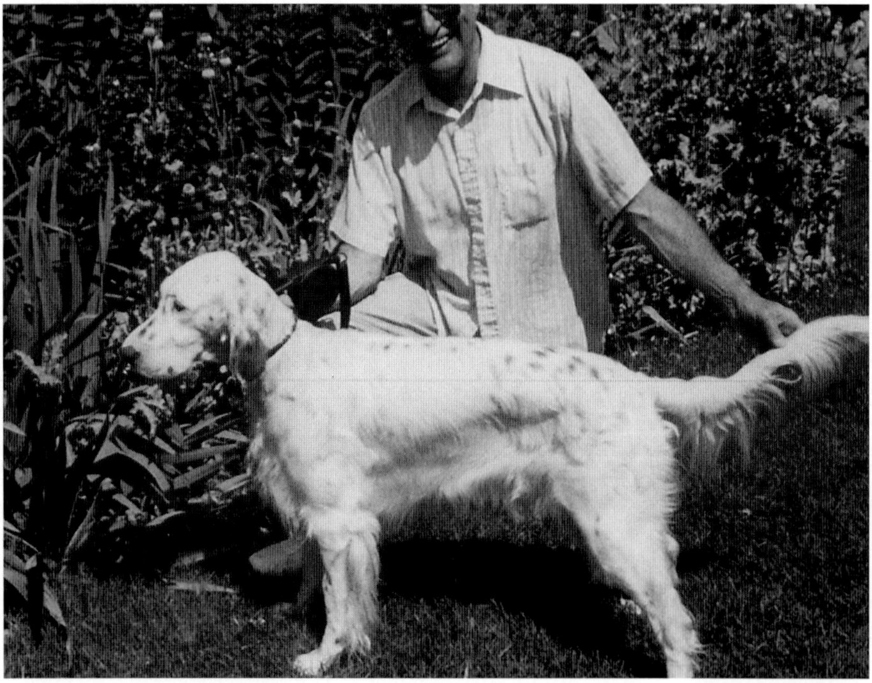

racing; so naming the colt after her was meant as an honour. When the new dog arrived, she ran so beautifully that I thought she deserved the name of Jenny also.

I received Jenny on one condition. The previous owner, when the time came, could breed her to another registered setter and take all the puppies but leave one with me. I readily agreed.

I had her X-rayed before she was to be bred and I discovered that she had hip displacia. The previous owner then wanted nothing to do with her and I never did get her registration papers. I did not want them anyway for I was quite happy to have the beautiful dog without the trappings. Andy and Jenny got along well for many years but once more the age factor interfered and I reached the stage where I had to carry Jenny's back end up the stairs as she walked up with her front legs. One more sorrowful trip to the vet.

I have had other dogs for brief periods of time. I was able to gain custody of a dog from a woman in Cobourg at the same house where I found the budgies. This beautiful black mix was living outside in the winter, tied up and sleeping on a bit of sacking in a garage. The children went past him back and forth to school and paid him no attention! Once a day he was given food and I had often gone over and found him without water. I had words with the woman and the dog landed at my place. He was used to the outside and it was winter so I made him the type of home that I made later for the cats, complete with heater. He was in absolute comfort. He played with my dogs. Late at night I remember watching from the sunroom window; the moon was bright, and he was running around and around the swimming pool as fast as he could go letting off steam — he was like a beautiful, silent, black wolf. I found a home for him with a retired music teacher.

Finally, I inherited a dog from my cousin when he died. My two cousins, man and wife, had had two little dogs which they absolutely adored. Each dog was so fat it was like a pillow with legs at each corner. The dogs used to sit, one beside each of my cousins at the dining table. A forkful would go in a human mouth and a forkful would go to a dog; it was unbelievable. Any way the dogs passed to their reward in good time. June and Art were lonely and they saw a cute little puppy and took it in. It turned out to be half Labrador and half Newfoundland and grew huge! My cousins were both in their eighties. I had promised to look after the dog if it ever became necessary.

On Christmas Eve I received a phone call. I was living in Cobourg. On Christmas Day I drove to Stratford and rescued the dog. The family waited dinner until I got back late in the day. My cousins had always been

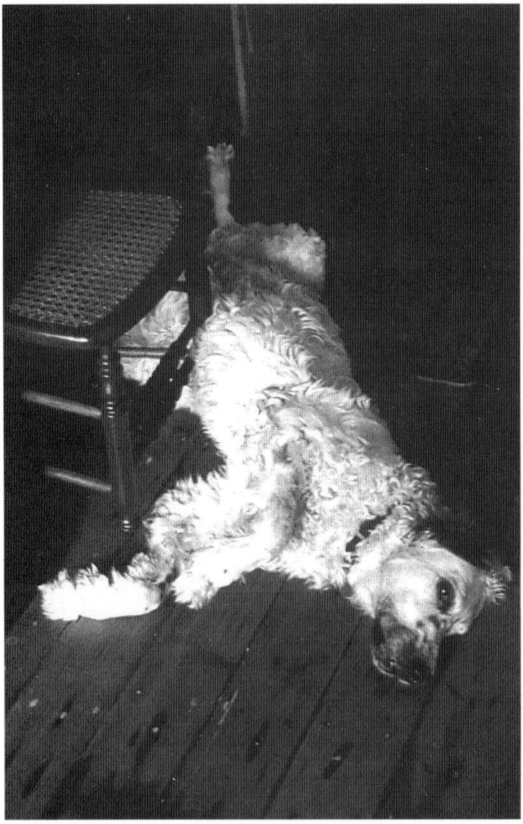

prosperous and had kept their beautiful home neat and tidy. But they had both grown old and frail. I was horrified to find their home a complete shambles. June did not come out to see me, as she was too upset at losing Robbie. When Art looked out the door at me putting Robbie in the car he had a haunted look, and I guessed that I would never see him alive again. I found out later that the two of them had been so worried that they might be separated and put into hospital that they hid their plight from everybody; neighbours, friends and family.

Two days later a neighbour phoned me. June had been found wandering down the road in her nightgown. It was winter weather and she was looking for help. Art was dead in the living room. I drove back to Stratford as quickly as I could. June was immediately put into hospital. She was my blood relative as our mothers had been sisters.

June and Art had moved from Montreal to Stratford to be close to me. They were rather strange because although we were in the same city, they did not stay in touch with me on a regular basis. Occasionally I used to buy them things at the Saturday market. Art would usually meet me at the door but I was not often asked into the house. Once a year, when my sister Joan came to Stratford to see some plays, we would be asked to lunch and the house would be spotless and the two of them very gracious. I had been named the executor of their estate and since Art's death I have been looking after June. I go to see her every weekday. She is in a nursing facility three blocks from my home.

I thought I might keep Robbie but when he started to fight with Andy I found him a good home in the country on two acres of land with a companion dog. I had met a woman who owned an ice cream parlour and greatly admired Robbie. I remembered her enthusiasm for the dog and went back to see her; she took him on trial and he made a great hit with the family. Since I had promised to look after Robbie that might have been interpreted as keeping him, but I was not able to do so. I did the best I could and I am sure that he is happy.

So ends the story of my pets, which can require a great deal of one's time, are expensive to maintain and often create a nuisance. But science has proved that people with pets live longer than people without them. I, for one, could not imagine an existence without the presence of these wonderful creatures.

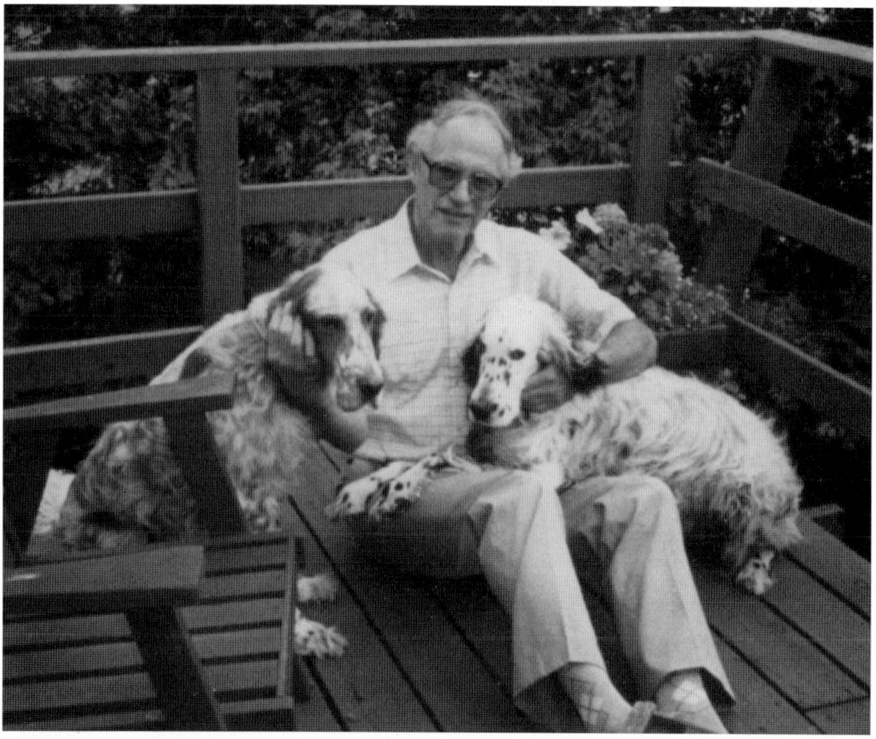

Chapter Seventeen

The Gallery Stratford, 1978-1984

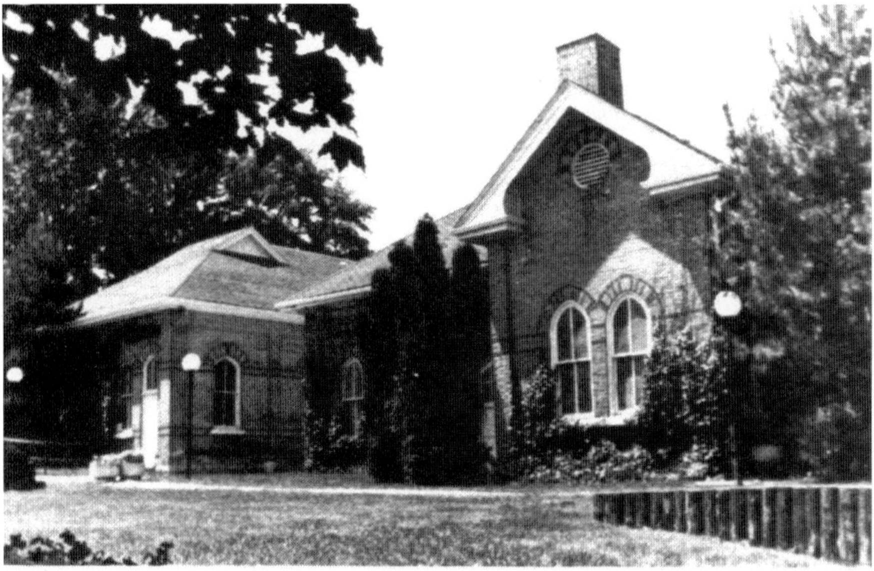

The first director of the Rothmans Gallery of Stratford was Robert Ihrig. He was followed by Robert Swain, who resigned in 1978. The position of Director was advertised in the Globe and Mail on June 23rd of that year. As I had left the O.C.C. I applied for the position in Stratford. The Selection Committee interviewed me at the home of the president, Mrs. Ann Gregory and I officially joined the gallery staff in the middle of October.

Before I move on to my work at the Gallery Stratford I would like to take the time to pay tribute to the best president that I was ever privileged to work with, Mrs. Ann Gregory. I have dealt with many Boards of Trustees. In our democratic society, the idea of a volunteer board to oversee and govern non-profit organizations is the standard approach.

This works well in the best situations but can be hell in the worst. Ann Gregory made my arrival at Stratford into a win/win situation. The professional staff had the confidence and cooperation of the Board and vice versa. There was an official Board meeting each month. Ann always asked me to lunch on the day of the meeting so that we could go over the agenda together, discuss it, and come up with possible solutions to present to the Board. Ann, herself, was gracious, could command respect with her quiet voice, had a good knowledge of the visual arts and was developing an excellent collection in her own home. She was interested in the programmes at the gallery and was usually present at gallery functions. I could not ask for a better president. Thank you, Ann Gregory.

The gallery itself had an interesting history. The Stratford Art Society was founded in 1945 to provide classes taught by well-known artists and an annual exhibition. It began a permanent collection and an art rental service. It needed gallery space but found that it had to be incorporated in order to receive assistance: so The Stratford Art Association came into existence in 1965.

The city had just bought a new pump station and had vacated the old 1880 Victorian/Gothic pump house on Romeo Street. The Association decided to make it into a centennial project: to renovate the two buildings and turn them into an Art Gallery. I had visited Stratford in those early days. I remember that after a lecture the executive of the Association took me over to Romeo Street to see the site. The entire group was excited and full of plans. A brochure was produced, eight thousand dollars was raised, and Robert Ihrig was hired as Director. Ihrig approached Rothmans. They became excited over the whole project and ended up funding the complete renovation.

Rothmans brought in an architect and the present single structure is the result of the imaginative joining of the two buildings. Over the years Rothmans donated more than a million dollars to the gallery. Funding ceased in 1974 with changing personnel and policies at the company. Funds were left however to assist in the transition period of the gallery into an independent public institution. The Rothmans Gallery of Stratford was renamed the Gallery/Stratford.

Rothmans presented some wonderful summer exhibitions during its tenure at the gallery. "Vasarely in Retrospect" was shown in the summer of 1971. Jack Pollock was its curator. The show toured Canada after leaving Stratford. Rothmans also funded and produced, using experts as guest curators, exhibitions on Realism, Art Deco, and Aboriginal Art, among others. Robert Swain became Director after

Robert Ihrig. He continued the tradition of special shows in the summer months. A number of times exhibitions were produced featuring costumes from the Festival itself as the Festival had a huge warehouse filled with costumes from past productions. Some costumes could be recycled, but others were kept as part of the archives.

Among the Festival shows produced by the gallery were the following: "Made Glorious, Stage Design at Stratford 25 Years — An exhibition of costume designs celebrating the silver anniversary of the Stratford Festival, 1977" and "Leslie Hurry: a Painter for the Stage", that opened at the Gallery Stratford in May of 1982 and then went to New York, Dallas and San Antonio as well as Cobourg, Kingston and Montreal. It also toured in England in early 1984. There was also a much smaller show called "The Trappings of Kings", curated by John Pennoyer and coordinated by John Silverstein, Curator of Exhibitions at the Gallery Stratford.

In the year, 1978, when I became Director, the Gallery presented Robert Swain's show, "A History of Children's Book Illustration, 1750 to 1940". The source of the books was the John Hayes Collection in Stratford. Swain's second show that summer was named "Fantastic Shakespeare". It was an exhibition of famous paintings using Shakespeare's plays as subjects. It had paintings by artists such as Singer Sergeant and was curated by Bryan Arnott and Dr. Richard Studing.

When I went to the Gallery Stratford I was able to take a summer Exhibition with me. I had worked for two years at the Ontario Crafts Council seeking funding for an Ontario Quebec Craft Exhibition. Finally the Crafts Council received $78,000 from the Ontario Quebec Permanent Commission toward such a show.

The Board of Directors of the O.C.C. asked me to continue my role as administrator for the exhibition. The show had its grand Quebec opening at the Salon des Artisans de Quebec in Quebec City on December 7th 1979, and travelled to four other Quebec centres in the following months. The Ontario grand opening was at the Gallery Stratford on June 2nd 1980. It stayed at that location until August 17th and then visited five other Ontario Centres

In 1979 Jerrold Morris acted as guest curator for the summer exhibition, "20th Century Canadian Drawings". He prepared an excellent catalogue. It was a difficult assignment because so little had been recorded on drawings in Canada. Ken Nutt of Stratford had a drawing in the show and also provided the front cover illustration. In the summer of 1981 John Silverstein produced a very beautiful exhibition with

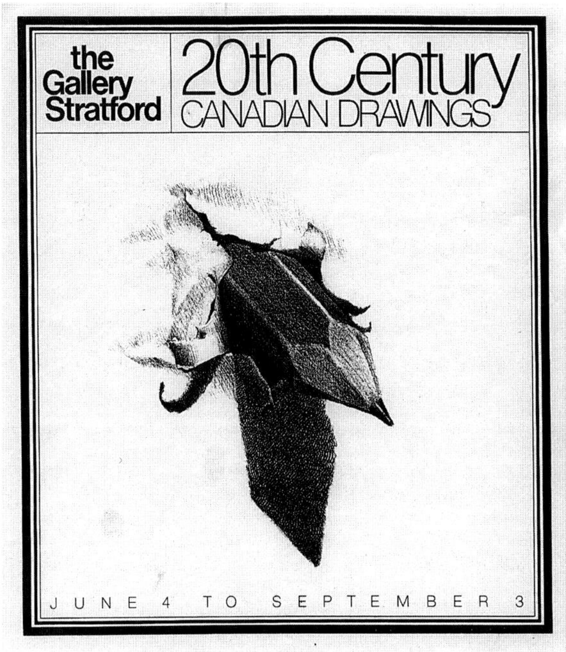

a wonderful catalogue. It was given a very poetic name, *Woven Winds, the Art of Textiles in India*. John had studied this subject in London, England and in India itself.

The Gallery Stratford programmes followed very much the pattern that I had used in Oshawa. We produced a monthly bulletin that went to every member. It listed the programmes, exhibitions and a calendar of events. Also there was a new concept that I introduced based on observations in Wales. The National Museum of Wales had ten thousand portable units travelling throughout the country each school term. Five catalogues were sent out on Geology, Zoology, Botany, Art and Archaeology. These went to the schools, the libraries, the art galleries and community centres. The units were small, sometimes consisting of only one item. An English teacher teaching Shakespeare could borrow a model of the Globe Theatre or filmstrips on English costume, weaponry or manuscripts. The emphasis in this programme was to give direct assistance to the very specific needs of the borrower. We started out in a very small way with local schools, we named the programme "Art Pack". The small units were not insured as we expected them to have a life of only two years. The emphasis was placed on the use of the object and not on its protection.

We put out Art Packs on Canadian Heritage — local, general, Indian, Eskimo, Man and his World, Man and His Cultures; items along with slide sets related to the school curriculum. The travelling exhibition was reduced to its smallest unit possible — often just one object, produced at an average cost of fifty dollars each. The programme was a first for a Canadian Gallery.

The Board was excited by the project. Funding was received from Wintario and a grant from Samsonite Luggage. Maggie Mitchell, the

Extension Officer, and Bruce White, the Extension Coordinator, did a wonderful job in organizing, publicizing and administering the programme. It continued for at least two years until funding ran out. Maggie Mitchell eventually left the gallery after many years of devoted work and became the Director of the Owen Sound Gallery. Bruce White went into Education.

One other programme, run completely by volunteers, is very much worth mentioning. John Miller, the Vice-President of the Gallery had been a High School vice-principal, but he left that position to administer the Stratford Summer Music programme. John suggested to the Board that we should have an art auction. I very strongly opposed the idea. All my life I have fought the ripping off of artists as a fund-raising idea: People always say, oh we will ask so-and-so to donate a painting. What they do not realize is that the painting might have taken only a few hours to complete but behind it is years of training in art schools followed by years of personal development as an artist. The Board finally decided instead of art to auction off services and gifts from other parts of the community, and it worked, very successfully.

The auction was called, and is still called, "The I Love my Gallery Auction". It is held on the weekend closest to Valentine's Day. It has now run for twenty years. The first year the profit was around fifteen thousand dollars — wonderful we thought! The profit now is in the neighbourhood of eighty thousand dollars! Surely this is a record for a fund raising project by volunteers in a small Ontario art gallery.

For months the volunteers collect the objects that are to be auctioned. A furniture store will give an armchair, a design studio will offer to design a business card, and a travel agency will donate a Caribbean cruise. For some years, artists volunteered to do a theme item, a birdhouse or a painted bird. I originally suggested that the committee go to a dentist and ask for a filling to be auctioned off or go to a lawyer and have him offer to make a will; professional organizations will not allow this to be done, but just about everything else has turned up over the years. One year I was attempting to write up the newspaper descriptions for the donations; we had been given a couple of cases of Coca Cola, and I wrote, "Have a coke Party" — It was soon vetoed by a more knowing member of the committee

Two days before the auction the *Beacon Herald* publishes two full pages of all the auction items, so many being auctioned off each half or full hour over the radio. Local celebrities working in pairs, for example the Mayor and the M.P.P., announce the bids over the radio as they are phoned in. There is growing excitement as two well known local people compete with each other over an item. In full view of the announcers are boards placed all around the room each with a volunteer marking down the bids as the bank of phone operators take the calls. It is a fun-filled day for all, with a great deal of excitement.

In the evening there is a formal dinner, usually held at the Church Restaurant. The really valuable items (such as cruises) are then auctioned, usually by an individual who knows everybody in town and can create competition. I remember that Eleanor Kane, one of the owners of the Old Prune Restaurant was very good as an auctioneer. Some years an actor from the Festival would volunteer for this job. In recent years, a silent auction has been added to the programme where twenty or so items are placed on view before the dinner, and people have a chance to view and write down their bids. The success of this programme has depended on the many volunteers over the years, the status of the gallery in the local community, and the generosity of the public. It is truly a magnificent effort and I applaud all concerned.

The Ontario Association of Art Galleries awarded me the Award of Merit for 1982. John Silverstein, the Curator at the Gallery Stratford nominated me for the award. This award was started in 1978 to show recognition of province-wide contributions to the visual arts in Ontario. It was later expanded to include individuals, foundations, businesses and corporations. One award is made each year. Anne Meredith Barry presented me with a scroll and a print at the annual meeting of the OAAG in Peterborough on May 7th of that year.

I donated a number of works to the permanent collection of the Gallery Stratford. First, in February of 1985 I gave a large Robert Downing sculpture "Double Exploding Cubes", aluminum and red arborite, 1968. This was followed in 1987 by eleven smaller works: two prints by John K. Esler, a work by Jack Pollock, three small drawings by Robert Downing, a photograph by Neil Newton and works by Jane Turnbull, Even Apostoll and David Bierk.

I have also, for the future, arranged for the donation after my death and my sister's death, for all my original children's book illustration by Ken Nutt (Eric Beddows) to go to the Osborne Children's Book Collection in Toronto. The Osborne Collection is building an archive on Ken Nutt. My Ken Nutt paintings and drawings are to go to the Gallery Stratford. I have a total of twenty-seven works by Ken Nutt in my collection. Also bequeathed is my collection of hand-made books by Gerard Brender à Brandis to the Gallery Stratford as the gallery collects works on paper and the Brandis wood engravings are superb and will add a wonderful dimension to the collection.

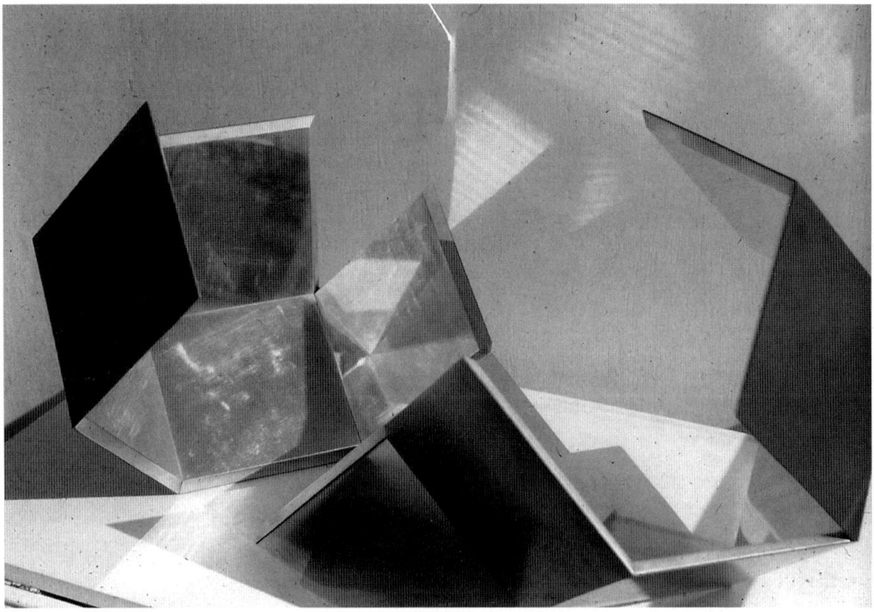

"Double Exploding Cubes" — Robert Downing

Finally, a negative aspect concerning my work at the Gallery Stratford. That ugly situation of Board versus staff reared its head. I know that Board members are volunteers and devote many free hours to organizational work. Sometimes, however, from my point of view as a professional worker, the amateur should be asked to take a course on the aims and principles of an organization before starting work on a Board. I have a copy of a letter that I wrote to Dr. David Leaney, President of the Gallery Stratford on December 5th, 1983. At Board meetings, the matter of loyalty of staff had been questioned because it was thought that a staff member was seeking another position. In my mind it is natural for a talented, competent young man receiving a minimal professional salary, who has already given five years to a position and has a wife and family, to attempt to advance his career opportunities. To me, he would be disloyal to himself if he did otherwise.

In this letter I pointed out that I would like to discuss loyalty with the members of the Board. The staff was putting in many extra hours in order to adequately cover the large array of programmes. Charles Trethewey, a part time employee, had given cello recitals free of charge and more than one hundred people had been in the audience for one concert. Only two Board members had turned up for one of the three concerts. Ken Nutt was a professional artist, also a part-time employee of the Gallery. His publisher gave a reception for the printing of the Children's book, *Zoom at Sea*, that Ken had illustrated. The event was very well attended, all staff were there voluntarily; only one Board member, an artist, had turned up.

Some Board members said that they did not know what was going on in the gallery! Obviously they did not read their monthly bulletins, the ads in the local papers or listen to my reports at the monthly Board meetings. The litany could go on but the point has been made and, of course, it is all past history. But how does one define loyalty?

The basic fact is, in a small art gallery the staff usually works there because they love the work. After all, the hours are long with many weekends being disrupted, and salaries are usually low. Such a staff needs encouragement and help; they must feel that they are doing a good job, are appreciated and people are grateful. I feel like this myself. I have given many speeches in my life, but still, as soon as I sit down after a speech, I turn to the nearest person and ask if the speech sounded alright. Am I wrong?

Chapter Eighteen

Ken Nutt

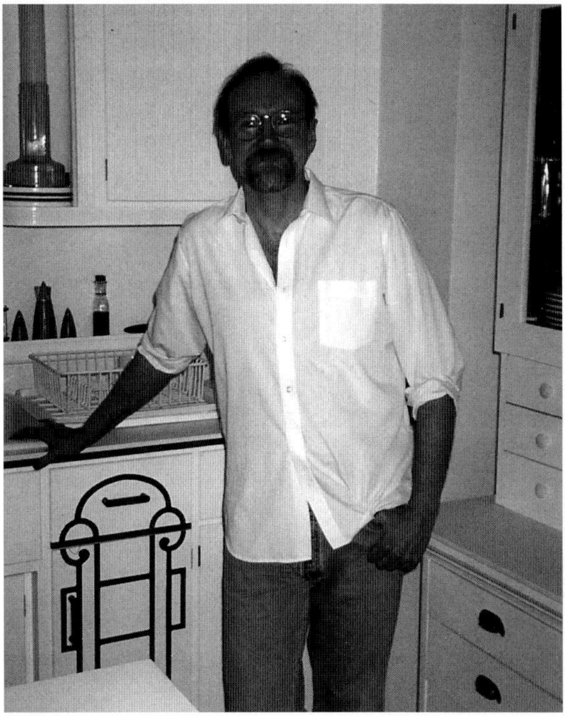

On January 30th, 1965, I arrived at the Woodstock Art Gallery in the middle of the afternoon. I was greeted by Lillie Telfer, the Director. I asked her if she would wish me happy birthday. I told her that I had been on the road for a week and I wanted to hear a friendly, familiar, voice say it to me.

I was then Director of the Art Institute of Ontario. In the two years, 1965 and 1966 I visited a total of one hundred and twenty communities. In 1965 I went on tours of one or two weeks to South Western Ontario, the Ottawa and St. Lawrence Valleys, South Central Ontario, East Central Ontario and Northern Ontario. I had my van full of ten paintings, easels, and spot lights.

I would usually try to arrive soon enough in the afternoon to set things up. Then I could go out to supper (or sometimes be invited to supper by my contact person), and then arrive back in time to greet the members of the audience who often arrived early in order to set up their paintings for the criticism.

That particular night three things happened that have always kept that date in my mind. There was a good crowd. I had known Lillie

Telfer for years. She was an excellent Gallery Director and not only would she have her gallery members and art club members out but, also, she would have advertised in the local paper. At the end of my talk, and after I had criticized the local work, the lights went out, the door of the hall opened at the back, and in came a lady carrying a huge birthday cake ablaze with candles. I was completely taken by surprise. We ate the cake with much merriment.

That same night a young boy, aged fourteen came up to me and told me that he wanted to be an artist. He asked me what training he would need, I told him about the Ontario College of Art and other art schools at the new Community Colleges as well as the Fine Art Courses such as I, myself, had taken at the University of Toronto. That young boy turned out to be Ken Nutt.

Then at the very end of a very successful evening I was called to the phone, the only time it had ever happened in all my years on the road. I was told that my Father was back in hospital and was dying, and so I packed up hurriedly and headed off to Toronto. Luckily I was on the last stop of my tour. Dad died two weeks later in February. It is because of my birthday party, and meeting Ken Nutt, and my Father's death that I so well remember this date.

I was Director of the Gallery Stratford from 1978 to 1984. When I first started that position I again met Ken Nutt. One day, early on, Ken came and sat in my office and reintroduced himself as the boy from Woodstock of years ago. He said that when he was a late teenager he had again attended a talk of mine, in 1969. I had just returned from Europe after my Canada Council grant. Ken was able to tell me about many of the slides I had shown that night. In fact when I was recently checking on the facts from him for this part of the story he told me about a slide I had shown where I was riding on a donkey and another slide of a villa high on a hill looking over the Mediterranean. Those slides were from my month in Morocco.

Ken took his art courses and attended York University. Then he became involved in an antique/gift store. He knew that he wanted to be a professional artist. He moved to the Stratford area and took on a part time job at the Rothman's Art Gallery of Stratford, later the Gallery/Stratford. He did installation work and he taught art classes, both adult and children's. I will never forget going into the gallery one Saturday morning and finding the children making phenakistoscopes. These were the first motion picture machines, invented in 1832 by Joseph Plateau. The children cut circles of paper; around the edges they drew stick figures of a man running and jumping, they cut in from the edge, bent each section upward, cut slits between the pictures and placed the whole thing on the turn table of a record player. Then the player was turned on at slow speed, the children would lie on the floor and look through the slits and watch the man actually moving and jumping up and down.

It was real magic. The more adventurous would then try cars crashing and other innocent motifs. The magic part to me, though, when I first went through the door was watching Ken, flat on his stomach with his face glowing and showing just as much wonder as I saw on the faces of the children. At that point I knew that Ken was a very special person with a wonderful outlook on life and a marvellous talent for communicating.

Ken started a Wednesday evening figure drawing class at the Gallery. There was no instruction. There would always be a good model. Ken arranged for the models, opened and closed the gallery, collected the five-dollar fee and paid the model. He did this as a volunteer. The classes still continue to this day, with Ken in charge. They attract many of the artists from the Festival who want to practice their drawing skills.

I consider Ken Nutt to be one of the most talented artists that I have had the privilege of knowing in my years in the Visual Arts field. He is an amazing academic and he has a wonderful drawing skill that he has been refining for years. He is constantly researching new projects. He loves the Art and Crafts period of the nineteenth century; he layers this with a love of the Mission Oak period in the United States, and the time leading up to the Art Deco period. His home has always been a wonder to me; it has imagination and fantasy interwoven with the basics of the three styles I have mentioned above.

He bought an old, large, Victorian home in Stratford. There was a fireplace in the living room; he simplified the mantel to match his Mission Oak furniture. I had my antique store at this time and he bought two large coloured glass windows from me. He had the walls cut out on each side of the fireplace, the resulting brickwork exactly matching the detail of the old brickwork around the top of his walls, and he placed the tall windows in these areas. The wondrous glow of light diffuses the room. He collects fossils and has cabinets and drawers filled with examples.

At one point he had a huge cupboard in his kitchen; when you opened the door a couple of hundred Mickey Mouse figures stared out at you in mischief and disbelief. Paul Howley of Howley Design and Building has recently completely rebuilt the kitchen on a model of the

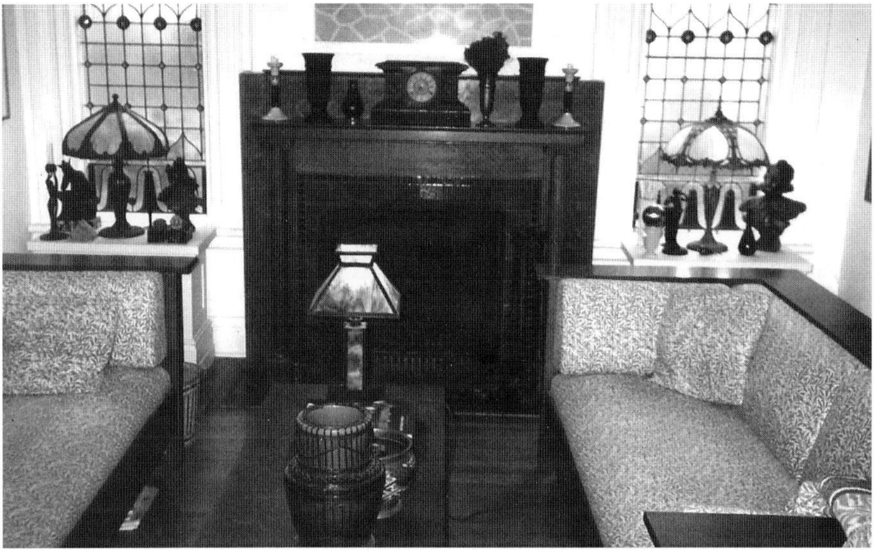

1920s. You look through the glass of the kitchen table and stare at hundreds of buttons in special little cubicles. The kitchen is in white, red and black. Ken bought from me large, white, hanging deco light fixtures. Almost every flat surface in the dining room and living room is filled with lady lamps, sinuous figures holding glass globes.

Ken has three studios in the house: two on the second floor are for his drawing; the finished attic with a special trap door to lift large canvases through from below, is where the painting and drawing from the models take place.

Ken's work has followed two career directions: his children's book illustrations, and his drawing and painting. Early in his career he took another name for his illustration work in order to keep the two aspects of his work separate. As an illustrator he is known as Eric Beddows, Eric being his middle name and Beddows being his Mother's maiden name. Year by year, book after book has been published showing his great talent as an illustrator: *The Emperor's Panda, The Cave of Snores, Night Cars, Shadow Play, Who Shrank my Grandmother's House,* and *Joyful Noise. Joyful Noise, Poems for Two Voices* won the Newberry Award in the United States and the book was placed in every children's library. The *Zoom* book series, text written by Tim Wynne-Jones, won the Canadian Library Association's Amelia Frances-Howard Gibbon Illustrator's Award twice.

The Zoom series of three books, *Zoom Away, Zoom at Sea* and *Zoom Upstream,* was a great popular success, published in 1983, 1985 and 1992. Zoom is a cat that loves water; in the first book he sets out to find

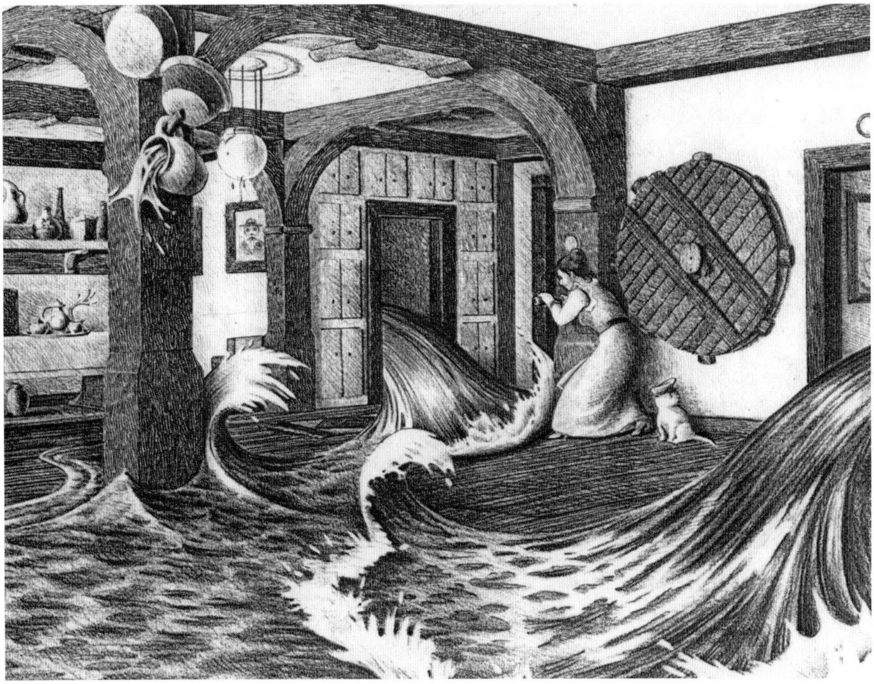

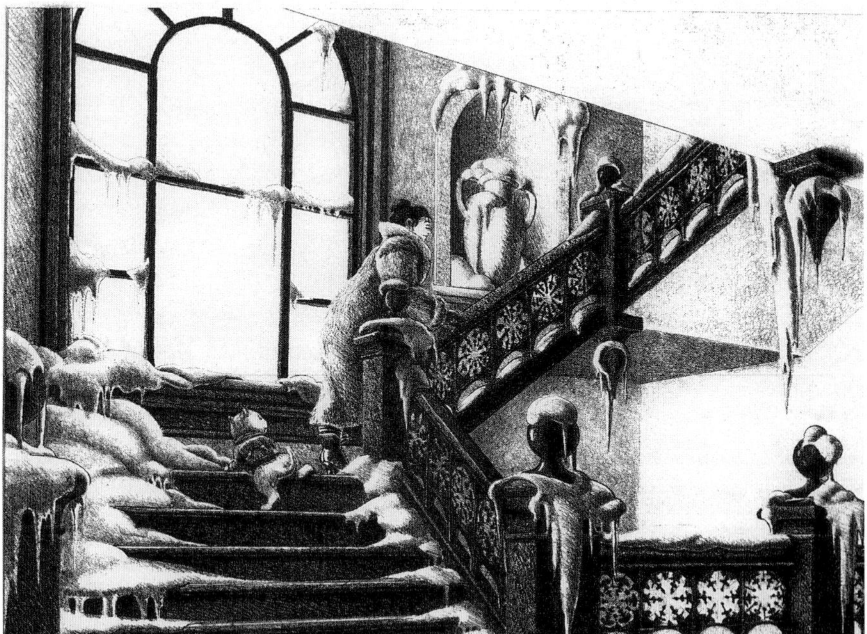

his Uncle Roy, a sea captain. He goes to an address he has found of Uncle Roy's, sets out and finds Maria, a wonderful woman in a magical house who creates for him the sea where he has a wonderful day of sailing. In the Second book he goes to see Maria again and learns that his Uncle Roy has set off for the North Pole. He climbs to the attic of Maria's house and reaches the North Pole where he does find his uncle's ship, but the Uncle has taken off south on an iceberg. In the third book he follows Maria down a stair behind a library bookshelf to the banks of a river that turns out to be a tributary of the Nile. He rescues Maria bound up in mummy's cloths and finally finds Uncle Roy who invites him to go exploring with him for the source of the Nile River.

Ken actually visited Egypt in 1991 in order to find the right detail for the last Zoom book. *Zoom Upstream* had wonderful end covers. There were two lines of elaborate cat hieroglyphs and cat tomb figures, some at war with dog warriors, and some paying homage to a cat pharaoh. Up in a corner were twenty-six small pictures representing the letters of the alphabet; a child, knowing this, could translate the story on the two lines of hieroglyphs. Wonderful stuff for children.

In 1996 Ken Nutt's artwork for the book *The Rooster's Gift* won the Governor General's Award in the English Children's Literature Illustration category. Ken received ten thousand dollars. *Maclean's* magazine in its December 9th, 1996 issue reported that whereas many of the award winners expressed pessimism about the future of the arts in Canada, Ken, in his acceptance speech at the awards ceremony, told the audience that although two people important to him had died in the middle of his project he found his work bolstered his optimism. His longtime partner, playwright Elliot Hayes, had been killed in a car accident and the author of the tale, Pam Conrad, had died of cancer. Wryly noting that while the book was not "War and Peace" nor the Sistine Chapel ceiling, Beddows said: "In those dark days, it never seemed like a trivial activity to climb the stairs to my studio in order to spend time with the smallest hen and her pompous rooster friend. It was, rather, a welcome escape into a happy place."

Ken has always built models as a basis for all of his book illustrations. Some of these have been very elaborate. This is a very ancient practice by illustrators. At the present time he is planning a series of books on one topic. He has just spent two years building a most elaborate model of an Edwardian mansion in perfect historic detail filled with turrets, bay windows, elaborate chimneys, arcades, walls, and a massive tower. He has just finished the final details of landscaping and street lighting. For the first time he is writing his own stories as well as

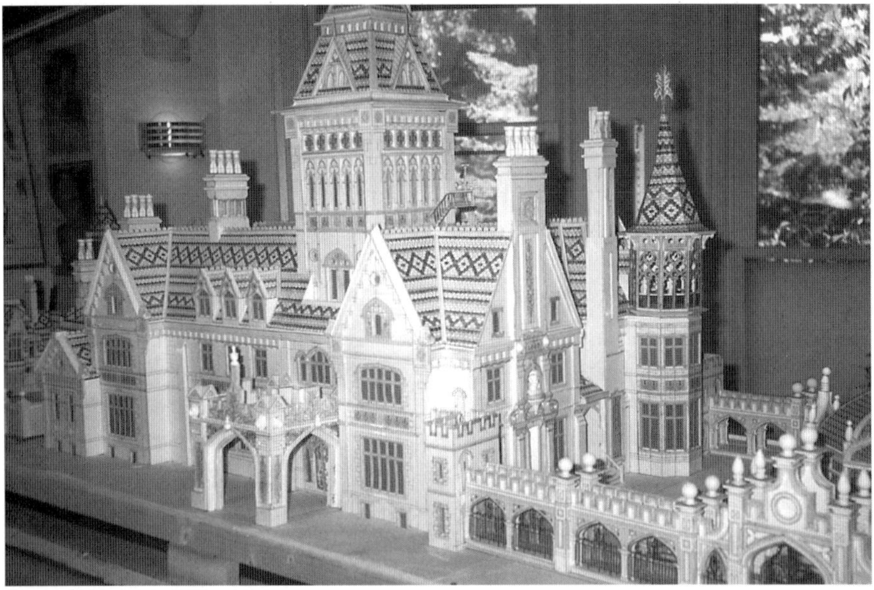

illustrating them. Now, after two years of preparations, the drawings will be completed very quickly.

I have followed Ken Nutt's development in drawing and painting for many years. I own twenty-seven of his works, almost equally divided between original drawings from his children's book illustrations and formal paintings and other drawings. He has won many awards, and has had many group and individual exhibitions. Various catalogues describe his work from the early days as ranging from beautifully crafted still-life compositions based on models of objects which he arranged from his own collections of "treasures" to works with a clarity of concept about them, a tranquility in the midst of multiplicity.

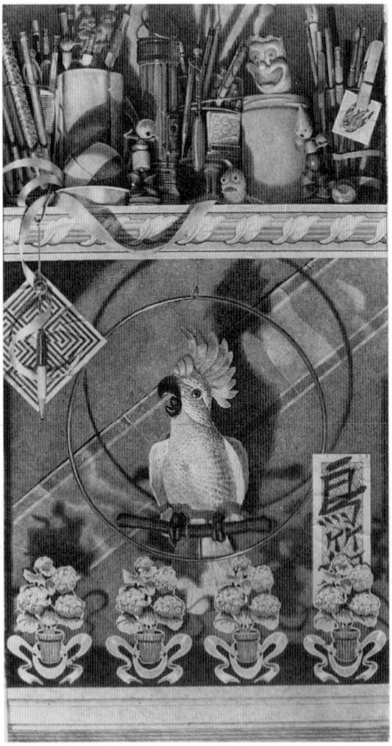

His later works have a more abstract theme, with Nutt's characteristic central focus point evident in all of them. Nutt uses realism but the objects function symbolically; the drawings are metaphors. These are surrealist works as they depict the merging of dream and reality. Nutt constructs a world from the external one; his are the objects that surround all of us and he places them in readable situations. In creating his works, Nutt proceeds from the outer world to the inner, personal world. There is a content to his work that transcends mere technique. He uses his technical strengths to lure us to his art, to bring us to the threshold of his boxes so that he can trap us; he addresses some of the darker places of the psyche. This is the "rubbish of civilization" being catalogued. The above is quoted from an introduction to a 1985 catalogue of Ken Nutt's work at the Art Gallery of Windsor, written by Marshall Webb. Also some quotations are from *Ken Nutt: the One Man Group Show. 1997*, an essay by Karen Mulhallen.

In his twenty-year retrospective, "Ken Nutt: the One Man Group Show" in 1997, Ken Nutt in the introduction very kindly wrote the following; "In reviewing the history of my work and my career, one name came up over and over. In High School, this person gave me advice about pursuing a life in the arts. Later as Director of the Gallery Stratford and my employer, he made sure that I was introduced to every visiting curator or gallery, owner. It was through his efforts that I secured my first commercial gallery, my first review in print and my first commission. He also collected my work, which is the kind of support an artist never forgets. Thank you Paul, for your support. Thank you for your friendship. This exhibition is dedicated to Paul Bennett."

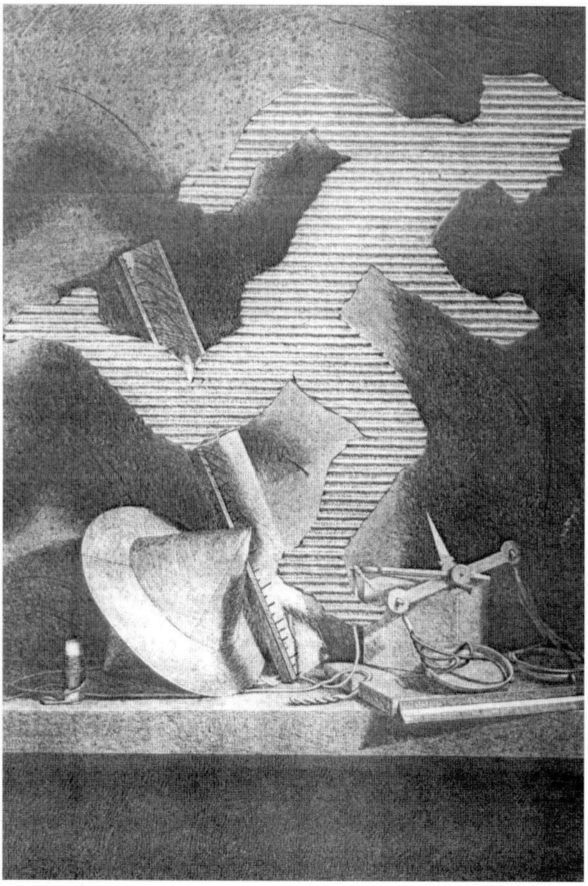

Chapter Nineteen

On Collecting

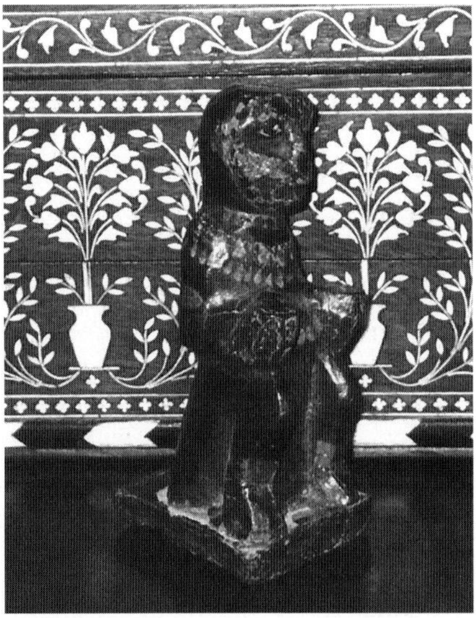

I am sitting in front of my House God. Not exactly mine originally, but I have owned him for thirty-seven years since my Father died. I take good care of him, for if I go away he is placed lovingly in my safe, and at other times he stands guard in a lawyer's stacking bookcase in my bedroom.

Back about 1875 when the British Empire ruled the world, an English army officer was going home on leave from India to England. The ship stopped in at what used to be Ceylon and there, somehow, this officer acquired the House God from the shrine of a native home. How he came into possession of something surely precious to its owner is a mystery. The House God was taken back to England and presented to my Grandfather and my Father brought it with him when he came to Canada. It must have had some significance or else he would not have carried it with him to the New World.

This little figure has watched over me all of my life, first in my parent's home and then in mine. He is a Monkey God; you can see where his tail emerged at the back of his body, curved upward and then gently touched the back of the head. It is missing. The figure is only six inches tall, made of wood and painted in dark vegetable dyes, the basic colour, as of the clothes, is a dark brown. The face, feet and hands are a dark scarlet and seem to be emerging from an elaborate robe, which is covering even the head and is decorated with yellow, green and black designs. The face has black stripes, possibly whiskers. Finally, the figure is sitting as if on a throne, his robe concealing the seat.

When we were children we always wanted to take off the base because we wondered if there might be a jewel hidden inside the figure. The base is attached to the figure by one handmade nail. Perhaps if the base were removed the figure would lose some of its mystery? Perhaps the power of the House God is strong enough that we have been willed not to touch it. I do feel that there is a deity guarding my house, with strange powers abroad, possibly ghosts hovering and waiting — that is enough.

Why do I start a chapter on collecting with the above object? Because the House God stands for collecting, it has worth in my eyes, it suggests a mystery from the past, it tells me about my roots, and it tells my who I am. So I collect.

When I was sixty I finally decided to collect beaded purses. I had always admired them but surely macho men do not collect such things and people might laugh. But gone are my inhibitions: now I am sure enough of myself, I know who I am and, I do not care what others think. Like me or leave me.

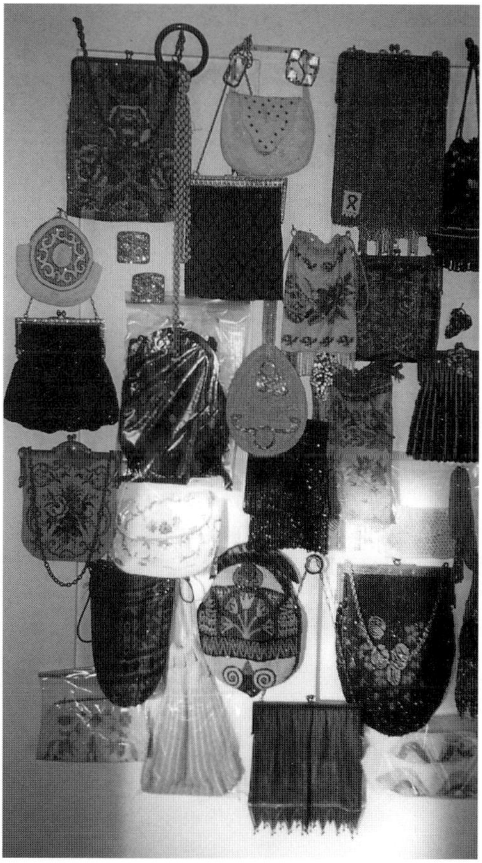

I am sitting in my study working at my keyboard. Behind me on the door to my clothes cupboard hang twenty beaded purses, from the Victorian times to the 1930s. There are also three pairs of buckles from the 1920s (one of them covered in brilliants) for lady's shoes and a few pieces of 1920s jewelry. In another part of this book I mention a particular bag given me by my friend, Kay Kritzwiser.

The collection seems to divide quite easily into bags from the Victorian period, and the Art Deco, 1920-1930 period. The Victorian ones mostly have drawstrings and are elaborately decorated in floral design favouring roses. The Art Deco ones have a metal frame across the top with a clasp in the centre and a chain attached from each end for holding-the purse. The Art Deco ones have much simpler designs in geometric patterns.

I almost destroyed my collection at one point by trading off five of the best purses in return for two Kilim, hand woven rugs for my study. Two friends of mine, Philip and Erna Fowler of Stratford, own an oriental carpet store, and also collect beaded bags. I was in their store, admiring the wonderful patterns of the flat weave kilim carpets, when the suggestion of the trade was made. I, as often happens, being short of cash, thought it an excellent idea, and I have certainly enjoyed the rugs. The chair I am sitting on while I type this chapter is resting on one of the carpets, but for a long period my poor little collection looked decimated until I had found a few more beaded bags to fill in the blank areas on the wall.

Finally, one Tuesday evening some years ago I sat in my usual spot, the first chair in the second row, at the Stock Auctions in Stratford. I was on tenterhooks. I had previewed the items for auction just before the beginning of the sale. Hanging on the wall behind the auctioneer's stand was a framed work that I had to have. There were a few desultory bids but I got it for just a few dollars.

The picture depicts a classical scene done in beads!! It shows a man leading a bullock in the foreground with a dog jumping at his feet, and two goats nearby. A tree in full foliage goes up the right side. In the middle ground there is a river with an outlet leading into the distance between two islands. There is a castle with a tower on the island to the left and a natural archway of rock on the island to the right. Two ships in full sail are heading out to sea beyond the outlet. A patterned border runs down both sides of the picture but not across the top and bottom. It possibly was part of something larger. The beading covers an area nine inches square, contained within an elaborately carved gold frame about an inch wide.

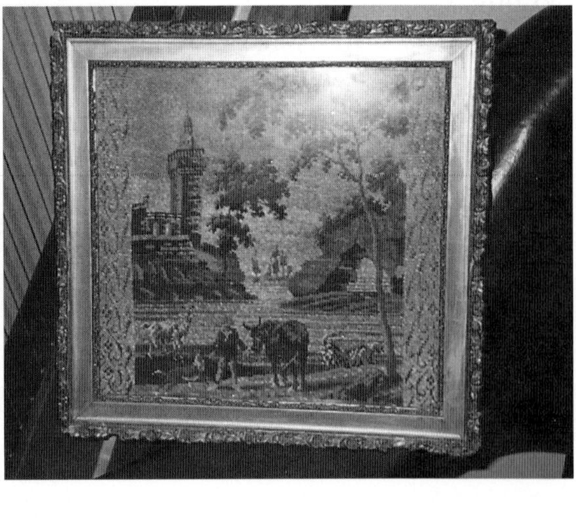

I have always thought that the work might have been done by a Victorian gentlewoman who might even have gone almost blind working on it, the beads are so fine! In fact it would have been impossible to thread a needle through the beads; they must have been individually placed on a waxed thread and then a needle added to work them into the picture. I cannot figure out any other way to do it. This beaded work is one of my treasures and I have it hanging on the wall beside my door of beaded bags.

While I was away on my European trip in 1968-1969 I seemed to collect objects a dozen at a time. I bought a dozen opal and gold rings, which I brought back and gave away to friends and relatives. I have already mentioned the large white opal ring that I bought in Florence and gave to my one niece, Beth. I gave another ring from this collection to my other niece, Rebecca, but unfortunately she had a robbery in her apartment and lost it; by that time I had none left with which I could replace the stolen ring.

I did keep one small Victorian ring that I acquired at that time, for myself, and I still wear it often. It had three fire opals on it, all oval, the largest one in the centre. It had the nicest colour of any of the opals in the twelve rings I had bought. One of the opals came loose and I took the ring into a jeweller to secure it for me. When the ring was returned it seemed to have lost some of its colour. The jeweller explained to me that the Victorians secured the opals in pitch or tar to make the colour seem stronger. Today when opals in old rings come loose it is necessary to replace the background with a modern adhesive.

I also collected a dozen beautiful calling card cases while away in Europe. There were, of course, no 'phones is the 18th and 19th centuries in England. The upper classes had a ritual of calling on each other where we today would simply use the 'phone. Ladies were always at home at certain times to receive friends. Often they in turn would go out on the same routine. and it was necessary to let the person know that one had called and nobody was at home. This might be fortunate if the visit was to somebody that you did not like but felt obliged by etiquette and protocol to call on. A simple card carried by the butler and placed in a tray could save you going back if you did not want to. There were rituals in the etiquette concerning calling cards: the visitor could turn down various corners to convey different messages. The calling cards were carried in elaborate cases, many of them made in the orient.

I collected a dozen of these cases; they were very beautiful, many being carved out of ivory. I had one, especially lovely, carved in ivory and dyed a deep scarlet red. All of the ivory cases had relief carving of great depth with various domestic scenes of people, animals, houses

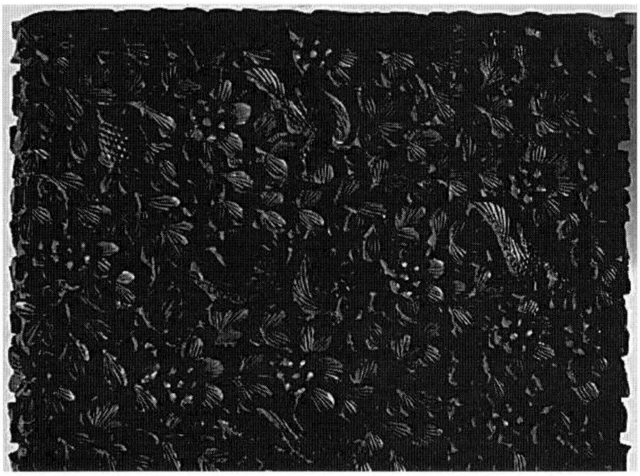

and mountains. I sold all the ivory ones at one time to an antique dealer in Stratford. I did keep five others. There was a calling card case in sandalwood, made in India. It depicted a tiger on one side in the middle of a jungle, with many herons and other birds flying through the foliage. This was given to me by my Auntie Chris, my father's twin sister, when I visited her in Bournemouth in 1969. She had a large collection of these lovely cases. I also still have four in tortoise shell and mother of pearl. My Mother gave one of these to me and later I secured one, which is obviously Art Deco as indicated by the geometric placing of the pieces of the mother of pearl. It must have held business cards.

In Chapter 5, I mentioned a small inlaid cabinet that I bought in Canterbury. I also have a writing desk, intricately inlaid with ivory, made in India that was given to my mother by my sister Joan and her partner. They bought it in Edinburgh. I love these Victorian cabinets, so beautiful and so useful.

For years I have been interested in the Art Deco style of design. I am very fond of small objects in that style but I would not necessarily want a home decorated entirely in Art Deco. Once I found a wonderful bookshelf that extended sideways more than a foot to hold books; it was made of brass with an inlay of exotic wood. The design shows peacocks in a tree with long weeping branches, the design itself being symmetrical with the two birds in reverse to each other. I found this beautiful object at an auction in Colborne.

Mrs. Schade, the lady from whom I bought my house in Stratford, gave me a simple green glass vase in a flaring Art Deco design complete with a glass frog inside it to hold the flowers in position. At an auction in Newtonville I found a second green glass vase, the same colour exactly, again in a flaring design, but in a slightly different shape. Obviously the same company made the two vases. They look nice together, on a hanging brass shelf, filled with Chinese lanterns and bitter sweet. One other object on that same shelf is a small bronze harle-

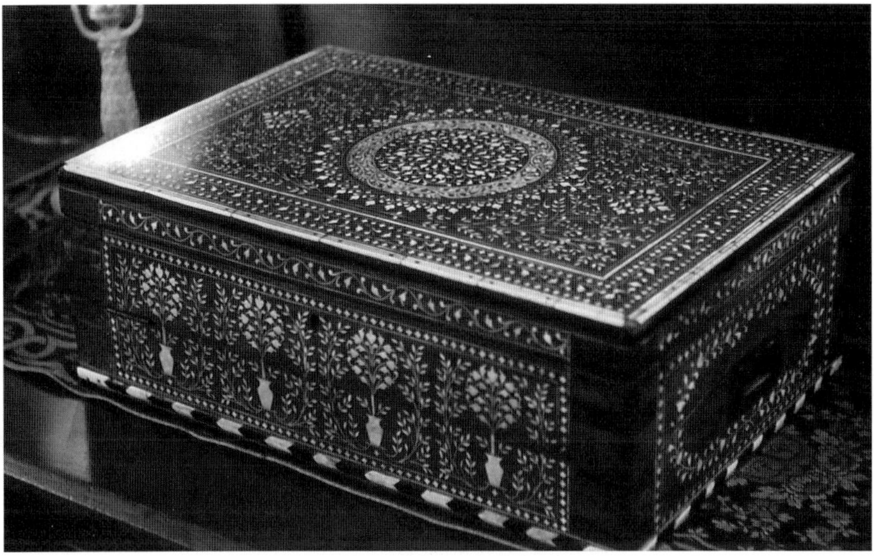

Mother's Indian writing desk

quin figure sitting down with a mandolin slung over his shoulders. His face is carved ivory.

One of the disturbing yet wonderful things about collecting is that one's taste keeps changing over the years. When I was a young man I was very interested in pressed glass goblets. I actually had two hundred of them at one time. It was fun to search out different patterns and find rare ones. I was turned off these when a number of large collections came on the market at once and you could actually go out and buy a dozen at a time if you wanted; and, at the same time, the number of reproductions proliferated. I did very quickly learn how to distinguish the fakes from the real ones. People some times tried to age the goblets by rubbing the bottoms on a brick and so causing wear marks but these were easy to detect as all the marks were running in the same direction. What could not be faked was a wear mark just under the rim at the top of the goblet. When a goblet is made there is a tiny bulge all around the upper edge. If the goblet is drunk from over many years just under that bulge a wear mark develops. This can actually be seen only in sunlight.

While in England I became ecstatic over the early English goblets with air twist, mercury twist, or spiral twist stems. I sought out and bought about a dozen of them. I am sure that some were likely fake. If fact I disposed of some before I even returned to Canada because I became more perceptive in my search. When I opened my own store I put them all into my stock and gradually sold them. From this collec-

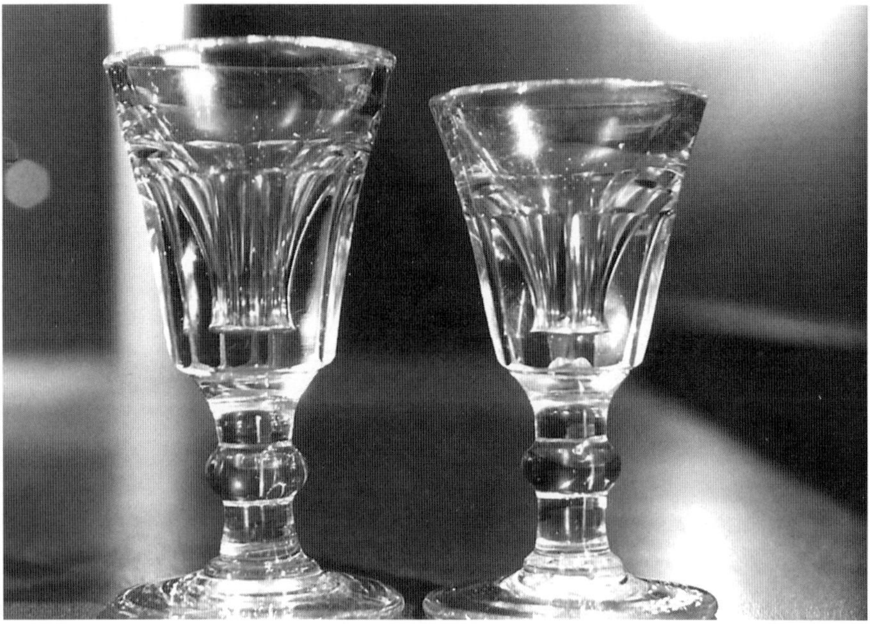

tion however two glasses remain because my Auntie Chris gave them to me. These small glasses were called toast master glasses and when you hold one up you realize that it holds only a tiny bit of wine, the rest of the bowl is filled in with glass. At a banquet in the old days the toastmaster had to stay sober so that he could carry on to the end of the long meals and keep making suitable toasts; thus he was only allowed a thimble full of wine with each drink.

At an auction I once bought a beautiful biscuit barrel of opalescent glass ribbed with sinuous lines of mauve glass. I found out that it was made by Kralic in Bohemia about 1880. I started adding other Bohemian glass (1880-1918) by firms such as Amphora and Palmme-Konig until I had more than a dozen pieces. The shapes were Arts and Crafts, and the colours reminded me of looking at an oil slick on the road in the sunlight.

I have collected oriental things for many years. Quite often beautiful handcrafted objects will appear at auctions or even garage sales. Two years ago I found a large soap stone Chinese carving of two urns, a flowerpot and two large plants of flowers. It measures seven inches in height by ten inches in width. I got it for ten dollars. I love cloisonné, the art practiced by both the Chinese and Japanese where thin brass wires are fixed to a brass plate to outline a design and then the spaces are filled with vari-coloured enamels. I found a beautiful little pin dish in cloisonné last year at a garage sale for ten cents. It has a

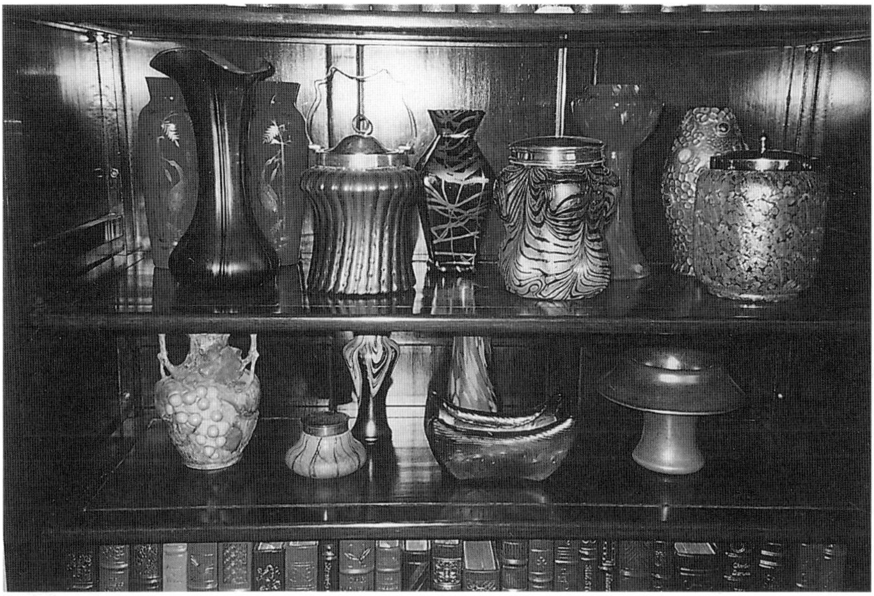

Bohemian Glass

wonderful design of vegetation on its surface. I also have a large cloisonné lamp with a shade that I secured from an auction in Owen Sound. The shade dates from the 1920s and is covered in gutta percha, which is rubber that over the years has hardened into a shell. The painted design is of swans and so bad that I love it. Both lamp base and shade are in exactly the same colours, one in a magnificent design, the other terrible. One day I had a man bring a Japanese four-section screen into my store. It has a red lacquer base with each panel depicting typical rural Japanese scenes of houses, mountains and roads with people, all inlaid in mother of pearl. It stands on a low bookcase in my living room. I could go on listing a wide variety of oriental objects that bring me great pleasure.

I attended the World Crafts Council Conference in Kyoto, Japan in 1972. I wanted to bring home Japanese robes for my sisters and women friends but I found that they were unbelievably expensive. Evidently a young man in Japan can practically bankrupt himself buying his bride a gown for their wedding. I had an idea. I phoned the tourist bureau in Kyoto and asked if there were any secondhand clothing shops in that town. There was one and I was given the address. A friend of mine from the conference and I grabbed a taxi and went to this shop. There were stacks of gowns all over the floor of the store. I bought eight of them for sixty-five dollars. Evidently the Japanese refuse to wear clothes worn by another person. I brought them through customs as used clothing and had presents for a number of friends. I kept one, with ikat weaving, for myself.

Now I come to one of my big collecting urges. The reason of course is the fact that my Father manufactured lamps and shades in the 1920s and 30s. I have always admired early electric lights whether ceiling fixtures, table lamps or floor lamps. As early as the 1950s I was searching for lights. I remember going to the old Crippled Civilians store on lower Jarvis St. one day where I found a bronze lamp with a mica shade for which I paid two dollars. That lamp still stands proudly in my living room fifty years later. I owned it for almost twenty years before I turned it over and discovered that it was a signed Handel lamp!

The Handel Company of Meriden, Connecticut was founded in 1885 and survived until the middle of the depression in 1936. It was famous for art glass, extravagantly decorated lamps painted with exotic designs and other objects for home use. It is interesting that my lamp collecting has gone full circle. Recently at the Covert Massie auction there was a beautiful old hanging ceiling fixture offered for sale, Joan and I are friends of the people who organized the auction and we both helped by doing surveillance duty on the viewing day. This was particularly necessary, as one well-known, very adroit and suspicious character had been circulating among the crowd of hundreds who were attending the sale. This light was in my room and I kept looking at it. A lady came in and said that she was going to bid on it; I said I too wanted it and would go up to five hundred dollars; she said she was going to two thousand.

At the auction, held outside in a large tent, Joan and I sat in the front row centre for two days and did not buy anything. Finally near the end of the auction on the third day "the" fixture came up. It went past my figure very quickly and I started to relax, then Joan said, "Go for it" and I did and I got it (For over six times my original intended price, but we split the cost between us). When I got the fixture home I took it apart and found the Handel signature on all six of the glass shades. I was thrilled. Now the light hangs in my living room a companion to my two dollar Handel of fifty years ago.

The fixture is made of brass with a highly decorated incised design in a hexagonal shape fitting close to the ceiling and narrowing down, after a short flare to an inverted finial. Six individual lights with amber shades cased in an intricate metal network are suspended on decorated metal rods about two feet in length. I feel that there is a slight

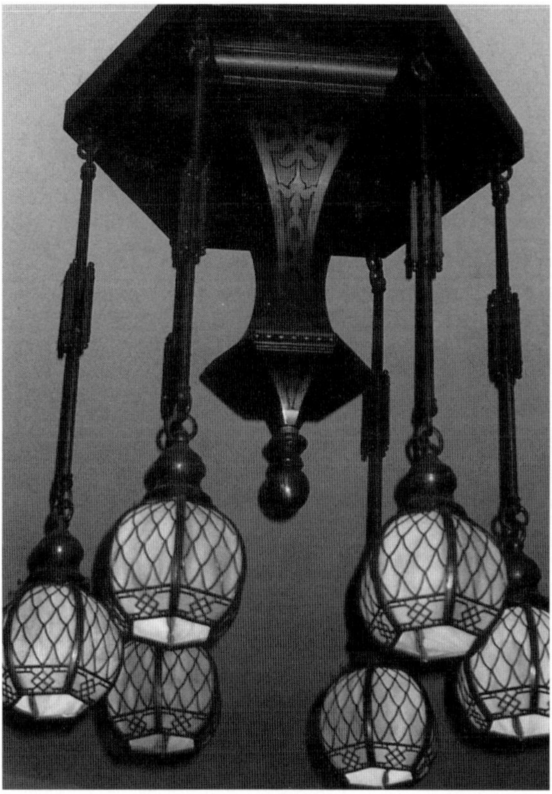

Charles Rennie Mackintosh influence in the design. An antique dealer friend of ours has told us that on the Internet, he could get us double the price we paid. We estimate that the fixture was made about 1910. We had it rewired for obvious safety reasons.

Between purchasing the two Handel lights I have secured an assortment of other lovely old fixtures. First I have a number from my father's old business, "The Art Novelty Studios", including the fixture that always hung in our dining room when I was growing up. It is a wrought and cast iron rugged type of light, somewhat Tudor in style, with six lights featuring rampant lions and requiring flame bulbs. Another fixture is the hall ceiling light with heraldic devices painted on its mica shade. There are a number of what Dad used to call bridge lamps — that is standing floor lamps from which the section holding the actual light and shade would stretch over a chair or table (perhaps a table for playing bridge and hence its name). I do not have any of Dad's original shades for these but over the years I have found a couple of good parchment shades from the 1930s period. ("parchment", normally denoting dried animal skin, here refers to a kind of heavy paper or cardboard made translucent by an oiling process)

I have a ceiling light in my study that is signed Verleys, France 1930s opalescent French shade hanging by three beautifully designed brass arms. Also there is a heavy brass light in my bedroom with thick chains and four brass arms. I have a table lamp that originally sat in the King Edward Hotel in Toronto. It is a large S-shaped dolphin with a brass shade engraved with a sailing ship. And there are others ———

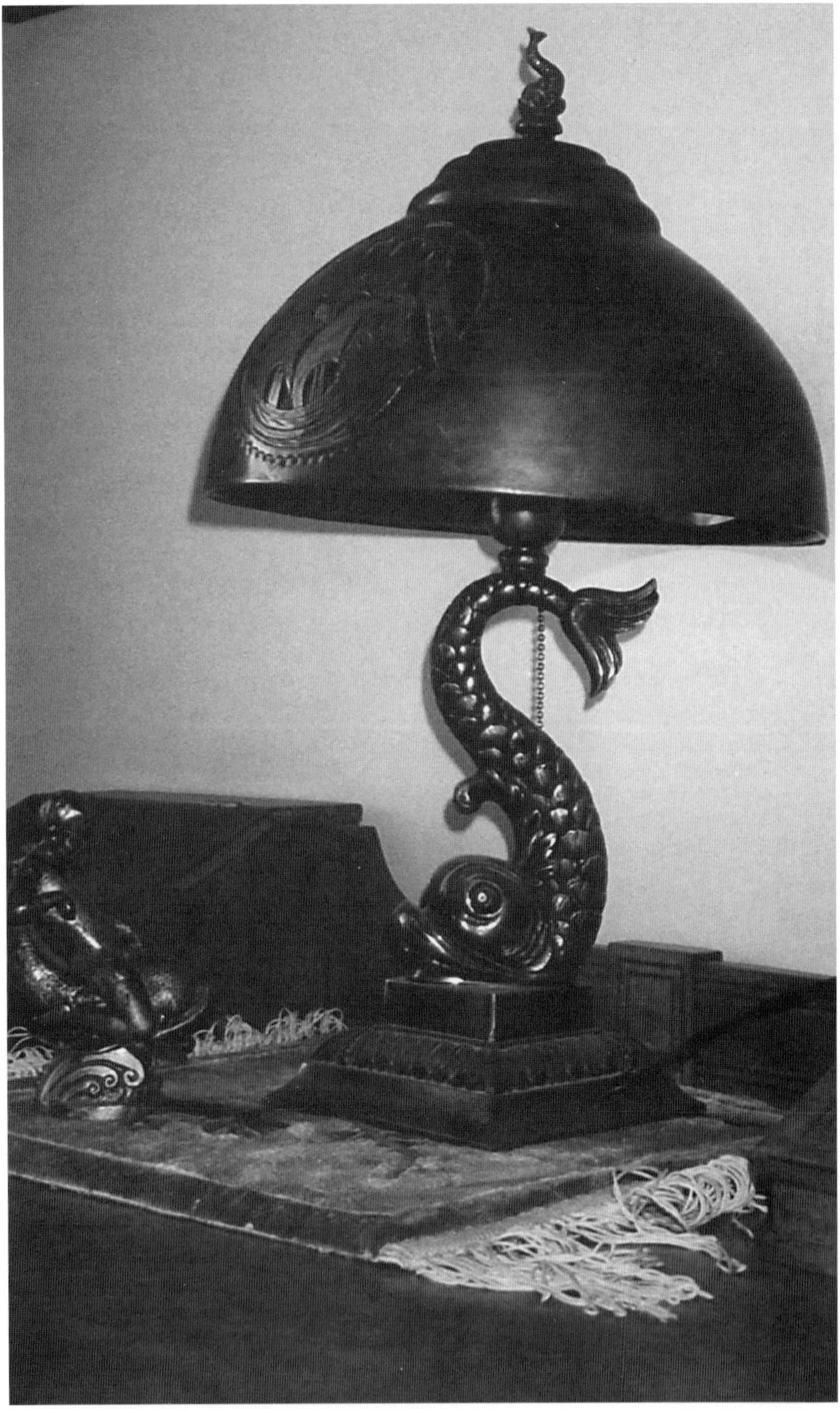

My greatest and longest lasting passion has been for collecting paintings, drawings and prints. I have bought and sold many such works. In some cases my tastes have changed in style and subject matter, but have remained consistent in others.

First of all I had my Father's own paintings as a measures of quality. I recognize the fact that my Father had two distinct phases. First of all, in his young days he was developing, along with many others of the time, a definite Canadian landscape tradition. This was shown in his small sketches that were very good and very much in the style of much of the Group of Seven early work.

Then the depression came and Dad lost his business, The Art Novelty Studios that employed more than a hundred people. Dad's partner was smart; he went back at night with a truck and removed enough equipment and supplies to start again elsewhere on a smaller scale. Dad was honest and lost everything and had to accept a job with another firm, the Florentine Company, importers of semi-quality art goods from Italy. My Father always remained the perfect gentleman; he was quiet, good natured and smiling. The true expression of his loss came in the diminution of his creative spirit; he stopped developing his painting style. The two landscapes he had had accepted for the Ontario Society of Artists Exhibition of 1929 were the best things he

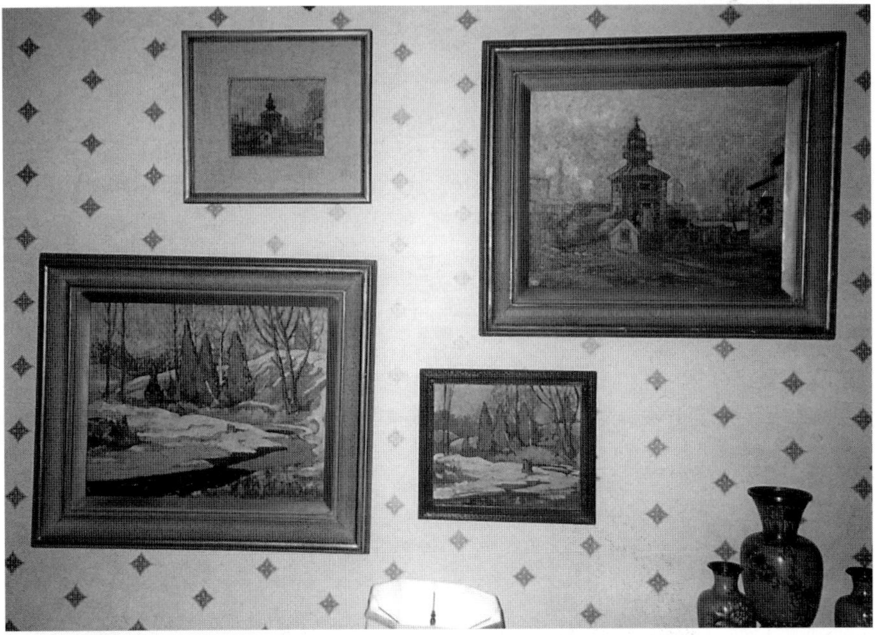

The sketches and studio paintings of Dad's two 1929 O.S.A. works

ever did. As he grew older his painting fell into a competent complacency and rarely recovered its spirit of excitement.

But to continue with my interest in pictures of all types. This collecting mania of mine was two-ended. At the lower end I place the little motto pictures of the 1920s; these were charming, with titles such as "Friendship". "Mother Dear" and "Home" They were printed in flat colour, with typical 1920s deco design, many of them dated and each with a motto in verse. I have a series of these in my bedroom.

At the other end are the fine art paintings by Ken Nutt. I have more than twenty-five of Ken's works. There are his drawings, in black and white or colour for his children's book illustrations and then there are his large painted works that cost thousands of dollars. These have been described in an earlier chapter and so I need say no more about them here.

I must point out that sometimes I think I am one of the few sane people in a crazy world. I am not a wealthy man but I have never thought it the least bit strange to buy a painting and take a year to pay it off; most other people in our society will buy a new car and lose thousands of dollars on it the day they first drive it around the block. With good judgment based on intuition and training I have always bought paintings and if I wanted to sell them I have always made money on my investments. That happens only occasionally in the field of transportation.

I have said earlier that I greatly admired the work of Peter Harris of St. Catharines. This man was crippled for most of his life and such a disability might have affected the attitude of most other people. But for Peter, somehow, it gave him a love of beauty that he transferred into his painting. His magnificent paintings of women are some of the strongest depictions of the female form that I have ever seen. His women are always strong people and absolutely feminine. At a 1986 exhibition organized by the Gallery Stratford I bought a painting of his called "Woman Reading", 1985 mixed media on paper. The colours are soft pastels, and

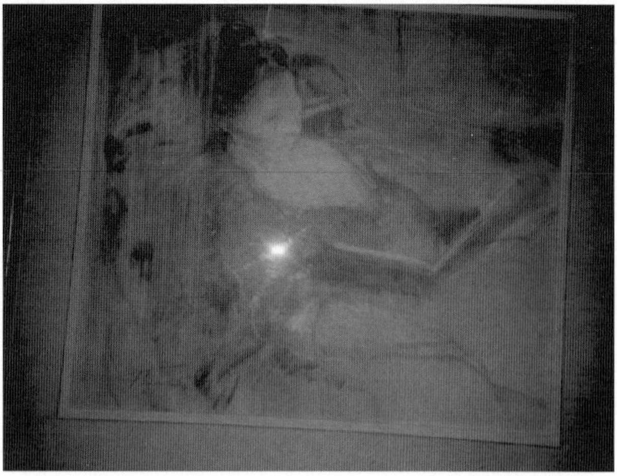

the relaxed pose of the figure suggests complete concentration on the book. I bought the work directly from Peter and he allowed me to pay for it, one hundred dollars a month for a year and a half.

Another artist I have admired and who stood the test of time is William Roberts. I bought four of his watercolours in the early 1970s and have never regretted the purchases. One picture I secured by trading one of my melodeons for it. I have always thought of Bill Roberts as the master of the empty spaces. He did a series involving apples, lemons and Victorian postcards. I have one watercolour of a postcard of a little Victorian girl and four apples. The rest of the picture is absolutely blank. The placing of the objects in the picture plane is such that every time you look at the work you fill in the empty spaces yourself with your own subject matter.

When I was with the Art Institute of Ontario I organized a small exhibition of L.A.C. Panton's work. Panton was Principal of the Ontario College of Art at the time of his death in 1954. I organized an exhibition of eleven studies and paintings to show Panton's work as a mature artist. His widow very kindly lent the works to the A.I.O. In the process of doing the show I bought one oil painting and two gouaches from her. I sold the oil and one gouache but still prize the last one. Panton was a realist in his early career but his work became more and more stylized as his career advanced until finally in his last few years he moved right into abstraction. His later works centred on the east coast. My picture is abstract filled with wind, waves and rocky coast and even a fisherman's hat. To my mind these abstract fragments give a much stronger story of the might of the forces of nature on the coast than a realistic picture could ever hope to portray.

Enough is enough. I have tried to show examples of my collecting fervor. But it has extended in many other directions also; for example a dozen wonderful Art Deco cups and saucers, two water colours by Tony Urquhart, a drawing by Peter Kolisnyk, my two gorgeous Brigit Riley prints, and so on. The reader by this time must realize that my house is overflowing with stuff. I must admit I thought so myself until two years ago. After renovations to the house, my sister moved in and three large moving vans arrived outside the door with her few belongings. That was the closest I have ever come to a heart seizure. Of course my melodeon collection was described in another chapter. I should add a note to state that somehow all of Joan's belongings found a home. Invariably people say, "There is so much to look at everywhere."

Chapter Twenty

Crackers and Crumbs

I was involved with arts organizations for more than twenty-five years. My field was the visual arts. I enjoyed meeting people ranging from the amateur right up to the top professional artist. In Canada our arts organizations are organized with a volunteer Board of Directors and, depending on the size of the organization, a professional staff. I was one of those people, a staff member. After many years I finally found it frustrating on a variety of levels; new boards had to be dealt with each year; raising funds from various government sources, private individuals and corporations became more difficult, and salaries in arts organizations lagged behind other professions. I decided to give up the security of a regular salary and go out on my own.

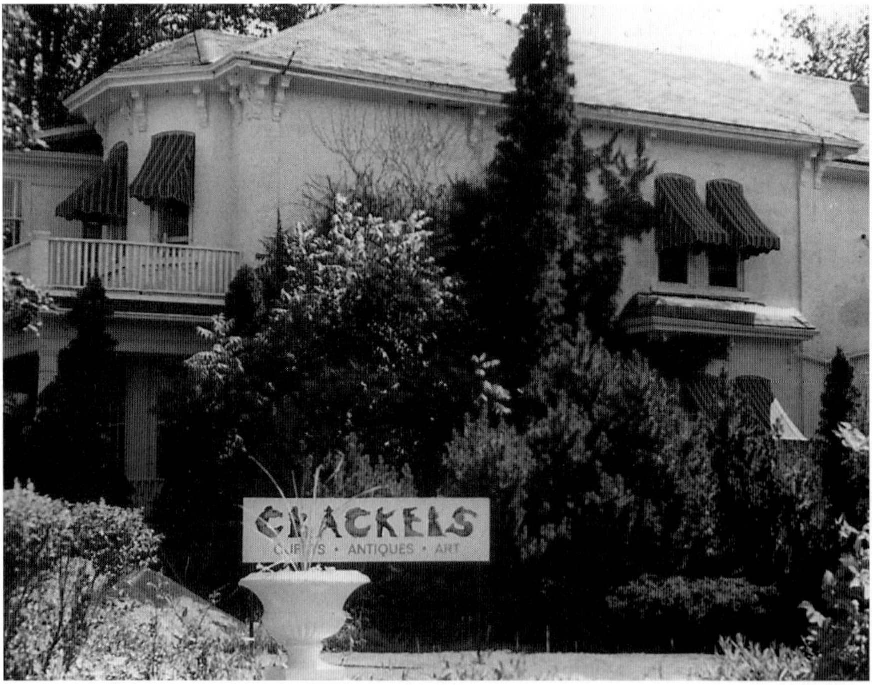

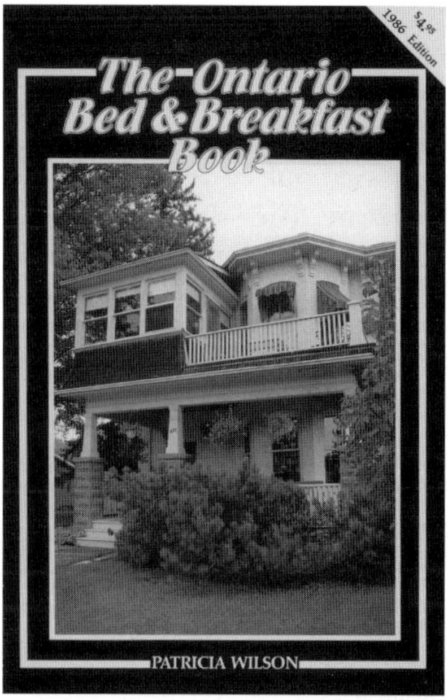

I bought a large, Edwardian style, old home on Erie Street, Stratford. I decided to open a bed and breakfast business combined with an antique store. My house had once been part of the building complex that was now the Leslie Cheese House. I thought I would name my establishment accordingly and called it, "Crackers". The B & B part and the main antique store were in the large house; the lesser antiques and collectibles were in the old converted garage, which was called "The Crumbs".

I did not know this fact at the time but some of my guests who came from the southern U.S.A. gleefully told me that the name Crackers in the southern U.S. referred to poor whites. Actually not quite a misnomer if referring to my first year of operations.

I was able to open at just the right time. By this I mean that there were only about a dozen bed and breakfast houses in Stratford in 1980. Later when the idea caught on there would be many dozens of them. In fact I eventually thought that there were too many. Many retired people thought that operating a B. and B. would be a good idea to add to their retirement incomes, meet interesting people and keep busy for a part of the year. Of course, all of these things were true. However the three theatres could hold only so many people. The main Festival Theatre seats 1,824, the Avon Theatre 1,117 people and the Tom Patterson Theatre 487 people, for a total of 3,428. That of course is the figure for full capacity, Take into consideration that the Festival runs for only part of the year, the shoulder seasons — the spring and fall — may have only half capacity; and many students who attend the Festival return home by bus at the end of the day. Then some plays may not be very popular, and the theatres regularly are dark on Sunday. You then have a considerably reduced number of people to draw on. I am not being negative, only realistic.

I had a very successful guesthouse. I had been to Cape Cod and I attempted to set up my house on what I had observed in Provincetown. I had a happy hour about 5 p.m. each evening. My customers could have sherry, cheese, crackers or biscuits, and enjoy conversation with my other guests. Then if they wished they would go to the theatre and have a leisurely dinner after the show. You learn by experience. I used to put out a full bottle of sherry until, one night I only had one couple in the house. Obviously they had never had sherry before. They drank the whole bottle, got drunk and missed the theatre. After that I used a decanter for the sherry and only put out enough for approximately two drinks per guest. These "Happy Hours" were a great success.

Stratford, since the Festival began, has attracted many artists whether they work in the theatre, an ancillary business or simply like the ambiance. I was delighted to find a wonderful designer for my logo, for my signs, stationary, etcetera. Scott McKowen had worked for another design firm in Stratford; then he struck out on his own and his talent and ability brought him work from far beyond Stratford. He has now worked for the National Ballet, and for some years he has been doing all the designing of brochures and related material for the Shaw Festival. I have been told that the Shaw has sent him to England to secure photoprops that are unavailable in Canada. For example, for the play *Private Lives* by Noel Coward an original photograph of Coward was found that was hung on a set in that play.

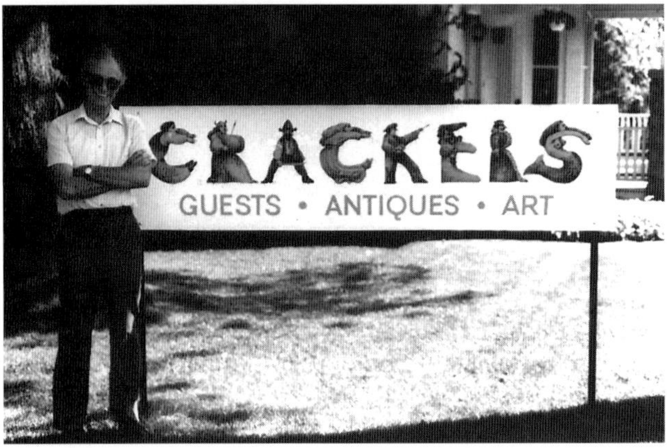

Scott took my name "Crackers" and designed it into a set of theatre figures, each letter being one figure. The "C" started out as a male figure falling backwards with his arms and legs thrown out in front of him and his back curved to form a "C. The "R" was a Wagnerian soprano of wonderful attributes; turned sideways with one leg forward.... the Logo was wonderful and attracted much attention.

In 1986 I received the first of a serial Christmas card from Scott and his wife, Christina. There were fourteen in the series, which ended in the year 1999. Each card was a letter in the greeting "Merry Christmas". The first, for example, was for the letter "M" and showed a couple, dressed in the fashion of the Pieter Breughel painting, "The Wedding Dance" from 1566, dancing and making merry. Other images were mediaeval, some modern. I was happy to live out the full fourteen years and end up with a window decoration. In 2001 I received the first of a new series on the twelve days of Christmas. Will I live so long?

Scott is a wonderful draughtsman. Last year I also received at Christmas copies of a series of sketches from a European trip, followed by the same this year. In his Christmas letter Scott told me that four of his drawings are in this year's annual exhibition of the New York Society of Illustrators. Stratford is indeed fortunate in having such talent in the local area.

Back to Crackers. It is amusing how one learns on the job. When I first opened I was a brand new host. Take simple little things: I had huge, hand-made mugs for coffee, which looked grand but emptied the coffee pot in one round. I then found that many people drink one cup of coffee only. I bought smaller mugs and the coffee went a great deal further. A guest could always ask for a second cup. The same with croissants, if I put a dozen on the table for five people, they would all disappear. I could put out six and add more later if needed.

One guest house in Stratford set up a formal dining room each morning for its eight guests. They would all come down and eat; the room, was pleasant and they would spend half the morning talking about the play that they had seen the night before. I had a better idea; my guests ate in the kitchen and I could seat only five with comfort. Other guests would come downstairs and seeing that the table was full

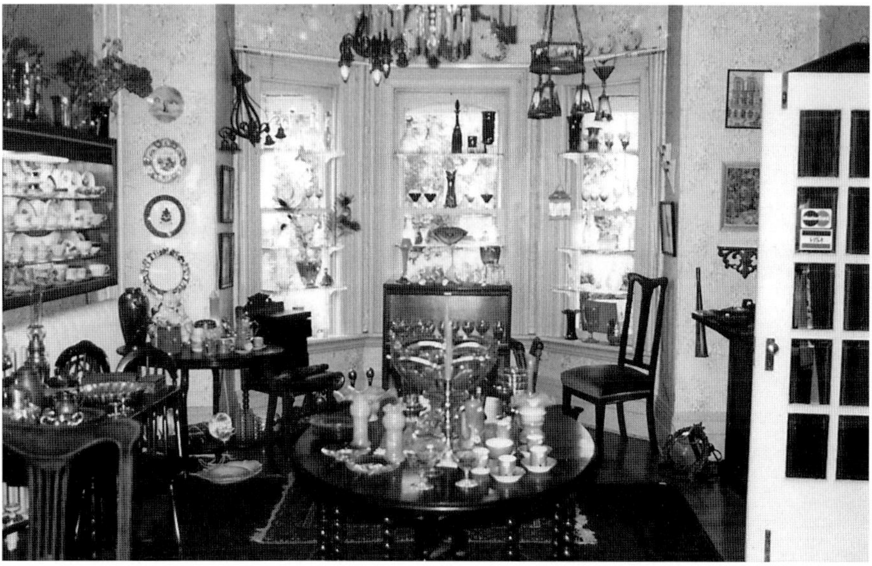

would then wander around my antique store to put in the time. You would be surprised how many items I would find waiting on the counter to be wrapped and paid for after breakfast! When there was a pile up the other guests tended to finish and then take their coffee out on the pleasant verandah where there was a vine giving shade and comfortable chairs. Some one might call it conniving, but I call it good marketing:

Over the five years I had many wonderful guests at Crackers. I especially remember a few who became good friends. Don and Phyllis Ketcheson used to book the whole house each year and then arrive with six other friends. They had enjoyed this outing for many years at Stratford. The whole group used to spend time in my antique store and invariably I sold a number of items. Don owned a design firm located on Clarence Square in Toronto. One year he was especially interested in a French Empire period desk that I had for sale. It was quite magnificent and had many secret drawers in it. I would love to have kept it myself if I could have afforded it. He sent one of his assistants back to Stratford the following week to see it and then buy it. He had it completely refinished and a year later he sent me a picture from a design magazine featuring the desk in a contemporary setting. Don retired a few years ago and now he and Phyllis live near me in Northumberland County. I quite often see the couple at local musical events.

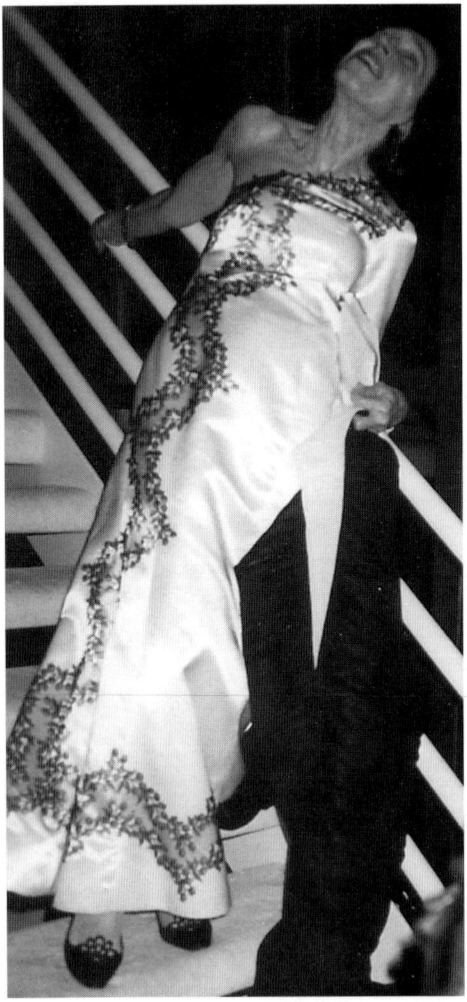

Another friend that I hear from each year is Louise Hodgson of Detroit. Louise would arrive with a friend, Terry Shea, a bank manager, who would do the driving. Louise was a strike negotiator for unions and, I understand, a very good one. She was also a great patron of the musical scene in Detroit. Louise had two apartments, one across the hall from the other in the building where she lived. She actually lived in the one and kept the other one for her costumes. Each time she would go to an opera or a musical event she would dress to suit the music. If it was Carmen, she dressed as Carmen and so on. Nobody ever knew what she was going to appear in next. She sent me three wonderful pictures in which she is posing in various outfits. On the back of one picture, a beautiful silk creation, she wrote, "Made by a friend of mine out of a garage sale sari, ribbons and safety pins, no sewing, puffed at neck in front." One time I had a large box of beautiful lace in my store. Louise went crazy over it and bought a great deal of it. She sent me a photo of herself posing on a stairway and looking upward; her gown was white with one shoulder exposed. The black lace she had bought looked magnificent;, it circled her neck and zigzagged down the right side, and went around: the bottom of the gown. There was a black train trailing along behind. Louise fell in love with my Grant MacDonald painting, "Boy with a Bicycle" and I sold it to her.

I remember the Peter and Mannie Marshall family from London. Peter was an art teacher who had advanced up the administration ladder in education. All the family had a good "eye". I remember the first spring when the parents with son Demetrius and daughter Mamueleta came into the shop. I was pleased to have quite a few interesting and reasonable items that I had obtained in the course of the winter months from auctions and garage sales. The family first bought some mud figures, those little clay figures that the Chinese place in their miniature gardens. Then they looked around and literally cleaned me out! The shop looked denuded after they left.

Dr. Chris Leung would appear from London also. He was a doctor, and I surmise that his first love was for his native oriental art objects, as he knew everything about them. He would come in and identify and date objects that I had bought more from intuition and my sense of design than from my knowledge.

Dr. Alan Preston and his wife, Mary, were frequent visitors. They lived in Toronto but also had a home in Renfrew. They bought one of my melodeons and now I understand that that particular reed organ is residing in Upper Canada Village. I will always remember the fact that they bought a set of George Barbier silk screen or pochior prints from me, dated 1922. This set came from a limited edition of a yearbook that Barbier had created for a client to give to her customers, probably for a fashion show. It was actually bad timing that made me sell them.

The day before the Prestons arrived to stay at Crackers I had received the bill for my annual fire and theft insurance premium. It was for a little over a thousand dollars. The prints were not in my shop but in my living quarters. Mary fell in love with the prints and offered me a thousand dollars for them. What could I do?

Henry and Marci Blumberg often stayed with me. Henry was a lawyer who was searching for a specialized line of collecting. Since he was interested in books I suggested that he pursue Canadian books that had been illustrated by Canadian artists. I had a couple of examples to show him from my own collection. However he settled on something quite different, American Civil War postcards. He eventually amassed an amazing collection, as I realized the last time I saw him a few years ago. He brought out his laptop computer to show me some examples. The above cross-section of extremely interesting people who were my guests could go on but I shall limit myself to just a few people I found fascinating.

Crackers gained great publicity. Pat Wilson featured a picture of the house on the cover of her Ontario Bed and Breakfast book in 1986. Kay Kritzwiser of the *Globe and Mail* featured my art collection in an article in 1981. *The Buffalo News*, the *Ottawa Citizen* and the *Montreal Gazette*, all mentioned Crackers when doing features on Bed and Breakfast locations. Magazines did the same, a picture of my house appeared in *City and Country* magazine in 1986, also in *Leisureways*, and *Ontario Leisure Magazine*. I have a scrapbook full of favourable notices.

As you can see from the above, it is hard to separate the B & B operation from the antiques. I had never been an antique dealer before although both Joan and Jane had been in the business for many years. I thoroughly enjoyed it. At first I used only the front room of the house for displaying stock. Of course more "stuff" arrived than I could handle and so I moved back a room and took over the old dining room. Then I realized that I often bought groups of things because I was especially interested in one or two items. So I took over the garage at the back and made it into "The Crumbs" where I could display and sell all this extra stock. I could not keep "The Crumbs" staffed, instead, I put up a sign asking customers to bring anything they found interesting into the main house, or else call a staff member to come out. Maybe at some time something was stolen. I am sure, however, that the cost of the stolen article was less than having a staff member on duty.

My sister, Joan, along with her partner, another Joan (Frith) and a Scotch friend, Ethel Mailer, opened an antique store in the early 1960s in the village of Newcastle. It was on the north-east corner of the main intersection, across from the Community Hall. A little later, they transferred their business, called "The Queen's Gambit" to Woodlawn Terrace in Cobourg. The business was most successful, and the proprietors became known far and wide as "The Girls". They specialized in buying whole estates. Many antique dealers traveling between shows, coming from Montreal or Toronto, would drop in to see the latest stock at any time of the day or night. Coffee would always appear, along with sweets. They operated the shop for many years.

I had two principal sources of stock. First of all, my sister Joan spent some time in Florida each winter. She was a born antique dealer. She visited stores, went to innumerable garage sales and sought out people selling things of interest. Florida was fruitful and a promising place to find stock; so often people would retire, leaving their big home in the north and move south to a smaller place, bringing their special treasures, usually small items, with them. Then (conveniently, from our point of view) they would die and their belongings would come on the market. Joan was only too ready and willing to purchase. I do not mean to make it sound callous but out of misfortune can come opportunity. Joan would collect stock all winter and bring it home to Canada. I appreciated having the first chance to buy from her. I remember especially buying art glass because I was interested in it myself. I also liked acquiring antique electric light fixtures, as previously mentioned, old oriental rugs and Art Deco items.

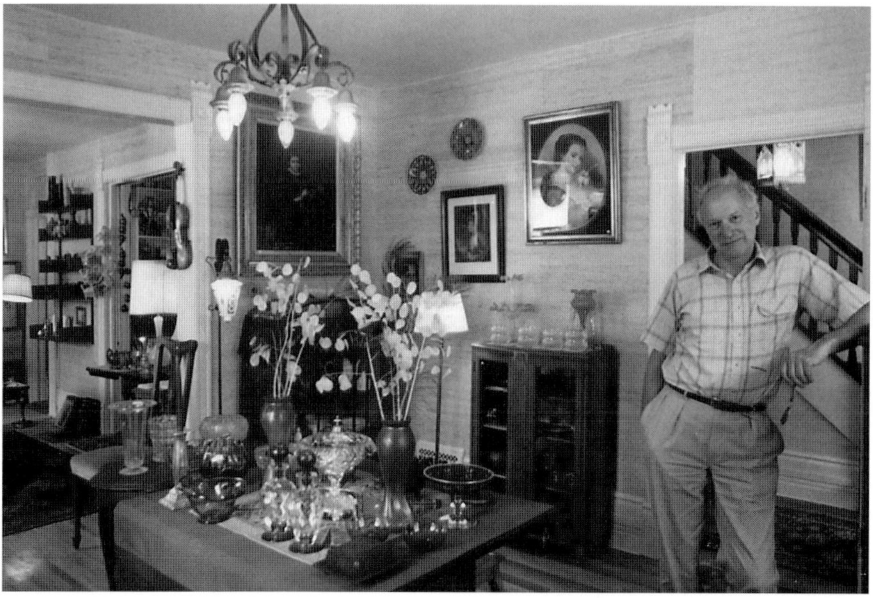

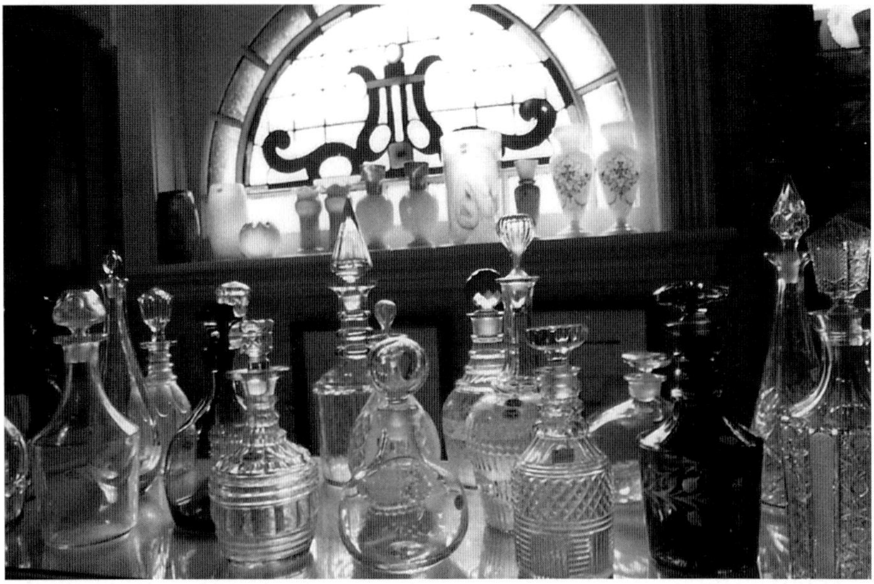

One of my other sources of antique stock was the evening auction that was held by James Stock each week at his sales barn. They were fun. There was an excellent food counter with homemade pies. I used to take a book and sit on the aisle seat in the second row. I could read my book, glance up as each item was brought forward and look down again without missing a word of my reading. I always previewed everything that was for sale the afternoon before. Many other dealers attended these auctions, and most of them tended to group at the back and swap shop talk. I knew them all but I did not join them as I liked operating my own way. James Bisback and Jonny of Jonny's Antiques in Shakespeare were the biggest dealers in these circles. At those auctions I bought many wonderful items. I grew to know, respect and like Ruth and Jim Stocks. I still correspond with them at Christmas. I found many bargains over the years, including many things that I kept for my own home.

In 1986 I sold Crackers; please see the chapter, *A Home of One's Own*, page 244. I moved to 286 Ontario Street, still in Stratford. I no longer operated a B. and B, but concentrated on antiques and art. I remember one couple of customers in particular; Jan Caputo and Ken Bruge from Michigan. They bought a huge walnut sideboard from me and they paid for it over a series of months; and then one Saturday they arrived with a truck to take it home. They brought friends with them to load it and had friends at home to help them carry the sideboard in triumph into its new domain; they sent me photos of the whole operation. They reported that they had no trouble with customs at the border. I had prepared them with a certificate of age. They had to assure the customs officer that they did not intend to sell it telling him emphatically, "Never".

I had sold the name of "Crackers" with the building so now I became "Paul Bennett, Antiques and Art". Scott McKowen once again designed my logo, this time with an Art Deco flavour. Unfortunately I had chosen a bad location. I had thought that it would be good because it lay between the downtown of Stratford and the Festival Theatre. I did not realize that people would be rushing along past my shop to get to the play, eagerly anticipating the performance and not even looking in toward my shop; people leaving the play would be gossiping about what had happened on stage and again would not even see my shop. I had only a driveway for parking and it would accommodate only one car, nobody wants to block somebody ahead of them.

I stayed there until 1994, but it was never as successful as Crackers at 433 Erie Street. Indeed I lost money my last two years in business, and somehow this did terrible things to my income tax. I was not allowed to claim that I had living quarters in the building and ended up paying thousands in back taxes. Live and learn: Finally with Jay married and a death in the family I decided to move east to be near my two sisters. It was time to retire anyway.

Before I leave this section I must mention some of the people who worked for me. Mike McDonald wrote me a letter of application on May 8th in 1983. He was a High School student who had spent two years working with the Stratford Summer Music Festival. He said he had confidence in meeting people. He also added that he was sure that he could handle housework. I quote from his letter:, "I feel that I would do more than an adequate job in tending to the needs of the house for here at home, in order to receive my weekly allowance, I must tend the housely duties of cleaning." He got the job and worked for me a number of years until he decided to move to Toronto where he first worked in Britnell's and then in other book stores, where he has done very well for himself.

Another employee was Judith Donaldson. I cannot remember how I met Judith but she first worked at Crackers and then later at 286 Ontario Street. She was charming, artistic, trustworthy and a good friend. Judith lived in St. Mary's with her companion in an old stone house that was transformed by her talents. She bought a number of pieces of furniture from me including a Queen Anne couch with wicker arms and back that I still covet for myself. She placed down cushions on it and made it extremely comfortable. Don, Judith's companion, is a retired journalist, if you could call him retired, for he still writes columns for the local papers. Judith writes me a letter at Christmas telling me about her painting, her children and grandchildren and many of her activities.

My years of living at 286 Ontario Street in Stratford are closely linked with the Linley family. The father, Richard, is a lawyer and a one-time alderman of the city of Stratford. Anna, the mother, is a nurse. This couple has four sons: Robin, Aaron, Andrew and Richard, and it is the most remarkable family that I have ever known. All four boys worked for me in some capacity or other over the years. It is a measure of the wholesome yet tolerant upbringing of these boys, that although they must have known that I was gay, from the eldest to the youngest boy, they followed each other in doing my garden work and other duties connected with my store.

I met Robin, the oldest, one spring night on the train from Toronto to Stratford. I was looking for somebody to work for me; he was looking for a summer job and he came to work for me. All four brothers were conscientious, honest and reliable. Robin went on working for me weekends and summer until he was finished high school. He went on to take Philosophy and History at Queen's University. He marked time for a while working as a waiter or server in a bar in Toronto. Then he decided to follow his father's footsteps and went to Law School at Dalhousie University. After working in Singapore and Toronto as a lawyer he received a scholarship to attend Oxford where he is now taking his Master of Law degree. In school breaks Robin wandered around Europe.

Aaron next appeared on the scene. He is quieter and more reserved than his brothers. He cut short his work for me at age sixteen when he went to Germany on a Rotary Club scholarship. Later he travelled around Europe and North America for a year and returned to attend the Chef's School at Stratford. He worked at Rundles Restaurant in that city, met Bronwyn, married and the couple now have a child, Liam. Aaron opened his own restaurant in Stratford, the Bijou. It is one of Stratford's better restaurants and is doing very well.

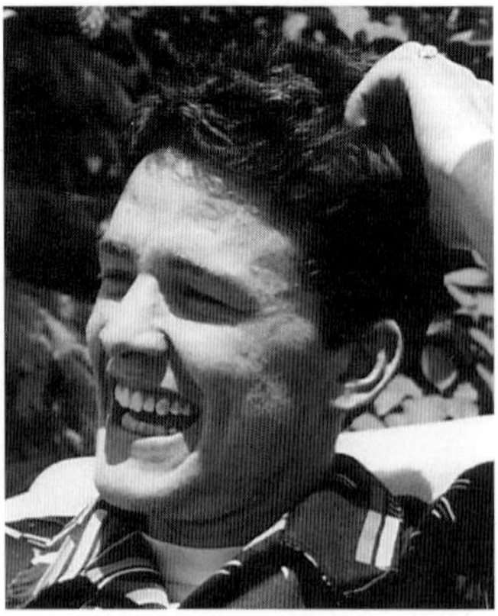

Aaron recommended his brother, Andrew, to me, to replace himself. I will never forget the day that Andrew came to apply for the job. Like Aaron and now Richard, he is very tall. At that age he was very slim. He came in my store and smiled a greeting and I do swear the whole room lit up. He has the most infectious smile of anybody that I have ever met. He was a great sportsman at school and into every activity. He went on to McGill because he wanted to experience the ambiance of Montreal. He took honours English with a minor in Religious Studies. In Montreal he was very active in volleyball but gave that up for drama as both an actor and a director. He travelled to Europe a number of times. He returned to Stratford and became an apprentice at the Festival for one season and then was on stage for the 2001 season. He would prefer being a director, which I think is wise. The roles for a six foot four hero are not numerous. He loves white water rafting and is going to be a guide this coming summer on the Ottawa River. Then he will be off to the Czech Republic to teach English for a year. He intends to come back and attend teachers' college.

Richard, the youngest, was a star tennis player in Stratford at a very early age. Actually he only worked briefly for me walking my dogs. I will always remember giving him five loonies the first time he walked Andy and Jenny. I gave him the five coins on purpose to make the fee look big. I watched as he went out the door. He bounced the coins up and down in his hand, gave his head a little nod and smiled as much as to say, "That's not so bad." Richard went to France on a Rotary scholarship for a year, returned and finished high school and then spent a year in Ottawa as a page in the House of Commons. He is now deciding (2002) what is next.

A wonderful family filled with an adventurous spirit and a love of life. With such young people coming along how can our country go wrong? Andrew is the one who has stayed in touch with me. About once a year he drops in to say hello, there is the occasional 'phone call, and a Christmas card comes from the whole family.

Chapter Twenty One

Robert, Mary, Violet, Kay

Robert Gage

I met Robert Gage at a dinner party one evening at Chris and Henry's home. Robert is a famous host and I had heard many stories about him a long time before I met him. Soon after we met he invited me to dinner. So began a five-year period when my gay social life largely hinged on this generous, friendly individual.

Robert is a hair dresser. He is very successful and his salon is considered one of the best by the social elite of Toronto. Everybody goes there, from the leaders of society, to visiting movie stars and important political figures.

Robert had a perfect background for his career. His mother had been a hairdresser for the fashionable figures of an earlier generation and she used to travel a great deal taking young Robert along. Robert spent part of his youth in Italy, England and other European locations. He met the rich and famous and tells great stories about such people as Rudolf Nureyev and Mick Jagger.

One such story tells how as a young man he started out with a woman friend in an old car from Italy and drove into Switzerland. The car broke down on a mountain road in the Alps, and along came an old truck loaded down with male agricultural workers. They waved at the girl, she grabbed her bag, waved at Robert, and ran over and jumped into the truck! Robert never saw her again. Robert went on waiting by his car, hoping for assistance, eventually along came an English lord driving a Rolls. He waved at Robert and beckoned to him. Robert grabbed his bag, jumped into the Rolls, went back to England and lived with the Lord for a number of years.

When I first heard about Robert's home in Warkworth, I was told that it was in a converted church. I pictured it as being straight out of

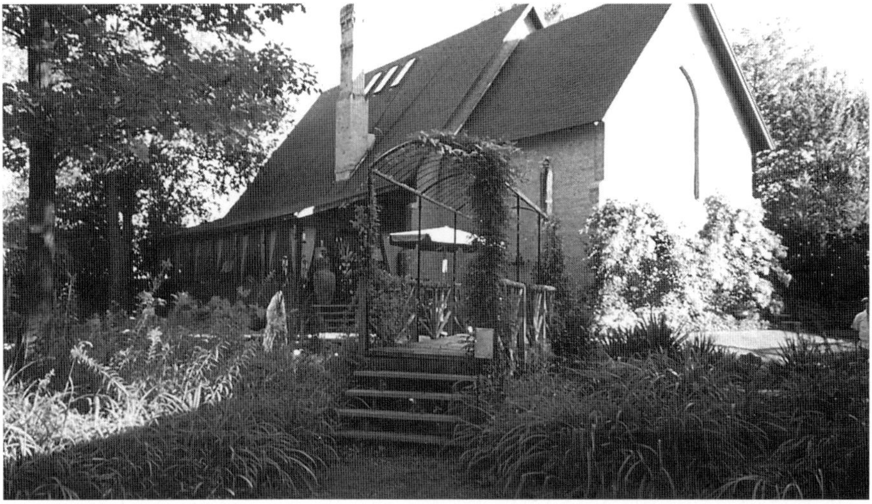

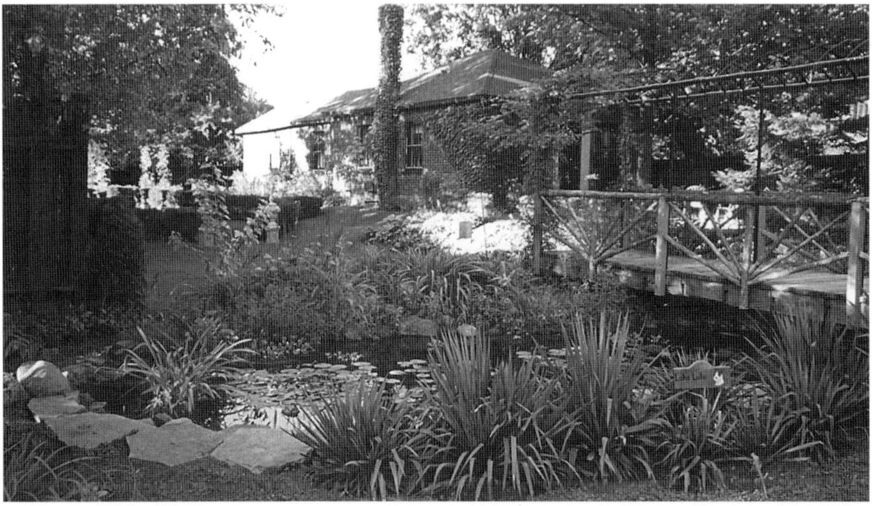

an interior design magazine. It is anything but; it has a human element about it that far outreaches anything a magazine can produce. It is, above all, comfortable, and the visitor immediately feels at home. It is filled with antique furniture, some pieces of which are especially beautiful. It is filled with art objects that suit Robert's taste, not fashion. Some of the oil paintings are fantasies of bad taste, I think of a portrait of Cleopatra clasping an asp to her breast, and a so-called pioneer portrait with a far too large head, secured from Ron Windebank's antique store. There are a number of small sculptures by E.B. Cox and a very soothing oil by Michael Bunn. There are good pieces of wrought iron about, and sections of architectural forms such as columns and bits of pediments.

The church itself was deconsecrated many years ago. Thank God, I am sure Robert would say. The chancel end is now the kitchen with huge freezers and stoves and ample storage. Guests usually come in through a side entrance into a vestibule at the south side and proceed down two steps into what was the main body of the church, now a wonderful living room complete with a huge fieldstone fireplace containing a fire that never seems to go out. The chairs and chesterfields are all comfortable, good quality and have a used, lived-in look. The ceiling here is low to accommodate two levels of bedrooms and baths above. There is a dining area at the east end of this room. Then you go through an arch and suddenly the ceiling soars up to its original height with a balcony looking down from above. This eastern end is another comfortable sitting area with partial columns, angels, and heavenly paraphernalia decorating the walls.

When Robert bought the church he had a tall wooden fence put right around the property enclosing a large, long irregularly shaped garden, a small manse, and the church itself. I understand, that after the fact, the town fathers passed a by-law prohibiting such fences. The garden itself is an evolving work of art. When I first came on the scene Robert was just going to put in a pond — and what a pond!, It is a small lake that stretches right across the property, with a bridge across the central area that within a year or so will be completely covered with wisteria. When Robert had the pond first built I was just downsizing my own lily pond, and I was able to give him many lilies, fish, and three fountains (that were attached to an old wrought iron fence sitting in the middle of the pond).

Robert loves pergolas. He has created a vista right down the centre of the garden that ends in a natural wood pergola covered with grape and other vines. There is an herb garden to one side, with magnificent hostas and small cedar hedges defining different areas. All the perennials are in large clumps with a huge mass of old fashioned orange lilies right across the lake in front of the old manse. There is also a pergola at the north end of the lake with a kind of dock waiting, I am sure, for a small boat or canoe to pull up!

So, we have the setting for wonderful dinners. In the warm months guests usually sit outside by the water or on the large enclosed verandah that runs right along the complete north side of the old church. Robert is a wonderful cook; often in the warm weather he will cook a large joint or roast in his huge barbeque. His dinners are not complicated. The vegetables, the salads, the desserts, are simple, but cooked to perfection with subtle flavorings and seasoning. Each time I have eaten there I have left, telling Robert that was the best meal ever, and I meant it.

There are many gay people living in the Warkworth area, some retired couples, others with weekend homes, other working from their homes. Always on weekends there are get-togethers of one sort and another. Each year there is a certain set of events that you can count on. First, Robert always has a huge Christmas Eve party, his "Orphans in the Storm Party". Everybody goes to it. He has been having these parties ever since he was a young man; new friends, old friends, mothers of friends, friends of friends, all turn up. Each year some old ones fail to appear and new people take their place. I have attended five of these events. . There is always a huge spread of food, large wheels of delicious cheeses, platters of wonderful entrees, and massive cakes. Drinks are poured, everywhere are dishes full of nuts, candies, chips, pickled herring, you name it. There is a huge tree superbly decorated, and there are other seasonal decorations: lights around the pool, lights on the verandah, and decorations across the mantel. A wonderful night that I would not like to miss.

In the Warkworth area there are regular seasonal get-togethers: the Halloween party given by Bob and Tom; the tobogganing party given by Meirion and Bob; the garden party in late summer hosted by Dick; my garden party way down in Port Hope in July, and so on.

I enjoy my visit to Robert's dinners very much. In Warkworth many social events are very casual and are called on the spur of the moment. Actually I have become something of an anomaly, I have to travel from Port Hope, a half hour's drive from Warkworth, I am single, I am a generation older than most people attending; in fact my age has cut me out of many conversations by Toronto people on business, theatre, the latest scandals and so on. Finally my participation has become somewhat limited and I miss it. Also since my sister has moved in with me I have been drawn more and more into the local social scene in Port Hope, particularly with regard to musical activities.

Robert has changed his weekend schedule drastically. He has found a wonderful partner, Justin, and rightfully his social life became centered on Justin. The grand dinners with dozen or more guests have become less frequent. There used to be a saying when an older man turned up at a gay social gathering with a younger man, that he was the flavour of the week. Well, I was an older man and very fortunate; I was the flavour of five years, and that is not bad.

Mary

Many years ago in Toronto I had my first cleaning woman, named Mary. Mary was also the cleaning woman for my sister, Joan, and went to her home the day after she had been to mine. That meant, of course, that I cleaned my apartment before Mary arrived just in case she talked too much to my sister.

Mary was a big woman with a somewhat gruff voice. She lived in an old house up under Casa Loma. She had a large number of dogs that she usually kept in the house when she was away. These dogs, for some unknown reason, kept having puppies and so the pack multiplied. One day Mary went home and found that she had forgotten her key, and nobody was at home to let her in. She called over to an obliging neighbour who agreed to go in the open front window and unlock the door from the inside.

He got half way in the window when there was frenzied barking and he was attacked by half a dozen dogs. Mary, in her wisdom, instead of pulling him out, pushed him in. He finally beat off the dogs and opened the door for Mary. In the meantime, she had found her key! I figured it was a scam — she simply did not have enough dog food that night to feed the dogs and thought that a juicy neighbour would do nicely.

One Monday afternoon I had a phone call from Mary. "Mr. Bennett, can I come and clean your house on Wednesday? I have to go to my husband's funeral on Tuesday". Her voice sounded like a foghorn over the phone as she always yelled into it. I was having guests for dinner on the Tuesday evening but I was gracious and agreed to her request. I decided to go to the funeral myself.

I arrived at the funeral home and went in. The funeral director, seeing me in a suit, came rushing over to greet me and handed me a bible. He thought I was the minister. It was a welfare funeral. I went into the funeral parlour, and there was Mary, wearing her usual work clothes for cleaning. The only other person present was her sister. Mary had told me about this sister, who was a prostitute. She stood there, her bleached blond hair sticking out from under a black pillbox hat. Her body was like a sack of potatoes with two toothpicks for legs. She was stylishly dressed in a very short black dress. There was a veil over her face. A minister did come in and stood over the casket and the service began. Suddenly it was interrupted by the big door opening at the back of the parlour. "Are you done yet? I ain't got all day?' It was the sister's latest client who had been waiting impatiently outside the door.

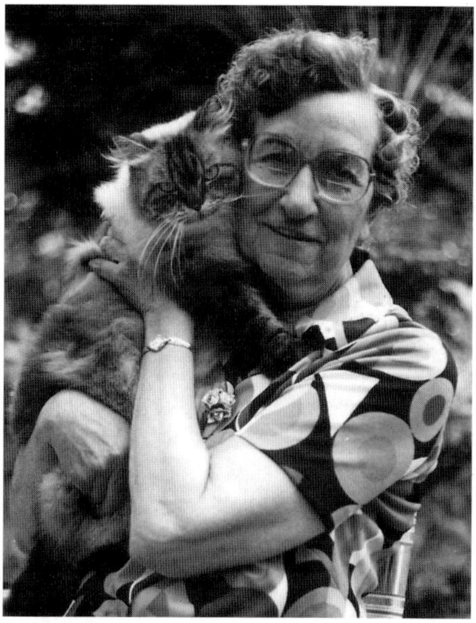

Violet Strohkirch

When I moved to Stratford, I lived on Water Street. My next-door neighbour was a maiden lady named Violet Strohkirch. Violet had lived in her house since the early 1930s when it was built by her parents. In her early years, she had lived in a large log cabin on the farm that her father owned. The Strohkirchs were of German background. Violet had a beautiful flower garden on her house's double lot. A maple tree planted at the front centre of her lawn grew to such a size that first the front flowerbeds lost the sun and then even the lawn did not prosper because of the dense foliage.

Violet has a lily pond. She had been given two white lilies back in the thirties and she still has the descendants of those original plants. Every year she takes these hardy lilies out of the pond, places them in green garbage bags and closes them up, and they hibernate in the basement with Violet checking them once or twice during the winter to see that they still have enough moisture. Violet's pond was built in the old way, with a cement base and sides. Each year a crack or two would appear and Violet would have it cemented over. Of course successive layers of cement over a period of sixty years plus have considerably reduced the depth of the pond, and now it is quite shallow and will hardly accommodate its flowers. However, she still manages to produce a half dozen extra plants that she sells each spring for a few dollars.

Violet used to ask me for dinner occasionally. She was a good cook and with the use of the original stove (plus a toaster oven) and refrigerator that were bought when the house was built, she would prepare a very pleasant dinner for me. I still use several of the recipes that she wrote out for me. I used to have to leave early after one of these meals in the winter because: she kept the house so warm that I found it uncomfortable. Violet was very frugal about her own needs, for her income was small, but and she was very proud of her house and would carefully put money aside for the next painting job or other major expense.

Violet once told me that she had had two offers of marriage. One was from a farmer, a neighbour of her parents, who was years and years older than she was; She refused this offer. The second was from a young man her own age who was killed in a car accident before they could be married.

Violet's great love in her life settled on her cats. First, there was Orie, that I never met, who had lived to a great age. Then came Nigel, black, beautiful, and quite intelligent. Violet would put him on a leash and walk him down to the corner, then release him and he would run home on his own. His death two years ago actually put Violet in bed for a few days. Now she has a gorgeous Himalayan, the most beautiful cat in the world, according to Violet. His prosaic name is Sandy Lee.

In 1934 when the family moved in from the farm, Violet was twenty-two years of age. Her father bought her a Studebaker car, and she drove it right down through the years until two years ago. Finally, she sold it last year. It had been repainted once, a few years back, in its original colours of blue and black. It still had its original upholstery and interior appointments. I do believe that the back seat was practically never used. That sixty-five year period must stand as a record for a one-owner, one-driver car. *The Stratford Beacon Herald* did a feature on the car back in the 1960s. Violet said "never again!" as she was pestered by every teen-ager in town wanting to buy it from her. Actually, I think that it pleased her just a little bit when she went over to the grocery store to find a young person or two hanging around the car asking her questions.

Finally, Violet only used the car for buying her groceries and going out to a friend's farm in the summer to pick up some vegetables. Violet told me one story once, and I still laugh about it. A couple of years back she was out in the country and her brakes gave way. She glided to a stop on the shoulder of the road and phoned from a farm to arrange for the car to be towed back to the trusted garage that she had used for years. She went to the garage with the car, the mechanic took off the wheel, looked it over and said, "Miss Strohkirch, when did you last have the brakes done." Violet thought for a moment, looked up in the air, did some calculations, and answered the man. "1954", she said!

Violet will be ninety this year. She is still in her own home with the assistance of a homemaker who spends a few hours with her twice a week. She is independent, feisty, and alone. Joan and I each Christmas put together a box of about two dozen small items, each one individually wrapped so that she will have the fun of opening several gifts. I arrange these small things in a box and sprinkle candies, in all the areas not filled. The plan was for her to open the box on Christmas morning when she wakes up. Instead, last year she received the gift two weeks before Christmas, when her homemaker was there, and they opened everything at once. So much for the Christmas spirit.

Kay Kritzwiser

Kay Kritzwiser joined the *Globe and Mail* in 1956 as a feature writer after a successful journalistic career in Regina. She covered a great variety of stories from battered babies to interviewing a young Elvis Presley. She kept up the hectic pace of several Royal Tours across Canada. Her features were considered journalistic gems of loyalty to the Crown. Also during this period she wrote a considerable number of articles about the developing visual art scene of the Sixties.

She was appointed the art critic for the *Globe* in 1965 after the death of Pearl McCarthy. She held the post until her retirement in 1975 but she continued as a free-lance writer long after, specializing in travel and art stories.

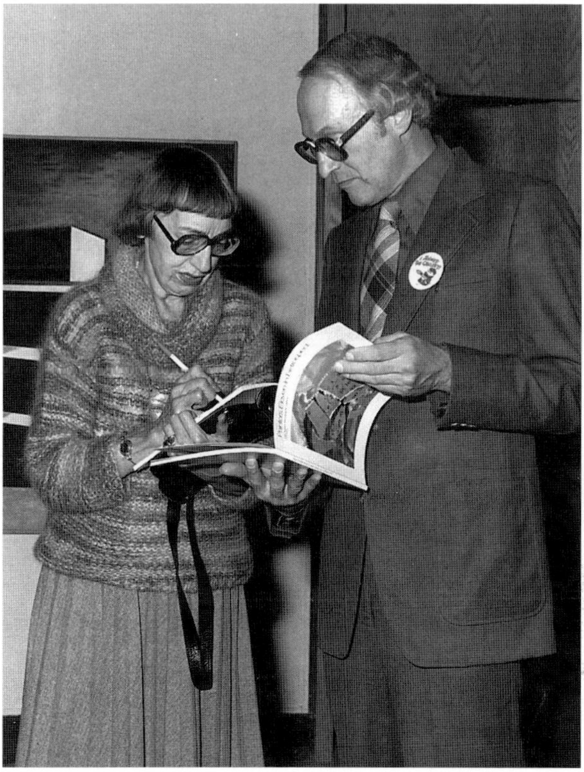

Kay was born in 1910 in Regina, third daughter of early Regina settler, Joseph and Lucy Mullan. She started her career early, being appointed, at the age of seventeen, as the editor of the *Leader-Post*, the young people's magazine. In 1933, she married Harold Kritzwiser, a legislative reporter and editorial writer. In 1947, the couple took a four-month-long trip around Europe, travelling by boat, train, bicycle, and foot. Kay's husband died suddenly at the age of forty-three, leaving Kay with a six-year old son. In 1956 it was time for a change and so she moved to Toronto at the invitation of the *Globe and Mail.*

Kay was an unusual person and a wonderful reporter. Her training in objective reporting always kept her in good stead. On top of this was overlaid her gentleness, her compassion for the individual, her genuine interest in promoting talent, her abrupt dismissal of the sham and insincere. Kay's insight and intuition in publicizing young talent and promising artists certainly helped in shaping the visual arts scene in Canada for many years.

Kay wrote a number of articles about my work over the years. In the process, we became good friends. She used to come and visit me once a year, especially when I was in Stratford. We would analyze the art world and rebuild it according to our own specific interests.

She wrote about the Art Institute of Ontario, about my research in Europe while on the Canada Council grant, about the Painter's Eleven project at the McLaughlin Gallery, about my work in Stratford and even about Crackers, my Antique store and Bed and Breakfast business. After she did her first feature on the A.I.O. I sent her an anonymous bouquet of roses, which arrived on her desk on the Monday after the Saturday feature. The card simply said, "Thank You" It took another article some time later before she figured out who was the giver of the gift.

The *Globe and Mail* acknowledged her contribution to the visual arts by organizing, along with a group of artists, a wonderful party to celebrate her seventieth birthday. Seventy artists, among them Charles Pachter, Ron Moore, Jack Shadbolt, Charles Comfort and Tony Urquhart, each gave her an original work of art, a truly amazing testimonial to her friendship and professional integrity.

Kay knew about my collection of beaded bags. (*See Chapter Seventeen*). In the summer of 1992 she came to visit me and the following week I received a parcel with the following letter "To Paul: For Saturday's welcome, which means welcome coffee, for my after-matinee moussaka, for my after-evening-performance's welcome nightcap, for my beautiful welcome bed, for Sunday's glimpse of Bennett the dexterous fishmonger? and finally for a second fleeting look at the lilies and ruffled poppies in his wondrous garden, and the leave taking Sunday afternoon with my beautiful china loot, all this and heaven too! I'll be in touch..,... and herewith, as promised the little beaded bag I carried on my wedding day on September 2, 1933 — that's almost 60 years ago ... does that qualify me to hang with your collection of Distinguished Bag Ladies?? .. Kay Kritz.

Unfortunately, as happens so often, I lost touch with Kay over the last few years. I believe that she moved to Vancouver to be with her sister, but I do not know for sure. Meanwhile I moved three times myself. She would now be in her nineties?

Chapter Twenty Two

Making Imprints

Teaching: 1985-1993, 1995-1997

I taught for three periods in my life: first of all from 1953 to 1958 in Etobicoke, then once again from 1985 to 1993 in Perth County; and as a supply teacher from 1995 to 1997 in Northumberland County. Rather than repeat myself as to my teaching approach, techniques, and projects I am only going to discuss the second last period of full-time teaching at Mitchell District High School in Perth County.

After my initial five years of teaching, I went back to university where I took group work techniques at the School of Social Work, University of Toronto. Then I went into adult education — to the Community Programmes Branch of the Department of Education and on to the Art Institute of Ontario. In all of my career I found that the three aspects of my own education, visual arts, teaching, and group work techniques all came together to give me the tools I needed for working with people.

I left the Gallery Stratford in 1984 to look after "Crackers", my guest house and antique store. I found that the summer kept me very busy but once the Festival Season was over, I was at loose ends. I mentioned this to my friend John Conroy and he suggested that I apply to the Perth Board of Education to become a supply teacher. I updated my teaching certificates plus my three Bachelor's degrees and one Master's degree, I was accepted, and in 1985 I started going to the various schools on call. Soon I was being called time and time again for St. Mary's District Collegiate and Vocational Institute. It was only a short drive from Stratford, the principal and staff were pleasant, and I had no trouble with the students. I was mostly supplying for English and History. The following summer in August I had a phone call from Eldon Alderson, the principal, he was short a half-time teacher in English and History and asked if I would like to apply. I did so and was accepted; the next year the same thing happened for full-time teaching in the same subjects. It seemed as if I was gradually returning to my old profession and I was enjoying it. Then the following year I was declared redundant, as there had been a cut back in enrolment. By this time I was used to an excellent salary, actually twice what I had been earning at the Gallery Stratford.

Just at that time the need for an art teacher was publicized at Mitchell District High School. It was thirty years since I had taught art. I asked for an interview and went happily up to the school one day, quite unprepared, and walked into a formal interview situation involving a panel of principals and teachers. I needed all the skills I had acquired over the years on the road to carry myself through that situation. I will never forget the last question put to me by the principal, who by the way is a good friend of mine now, He said, "Tell me, Mr. Bennett, why do you want to teach art?" I thought in my mind, what a stupid question and, tired by this time, I answered, "Because of the salary", I knew I had blown it. The school advertised the position. Suddenly it was realized that redundant teachers had to be placed before new teachers were taken on if they had the qualifications. I 'phoned the Director of Education (who just happened to have stayed at Crackers when he first came to town and was looking for a house). A 'phone call later and I was informed that my superior merit had made it obvious that I should have the position.

Once back to my old subject I was away, I had a wonderful time. To begin with I had a small art room and a small number of students„ By the second year I had been moved to one of the old large Family Studies rooms with a large supply cupboard, and students were pouring in. It was only after I retired that the principal, Terry Boyce, told me that every roughneck that they had in the school and could not place elsewhere was directed by the Guidance Department to take art. I could handle them all. I gave personal attention. I always criticized the same way I had used for years with adults — say the good things first and then advance the student with a small criticism that made that student reach, but never too far. I had projects for the individual, for pairs — I would team a rough boy or girl with a quiet one that had talent but was afraid to speak out. We had group projects where we had to work up and down the halls outside the classroom; we had projects away from the school.

Amusing things happened. I once had the grade nine class doing a detective project on textures, which is defined as "the surface quality of something". The students had to see how many textures they could find in the room and draw them carefully in a free form squiggle that

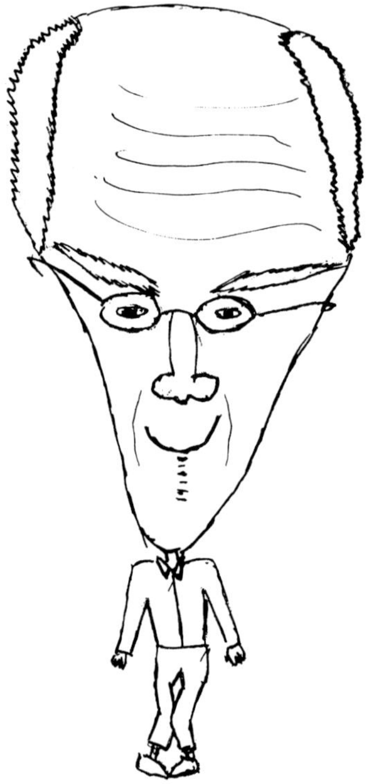

they had just drawn at my direction. One smart alec came up to me and asked if he could draw my tie. I looked down and saw that I was leaning over the paper cutter, I said of course he could, raised the handle of the paper cutter and one down stroke and the boy had a piece of my tie to draw accurately.

One day, about 1992, in a grade 12 art class I was discussing some modern paintings with my students. Always these classes were difficult as the students found it hard to understand contemporary concepts of art. Barry Waddell, one student, suddenly held up the back of his binder on which he had cleaned some brushes. He asked me if I considered it modern art, Going along with the obvious fun, I said of course it was. He asked how much it would be worth. I suggested about twenty dollars. He asked if I would buy it. I said yes, asked him to take the binder to the paper cutter, cut the back off his binder, and bring it to me. He did so. I took a twenty-dollar bill out of my wallet and handed it over to him. The class was in an uproar. The story was all over the school by noon. After school Barry, actually a good friend of mine, came back to the art room and suggested that he would return the money back to me. I refused. His painting is now in my book of archival material.

When I retired Barry slipped into my room the last day and when I was not looking placed a card on my desk: After he left, I opened it. The following note was inside; "Dear Mr. Bennett, In my eyes as a student of your teaching, your retirement is a disappointment, because you are much more than just a teacher, but also a friend. Your wisdom of art has broadened my horizons and opened my mind to new concepts, and for this, you will be missed. All of your students could rely on a clever story, and an ever-present smile when they came into your room, and for all of this, I thank you. Good luck on your retirement. —And you had better keep that painting. You never know, a Barry Waddell original might be worth something someday! Sincerely yours, Barry Waddell."

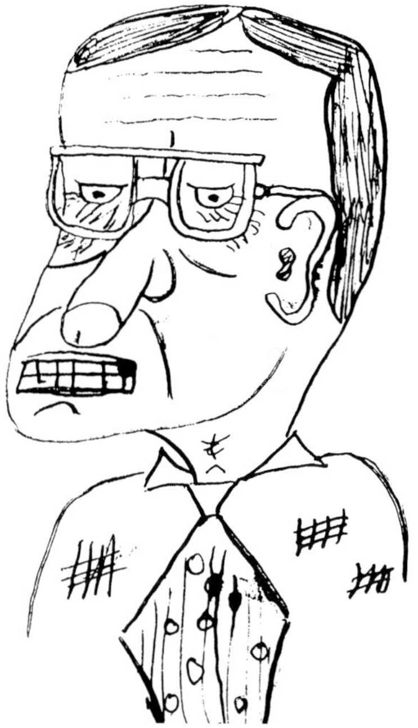

I had a nickname. It actually started when I was at St. Mary's. One day two large boys got into a fistfight just as they were coming into my class. Without even thinking, I pulled them apart at arm's length and braced one against the wall while I held the other away from him. Then my strong voice came into play and I marched the two of them down to the office. I now know better; policy says a teacher should never touch a student. One of the boys in my class was the son of another teacher and he went home at noon and told this tale at the lunch table; only he was a student of wrestling and knew exactly what holds I had used in wrestling the two fighters apart. The story improved with the telling. Next thing I knew I had been given the nickname, "Basher". It was only used in front of me in fun, but occasionally I would hear it echoing down the hall, "Basher Bennett".

I was never afraid to place myself in a position where a student might actually realize that I was not super human. So many teachers are afraid to let themselves go in any way in class because the students might think it a sign of weakness. For example, I suggested that the students in grade nine use me as a subject for drawing caricatures. We had studied what such a drawing was; the grotesque representation of a person or thing by overemphasis of characteristic traits. I described myself; thin hair on top of head, a cane — I had just had a knee replacement, — my love of art and music, et cetera. The students set to with a will and in the excitement drew some amazing likenesses.

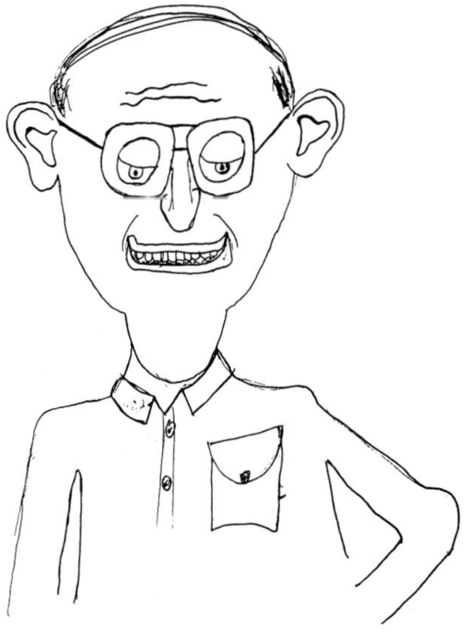

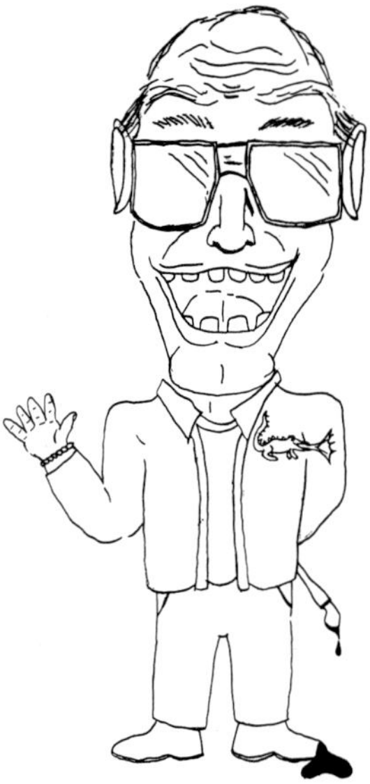

When we did figure drawing, I would often stand on top of a desk and act as the model. From my vantage point, I could see every drawing board in the room. I used to take newspapers to school and give them to the students for the first fast drawings, the paper was ruined already, and so they did not have to worry about wrecking it. We started with twenty-second drawings with me whipping them into action with my voice constantly telling them to loosen up, to make the heads smaller, et cetera. The drawing were thrown on the floor as we went on, none were saved. Gradually through a week of drawing the sessions would be lengthened until we were doing gesture drawings and contour drawings with freedom and some semblance of authority.

One of my most successful projects in grade nine was having the students draw portraits of their partners across the desk from them as playing card figures. That is the drawing had to look like a king or queen in a deck of cards. A head at each end, the arms coming down and joining in the middle. They could choose any subject: a girl who loved horses might incorporate a horse's head behind her and the hands could be holding the reins, the same subject could have the rails of a corral and the hands could be holding a saddle. One girl loved birds and asked if she could use her budgie as a subject. The budgie was turned away from the centre, reversed at the other end and both were standing on the same branch of a tree.

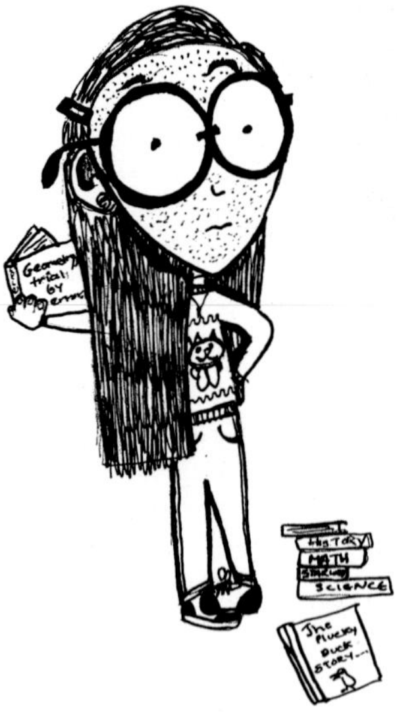

A grade ten project that needed great dexterity was to take a reinforced grocery box and paper the interior with black bristol board. Then create a scene of great perspective and depth by stringing white thread back and forth across the box, starting at the back and working forward. Wherever you did not want the thread to show you blacked it

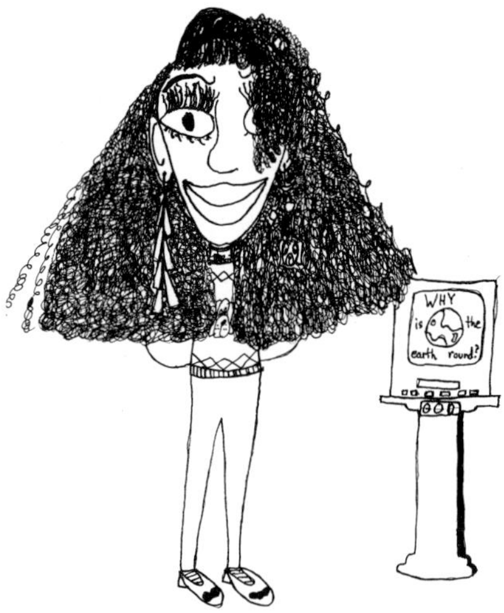

out with a black marker. I have had amazing street scenes.

A number of times the grade twelve classes painted murals around the school. The grandest and best was one that covered a whole wall of the library. The seventeen students first did figure drawing of school activities. We looked at these and picked out the best. Then we talked about the fact that the students were not good enough artists to paint realistic figures and so we worked toward the idea of a mural of a flat pattern that respected the two dimensional quality of the wall; the girls would all be in curved line painted silhouettes in a flat tan with dark brown outline, the boys would be in straight line painted silhouettes in a light green with a dark green outline. The mural actually had twenty-three full or partial figures in it representing school activities from studying to basketball and dancing.

I have always loved paper sculpture for stage sets. A number of times I was able to create sets that gave an interesting look to a glee club concert or a play. I like the crisp way that you can cut paper so that you have a sharp edge to a design and clear colour.

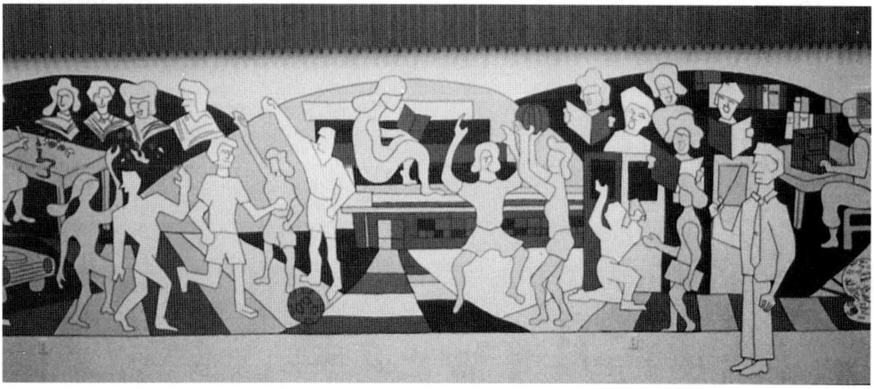

The last major project that I did before leaving Mitchell was to create two complete sets of books, one for each grade of art class, complete with the total list of projects and backup material. Also included were examples of student work for each project. The teacher hired to take my place had just graduated from teacher training and I thought she might appreciate the back up of a complete set of courses. I also, in my characteristic way, kept one complete set for myself in case I needed future reference.

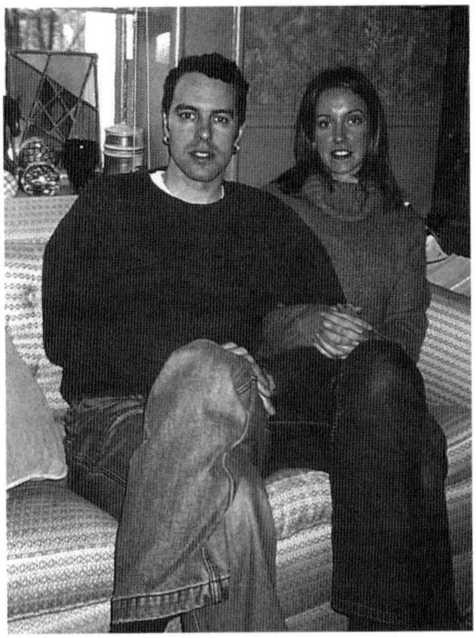

One former student, Mark Bovey of Mitchell, has kept in touch with me since I retired. Mark went on to college training in art and procured a very good position in London. Recently he moved to Toronto where he is excited about his new work and environment. He is designing for an advertising agency. Every now and then Mark and his girl friend will drop in to see me in Port Hope when he is travelling down to visit his grandmother in Gananoque.

After I moved to Cobourg in 1995, I applied to the Northumberland Board of Education to see if I could again supply teach. I was accepted. It took a while to be recognized as a competent teacher. I never sent a student to the office in the whole time I was doing supply work. My diaries show that on September 29th I did my first supply work at Cobourg West Collegiate in English and History. After a while I was asked to that school quite often because I lived practically across the road from the school and could be called in very quickly. I was thrown into just about any class situation from girl's gym to teaching canoe building. I supplied in High Schools in Cobourg, Port Hope, and Campbellford. The number of calls kept increasing until Christmas, 1997. At that time, the husband of a cousin of mine died in Stratford. I was executor of the estate and had to look after my cousin, his widow, and dispose of the house and contents. This all took time and I gave up the supply teaching with great reluctance.

I believe that I had a natural aptitude for teaching. On top of this of course was training in three diverse disciplines. I do know that the centre of my work in my total career was working with people; teaching was simply one manifestation of that principle. I personally received great satisfaction from this aspect of my work.

Chapter Twenty Three

My Water Worlds

My interest in lily ponds goes back to the summer of 1942. The Second World War was into its third year. My Father was a Major and the Adjutant of A10 Training Centre at Camp Borden. Camp Borden was a huge training facility for the army. I had just finished grade nine at Belleville Collegiate Institute and the family lived on the Trent Road in Avondale.

Dad arranged my first real job for me for the summer. I went to Camp Borden, slept in a tent on metal bunk beds with a large group of other boys most of whom were the sons of officers. We worked out on the ranges building tank traps.

This was my first time away from home. One weekend Dad took me to Wasaga Beach. We rented a small cabin, swam, sat in the sun, and ate in restaurants. It was a completely new way of life for me and I loved it. I even had my first milk shake. I remember Dad telling me to order one and my surprise when it was placed in front of me.

Even in an army camp, Dad had to make his artistic imprint. He had created a large pond at the front of the officer's mess. It was quite elaborate with a flagstone walk curving up to a parapet at the front. It must have been made of cement, there were stones lining the sides leading to the back with a large rockery. At one end was a small waterfall with a cave lurking under it. In the middle was a small island with an old stump placed on it. There were cattails and Siberian iris, flowers in the rockery and wooden armchairs placed at one end. It had gold fish in it but I do not remember seeing any water lilies. The pond, in my eyes, was huge. It was well looked after by an army corporal. He was a veteran of the First World War and had a row of ribbons on his chest. The pond was quite lovely and looked incongruous against the background of a drab army hut covered in tarpaper.

Dad showed me the pond with great pride. I do hope that I showed him that I was impressed, as I must have been to remember it now more than fifty years later. Likely it was the first inkling in my subconscious of that desire that led me to make a series of lily ponds later in life. In August of that summer, one day while working, I stepped on an old rusty nail that went right through my running shoe and foot and I was sent home for the rest of the summer.

For convenience we moved to Toronto to be near Dad, at Camp Borden (and later at Longbranch) and Joan, also, who was starting English at Victoria College at the U. of T. I finished my high school work at Harbord Collegiate and then took Fine Arts at the U. of T. After the war had ended, Dad had left the service and began working with the Department of Veterans' Affairs. One weekend Mother and Dad started driving down the highway looking for a house outside of Toronto. They arrived in Newcastle and found what became "The Hollows", named after Dad's home in St. Albans, England.

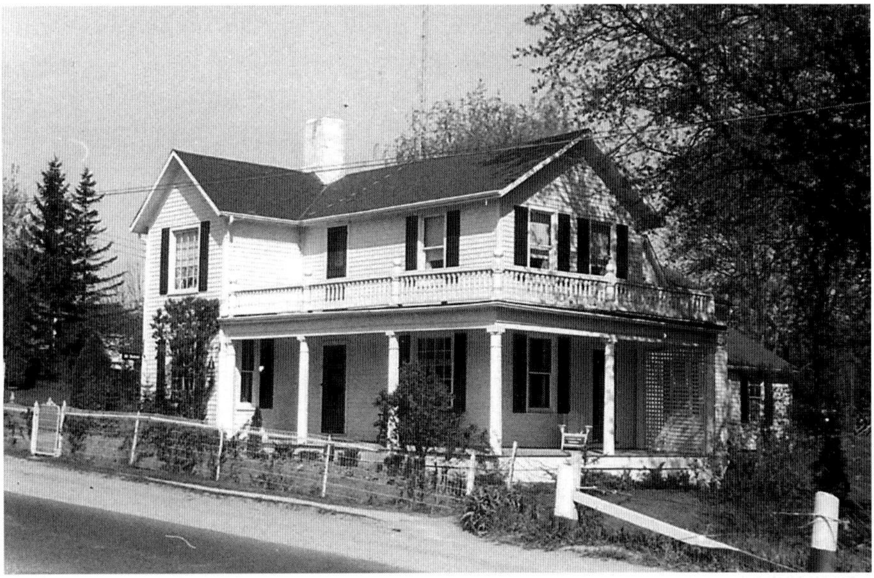

The house was large, with exterior clapboard that had that lovely grey patina found in older homes that had never been painted. We named it well, as it stood at the bottom of a hill and in the ravine there was a small stream that went right under the road. One of my first summer jobs was to give the house two coats of white paint. Dad started working in the garden and, of course put in a small lily pond with a weeping willow tree nearby. The pond had a cement base and was wide at the north end narrowing in to a small basin at the south: There was, once again, a small waterfall that you could hear through the kitchen and dining room windows nearby. This time I do remember there being water lilies. A door coming out from the dining room on the western side of a small patio led to the pool. There was a rockery protecting the western side of the pool and built up against the driveway. Dad was rightly proud of his work and it was much admired.

We all worked hard at The Hollows. As well as painting the house I moved the driveway: I dug it down six inches, put in a base from a mountain of ashes that I had found at the back of the garden and then laid a layer of gravel. The drive originally came in right beside the house, but now it curved around the pool — much more attractive.

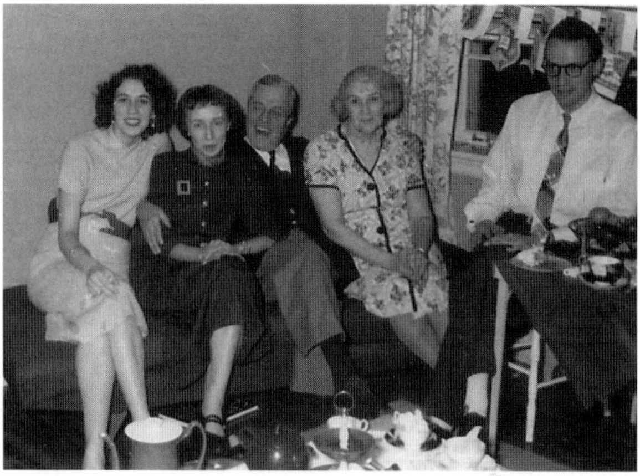

I vividly remember one incident the week we moved in. It was Sunday and Dad had decided that we should clean the old finish off the dining room floor, I was working with paint remover at the east end, Dad, with Joan's assistance was using a blow torch at the west end. Like most old houses, the floor had a slight slope — from east to west. Need I say more! The paint remover caught fire from the blow touch and a huge wave of black, sooty smoke filled the room. I ran to the front stair and yelled up to Mother. "Mother, Mother, the whole house is on fire!"

Mother came down the back stairs into the kitchen, wearing a dressing robe, but she was, as she said later, dressed underneath. She was carrying some dirty clothes and her jewelry in one hand and an empty suitcase in the other. Jane, in the meantime, had grabbed a large pan of water in which she had just finished washing the dishes. She threw the water over the fire and somehow managed to throw it exactly the right way, for it blanketed the flames and put them out. While all this was going on Joan was standing at the old phone (the kind you used to have to crank) furiously turning the handle — we found out immediately after that it was still disconnected.

We opened all the windows to let the smoke pour out. We had planned to wallpaper the house one room at a time; instead, we were forced to decorate the house as soon as possible because of the smoke residue that covered the walls. The horror of the whole story is the fact that we had just moved in, but we had not moved our fire insurance

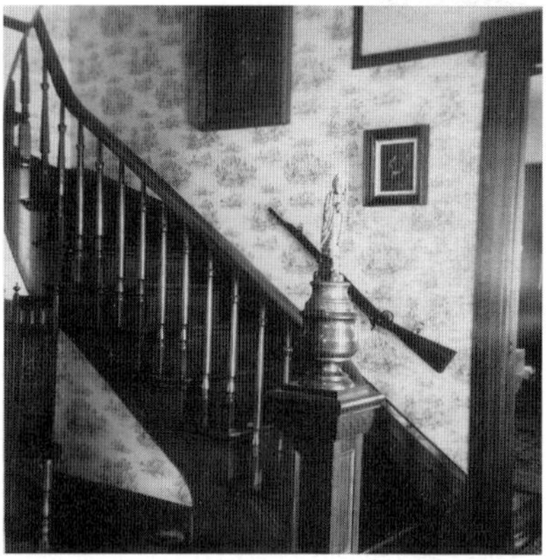

yet from our Toronto home to Newcastle!

A fine house had been built by a master carpenter for his own family. Our kitchen and pantry with a quaint old narrow staircase rising to a low-ceilinged room above was obviously of early nineteenth century construction. To this pioneer cottage in the early twentieth century had been added the fine front part of the home. It had one interesting feature. At the time of the building there had been a very severe winter when all the sweet chestnut trees had been killed. All the woodwork had been made of this wood, including the high wainscoting in the dining room, the curving staircase from the front hall to the second floor, the trim in all the rooms, and the doors. It was a warm grained wood that was very attractive.

It was years before I again had a lily pond, or water garden, as they are now called, enter my life. I moved from Toronto to Stratford in 1978 to become the Director of the Gallery Stratford. The wife of one of the members of the Board of Directors of the gallery was in real estate. Mary Swerdfager took me under her wing, promising that she would find me the right house to suit my needs and position, and she did so. The house was on Water Street and is now the home of Peter Mansbridge and Cynthia Dale.

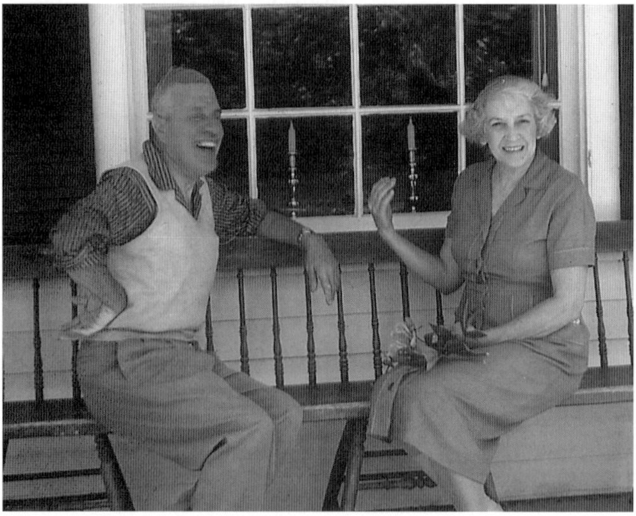

In that garden, I developed the formula that I have used for four other homes right up to my present one. First, I had to have a dog run because I have had a dog, or dogs, since that time. Then I had to have a lily pond, and finally there had to be

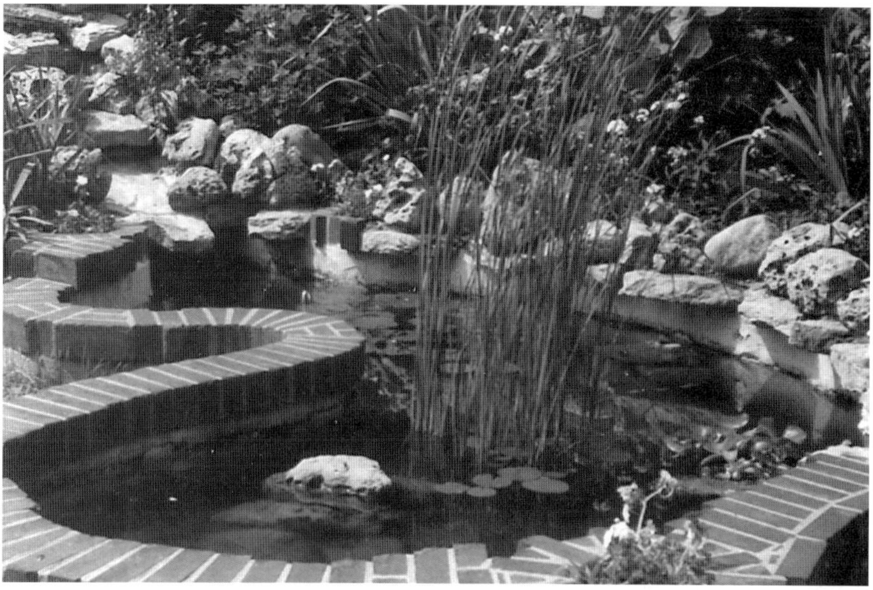

pleasant flowerbeds. Now the pond on Water Street was so small and insignificant that I do not remember much about it. I do know that it was part of the flowerbed on the West Side of the small garden where it got the best sunlight. Actually, I was more concerned with a dog run as I had just secured my first English setter.

When I moved to Erie Street in Stratford and opened my guesthouse and antique store in "Crackers" in 1981 I finally had to take water gardens seriously. The previous owners, the Schades had owned the house since the 1930s. The house had been built in the Edwardian period.

Six ponds on the hillside at the back of the house had been filled in and covered up, and I opened up all of them! The top one stood by itself in a flowerbed, and used to hold turtles. It had high ledge that you (and probably the turtles) could sit on. The other five ponds were varied in shape: at the top was a kidney shaped one, next a rectangular one with each corner turned inward, then came a round one with a three tiered fountain, followed by another round one and finally a quite deep square one. The five hillside ponds were all connected underground so that the water started at the top and flowed downward to each one successively and was then returned to the top by a pump. They were all made the old way with thick cement at bottom and sides; each had a ledge about a foot above the ground emphasized by a top covered in red brick laid side by side and securely cemented in place. The bricks were shaped to follow the curves of the winding edges. The Schades loved variety in their gardens putting in each pond a different type of creature or fish. I never did get the fountain to work properly unfortunately, and I found out later that making it work would have been relatively simple. However everything else was operating.

I filled in the isolated pool at the top, making it into a raised flowerbed. The rest of the ponds were filled with water lilies and fish and backed by a large blooming flowerbed. I remember on Sunday afternoons, when it was quiet and I had a staff member on duty to look after both guests and antique browsers, that I would sit under a garden umbrella by the ponds and watch them. I especially enjoyed the dragonflies that would hover on the surface and then dart away.

I operated my combined guesthouse and antique store for five years. Then I sold the place for a profit and moved closer to the centre of Stratford into an old house that I renovated on Ontario Street between the downtown and the Festival Theatre. I opened an antique store only; the shop was downstairs and I lived upstairs with my study being located in the old kitchen area at the back of the downstairs. I developed a small garden, overlooked by a deck on the second floor at the back. There was an outside stair down into the dog run where I built a large complicated doghouse that my two dogs never entered. My ponds were not too ambitious. At an auction, I bought a brand new, pale blue bathtub, which became my only pond for the first year. I made the pond look a great deal larger than it actually was by building a large rockery around the three back sides.

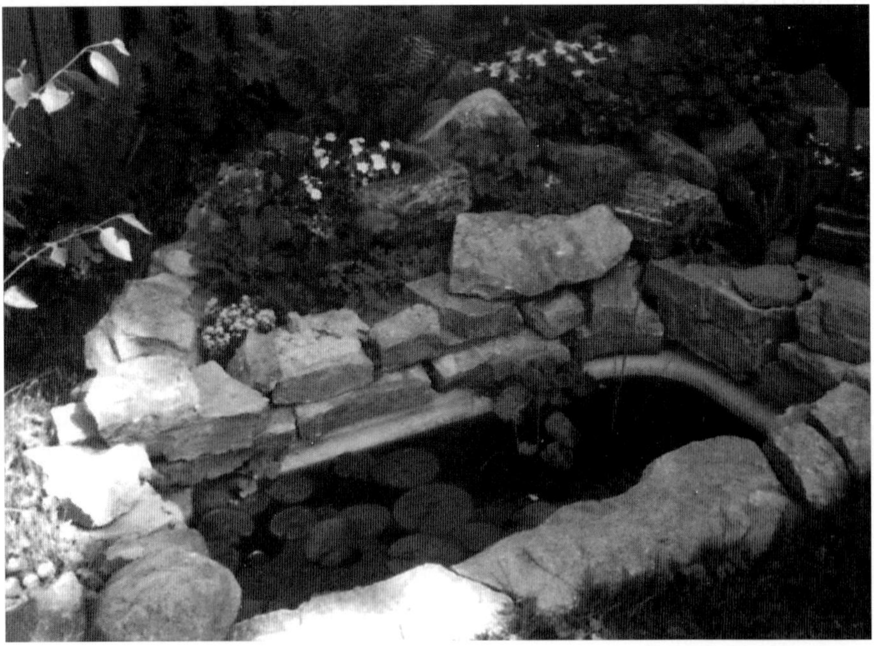

The second year I bought two large free form preformed plastic liners, and created a very pleasant corner of the garden with the two ponds and connecting rockeries.

Now I move on to my greatest creation in the water garden field. I moved to the town of Cobourg in 1995 to be near my family: Jay had been married; we were all growing older; and recently I had had a dear and close friend die. I bought a "Jackson" house close to the downtown. A family by the name of Jackson in the early 1900s had built great many homes in Cobourg.

This house was quite small but the magic thing about it was that although it was downtown, it was on a large lot that ran toward the lake at the end of the garden and it boasted a large 36′ by 16′ swimming pool close to the house at the back. I love swimming and for years I have been swimming three times a week at the local "Y". However I did not need the harassment of looking after an outside pool for twelve months a year for the pleasure of swimming in it for two or three months, in the summer. I decided to make the pool into a water garden.

My first decision was to have an angle iron platform made, four feet by six feet, with a wire net, to stand on five foot legs in the deep end and secured by airplane wire to the sides of the pool, as water plants cannot grow properly in eight feet of water. It was a success and a fountain of leaves and flowers completely filled the platform

The next year I extended this growing area to ten by twelve feet with a much larger platform that sat on the first and again was secured to the sides of the pool. Containers of water lilies, cattails, pickerelweed, and oxygenating plants completely filled the platform.

At the pool's shallow end I upended an old bathtub and created an island. A fountain was pushed through the old drainage hole. Rocks hid the tub and flowers covered the area above water. Containers of water plants were, anchored by wires to the old tub legs. A stained glass and iron sculpture graced the island. Birds loved to sit on it and fly in and out of the three bell fountains.

The shallow end of the pool was just three feet deep. Bog lily, bog bean, creeping Jenny, parrot's feather, bog mint, dwarf cattail, arrowhead, flowering rush and horsetail were placed in containers on the tops of plastic milk crates. Water hyacinth and water lettuce floated free in the sun and shadow. Three large tubs of hardy red, yellow and white water lilies provided leaves and blooms on a continuing basis. I filled the steps leading down to the pool with pots of flowers and left a narrow path down the steps on one side so that I could enter the pool for maintenance of my water jungle.

The aristocrats of the pool were the five Golden Orf, each about a foot long. The fish come up at dusk to do a ballet around the pool looking for surface bugs. There were about one hundred Shubunkin and many goldfish to add life and colour. Spawning each spring created hundreds of fish fry that grew and assumed bright colours as the summer moved along. I had no Japanese koi in the pool because they have a reputation for digging and rooting out plants. I could not have the containers knocked off the platforms.

The fish stayed in the pool during the winter. A bubbler was placed in each end so that a small section could be kept free of ice. Noxious gases form in the winter from decaying vegetation and, if not allowed to escape, could kill the fish. In the winter I simply dropped the tubs of hardy lilies to the bottom and raised them again in the spring. The cattails and bulrushes would be cut off just a few inches above the level of the water. If you cut them below the water, they would drown. Any exotic plants like bog lilies or lotus I would take into the house and place on shelves in the cool basement. You had to make sure that they were kept moist during the winter months.

Of course, there were problems. I always worried that the plastic liner of the original pool might be punctured and I would not be able to find the hole; but that did not happen. For the first two years, I used the original pool pump to power the fountains. The excess water going through the system was simply allowed to flow out into the pond. I tied a towel around the outlet to try to prevent the current being too strong. Then I discovered that the swimming pool motor was delivering a flow of twenty-four hundred gallons of water an hour and I needed only twelve hundred. My electric bill was astronomical. I closed off that pump and bought an underwater Mag 1200 that was energy efficient. My fountains worked beautifully and I saved the cost of the pump on my electric bill in a very short time. After all an ordinary swimming pool uses a pump for a maximum of three months a year, I was using mine for seven months.

My water garden was a magic place. It was a complete world in its own right. It attracted visitors and offered a home to its own denizens. It was alive and responded to all of nature's cycles of procreation, survival, and death. In the spring, the toads arrived. They alerted the neighbourhood with their mating calls. These creatures layered in their breeding rituals, laid their eggs in silver chains, and then disappeared into the night. The large fish ate well for two days.

In the spring also came the mallards, the male ducks doing their bachelor- companion bit while their mates sat on their nests. They

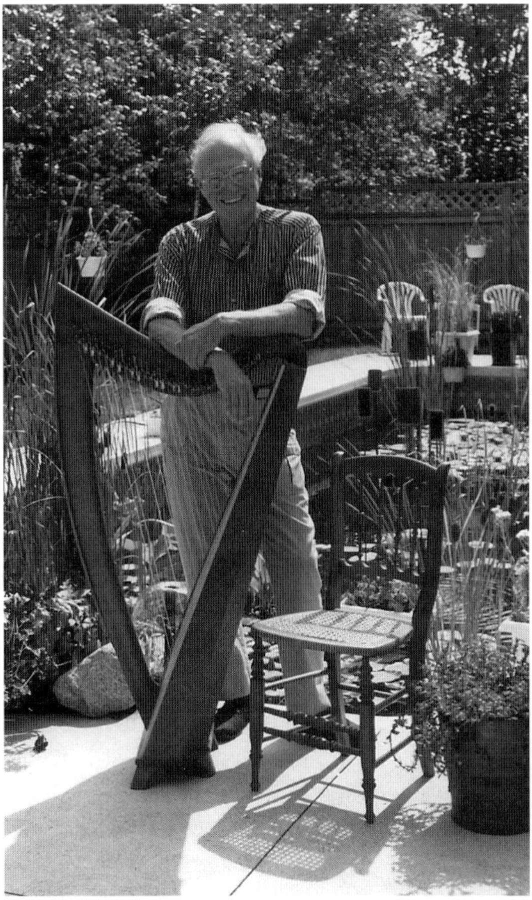

would gracefully alight on the water, causing the lily pads to rise and fall in ever widening ripples. Decked in their finest for the mating season, these birds, glossy green, Prussian blue and purple, moved in a funny erratic way. They would not touch the domestic plants that had been secured from the local marshes. But instead these gourmets unfortunately enjoyed eating the expensive imports! They had to be discouraged so I allowed my two dogs to patrol the edge of the pool when the ducks arrived.

Sparrows would line up along the edge of the pond and look down at the green surface of the duck weed and frogbit; the adventurous would fly in a circle and attempt to land on this inviting "lawn". Then there would be a great fluttering of wings as they would break through the surface of the water, and then they would lift off and hang on the stem of a cattail.

There was menace in the pond as in all life. Often one would find a dead sparrow floating among the lily pads, the victim of a raven attack. A pair of these black frightening creatures called raucous challenges to the world from the top of the elm trees on the edge of the property.

Maybe I created too close a copy of nature. One spring I found two of the Golden Orf had attempted to go up river to spawn. The closest river was the waterfall I had constructed down part of the steps into the original swimming pool. There was a bell fountain at the top of the steps and the water then ran down into the pond. I went out early one morning and found two of the fish stranded at the top of these steps. I lifted them gently and slipped them back into the water.

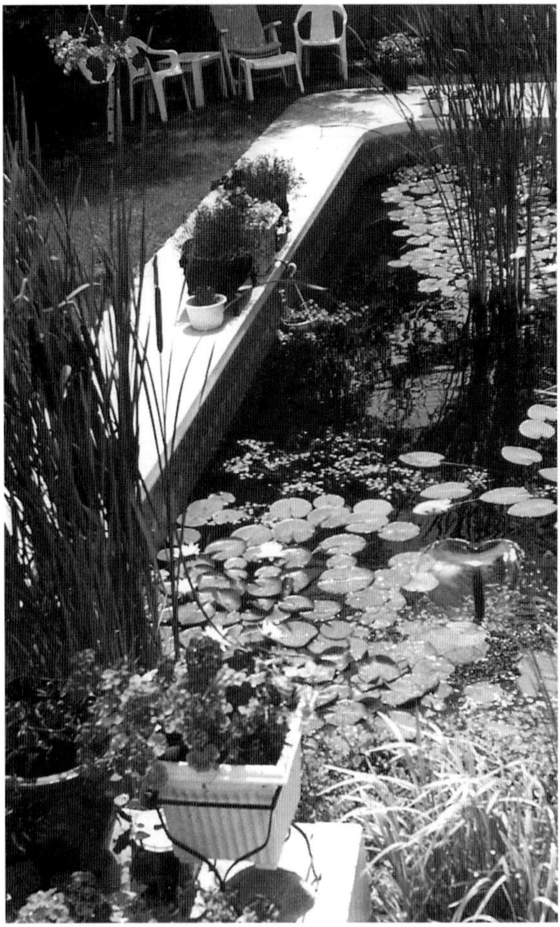

I did not know what the activity was below the surface of this magic water. I was sure that it was as incessant as the parade in the air above. I could sit for hours watching the changing light on the plants, seeing the movement of the creatures above the surface and wondering about the life below the surface. I felt I was part of that life and I felt honoured.

Chatelaine Gardens printed a feature on my water garden in the Spring/Summer issue of 1997 and Tropic Fish Hobbyist did the same in May of 1997. I had written each article and there was some local notoriety. After all, a swimming pool is a status symbol in the Canadian psyche, and one does not destroy a pool lightly. The pond was on a garden tour and many people dropped in to see it. I had this pond for only three years. The last year the growth was quite extraordinary. The rushes must have been eight feet tall; all the plants were expanding, luxuriant, and exuberant, it was wonderful. You could walk along the edge and seem to be surrounded by it all. Thank goodness, I have photos of it.

James Hoffman, a local developer, had wanted my property almost from the time that I bought it. Finally I sold him the lower, south field and considered his offer to buy the rest of the property. Within a few months I had a chance to buy a beautiful, large Georgian home that had once been a tavern, on Dorset Street, in Port Hope. I bought this house and sold to Hoffman; within two weeks of my moving he had bulldozed the pond out of existence, as he was afraid of children get-

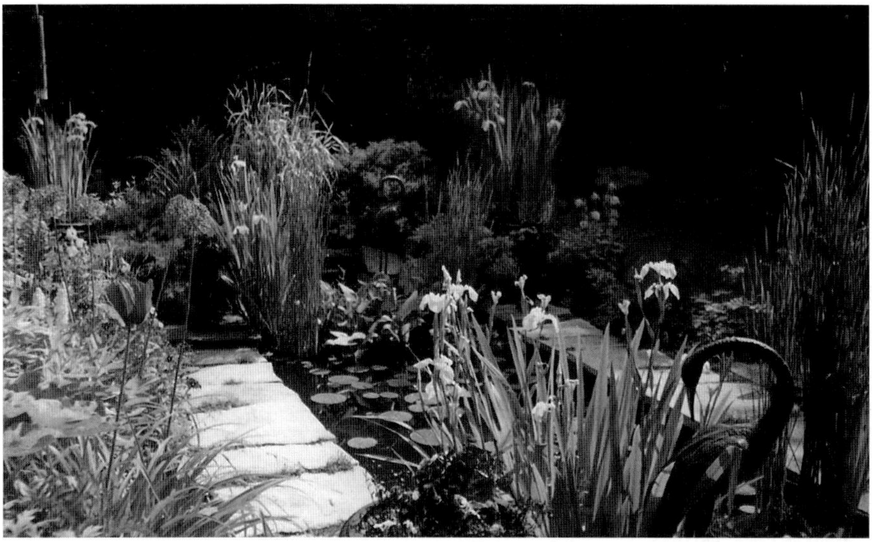

ting into it and drowning. I had removed most of the plants and almost all the fish. Many of these I gave to friends who had ponds of their own.

Before I moved to Dorset Street, I had a pond dug for me in my new garden. It was twelve feet long, six feet wide and three feet deep, with a shelf for plants at each end. It was an anticlimax after my Cobourg pond but certainly did not require as much work and it is very pleasant. I bought a double strength liner and edged the top with cement blocks.

Last year my sister, who had come to share my house, bought lovely flag stones for the edge, the walks and a small patio area near the pond with a bench placed on it. Joan has a strange middle name, St. Albans, after the birthplace of my father in England. I had named the pond Lake St. Paul (my sister did not move in until I had been here two years), the pile of earth at the far end that was transformed into a rockery became Mount Bennett:. The torrential cascade of water that pours from Mount Bennett: into the depths of Lake Saint Paul bears the impressive appellation, after my sister, of the St. Albans Rapids. This year we were once again on a garden tour.

Chapter Twenty Four

A Home of One's Own

In 1972, I was forty-four years of age. I had never actually owned a home of my own as I had always rented an apartment, or in the case of Bedford Road, a full house. Now I was living in Apt. 408, 30 Hillsboro Ave., in Toronto. I was Director of the Canadian Guild of Crafts, Ontario.

An opportunity arrived and I was able to buy a condominium. Since that time, with the exception of one last stint in an apartment, I have owned and lived in six different homes.

On the 7th of November 1972, I had renewed my lease for a year at 30 Hillsboro where I was paying two hundred and ten dollars a month for the apartment and parking. Then, in that month, I saw an advertisement in the paper claiming that I could own my own apartment home for as little as two hundred dollars down. It seemed unbelievable and I decided to check it out.

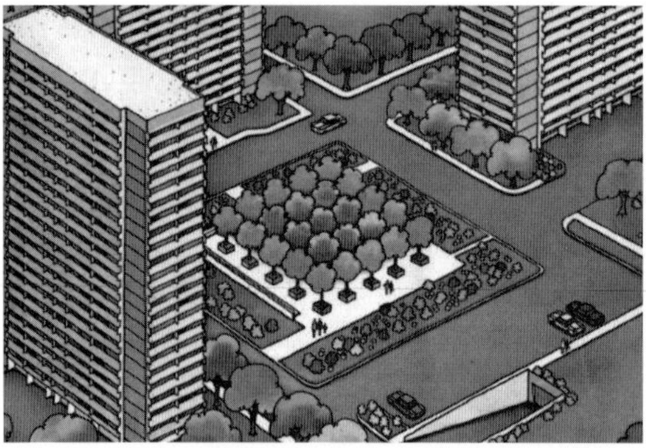

Chapel Glen was on Don Mills Road, south of the Ontario Science Centre and close to wooded ravine areas. At that point the Don Valley Parkway comes from the north and turns gradually to the west. I investigated quite thoroughly. I got the story that condominiums were a new concept in Toronto and the owners were trying to sell this complex as fast as possible so that it could be registered and the occupants, the new owners, could start the organization necessary to formally govern the building. I already knew that it was a successful concept in Europe.

I even went so far as to drive up the Parkway early in the morning and then drive down again the in the morning rush hour to see how long it would take me to get to work. I bought in, and never regretted it. On February 1st, 1973, I took possession of a two-bedroom suite, Apt. 2106, 735 Don Mills Road. I paid two hundred dollars down, the total cost being twenty-one thousand, six hundred. I had to break my new lease at 30 Hillsboro where I lost my last month's deposit and the apartment was re-rented for me. For my new home I had to buy stove, refrigerator, curtains and so on.

My belongings looked very nice in that bright, cheerful place. I made an extensive super eight film of the suite, and later I had the film transferred to video; on watching it I am sorry that there are so many works of art that I allowed to pass through my hands: for example, a Jack Bush painting, a Grant Macdonald picture of a boy with his bicycle, three small Jock Macdonald watercolours. I removed the doors of the coat cupboard in the vestibule and placed my handsome Bell melodeon in that area. I papered the hall and cupboard in the same dark stylized lotus type of paper.

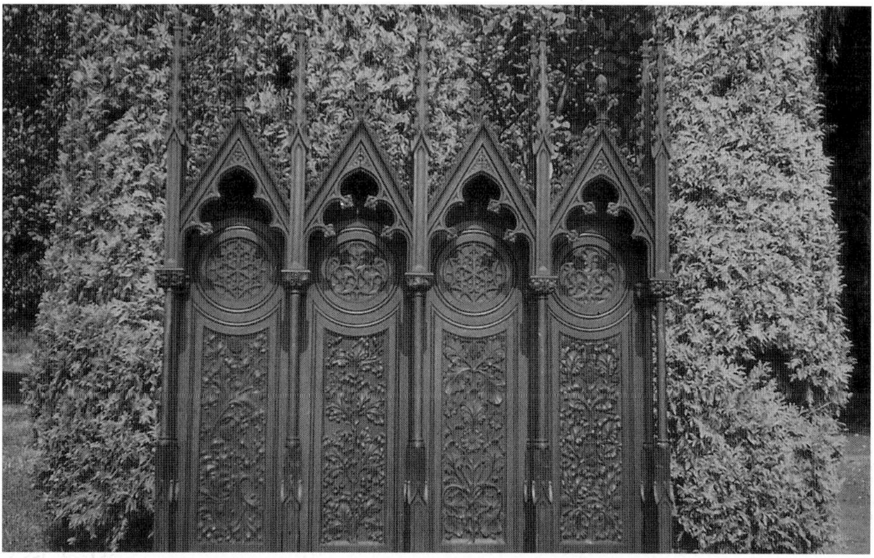

My altar screen or reredos I placed on the wall of the dining area attached to the kitchen. The living room had a predominance of bright red and black. There was a black leather chesterfield. From the ceiling, I had a large glass fish bowl hanging full of guppies. The main bedroom held my bed, a Victorian maple chest of drawers, a small six-drawer, lingerie chest from my Father's business and my grand piano.

The second bedroom became a study with a pullout bed hidden in a chesterfield, a tall Victorian desk/bookcase, a wall full of books, a large aquarium and Dad's three sided leather screen, there were art objects everywhere some of which I still have.

I enjoyed using the swimming pool and sauna. From my windows on the twenty-first floor, there was a feeling of space and open tree land, punctuated by high-rises and roadways. On July 15th, 1975, I sold the place for thirty-five thousand dollars, making a profit of seven thousand, six hundred odd dollars. I paid off some debts and with the remainder, I bought myself a good Heintzman piano. My poor old refinished Night Club grand went to a smart piano salesman, who knew how to bargain, for two hundred dollars. I have consistently been lucky with real estate. I sold the condominium to the second person that looked at it. I do believe that sometimes places like mine sell because people think that they are buying your life style, and an arty interior helps. I moved back to my old apartment building at 30 Hillsboro Avenue, a two bedroom this time on the fifteenth floor.

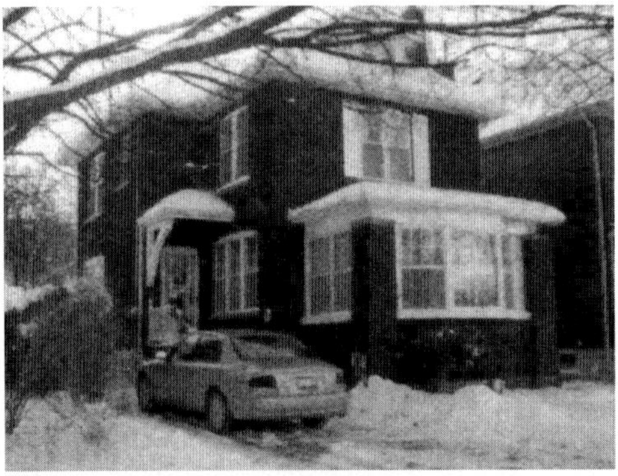

The next home I bought was in Stratford. I left the Ontario Crafts Council and became the Director at the Gallery Stratford. Mary Swerdfager, realtor and friend for all my time in that city, took me under her wing and helped me to find a place. She said it had to be suitable and in the right location befitting my position at the art gallery. I ended up with a pleasant home at 11 Water Street, looking through the tennis courts at the Avon River. The house was forty-eight thousand, five hundred dollars.

The house was exactly the right size for me. It was built in the 1930s. There was a fireplace in the living room that I enjoyed. When I took down the large mirror that had been placed over the mantel, I found wiring for two light fixtures. I placed two wrought iron lights there, one on each side of one of my father's, Ontario Society of Artists paintings. Double doors led out of the living room into a small sunroom, which faced north and had a seat all around the wall. I always wanted to insulate that room and incorporate it into the living room. A later owner did just that. The kitchen was small but suitable, the dining room the same. There were oak floors throughout. A sturdy staircase led around a landing and up to the second floor. There were three bedrooms, with the front, larger one stretching right across the width of the house. I now had a regular guest room and a study. The bathroom was typical of the thirties.

A door opened from the central hallway onto a full stair up to the attic. I would have finished that room for a music room or a studio if I had stayed there long enough. In the attic, a single dormer window faced north. There was also a small porch off the kitchen onto the garden. A door from the study opened onto a small deck above the porch.

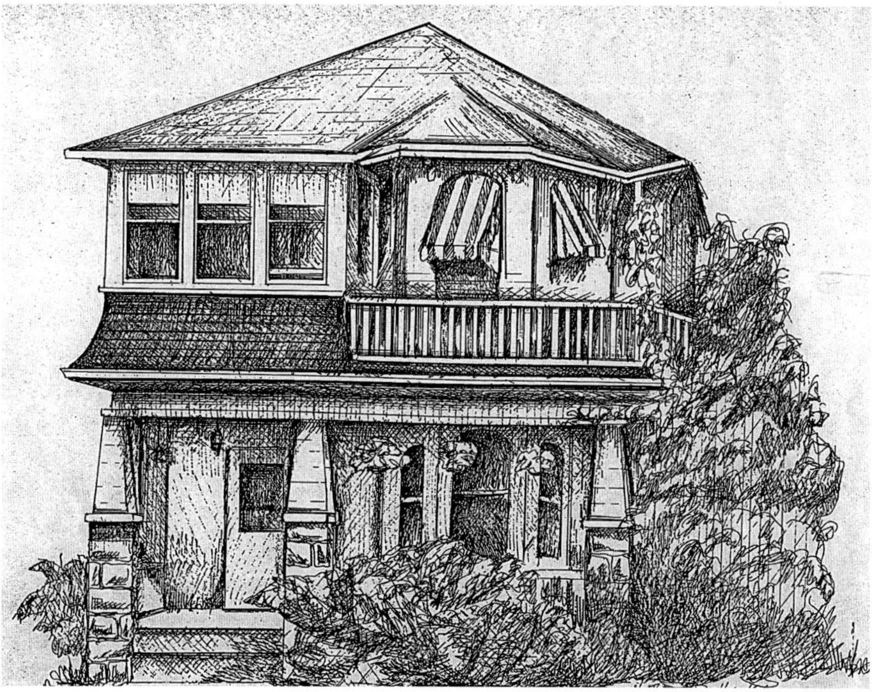

Next I found a house on Erie Street that had business possibilities and I took a flying leap into the unknown. I listed the Water St. house for fifty-seven thousand, nine hundred and it sold in June 1981. I had listed with Mary Swerdfager's Company of course but a real estate man from another company showed it and liked it so much that he bought it for his own use at fifty-two thousand. The asking price had dropped because the real estate company waived the commission payable by me and therefore the purchase price could be reduced by that amount. There was a sad sequel to this sale; a year or two later the real estate agent who had bought the Water St. house committed suicide on the stairs. There were marital problems and he had lost his driving license (awkward for selling property) for impaired driving.

Frank Leslie of Leslie's Cheese House introduced me to Emma Schade. Emma owned the large Edwardian house that was right beside the cheese house. In fact, in early days the two buildings had been one property, which was bought by the Hergott Brother in 1887. The cheese house had been a brewery and the Schade house was the brew master's house. In 1896, the Kuntz Co. Ltd. of Waterloo divided the two sections for assessment purposes following the purchase of the brewery. After the closing of the brewery, the building became a cold storage warehouse and then a soft drink depot. Finally, in 1952 it was sold to Frank Leslie who opened the cheese house.

Mr. Albert Schade had run the cold storage plant and the soft drink depot. Emma was his secretary; they married and lived in the big house along with Mrs. Schade's mother. The Schades travelled a great deal each year and were often away for months at a time on ocean cruises.

Mr. Schade died in 1980 and Emma Schade decided to sell and move to an apartment. She did not want to advertise and have various strange people going through the house. Frank Leslie knew that I wanted a business opportunity and so introduced me to Mrs. Schade. We seemed to get along very well. Emma was reputed to have a great deal of money.

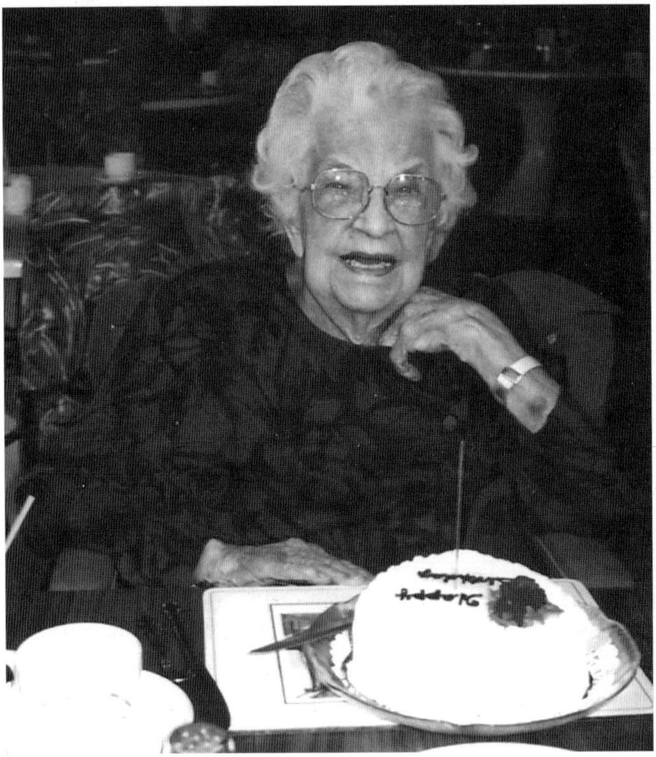

Her husband later in life had been in the hotel business. She wanted more than ninety thousand dollars for the house with its extensive gardens at the south side and land extending a long distance to a ravine and small river to the east at the back. I had the audacity to offer her fifty-five thousand. I also agreed to look after her two cats that she could not take to her new apartment and to work intensively on the gardens to return them to some of their former glory.

Mrs. Schade accepted my offer and we became friends — a friendship that lasted right up to her death at the age of ninety-eight in 1994. Emma showed me things in the attic that she wanted to get rid of. I bought a handsome light fixture for sixty-five dollars. A few years later Emma's niece said how much she liked it. I sold it to her for the same sum. I bought a lovely pair of old snowshoes that now are hanging on the wall of my guest room with two other pairs. Foolishly, I refused a large jardinière that brought a huge price from Jonny's Antiques at the estate auction later.

When I first moved in a long dilapidated chicken coop ran along the back edge of the five lily ponds. I cleaned it out and found many metal beer and soft drink signs that I sold at a garage sale for ten dollars each. Some of these were turning up at flea markets for months afterwards at prices up to a hundred dollars. Many of these signs were brand new with paper liners between them. In that coop, there was also a small bar complete with metal spigots and other equipment. A collector of beer memorabilia was delighted to secure it.

I was able to redecorate a couple of rooms with what I earned from the garage sales. I later tore down the chicken coop and created a parking area for five cars.

I took Emma Schade out for lunch the day that she moved to her apartment. She was feeling blue and appreciated the thought. This lady became a very special friend to me. In many ways, she remanded me of my Mother. She had had a driver for her car, but when he became too old to drive, she had to sell the vehicle. I used to take her for a ride in the country about once a month and we would stop at some restaurant or hotel that she remembered from the old days and have lunch or dinner. She always insisted that we each pay our own way.

Emma seemed to have three guiding principles which I hope, if I live so long, I can emulate; She always accepted every invitation to go out; she read the local paper every day from end to end so that she could be current on what was going on and could talk about it; and she never talked about her health. Three golden rules. After she had moved from her apartment because of failing health, I visited her every day, first in a nursing home and then in the hospital, for two years until her death. I remember two incidents in the home that amused me. One day, an old lady resident, came up to me and with a wink asked what room it was that I was living in! Another day, while waiting for the elevator, I heard three women sitting in the window seat behind me discussing me, saying how broad my shoulders were and how they appreciated my rear end!

I very much appreciated at Emma's funeral the fact that the nieces, that I had come to know quite well over the years, specifically mentioned my name and thanked me for my care of their aunt. As they lived in Toronto, they used to see her only once a week.

Crackers Guests, Antiques and Art was very successful. Eventually I did find it a big undertaking by myself. Much of the money I was taking in was going out in wages. One day Tom Hodgins, a courtly, gentle man, who was one of Mary Swerdfager's real estate agents, dropped in to see me. It was a time of high property values. In Toronto many people were selling their homes for a great deal of money and leaving the city to move to smaller locations where they could buy equally nice homes for half of what they sold for in Toronto. In Stratford, the Bed and Breakfast craze was in full swing.

Tom asked me if I had ever considered selling. I said no. He asked what kind of price I would want if I did? I rapidly added my cost of renovations to the original cost and said I would want one hundred thousand more than I had invested in the place. He said I could get it and I just about passed out. I signed up.

Doug Chamberlain was a popular actor at the Festival. He and a friend owned a beautiful, big home in St. Mary's. He was looking to open a business away from the theatre. He had come into Crackers a number of times and asked me questions and admired my operation. I phoned him and told him that I had put the house on the market. I suggested that he come by one Saturday morning (when I knew that the house would be full of guests).

I will never forget the setting. There were five, excited, adoring, Stratford devotees sitting at my kitchen table having breakfast. Doug was leaning against the refrigerator. He was personality plus as he talked to his public. Meanwhile I prepared breakfast, served it, cleared the table, excused myself, and went upstairs where I changed or made up the beds and tidied the rooms. I returned downstairs, put on the lights in the antique shop, and prepared for the day. Finally the group in the kitchen broke up and Doug came to me and said he thought that a Bed and Breakfast operation was just what he wanted. Early the next week after Doug and his partner had examined my books, I had an offer. There was a bit of a delay while Doug arranged financing and I found myself a new home. On January 9th, 1987 I sold Crackers for one hundred and seventy thousand dollars.

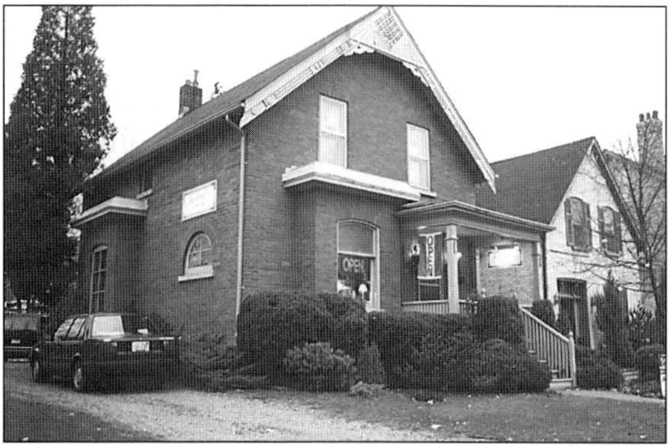

I then moved up to the centre of Stratford, to 286 Ontario Street where I bought an old home on the north side of the street for one hundred and thirty thousand dollars and then spent approximately thirty thousand dollars on renovations.

286 Ontario St. was a much smaller house than 433 Erie St. This suited me because I had decided to concentrate on the antiques and art only and not have guests. My living quarters comprised the upstairs as well as a study at the back of the building downstairs. Upstairs I had a living room, one bedroom, and a large kitchen that held my dining area as well, and a large bathroom.

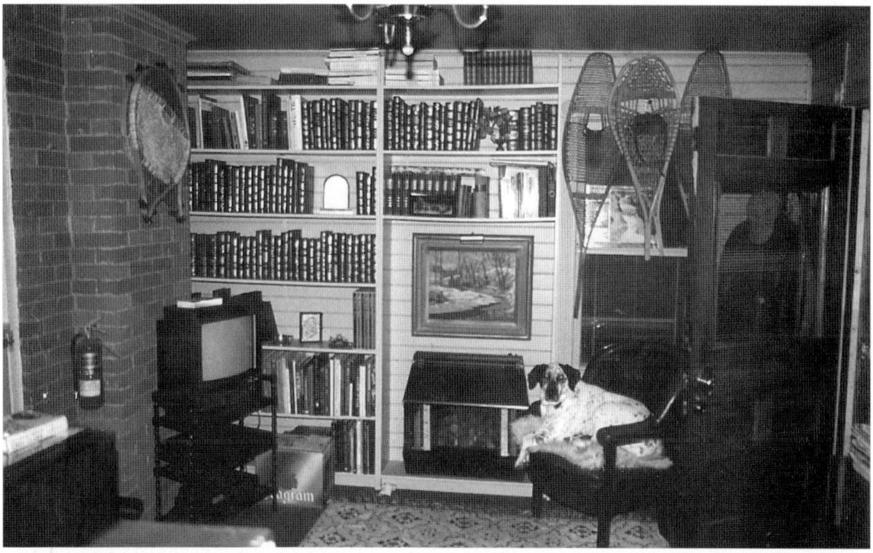

In the bathroom, I originally took half for a storage room, but later I changed this and made the whole room into a very pleasant bathroom with a six-foot whirlpool. I would guess that the upstairs held four bedrooms in the original plan of the house. There was a door in the kitchen that led to a large deck above my study area downstairs. There was a stairway down to the dog pen at ground level.

On the first floor, I could use three rooms for selling antiques. I installed a two piece powder room in the back corner of one room. The large back room that had originally been the kitchen made a wonderful study/office, in which I installed a gas fireplace. There were some very nice features left from the original 19th century house. There was a semi-circular piano window of coloured glass in the front room on the west side, two bay windows, maple hardwood floors, original woodwork including the stair balustrade and newel post, and one set of sliding doors. The exterior bargeboard was restored and repaired during renovations.

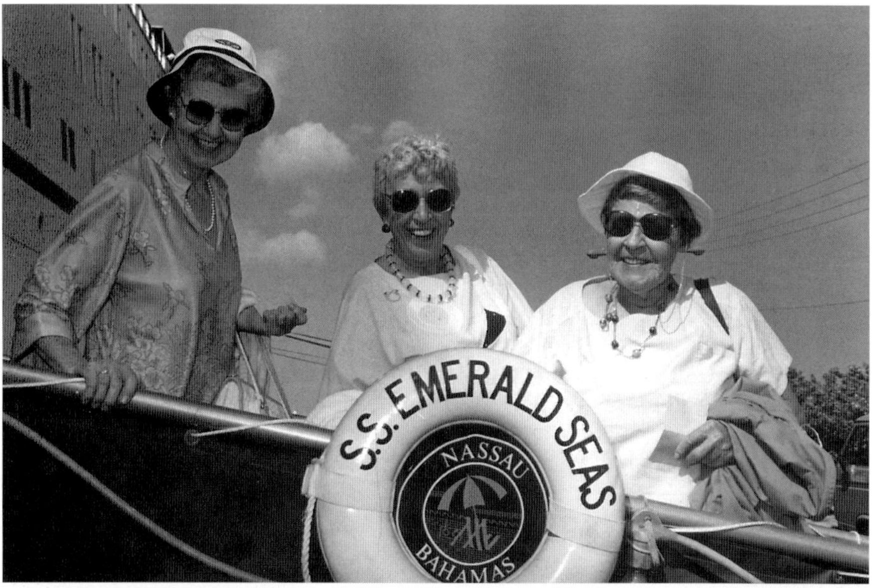

"The Girls" — Ethel Mailer, my sister Joan, Joan Frith

It was a nice compact building and I enjoyed living and working there. However, it came time to move on. Jay, my friend, had been married. Ethel Mailer, a great family friend, who had lived with the two Joan's, had died. Suddenly time seemed to be closing in and I decided to move back to the Cobourg area to be near Joan, Jane, and their families. (I forgot to ask them if they would like me to move closer to them!) I sold 286 Ontario St. for one hundred and sixty-two thousand, five hundred dollars on January 25th, 1995 and moved east.

On January 16th, 1995, I bought 107 Albert Street in Cobourg for one hundred and sixteen thousand dollars. It was a Jackson house as I have already mentioned. A family; a father, and a number of sons, had built it between 1911 and 1930. I heard the story that each of the sons had a special trade: carpentry, plumbing, electrical work, and they all combined their efforts to build homes in the Cobourg area. The house was small but had a later addition, a wonderful sunroom across the back of it, facing south.

As usual, I painted and papered. I was becoming more daring in my papers and put in some bold and exotic designs. There was a wood fireplace in the living room. My bedroom had two windows facing north onto the street. The small bathroom had a skylight.

I did find that the house was certainly small. However, the garden compensated for this. There had been a handsome whirlpool in the sunroom when I arrived, but I moved this outside and eventually sold it because I do not enjoy the financial and mental upkeep of balancing chemicals. The crowning glory of that location of course was the water garden that I created out of the swimming pool. This has been described in detail in another area of this book. I had some great dinners and parties there as I came to know the gay community in the area. An old lady who lived next door evidently had listened over the fence at one of my garden parties. She loved to do a grotesque dance on her lawn when I was walking by or looking out the window. She would bend her wrist and ape the characteristics of a stereotypical gay man and sing la de da as she pranced around. I stopped shoveling her walks in the winter.

James Hoffman was the developer directly to the south of me on the lakefront. First, he had built a number of three storey condominiums, then some streets of town houses, very smart with back garden/patios and landscaped streets. I went down and inspected a couple of them. James spoke to me personally and asked if I would be interested in taking one of the town houses in exchange for my property; he was especially interested in my long narrow back lot that ran down toward his property on the harbour. I declined. In April of 1997 he made another proposal: he would pay me one hundred and fifty thousand dollars for my property; The south lot was to be severed as soon as possible, with a deposit of thirty-five thousand dollars and I had the option of staying in the house for up to five years if I wished before the deal was completed. When I left, I would receive the remaining one hundred and fifteen thousand dollars. He could not ask me to leave before the five years was up but I could leave at any time with three month's notice. I took the option of leaving just over a year later May 29th 1998

Shortly after James Hoffman and his enterprise went bankrupt. He cited the fight he had with city hall in changing by-laws, the bureaucracy that was constantly badgering him, and the difficulty he had in receiving decisions on important issues, as being a great deal to blame for his problems. I found James Hoffman to be a man of vision, a very just and kind man who did all he could to help me in making fair decisions in my favour. Soon after I left, the lily pond/swimming pool was filled in for fear of children falling in and drowning and, a fence was put up across the garden, giving the house just a few yards of backyard space.

The reason I left Cobourg and moved to Port Hope in the spring of 1998 was a simple one. I fell in love with a house. Actually it was not a sudden thing; I was led up to it and predisposed to it because I have always loved the simple lines and elegance of the Georgian period of architecture. My cousin Grant Maidens, had owned a house in Port Hope for a couple of years. He also owned a thirty-five unit apartment building on Eglinton Avenue in Toronto. He was a very efficient landlord and he lived on the premises so that he could keep on eye on thing. He loved to come to Port Hope and work on renovations to his house here but it was very frustrating because he was frequently arriving late and having to return early to Toronto.

The house is at 43/45 Dorset Street West, Port Hope, and just up the hill from the Canadian Tire store. The two storey plus attic Georgian building was originally built as a tavern in 1860.

It was first Martin's Hotel and later Blackham's Hotel. The building suffered a number of fires and, by my estimate, a firewall was added right through the middle of the building when it was turned into a duplex just before the turn of the 20th century. For almost a century, it housed a large variety of tenants.

Not only was it difficult to carry out renovations on the property, but my cousin had trouble as a long distance landlord; people were always moving in and out of both sides. He had difficulty arranging the showing of the building when it was advertised. He suggested that we have the ownership of the building separated; I could buy the eastern, larger side of the building to live in, and he would keep the western part as a weekend home. First, he suggested a ridiculously low price. Obviously, he had not thought the situation through. Then he started raising the price each time I saw him. I went to the Town Hall and discovered that it would cost thousands of dollars to separate the two halves; for example, a completely new sewage line would have to be installed. By now, I liked the ambiance of the old building. So finally, I bought the whole building from Grant for one hundred and seventy-five thousand dollars. I had sworn that I would never again have a mortgage and there I was right back with one! However I did have excellent tenants next door; the first one moved out and Mrs. Barbara Klintworth moved in.

I spent almost thirty thousand dollars on restorations that first year. As part of our deal Grant had agreed to go ahead and have the brick pointed at his expense. It cost nine thousand dollars and was done very badly. I had a new roof put on at the back. It was stripped right down to the rafters and practically rebuilt. Three skylights were put into the south side of the roof in preparation for the attic being finished one day. Also in the attic, on the east and west ends, two small windows, mere slits, were replaced with large six over six windows that matched the rest of the house. A two piece bath was placed just inside the back door of my kitchen.

When I moved into the house I actually made fifty-two trips with my van, one or two trips a day, bringing my possessions over from Cobourg to Port Hope. Finally, I had only five or six large items left; the piano, chesterfield, et cetera, for the movers to transport. During the month or more that I was doing this I gave up swimming at the YMCA, I was honoured in 1999 by having my house chosen as one of nine homes on the Port Hope Annual House Tour sponsored by the Port Hope Branch of the Architectural Conservancy of Ontario. The event took place on Saturday, October 2nd. It was extremely well organized. There were two shifts of eight guides to handle the fifteen hundred people who came through the house.

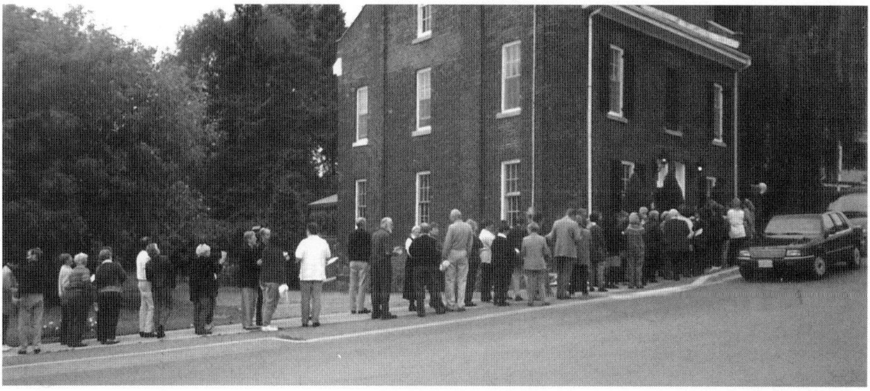

Joan Frith, my sister's companion of fifty years, died in September of 1999. Joan was now living alone at Rice Lake in a very large house at the bottom of a hill that was most difficult to navigate in the winter. Joan and I decided that she should move in with me, we would share ownership and we would restore the building to one unit. Barb Klintworth, who had become a good friend by this time, agreed to break her lease although it still had almost a year to run and she moved out. I will always be grateful to her because if she had rightfully insisted on staying I would have had to sell and move out myself.

I packed up my furnishings into two rooms, covered everything, and moved out to Joan's home at Rice Lake in November of 1999. I had thought that we would be able to serve the family New Year's dinner back in Port Hope. What a laugh! We finally moved back to Port Hope in the following April and, at that time, we did not have a single appliance in the kitchen! I have been told that when you start restoration work you figure out how much it will cost and how much time it will take and then double each figure; actually that is a conservative estimate. In our case, everything multiplied. For example, we took up the floor in the attic and I did not like the look of the old wiring and asked that it be completely replaced. It turned out that the electrical work in the house went down from the attic and so we rewired the whole house

We had major work done. Now a new staircase goes up to the attic, which has a guestroom, a bath and a large library that holds Joan's seven thousand books. There are four huge closets under the eaves for storage. The old, two sets of stairs to the attic that forced one to double up at the top in order to get out from under the roofline are now closed off and make wonderful linen cupboards.

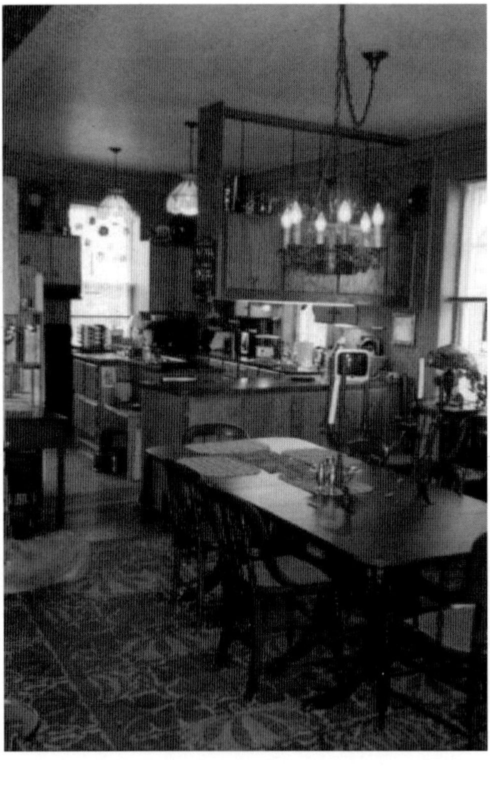

We left the stairs on each side of the house; one stair goes to my own area of study, bedroom, and bath, the other to Joan's area of guestroom, bedroom, and bath. In fact, we are calling the house "Two Stairs", as it is a distinctive architectural feature having the two stairs beside each other, one on each side of the old firewall. We punched three doorways and an arch through that wall.

On the main floor, the rooms were left the same shape on my side, the east. My living room remains, the dining room has become a card room, (we play a great deal of bridge) and my old kitchen

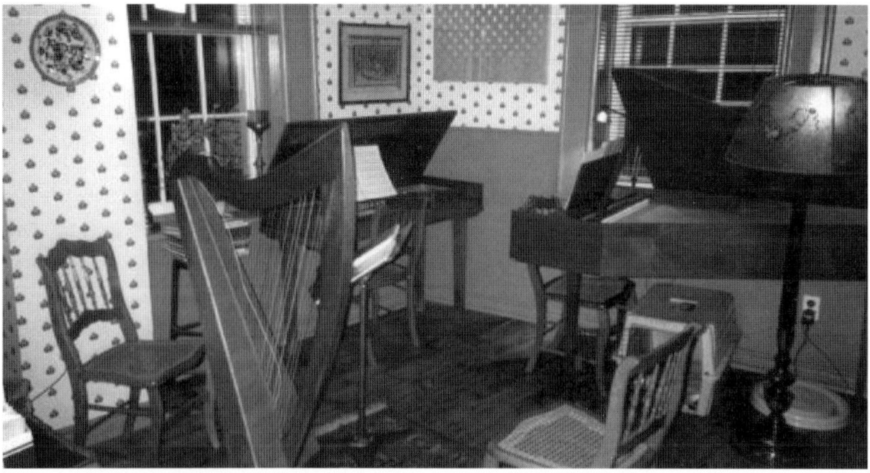

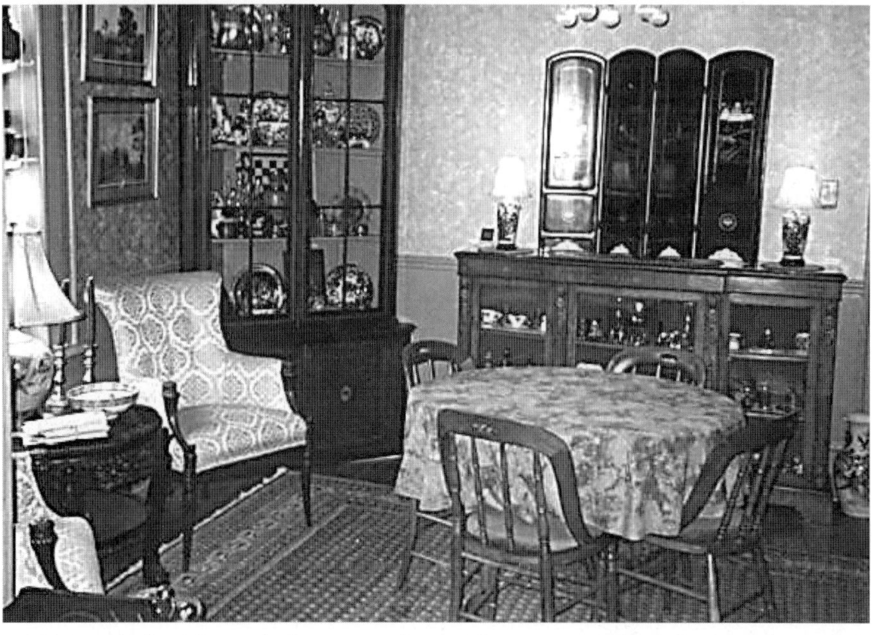

was emptied and made into Joan's music room and study. On the other side of the house, the west, most of the interior walls were removed to make a much larger kitchen that incorporated all the cupboards from the two original kitchens, a dining area and a TV/living room. The house is much lighter now. The attic has the three skylights and the windows mentioned above. We also added two more six-over-six windows at the back of the ground floor, on the south wall of the kitchen and the music room. In addition the two back doors had their top panels removed and windows inserted. Now we can look out on the garden.

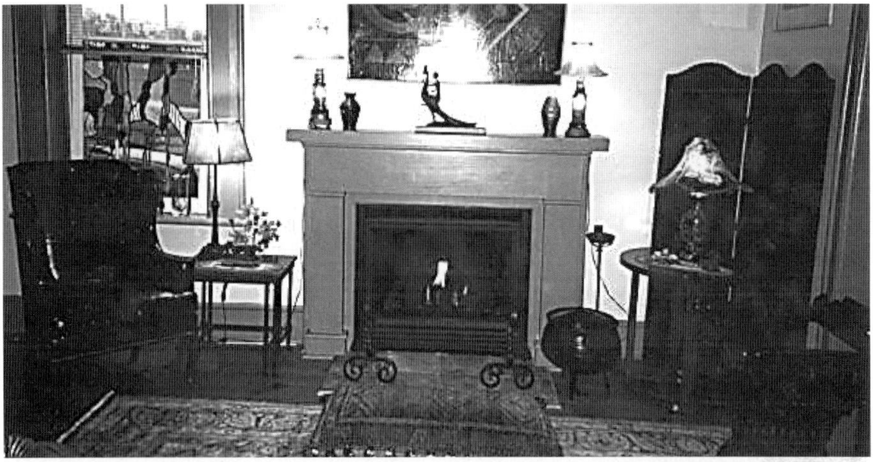

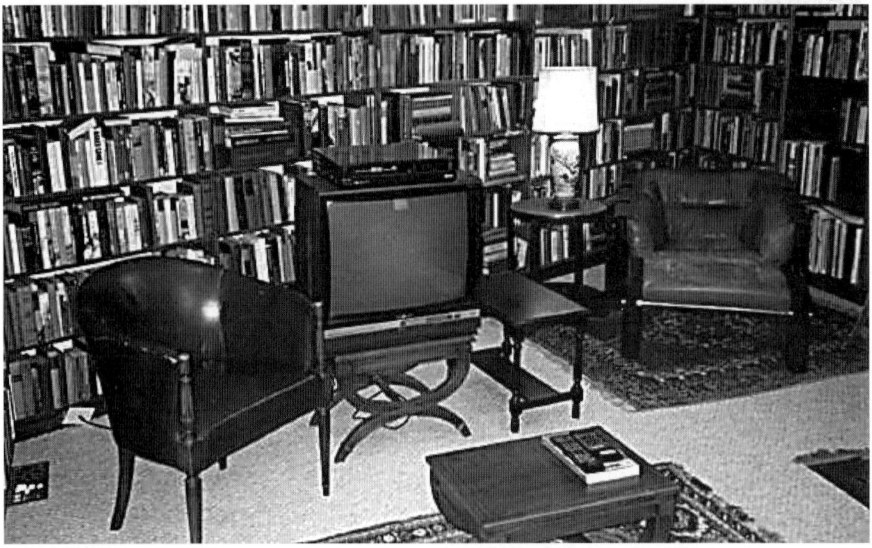

In the cellar, one room has been finished on each side. On the east, Joan has a sewing/craft/laundry workshop. Below the kitchen is a food pantry with many shelves and some cupboards. The small closet in the kitchen itself now has a turntable on each shelf. (perhaps the largest lazy susan in domestic use)

I was on site every day, bothering the workmen. (Actually, I performed an important function as they constantly referred to me with contracting problems — Ha.) My first important task was to carry Joan's books down from Rice Lake. I carried about thirty bags a day and had to store them wherever they would not be in the workmen's way. I filled every cupboard and then finally had to place five carloads in Joan's camper. (We had to replace the tires in the spring.) I also painted all the new windows.

My chief joy was painting three wild murals in my new bathroom. Originally, there was to be a small guestroom beside the bath. The wall had to be moved and when it was taken out and I saw the large space with two windows, one facing south, and the other east, I decided that the bathroom had to occupy the whole area, and I do not regret the decision. The murals are based on a 1930s stage set from Paris. They

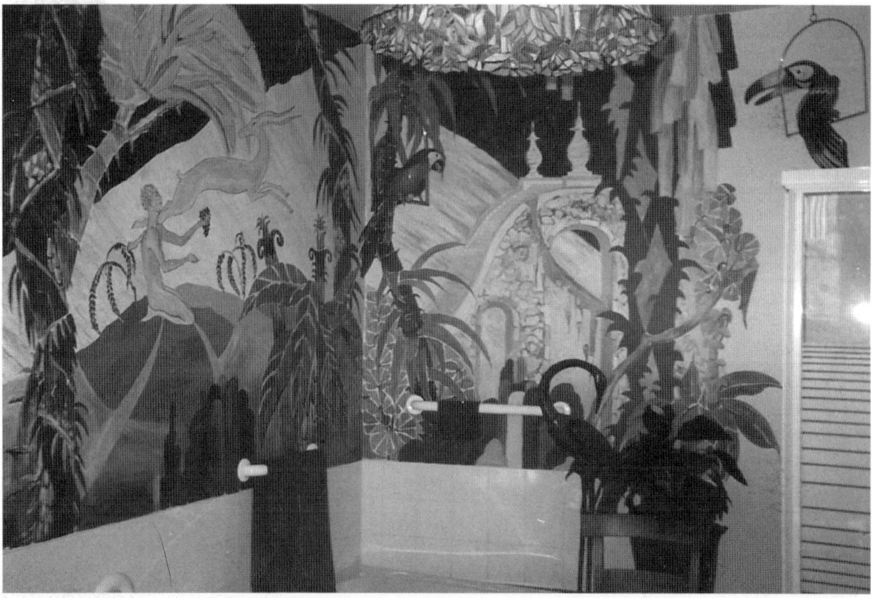

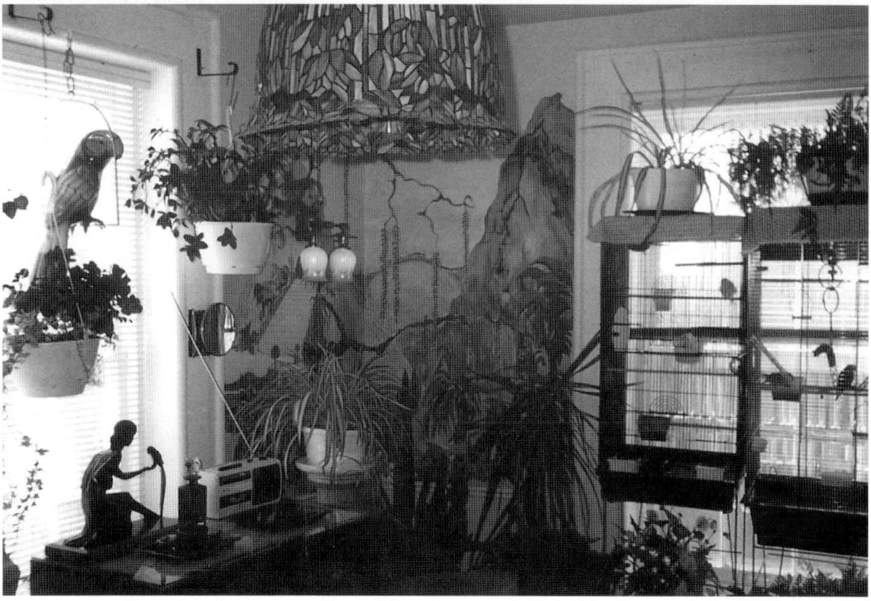

are jungle scenes in very stylized plant forms with black skies. I placed the figure of Nijinsky playing the role of the satyr in the "Afternoon of a Fawn" ballet in one of the panels. I copied the pose from the Barbier print of 1912. Nijinsky is kneeling, head thrown back, his horns protruding from his blond curly hair, his hands held forward holding a bunch of grapes. I did not have a fawn receiving this gift, but I did place a spotted antelope bounding across the distance right behind. I have added Art Deco detail to the rest of the room. I used water-based acrylic. It took one evening to draw each of the murals in chalk on the walls and a week to paint each one. I had not painted on such a large scale for some time and I found that I grew bolder as I went on.

We added the final detail to the house in October when Joan and I attended the Covert Massie auction in Cobourg. We were able to secure a beautiful 1910 Handel hanging light fixture that now hangs in my living room and pulls all the early 20th century elements of the room together. The furniture, lamps, leather screen from my Father's business and paintings never looked better.

In August of the year, 2000, we had a grand garden party to welcome everybody to our finished home. More than one hundred and thirty people attended – friends straight and gay, relatives, everybody. We saw

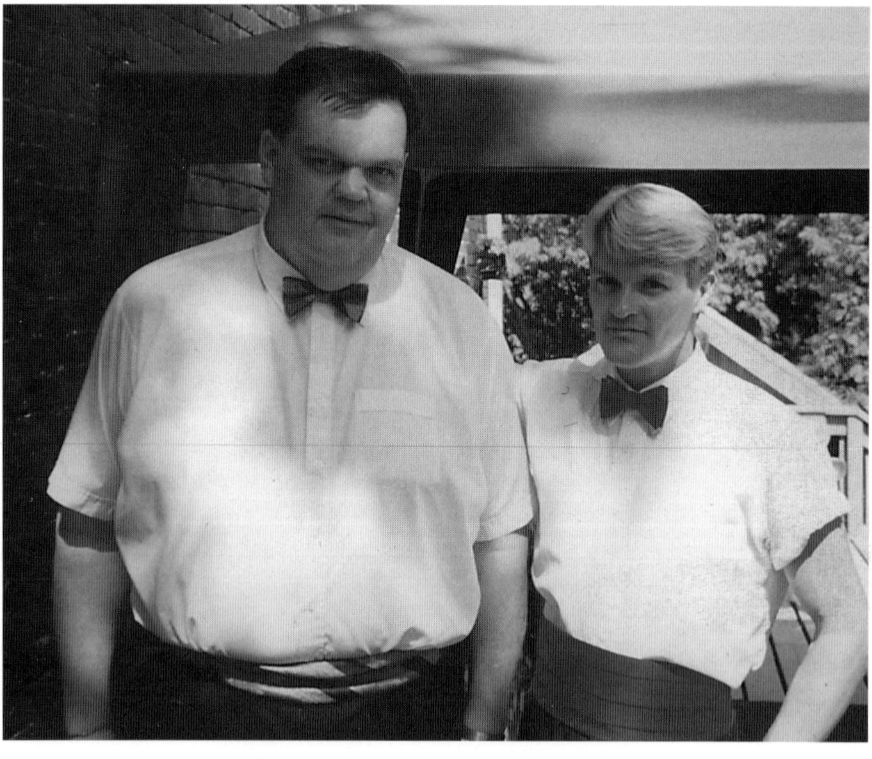

Richard Randall and Alex Smith

some cousins from western Canada that we had not known since we were children; Joan met a cousin from Toronto that she had not seen in fifty years. At that time I had only a few water lilies in bloom and so I faked some, — I dropped in the blooms of large begonias and I was congratulated on my exotic lilies!

I must mention that Joan and I had a number of large parties; in the house or in the garden. We were only able to do this with the assistance of two very good friends. Richard Randall of Cobourg often prepared and served food for us. Alex Smith of Port Hope helped set up, clean up and serve drinks.

That completes my overview of my six homes. In each case I have reported how much I paid for the house and how much I sold it for. It is interesting to see the growing amounts as years added inflation and larger premises to house prices, and my own tastes changed and multiplied. In the last case I have to be more obtuse as Joan dislikes having her finances discussed. She did move in with me and we split the cost of all house expenses evenly at the end of each month. On the house buying and restoration, Joan has paid for more than I have. I will state that we do not have a mortgage and that the renovation costs were greater than the initial cost of the house. Enough said.

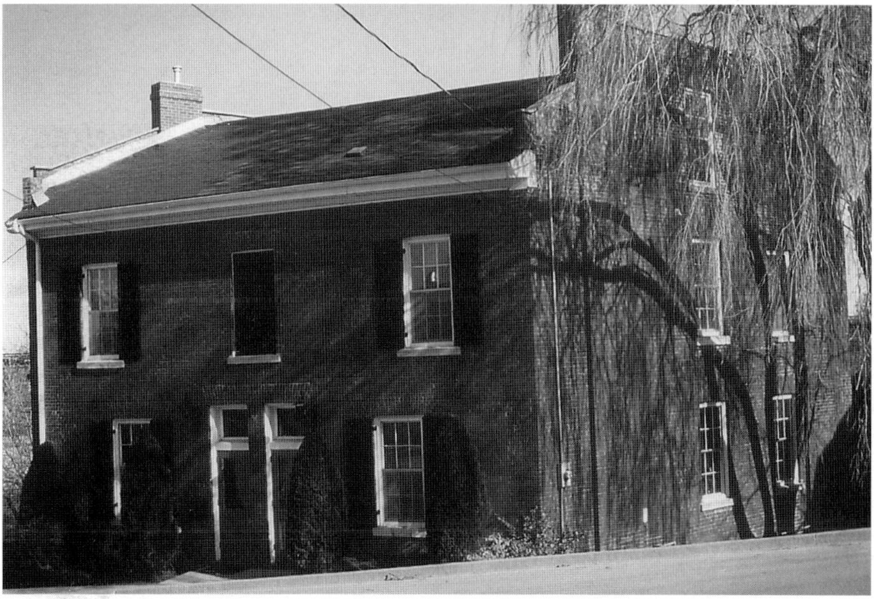

Chapter Twenty Five

The Cuban Connection

I am sitting in my study and staring out the window at the grey January day in Canada. I am just starting to write a chapter about my interest in Cuba. Suddenly I think that I should be able to print that chapter on bright yellow paper. Cuba makes me think like that; it is a country of great beauty, strong colour and music, wonderful handsome people, wealthy land, ancient history, despair and apathy.

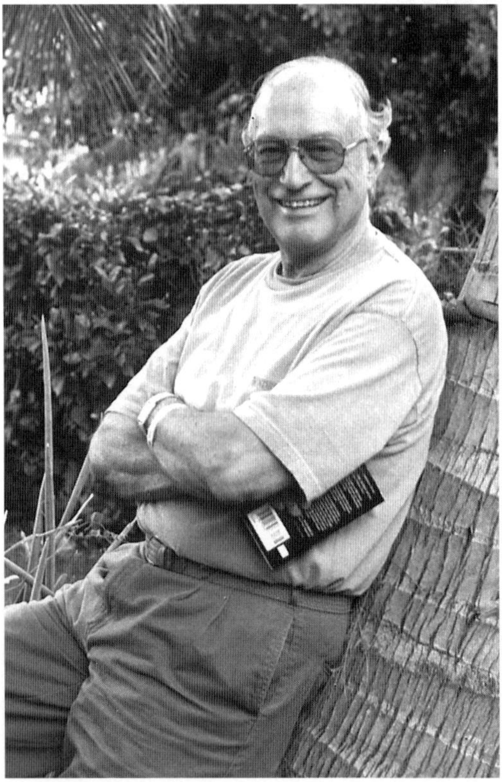

John Conroy introduced me to Cuba. I first met John in the Hart House dining room at the University of Toronto. I had returned to university after a few years' absence; he was an undergraduate student, and I was eight years older than he was. We became friends and kept in touch down through the years.

John has been a wonderful history teacher. Every holiday through his life he would travel, and he has covered the world. He can tell fascinating stories about taking the Trans-Siberian railway or visiting a glacier lake in northern Canada. Gradually over the years, he developed two interests, Russia and Cuba, both of which he visited many times. He has a natural ear for language and very quickly can learn the nuances or accents of a dialect so that with a few words he can speak and sound like a native.

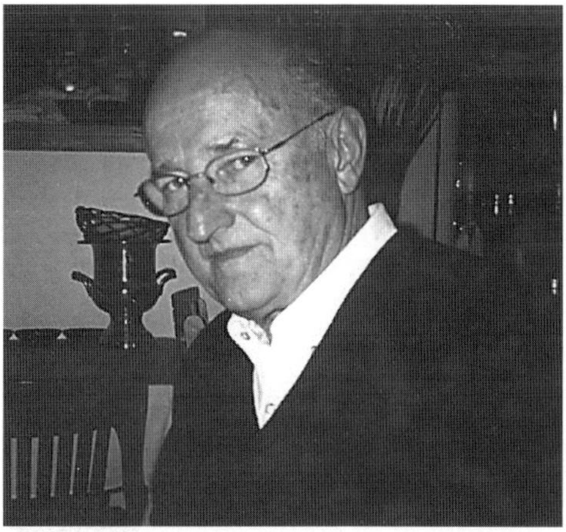

I always remember the story about one of his last trips to Russia when he was carrying medical supplies and a collapsible wheel chair for a children's hospital situated many miles from Moscow. Somehow he got through the red tape and confusion of train travel and arrived at the hospital with his gifts. He was greeted as a hero and the local authorities insisted on giving a dinner in his honour. A large group of dignitaries arrived, and each solemnly stacked his rifle and other weapons just inside the door. Then they started to drink, and drink, and drink vodka. There were innumerable toasts to John and to Canada. John had to match drink for drink or appear rude. He did so, meanwhile breaking off chunks of bread and eating as much as he could to absorb the alcohol into his system. The time for speeches was almost over and John was called on to respond. He spoke in Russian, although he remembers nothing about it, and appears to have impressed his hosts. He finally escaped from town.

After the fall of Communism in Russia, John turned more of his attention to Cuba, which he had been visiting for twenty-five years. He has made almost fifty trips to that island, always carrying letters, medical supplies and gifts for the ever-widening circle of friends he has made. He took down much needed medical supplies for an Aids Clinic. Cubans now living in Miami would entrust him with gifts to give to relatives and friends. For some time he operated a phone system before the embargo on communications was lifted between the U.S.A. and Cuba. He had a three-way-set-up whereby a call would come from Miami, he then would dial a relative in Cuba, and the original caller could then talk by way of Canada to mother, father, or whomever in Havana or somewhere else on the island. There was an individual doing this very thing in Toronto on a commercial basis and Cubans were so eager to speak to relatives that they would pay double to make such a call. That person ended up making a fortune. John made only his expenses and sometimes not quite those. He would often be awakened in the middle of the night to put a call through.

I entered this scene when John asked me in January of 1994 if I would like to drive to Florida with him for a short holiday. I gladly agreed. We drove east, crossed over into the U.S.A. at the Thousand Islands Bridge and right into a horrendous storm! I remember that John had suggested that we drive through Washington and see the sights. We were in the middle of the city rush hour and it took forever to get out. We finally stopped at a roadside restaurant and each of us ate some meat loaf for dinner. When we finally found a motel, turned on the heat, and went to bed we woke up with food poisoning. It was not a pleasant night.

As we went south, we kept stopping at the homes of Cuban expatriates; John was always greeted loudly and treated to a grand meal, with Cuban black beans and rice. John then exchanged information and picked up many letters that he could forward through Canadian visitors going to Cuba. We visited the Florida Keys and then headed north up to Houston, Texas and so back home.

Then I was asked to accompany John to Cuba. He always carries a mountain of luggage. In the past he has taken up to four large canvas bags; he would go up and down the line and find a businessman who travelled back and forth frequently and was carrying little. A little explanation and persuasion and that person would put a bag on the plane in his name. This time I was the extra bearer of gifts.

We got to the airport and John asked how I was feeling; I thought this a rather strange remark but I had recently had knee surgery and so I did not question it. Then he suggested that I should sit in a wheel chair. He produced one from the airport stock and I sat in it. He draped the chair with a variety of bags. He checked our four large suitcases and started to push me to the departure lounge. I was carrying a small Irish minstrel harp that I meant to practice while I was away the two weeks. There were four attendants on duty. I should mention that John speaks Spanish fluently. When the first call went out for children and cripples, we went up to the counter. There was a great discussion over the fact that I could not carry the harp on board the plane as it had to be checked. There was much gesturing of arms and John was most eloquent about how much this instrument meant to me. Finally two of the attendants took the harp between them (it weighed all of ten pounds) and promised that they would see that the harp was put in a safe place on the plane. That left two attendants to look after more than two hundred passengers. We were quickly let on board draped in our multitude of parcels. On the plane, we were about half way to Havana when I realized that I had to go to the washroom. We were near the front of the plane and so I stood up and started walking rapidly toward the back. Suddenly I realized that I was supposed to be a cripple! I immediately started to limp. No one seemed to have noticed anything odd.

We landed at the old Havana airport. A stairway was wheeled into place and the passengers disembarked. As John and I were held back until the last I really wondered what was going on. Suddenly a nicely dressed attendant came up the stair, came over to me, and lifted me out of my chair. I was helped carefully down the steps, she going first in case I should fall. At the bottom of the stairs, an ambulance was waiting for me! We rode in triumph past the long line of travelers walking the distance across the tarmac and were taken through the VIP door. We went through customs like a shot. There was only one hitch; John was carrying office supplies for friends who worked at the Oceanographic Institute and the customs official started to open the box. John pulled out a letter that he had secured from his local M.P., complete with the Canadian insignia at the top, the flag, and two imposing signatures. He waved this in their faces, threw his arms about, the box was quickly sealed and we processed right through the other people in the airport.

By this time, John conveniently had a ten-dollar U.S. bill sticking unobtrusively from his hand. Such an amount equals three weeks' pay for a Cuban professional worker. Our procession, John at the head, me following carrying my precious harp and being pushed in my wheelchair by my nice compassionate guide, three air port attendants carrying our bags - all made our way out of the building to the car that John had waiting for us directly at the front of the terminal. The last kind gesture that I received was the guide lifting me tenderly out of the chair, then putting her hand in blessing on my head and lowering me gently into the car where I went into hysterics. John, meanwhile, gave the ten dollars to the head porter who would divide it with his assistants.

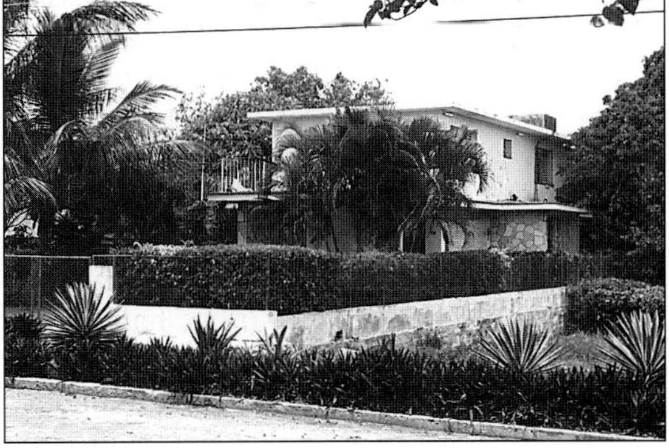

So with such fanfare, we arrived in Cuba. We immediately drove out towards the village of Guanabo to a very pleasant home where we had rented the second floor for two weeks. I remember especially two things about that car trip. First, the Russians had left Cuba only a short time before, depriving the Cubans of all the foreign aid from their previous ally. Consequently they were very short of fuel and were using an extremely low grade of gasoline. The exhaust, from the trucks especially, was unbelievable —just a black cloud that obliterated all view of traffic coming from the other direction.

The other thing I remember was the strange impression I had while we were driving through the centre of Havana in the dusk, I felt as if we were driving through Atlantis under the sea. There was street after street of palaces and magnificent homes in a great state of disrepair; evidently they had been turned into apartments for the proletariat, and laundry was hanging out at every conceivable location to dry; it looked like seaweed in the half light. I later learned that Havana has a very old history: it was a great metropolitan city, the cross roads for trade routes and gold shipments between Spain and the New World when New York was just a village on an island.

John had a friend, Julio, who lived in Havana and worked at the Oceanographic Institute. He took holidays while we were in Cuba and came out by bus from Havana to stay with us.

One day, John and Julio took me into Havana. We toured "El Morro", the ancient fortress across the harbour from Havana; then we visited the Cathedral, toured areas of the old city, and finally visited a huge street craft show. I thought, overall that the crafts were of very poor workmanship and intended for the tourists. There was nothing that I wanted to buy.

There were many prostitutes in evidence. One in particular, a very large woman who reminded me of an army tank, seemed to take a fancy to me, or perhaps my money although that thought hurt my manly pride. She pursued the three of, us relentlessly through the fair. She was hard to miss, being dressed in scarlet spandex from head to toe. She looked as if she had been poured into this outfit. We finally went, into an antique store to avoid her, but she followed us in. I remember that John stood on one side of me and Julio stood on the other side as we leaned against a counter. This lady of pleasure was not going to lose her prey so easily; she managed to brush against me and pinch me in an unexpected place.

One day John decided to rent a car and take Julio, a friend of his named Carlos Julio and myself on an over night trip to the city of Trinidad, a good way down the island. We picked up the car and drove it back to Dorita's and Leonel's home where we were staying. We took it inside the locked gate and parked it right beside the front door.

Suddenly late that evening Dorita called to John to rush downstairs as the car's trunk and been opened and the spare tire stolen. Early the next morning John drove the car back to the rental agency and we had to pay seventy-five dollars to get a new tire. I told John afterward that I thought it was all too neat. It was a Korean car that we rented, we were in a small village where tires were not available, and yet we were able to easily obtain a new one. I am sure that the agency had arranged for our tire to be taken, as the trunk had not even been forced, and we bought back the same tire.

The four of us drove to Trinidad and had a very pleasant time. We stayed in a private home rather than in a hotel as we had been flagged down by a man at the edge of the town who told us he was operating a guesthouse to which he guided us. It was neat and tidy and his wife gave us a wonderful evening meal. The next day we toured the city, supposedly the landing place of Columbus when he visited Cuba. The old square was quite magnificent, Spanish, and grand. We returned to Havana that evening.

A note about cars in Cuba. There are three types of cars: the old pre-Castro, 1950s-built large American ones that have been rebuilt so many times that almost the total car has been replaced (the Cubans are experts at making car parts); then there are the Ladas, the Russian cars that were introduced - during the Russian period; finally came the new Japanese and Korean cars that represent the new rich from the hotels and car agencies, et cetera. There are no new American cars on the island.

A couple more of my observations. The first time I visited Cuba there were hundreds of dogs running the streets: small, many looking if they were from the same gene pool; many emaciated as if they had a background of Italian greyhounds; many ill, with fur falling out and even limbs missing. The next time I went to Cuba, they were all gone. There had been a campaign to eliminate them.

The first couple of times I was in Cuba, on every street corner, outside every hotel, on every road, hitchhiking, were young girls, obviously prostitutes. Everybody is after the American dollar however it is available. I remember one scene at my hotel where four young handsome Italian boys from New York, obviously on a holiday to let off steam, were being seen off on their return home by three quite gorgeous young girls. So much arm waving, so many promises, such boisterous good will, such sadness. Two trips later the girls had disappeared, the result of another purge. They are still there, however, only a little more difficult to find.

Such an amazing island. Castro shouts hate at the Americans just across the water; because of them he can tell his people that he must keep a huge army. The fact is, the U.S. could walk right across Cuba any day that it might want to. The main reason Castro has the army is to control his own people. He can blame the embargo for everything that goes wrong on the island, a rich island with fertile land and yet people go hungry. Cuba boasts universal education yet few can find a job, You ask any employee in a hotel- they all have university degrees and yet they are desperate for U.S. dollars. The average wage for a doctor is twenty U.S. dollars a month. On my last visit, the girl who flipped the eggs in the morning and made my omelet was a university graduate in languages. She could speak four of them. Cuba has free hospital care and yet, the hospitals are without necessary drugs. Meanwhile, Castro is reputed to be one of the richest men in the world.

The generation represented by Julio and Carlos Julio is in a sense a lost generation. Julio, with John Conroy's help, came to Canada as a refugee; he is now a Canadian citizen, holds down a responsible job, is a card-carrying member of a political party, speaks English fluently, dresses with great taste and has likely travelled more in Canada than most native born Canadians. On the other hand, Carlos Julio is mired in the Cuban system. He works at the Oceanographic Institute and makes fifteen dollars U.S. a month. He wants to leave Cuba but he is having trouble learning English. He is looking after an aged grandmother. The future is bleak for his generation in Cuba.

While in Cuba on my first trip we were invited to a birthday party in an apartment in Havana. It was given by Libertad and Bibi, a commercial gallery director and her assistant, for an artist named Giraldo. The interesting thing about that group was that everybody there was a professional by training — an architect, a teacher, a lawyer, et cetera, but all were working in the tourist trade attempting to bring in U.S. dollars. For example, I was talking to a thirty-year-old architect who was a guide for Italian tourists because with his family background he could speak Italian. At the party everybody was in a happy mood, the music was loud with a strong beat and one man with a luxurious black moustache did some wonderful dancing. We learned that he was a choreographer for the National Ballet of Cuba.

I had a long talk with Giraldo. He was an interesting artist and he brought me some slides of his work to show in Canada. I did so but I found out, as I suspected, that the public galleries in Canada were on limited budgets and wanted to show and collect only Canadian works. I felt that Giraldo might have only limited success in Cuba, as some of his work depicted the boat people trying to escape to the United States.

There was some impromptu folk singing at the party that was very melancholy. The son of my landlady in Guanabo, Leonel, was present. He is about twenty-five and a photographer by profession. He is extremely handsome, dressed in a white shirt with a small lace detail. I played my minstrel harp for him and his mother later. They enjoyed it.

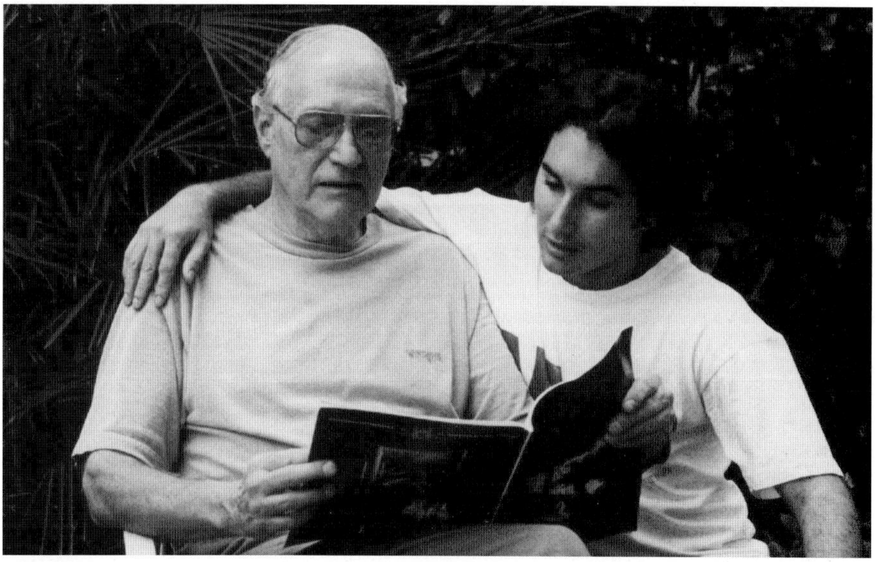

I have visited Cuba once a year now for six years. After the first year, we were not allowed to stay in a private home. The government decided that such situations made the common people dissatisfied with their lot. We stayed for three years at the Hotel Tropicocas a few kilometers from Guanabo, just along the coast. In the second year Julio made it to Canada, was living in Stratford and learning English just as fast as he could.

He worked as a gardener the first summer and then took a position in a health food store, The Gentle Rain, where he has done very well. John and I went to Cuba alone and teamed up with Carlos Julio for trips to the beach.

A recent trip was made famous by the "flying lettuce" episode. The first day of our holidays John always makes a trip into Havana. He is gone all day travelling around, delivering presents and letters that he brought from Cubans living in Canada, On the last day of our holiday I usually go with him to pick up letters that people want him to mail in Canada. Usually, wherever we stop these kind people give us refreshments that we are sure sometimes must take a large chunk of their rations.

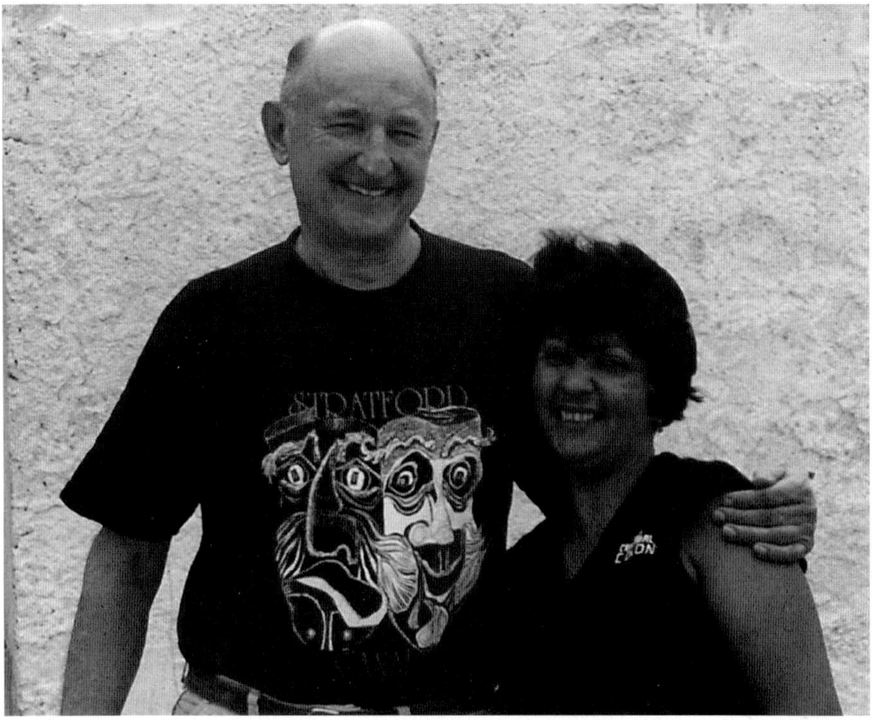

In this one case, a lady, a great friend of John's, who owns a home where a son and family live upstairs, always prepares a full banquet. John always tells her not to do it but she does it anyway. We were forced to sit down and a salad appeared made of shredded lettuce and other ingredient. John was talking to one son, a sea captain, who was asking questions about Canada. There were quite a few flies around and so the hostess asked another son, a doctor, to bring out two floor fans. He did so and trained them right on me. Every time I would take a forkful of the salad the wind would blow it off and it would hit the wall beside me. I started to laugh and as soon as the others saw what was happening, there was general hilarity. Since then, to John and myself, this lady has been known as "the flying lettuce lady". She was a widow and I think she rather liked me. The next time we visited on the following year she presented me with an orchid that she had grown in her own garden. This last Christmas I received a card from her, the first letter I have had sent successfully from Cuba.

I cannot close the story of my connection to Cuba without mentioning, "Condesa" Miraida Figueron — "The Countess" as we called her. Miraida lived in Guanabo and was a local character who taught English in the local school. Leonel learned from her and he speaks English very well. John Conroy had known Miraida for years; he was the one who gave her the name, The Countess. Miraida lived in an apartment right down next to the ocean. She had always hoped to leave Cuba. After she made friends with some people visiting from Denmark, she dyed her hair blond hoping to go to that country. As a blond, she looked grotesque with her dark complexion. One of the reasons for visiting Guanabo was to see Miraida. Two years ago she decided to go and visit her son who was at school in another town. She had bought a very old car and was very proud of it. She went with her young boy friend at night, with another man driving. The roads in Cuba are in dreadful condition. They were driving fast, they came up on an old truck that had no back lights, and went right under it decapitating all three of them in the car. The authorities did not find the wreck until the following morning by which time the clothes and jewelry of Miraida and the two men had been completely stolen!

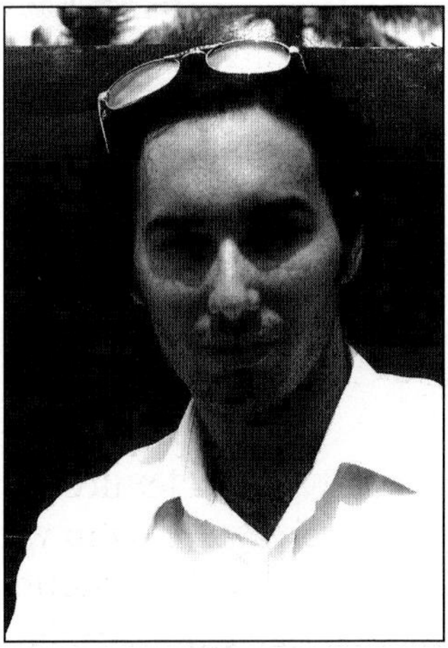

Leonel

Over the years, I have made two particular friends in Cuba. Leonel, the son of our first landlady, speaks English well and is a photographer, as I have said. I had inherited a great deal of photographic equipment from a cousin who died, including cameras, lens, tripods, et cetera. I took it all down to Leonel who was delighted to receive it. It is hard to believe that he went right through a photography course at college level without there being a single book about photography in the school. I have since taken down to him a number of books -about photography. I also take him a fair number of black and white films each time I visit Cuba. One year when I arrived, he had let his hair grow long. I told him that he looked like the American singer, "Tiny Tim". The next time I went his hair was cut short again. Leonel's mother, Dorita, spends a great deal of time in Miami visiting her daughter and grandchild.

She has dual citizenship and can go back and forth freely. Leonel loves his home and will not leave it and so he stays at home while his mother is away and looks after things. No one would dare leave a house unattended in Cuba. He is frustrated, however, as he sees no future there for himself.

Carlos Julio has also become a good friend of mine. I send him thirty dollar U.S. a month; this is double his salary. It allows him to buy cooking oil, toilet paper, and other necessities in the stores (that take only American dollars) for his grandmother and his uncles. His grandmother is well over ninety and likely would not survive without the vitamins that John takes down to her and the extra food that I provide. Carlos writes to me in Spanish. I do not speak the language but I have learnt to translate the letters quite quickly after five years of doing so. I write him in English and he does the reverse; he translates my letters into Spanish. Maybe some day we will be able to speak to each other directly. I take quite a few clothes down to Carlos; Leonel's mother brings him stylish clothes from Miami.

This chapter is open-ended. I do not know what will happen to my two friends in Cuba. I will try to support them as much as I can and hope for the best. John Conroy has a wonderful idea for the future concerning Cuba. It is far-fetched but someday anything could happen. He thinks that Canada should accept Cuba as a province of our dominion. It would send its representatives to parliament just as any other province does. Why does he propose this? There are many practical reasons. Cuba has rich agricultural land from which we could import all of our citrus fruit, it being apart of our own country using the same currency. We could go south in the winter and holiday in the

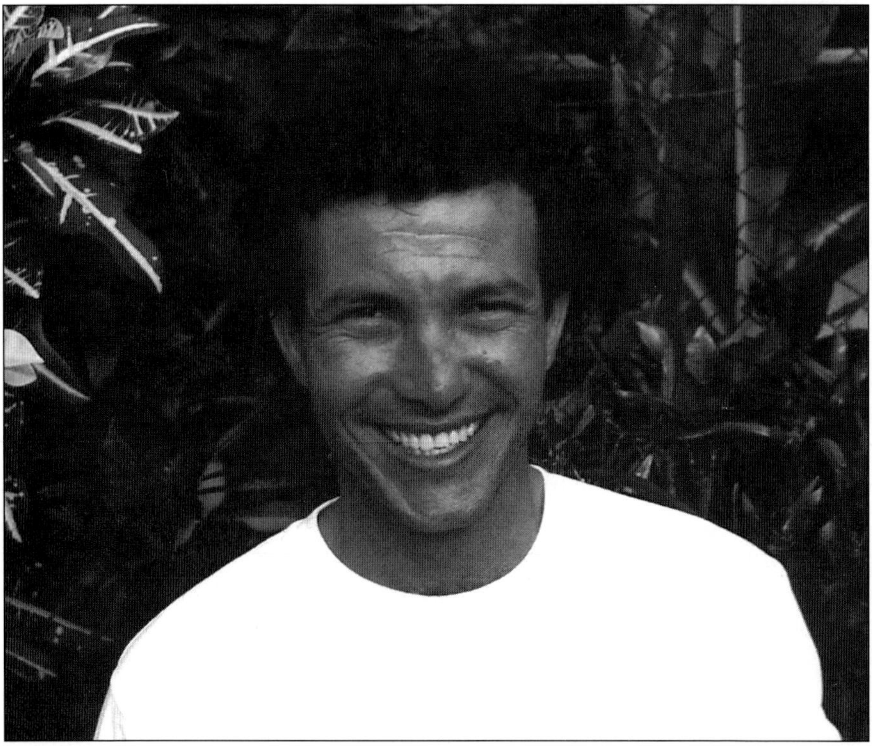

Carlos Julio

Caribbean and still be in our own country. Cuba could make use of our manufactured goods after so many years without direct access to these markets, and that trade would be tariff-free, being within our own country. Our raw materials could benefit Cuba. The trade between the two parts of the country would be of great benefit to our ports on the east coast, and so on...

Chapter Twenty Six

Awards

In 1998, I was nominated for an award. William J. Withrow, C.M., Director Emeritus, Art Gallery of Ontario, wrote a letter of commendation: "Paul Bennett was Director of the Art Institute of Ontario from September 1964 to August, 1968. It was an affiliation of 13 professional visual arts organizations in Ontario. Its mandate was to take exhibitions of the visual arts out to the people of the province and was, therefore, the forerunner of the Extension Department of the Art Gallery of Ontario. During this time Paul lectured to approximately 200 Ontario communities including out of the way ones in the north such as Chapleau, Red Lake and Hearst."

He went on to say that I had been in charge of the Ontario Centennial Arts program and ends the letter stating, "This important pioneer work in our province during the early years of the growth of art galleries, especially in the north, deserves recognition."

Doris McCarthy, C.M., O.O., F.O.C.A., R.C.A., O.S.A., C.S.P.O.C., L.L.D., (Calgary), L.L.D., (Nipissing U.), stated: "In the early sixties when I was president of the Ontario Society of Artists, he (Paul Bennett) was engaged in a one-man job of taking the visual arts to the hinterland of Ontario. I consider him to have been the greatest single factor in the rapid development of awareness of the visual arts beyond the major cities. There are now few small centres without an art gallery or art museum for which he planted the seed."

Gordon McFarlane, former Co-Coordinator of Visual Arts, Peel Board of Education, stated, "He did invaluable service for the people of the province by making sure hundreds of art exhibitions travelled to every part of the province." He spoke of the Ontario Centennial Art Exhibition and also of my work at the Robert McLaughlin Gallery in introducing the Painters Eleven project. He went on to mention my raising the level of crafts to that of Fine Art, and exposing people to works of beauty and fine craftsmanship.

Naomi Lightbourne, former Executive Secretary of the Ontario Arts Council, stated, "Paul, almost single handedly addressed the problem of art-deprivation in Ontario. From various galleries and collections, Paul amassed an exhibition of original artwork, which he carefully packed into a secondhand van and took to communities throughout the province. In these communities Paul would set up the exhibition and lecture about the various works — students during the day and adults in the evening. In addition, he gave workshops and, if asked, would offer critiques of work done by local residents. He was a true pioneer. In 1979, I became the Community Arts Development Officer of the Ontario Arts Council, a position that I held for seventeen years. This new responsibility required visits to communities all over the province. On many occasions, I heard people recalling Paul's visits so many years before. It was thrilling to realize how he enriched the lives and widened the horizons of countless people. I know that Paul's infectious enthusiasm and his comprehensive knowledge of the visual arts have left indelible impressions throughout Ontario."

Joan Murray, former Director of the Robert McLaughlin Gallery, stated, "I have known Paul Bennett for over thirty years. He has been a seminal figure in the development of culture in Ontario, as Director of the Art Institute of Ontario, Director of the Robert McLaughlin Gallery, and Director of the Canadian Guild of Crafts. There are personalities in Canada who make a difference, and he is one of them. We need more like him in Canada at this time."

Terry Boyce, former Principal, Mitchell District High School, said, "Single handedly he created a dynamic department that students wanted to be in. His use and mixture of different media and his focus on the students' world made visual art appealing to many differing students — including ones that I could not imagine as being interested in the artistic world. As a teacher Mr. Bennett set high standards and made them attainable'. He had an excellent rapport with young people based on an egalitarian manner. He was respected by the students and staff alike. His student-planned and student-executed murals continue to enliven the hallways and resource centre of the school. His influence on the several hundreds of students that he taught was significant."

Mark Bovey, Designer for an advertising agency, stated, "Paul Bennett was my grade 10-12 Art Teacher at Mitchell District High School. Paul was always enthusiastic about art; he even managed too keep art history interesting. Paul had an interest in our opinion of what art is and why or why not some of the classic artists, movements or pieces should be important parts of art history. Personally I had a battle with Paul over "The Red Square" as a worthy piece of influential art. Even when it came to projects it was interesting; he was forever having us work in different mediums from watercolours to salt licks. Depending on the project, Paul would have us work solo, in groups to complete pieces and we even worked as a whole to design and paint a mural in our library." "There is a larger, more important picture to be seen here. Paul had a talent for handling people; every problem student who was evicted from other classes somehow managed to end up in his art room. He did not push them away or allow them to become a problem, he just dealt with them in his own gentle way and they quit being a nuisance and actually learned something. From my perspective, Paul was a source of inspiration because he never inflicted his opinion on the artwork that I was producing. Paul gave an individual the freedom to produce art that expressed themselves but he pushed you to explore boundaries of your own talent and style. He was always happy to see students excited about pieces they were working on -let's face it, the only way you are going to produce great art is if you are truly excited about the work that you are doing. Sometimes Paul even put his own money into buying supplies for us to create projects.

"Currently I am designing for an advertising agency in London, Ontario. The basic principles of design that I first took with Paul still apply to my daily life as they did in high school and college. More importantly I value the lessons that Paul taught me about teamwork and how to tactfully deal with others. These values of Paul's unique personality were as great a lesson as his knowledge of art and benefit me most in the highly competitive industry of advertising."

I have read these letters over many times during the past years. As one grows older it is easy to think that with declining mental and physical powers, one has not accomplished anything in one's life. In my own life, especially with grass roots development I tended to move around and go sideways rather than staying in one place and going upward. Those letters have been my reward. There have been individuals who believed in what I tried to do. Perhaps the grass roots did develop some beautiful water lilies.

Chapter Twenty Seven

Postlude

Ghosts, portents, things nocturnal, things that go bump in the night. It is four a.m. on a morning in May. It is dreary outside, the rain is pelting the window. I cannot sleep. Marmie is once again guarding the crook in the hall looking over the stairwell, Andy is still asleep under the clavichord. I know that all is well, the very walls of the house are in a deep sleep.

However last December I had a premonition; these things do happen in my family. I was absolutely sure that something dreadful was going to happen to me. I had always wanted to write about my life and work and so I started frantically to do so. I would sit at the keyboard night after night until two in the morning. I told nobody the reason for my rush. Joan often chided me; she said that I should take my time; books are never written overnight. I worried about my health. I had a ringing in my ears and I rushed off to the doctor to have my blood pressure checked. I threw my hip out, the doctor said that I did not need a replacement just a new chair in front of my desk.

I started out reading one chapter of the book at a time to Joan. She became very interested, as I had hoped she would, and offered to edit it for me. She did teach English in High School so I told her that she had had a wonderful idea. She sat at the dining room table day after day. I finished the book in record time in just over three months. Then started the laborious rewriting. She was iron willed, as ever. The Crafts Council was interesting to me but would bore the pants off an ordinary reader. The pages in that chapter dropped from thirty-seven to seventeen. She said that I had talked about the Linley brothers for years, where were they in the book? And so it went, chapter by chapter, with three rewrites, I was just ahead of her all the time.

Joan has always been an organized person. On April the fifth she came down to breakfast and insisted that we go to the lawyers that day, along with her business partner, and reorganize her finances. We did so. On Monday, April 8th she announced at noon that she had just added the last expression marks to a piece of music that she had been working on for a month. We laughingly had called it "Waiting for Paul" as she had composed it, over a number of weeks, sitting at the piano with her coat on while waiting for me to get ready to go out. At noon that day we had a lovely lunch, Joan had made a tomato aspic, she added some cold chicken and dressing from the night before and I had made a potato salad. She announced that she had just finished editing the last paragraph of the last chapter of my book. The chapter was sitting on the steps waiting for me to take upstairs and add to the total manuscript. I did so after lunch. I came back down. Joan was stretched out on the floor in the living room, in a coma showing no vital signs. The paramedics arrived within minutes and she was rushed to the hospital where she died three-weeks later without regaining consciousness.

We always recognized that Joan was my father's favourite child, she was the eldest, there was no sibling rivalry in this. Her attack came on the eve of the anniversary of Vimy Ridge. A coincidence? Perhaps. My foreboding or premonition, perhaps another coincidence. It certainly was misplaced but it did hit the person closest to me. This old hotel may still hide many secrets in spite of all our renovations.

I do feel that Joan is very much a part of this book and I dedicate it to her. By the way, she did not edit this particular chapter.

Index